The Female Ruse

Hebrew Bible Monographs, 74

Series Editors
David J.A. Clines and J. Cheryl Exum

Editorial Board
A. Graeme Auld, Marc Brettler, David M. Carr, Paul M. Joyce,
Francis Landy, Lena-Sofia Tiemeyer, Stuart D.E. Weeks

The Female Ruse

Women's Deception and Divine Sanction in the Hebrew Bible

Rachel E. Adelman

Sheffield Phoenix Press
2017

Copyright © 2015, 2017 Sheffield Phoenix Press
First published in hardback, 2015.
First published in paperback, 2017.
Published by Sheffield Phoenix Press
Department of Biblical Studies, University of Sheffield
45 Victoria Street, Sheffield S3 7QB

www.sheffieldphoenix.com

Cover: 'Isaac Blessing Jacob' by Gioachino Assereto, 1640
(early Baroque, Italian painter 1600–1649)

All rights reserved.
No part of this publication may be reproduced or transmitted in any form or by any means, electronic or mechanical, including photocopying, recording or any information storage or retrieval system, without the publisher's permission in writing.

A CIP catalogue record for this book
is available from the British Library

Typeset by the HK Scriptorium
Printed by Lightning Source

ISBN 978-1-909697-94-2 (hardback)
ISBN 978-1-910928-25-7 (paperback)
ISSN 1747-9614

*To my parents, Howard and Margaret,
for their loving support*

Contents

Acknowledgments	ix
Abbreviations	xiii
Transliteration	xvii

INTRODUCTION: THE FEMALE RUSE	1

Chapter 1
READING REBEKAH UNVEILED ... 11

Chapter 2
THE COLLUSION OF SISTERS: A STUDY IN
THE LEAH–RACHEL–JACOB TRIANGLE ... 38

Chapter 3
OF VEILS, GOATS AND SEALING RINGS, OF GUARANTORS AND KINGS:
THE STORY OF JUDAH AND TAMAR ... 68

ADDENDUM: THE SIGNET, CORD AND STAFF ... 87

Chapter 4
WEAVING THE MESSIANIC LIGHT: LAW AND NARRATIVE
IN THE MAKING OF THE DAVIDIC DYNASTY ... 90

ADDENDUM 1: DAVID'S INHERITANCE ... 122
ADDENDUM 2: A COMPARISON OF THE THREE NARRATIVES ... 124

Chapter 5
DAVID'S WIVES AS WOMEN OF OATH ... 126

Chapter 6
MICHAL: THE KING'S DAUGHTER OR THE KING'S WIFE? ... 137

Chapter 7
ABIGAIL: WOMAN OF VALOR OR WOMAN OF WILE? ... 151

Chapter 8
BATHSHEBA: WOMAN OF OATH											162

Chapter 9
'PASSING STRANGE': GENDER CROSSING IN THE STORY
OF JOSEPH AND ESTHER											198

ADDENDUM: ANALOGIES BETWEEN THE JOSEPH
AND ESTHER NARRATIVES											228

Bibliography											231
Scripture Index											243
Author Index											254

Acknowledgments

The idea for *The Female Ruse* had its inception, perhaps, on my father's knee when I first learned about Eve's role in the Garden of Eden. Though I was just a girl, my father's reading remains with me. Eve impelled the first human beings into history by listening to the words of the Serpent and presenting Adam with the fruit of the Tree of Knowledge. This was really the first female ruse. The pivotal verse reads, 'So when the woman saw that the tree was good for food, and that it was a delight to the eyes, and that the tree was to be desired to make one wise, she took of its fruit and ate; and she also gave some to her husband, *who was with her*, and he ate' (Gen. 3.6 NRSV). The central question is whether the man knew what he was eating? And, therefore, did he not equally bear the blame? According to my father, not a Torah scholar but a Hegelian philosopher, the fruit offered sexual knowledge and the Serpent represented the Phallus (perhaps I was not quite so young after all). The man and the Serpent were one, split between mind and body, and Eve presented the possibility of synthesis, the integration of mind and body over which man was (and is, peculiarly and perpetually) divided. So Adam knew, but he didn't know. After all, the verse states, '*he was with her*'. According to my father, only his body was really 'aware'; his mind was in denial. Eve was the catalyst for the human move into maturity, where desire (the life of the mind) and body (sexuality, procreation and the recognition of responsibility) come together in nurturing life in this world.

Unfortunately, most of history is just that, *his*-story, and male theologians and Bible scholars have misread Eve's intent ever since. 'The Fall', the cause of the banishment from Eden where humanity was once one with nature, has been radically misunderstood for the past few millennia, framed as a vertical drop instead of a transverse slide. I maintain that Eve was not the first (or last) woman to be misunderstood. Freud, in a way, got the question wrong. It isn't: What do women want? But, rather, what do women know? This book is an attempt to address that question by exploring the unique role that Eve's handmaids have played in the Hebrew Bible ever since, those women who have instigated a particularly *female* ruse, bringing the life of the body to bear on the mind.

This project began to coalesce five years ago, when I was a research fellow at Harvard Divinity School in the Women Studies in Religion Program (WSRP), during the academic year of 2011–12. I wish to acknowledge the insights of my colleagues in the WSRP who read, commented and discussed early drafts of the first chapters, including Bernadette Brooten, Julia Watts Belser, Azza Basuradin, Michelle Wolfe and Hauwa Ibrahim. I am especially grateful to Ann Braude, the director of the program, for her unflagging support. She urged me to safeguard my precious research and writing time, and encouraged me to complete the work for publication. I am also grateful to the students at Harvard Divinity School who participated in my course, 'Women and Deceit in the Hebrew Bible' (spring 2012), which was based loosely on the premise of this book. They became my first informal readers and teachers in helping me articulate the workings of the female ruse in the Hebrew Bible. I have had many opportunities to teach this material since: to the students at Maayan, Torah Studies Initiative for Women (centered in Boston), and to the Kent Street group (a post-Meah class in Brookline, Massachusetts). All of my students have inadvertently become my teachers, as the rabbinic dictum goes: '"And all your children [*banayikh*] shall be learned of the LORD" (Isa. 54.13)—do not read "your children" [*banayikh*, lit., sons], but "your builders" [*boniyikh*]' (*b. Ber* 64a). Indeed, they must be read as the mortar between the lines of these pages.

Several of these chapters, in one form or another, have undergone editorial revision since their first public appearances. The first chapter, 'Reading Rebekah Unveiled', arose as a paper for a panel at the AJS Conference in Boston, December 2010, which was subsequently published under the title 'From Veils to Goatskins: The Female Ruse in Genesis,' in the online journal *Textual Reasoning* (6.2 [March 2011]), under the rubric of 'The Female Ruse: Women's Subversive Voices in Biblical and Rabbinic Texts' (http://jtr.lib.virginia.edu/volume-6-number-2/). The basic ideas first articulated there have undergone a great deal of expansion since then. The fourth chapter was originally presented as a paper, 'Ethical Epiphany in the Story of Judah and Tamar,' for a comparative literature conference at the University of Toronto, April 2008, and subsequently published in a collection of essays: *Recognition and Modes of Knowledge: Anagnorisis from Antiquity to Contemporary Theory*, painstakingly edited by Teresa Russo (Edmonton: University of Alberta Press, 2013), pp. 51-76. The fifth chapter found a home, in an earlier draft, as 'Seduction and Recognition in the Story of Judah and Tamar and the Book of Ruth', in *Nashim* 23 (2012), pp. 87-109. A selection from the final chapter, on Joseph and Esther, was also published as '"Passing Strange"—Reading Transgender across Genre: Rabbinic Midrash and Feminist Hermeneutics on Esther', in *JFSR* 30.2 (2014), pp. 81-97.

But many of the chapters and selections of these chapters have never seen the light of publication. This is the first time that the theme of women's deception as a means of advancing the divine plot has been addressed systematically in the Hebrew Bible. Thank you to Sheffield Academic Press, and the series' editors, David Clines and J. Cheryl Exum, for recognizing the merit of bringing these essays together, for the first time, under the common theme of the female ruse.

I have shown drafts of many of these chapters to colleagues and friends for comment. I would like to thank, especially, Avivah Gottlieb Zornberg for her reading of earlier versions of the Judah and Tamar chapter, and for feedback on Esther and Joseph (Chapter 9). Her scholarship, creativity and depth, as a teacher and mentor, have been a pervasive source of courage and inspiration all along the way. In addition, I'd like to thank Judith Kates for her editorial suggestions on many of the chapters, and her unflagging encouragement of my scholarship. My brilliant rabbinical student at Hebrew College, Gray Myrseth, has also inadvertently contributed to these pages, in particular to the final chapter on 'Gender Crossing'. My friend Bracha Rosenberg also lent her keen eye to editing. I am most grateful to my compassionate and astute rabbinical student, Jordan Schuster, for his thorough editing and depth of insight as he read and commented on every line of this book. Without him, I could not have pushed through those last days of labor in the painful transition toward birth. He is the midwife of this book. But I attribute the conception of this book, ultimately, to my father, Howard Adelman, and to my mother, Margaret Adelman. They have been so much more than parents. Each, in their own way, has inspired and encouraged this work, with deep faith in me and in the knowledge underlying the female ruse.

Abbreviations

AB	Anchor Bible
Ag. Ber.	*Midrash Aggadat Bereshit* (ed. Buber)
ANET	*Ancient Near Eastern Texts Relating to the Old Testament* (ed. J.B. Pritchard; Princeton, NJ: Princeton University Press, 3rd edn, 1969)
ARN A and B	*Avot deRabbi Natan, Aleph and Beit* (ed. S. Schechter, Vienna, 5647/1887)
b.	*Babylonian Talmud*
BDB	*A Hebrew Lexicon of the Old Testament* (ed. Francis Brown, S.R. Driver and Charles A. Briggs; Oxford: Clarendon Press, 1907, 1966).
BI	*Biblical Interpretation: A Journal of Contemporary Approaches*
BR	*Bible Review*
Cant. R.	*Canticles Rabbah* [also *Shir haShirim Rabbah*] (standard printed edn, Vilna, 1878)
CBQ	*Catholic Biblical Quarterly*
Eccl. R.	*Ecclesiastes Rabbah* [also *Kohelet Rabbah*] (standard printed edn, Vilna, 1878)
Eliyahu R.	*Seder Eliyahu Rabbah* [also *Tanna de'bei Elyahu*] (ed. M. Ish Shalom; Vienna, 1902; reprint, Jerusalem: Wahrmann, 1969)
Est. R.	*Midrash Esther Rabbah* (standard printed edn, Vilna, 1878)
ESV	English Standard Version (Wheaton, IL: Crossway Books/Good News Publishers, 2001)
Gen. R.	*Genesis* [*Bereshit*] *Rabbah* (ed. H. Albeck and J. Theodor; 3 vols.; Berlin: Bi-defus Ts. H. Itskovski, 1912–31; reprint, Jerusalem: Wharmann, 1965)
GKC	*Gesenius' Hebrew Grammar* (ed. E. Kautzsch; rev. and trans. A.E. Cowley; Oxford: Clarendon Press, 2nd edn, 1910)
HALOT	*The Hebrew and Aramaic Lexicon of the Old Testament* (Leiden: Brill, CD-ROM edn, 1994–2000)
HTR	*Harvard Theological Review*

HUCA	*Hebrew Union College Annual*
Ibn Ezra	Abraham Ibn Ezra's commentary on the *Torah*
Jastrow	M. Jastrow, *A Dictionary of the Targumim, the Talmud Babli and Yerushalmi and the Midrashic Literature* (New York: Judaica Press, 1992)
JBL	*Journal of Biblical Literature*
JBQ	*Jewish Bible Quarterly*
JFSR	*Journal of Feminist Studies in Religion*
JNES	*Journal of Near Eastern Studies*
JOFA Journal	*Jewish Orthodox Feminist Alliance Journal*
Josephus, *Ant.*	*Antiquities of the Jews*, from *The Works of Flavius Josephus*, based on the 1890 Niese edition (BibleWorks, 2003)
JPS	Jewish Publication Society
JPSV	Jewish Publication Society Version
JQR	*Jewish Quarterly Review*
JSOT	*Journal for the Study of the Old Testament*
JSOTSup	*Journal for the Study of the Old Testament*, Supplement Series
KJV	King James Version, 1769 Blayney edn of the 1611 King James Version of the English Bible
Lam. R.	*Lamentations* [*Eikhah*] *Rabbah* (standard printed edn, Vilna, 1878)
LXX	Septuagint
m.	*Mishnah*
Maharal	commentary of the Moreinu HaRav Loew, otherwise known as the Maharal of Prague (1520–1609)
Maharsha	Moreinu Ha-Rav Shmuel Eidels (1555–1631), commentary on the Talmud
Mek. Ish.	*Mekhilta de-Rabbi Ishmael,*
Midr. Teh.	*Midrash Tehillim or Shoher Tov*
Midr. ha-Gadol	*Midrash ha-Gadol*
Midr. Yashar	*Midrash Yashar*
MT	Masoretic Text
Netziv	Rav Naftali Zvi Yehuda Berlin (otherwise known as the Netziv of Volozhin, 1816–1889), commentary on the Torah
NJPS	New Jewish Publication Society Version
NRSV	New Revised Standard Version, 1989
Num. R.	*Numbers Rabbah* [also *Bemidbar Rabbah*] (standard printed edn, Vilna, 1878)
Pes. K.	*Pesiqta de-Rav Kahana* (ed. B. Mandelbaum; 2 vols.; New York, 1962)

Pes. R.	*Pesiqta Rabbati* (ed. M. Ish Shalom, Tel Aviv, 1951)
Peshitta	Peshitta, the Syriac translation of the Pentateuch
PMLA	*Publication of the Modern Language Association of America*
PRE	*Pirqe deRabbi Eliezer* (Venice, 2nd edn, 1544)
Radak	Rabbi David Kimḥi's commentary on *Tanakh*.
Ramban	(also known as Naḥmanides), Rabbi Moshe ben Naḥman), commentary on Torah
Rashbam	Rabbi Shmuel ben Meir's commentary on Torah
Rashi	Rabbi Shlomo Yitzḥaqi's commentary on Torah and Nakh
RSV	Revised Standard Version 1952.
Ruth R.	*Ruth Rabbah* (standard printed edn, Vilna, 1878)
S. 'Ol. R.	*Seder 'Olam Rabbah*
t.	*Tosefta*
T.	*Testaments of the Twelve Patriarchs*, in *The Old Testament Pseudepigrapha,* II (ed. James H. Charlesworth; (New York: Doubleday, 1985)
Tanḥ.	*Tanḥuma: Midrash Tanḥuma-Yelammedenu* (Constantinople, 1st edn, 1520-22; reprint, Jerusalem, 1971)
Tanḥ. (ed. Buber)	*Midrash Tanhuma HaKadum ve'haYashan* (ed. S. Buber; Vienna, 1885)
Targ. Jon.	*Targum Jonathan ben Uzziel*
Targ. Neof.	*Targum Neofiti*
Targ. Onq.	*Targum Onqelos*
Targ. Ps.-J.	*Targum Pseudo-Jonathan*
VT	*Vetus Testamentum*
WBC	World Biblical Commentary
y.	*Palestinian Talmud* (or *Talmud Yerushalmi*)
Yal. Shimoni	*Yalkut Shimoni*
ZAW	*Zeitschrift für die alttestamentliche Wissenschaft*

TRANSLITERATION

א	ʼ (closing quotation mark)
ב	b (with dagesh) or v (without dagesh)
ג	g
ד	d
ה	h
ו	w; o/u (as a vowel)
ז	z
ח	ḥ
ט	t
י	y
כ	k (with dagesh) or kh (without dagesh)
ל	l
מ	m
נ	n
ס	s
ע	ʻ
פ	f (without dagesh); p (with dagesh)
צ	tz
ק	q
ר	r
שׁ	sh
שׂ	s
ת	t

Introduction

THE FEMALE RUSE

There are more things in heaven and earth, Horatio,
Than are dreamt of in your philosophy.

Shakespeare, *Hamlet* I.v

Oscar Wilde once wrote that 'Man is least himself when he talks in his own person. Give him a mask and he will tell you the truth.'[1] The truth the writer alludes to is an alternative truth, which the given identity of face and name cannot convey, a deeper truth that can only emerge through subterfuge. The guise uncovers a psychic terrain that not only unmasks others who might say and do what they otherwise would not, but also reveals desires inchoate to the self. This book centers on biblical plots of female subterfuge, which entail a journey below the surface of things (*subter*, in Latin), but also an escape or flight (*fugio*) from social and cultural norms. In folk tales and myth, the trickster is often the weaker party, subordinate within the social hierarchy, compelled to use artifice in order to circumvent authority or evade consequences. Like the story of Br'er Rabbit outwitting the wily fox in American folklore or Prometheus stealing fire from Mt Olympus, the female trickster in gendered tales of subterfuge in the Hebrew Bible is compelled to deceive in order to gain the upper hand over the man, who otherwise holds the reins of power.

Consider the daughters of Lot lying with their drunken father, who then conceive the founding fathers of Amon and Moab; Leah and Rachel, the mothers of the twelve tribes of Israel, duping Jacob on their wedding night; Tamar's seduction of Judah, her father-in-law, who then bears the progenitor of the Davidic line; Naomi sending Ruth to the threshing floor to seduce Boaz by night; and Queen Esther concealing her Jewish identity in the Persian imperial court. Wendy Doniger has aptly dubbed these scenes of

---

1. Oscar Wilde, 'The Critic as Artist', in *The Artist as Critic* (ed. Richard Ellman; Chicago: University of Chicago Press, 1968), p. 389.

deception 'the bedtrick'—sex with a partner whose identity is somehow obscured.² They take place in the most private sphere of encounter, in the bedroom, cave, or tent, where identities shift in the dark. What is most striking about these tales of feminine wile in the Bible is that the divine will allies with the women. The question is why. What role does the female ruse play in advancing the divine plot?

According to folklorist Victor Turner, the trickster figure inhabits a 'liminal space', betwixt and between social categories.³ He or she plays a morally ambiguous role, resorting to trickery, the 'power of the weak', in opposition to those who hold authority. With regard to the Bible, the question is whether deceptive women, as the weaker party, are deemed 'wily' by nature, thereby reinforcing power relations, or whether their use of subterfuge undermines that power hierarchy.⁴ Of the eleven central female figures in Genesis, six resort to deception.⁵ Yet not all are condoned. As Joshua Levinson points out, 'when her actions are perceived as undermining the patriarchal order she is deprecated, but when her actions promote providential plans or national aspirations of continuity, she is praised or at least justified in her actions'.⁶ This is certainly true for the matriarch Rebekah, when she dresses Jacob up in goatskins to steal the blessing, and for the midwives of the exodus, who defy Pharaoh's orders to slay the Hebrew infant boys, and for Rahab, the harlot, who enables the two Israelite spies to escape from Jericho. All these women are lauded for lying. This book, however,

---

2. Wendy Doniger, *The Bedtrick: Tales of Sex and Masquerade* (Chicago: University of Chicago Press, 2000).

3. Victor Turner, *The Ritual Process: Structure and Anti-Structure* (Chicago: Aldine, 1969).

4. Esther Fuchs argues that these narratives of deception are not just descriptive but prescriptive of patriarchal values, reinforcing the subordination and silencing of women ('Who Is Hiding the Truth? Deceptive Women and Biblical Androcentrism', in *Feminist Perspectives on Biblical Scholarship* (ed. Adela Yarbro Collins; Chico, CA: Scholars Press, 1985), pp. 137-44; '"For I Have the Way of Women": Deception, Gender, and Ideology in Biblical Narrative', *Semeia* 42 (1988), pp. 68-83; and *Sexual Politics in the Biblical Narrative: Reading the Bible as a Woman* (Sheffield, Sheffield Academic Press, 2000). Contrast Fuchs's claim that 'motherhood is a patriarchal institution', which only advances the birth of the male heir (*Sexual Politics*, p. 73), to Tikva Frymer-Kensky's discussion of the Rebekah narrative in *Reading the Women of the Bible* (New York: Schocken Books, 2002), pp. 5-23.

5. The daughter of Lot, Rebekah, Rachel, Tamar and Potiphar's wife.

6. Joshua Levinson, 'Dialogical Reading in the Rabbinic Exegetical Narrative', *Poetics Today* 25 (2004), pp. 517-18. This same point is made by Toni Cravens in 'Women Who Lied for the Faith', in *Justice and the Holy: Essays in Honor of Walter Harrelson* (ed. D.A Knight and P.J. Paris; Atlanta, GA: Scholars Press, 1989), pp. 35-59, and Ora Horn Prouser, 'The Truth about Women and Lying', *JSOT* 61 (1994), pp. 14-28, and Susan Niditch, *Underdogs and Tricksters: A Prelude to Biblical Folklore* (San Francisco: Harper & Row, 1987).

urges the reader to look beyond either/or, and the question as to whether deception is condemned or condoned. Trickery may present an opportunity for change, a shift in consciousness, or even an alternative interpretation or adjudication of law. Drawing on the structural anthropology of Lévi-Strauss, Mieke Bal suggests that deceptive women 'enable a culture to interpret and overcome its own dichotomies, contradictions, and suppressions'.[7] My study is necessarily selective; I am interested in those narratives that promote the 'providential plan' and, thematically, explore how the nexus of truth becomes gender embodied. I argue that, because the female trickster plays a morally ambiguous role, in violation of social norms, she enables renewal or transformation.[8]

The female ruse in the Hebrew Bible can be read as a subset of narratives of recognition, where the main player is propelled from ignorance to knowledge over the course of the story. The reader is drawn into this 'drama of knowledge' (Meir Sternberg's term) through various techniques of revealing and concealing, and comes to identify with the omniscient deity in the end.[9] Sternberg, however, does not systematically address the role of gender in the crux of the drama, contingent upon the gap between the 'best laid plans' of men and the divine will as forwarded by women. While my discussion is not restricted to sexual encounters, the stories do hinge upon knowledge concealed in the recesses of the female body, the site of conception and pregnancy. In the womb, the identity of the father is known, with certainty, only by the woman (and the omniscient deity). Anxiety over paternity indirectly underscores these narratives of deception, granting the heroine an advantage in the realm of *knowing,* both carnal and conscious. For the reader, secrecy is engendered in the act of conception and gives rise to the 'hermeneutic chromosome',[10] in which the advantage of knowing *more* than the male protagonist is engendered in the woman and reader alike. It is the inner workings of God through the female body that beckons the question: what does *she* know that the man does not, and why is this knowledge withheld from him? It prompts us to engage in a game of interpretation at the level of genetic selection. This selective force forms a helix,

---

7. Mieke Bal, 'Tricky Thematics', *Semeia* 42 (1988), p. 137.

8. See Kathleen Ashley, 'Interrogating Biblical Deception and Trickster Theories: Narratives of Patriarchy or Possibility', *Semeia* 42 (1988), p. 108.

9. See the discussion of the 'omnipotence effect' in Meir Sternberg, *The Poetics of Biblical Narrative* (Bloomington, IN: Indiana University Press, 1985), pp. 98-105.

10. Sanford Budick coined this term (oral communication), in response to Chanita Goodblatt's paper, 'Why Ruth? Interpretive Potential in the Biblical Text', at a conference: 'The Biblical Literary' (Hebrew University of Jerusalem, June 14, 2010). Whether Budick meant to convey a confluence between the reader and the woman's body as a locus of interpretation, I cannot ascertain for sure, but I adopt the term in this evocative sense.

like the DNA itself spiraling around its own axis, translating from code to physiological form. We are compelled to spin out the story-yarn, telling and retelling it in our attempt to ascertain the mystery of the father's seeding.

A Prospective

In the first section, I explore three stories of female subterfuge in the saga of the Israelite patriarchs: the story of Rebekah in finagling the blessing for Jacob from his father (Chapter 1); the collusion of sisters, Rachel and Leah, in duping Jacob on his wedding night (Chapter 2); and Tamar's seduction of Judah, her father-in-law (Chapter 3). In each story, a tension between the progression of lineage and the process of selection propels the plot forward. In Genesis, for example, the grand theme revolves around *toledot* ('all those begats'), the genealogical passage from father to son. Yet that simple progression is thwarted through barrenness (ubiquitous among the matriarchs), doubts as to who should be the chosen son under the rubric of God's covenant, and difficulties in settling the homeland. These conditions all obstruct the process of establishing the rightful heir, and women are ultimately pivotal in determining the selection. Drawing on the insights of classic midrash, medieval exegesis and modern literary readings, I outline the unique role that women play in deciding who should be the recipient of the patriarchal promise, the heir to the monarchy and the progenitor of the messianic line.

In the first chapter, 'Reading Rebekah Unveiled', I trace the role that the matriarch plays in promoting her favorite son, Jacob, as the recipient of the patriarchal blessing (Genesis 25 and 27). From the moment of first meeting, Rebekah's relationship with her husband, Isaac, is veiled, marked by an asymmetry of sight; she sees more, both literally and figuratively, than the myopic man. She alone is privy to the divine oracle on the fate of Jacob and Esau, her two sons, yet does not confide in her husband. She then guarantees the fulfillment of that oracle, dressing Jacob in goatskins to present himself before his blind father. Rebekah's active role in determining the heir to the covenant is read in the light of the near-ubiquitous theme of the overturning of primogeniture in the Hebrew Bible, where the younger son is favored over the firstborn. The question is why she never reveals the prophecy to her husband. What purpose does the obscured knowledge serve in advancing the divine plot?

The consequences for the deception carry over into the next generation, for the patriarch suffers, inexorably, as a result. Measure for measure, Jacob is duped on his wedding night, when Laban's older daughter, Leah, replaces Rachel, the beautiful and beloved younger one. According to the biblical account, the nefarious uncle is the agent behind the deception, whereas the midrash conceives of a collusion between the sisters. In this rabbinic reading, the women plot a 'bedtrick' before the marriage, which entails Rachel's self-abnegation and Leah's actively choosing Jacob. Though they mirror him, prick his conscience, neither of the sisters is rejected by the patriarch in the aftermath. In this reading, all twelve sons consequently become united under the rubric of the divine promise. This second chapter considers the critical role the matriarchs play in determining the heirs to the patriarchal covenant, and the havoc that ensues as a result of their later absence from the narrative of Joseph and his brothers. With Rachel's early demise, the plot devolves into near fratricide and exile (though this, too, is part of the divine plan).

The third chapter engages in a close literary reading of the Judah and Tamar narrative (Genesis 38). Flanked on either side by the stories of Joseph's sale into slavery and the attempted seduction of Potiphar's wife, it seems to interrupt the plot line. Rather than disjuncture, I read this story as integral to Judah's character development, where Tamar plays a critical role in his transformation from a rather odious character, who advocates for the sale of Joseph, to a man who later stands up as a substitute for his younger brother. The rabbinic tradition makes the causal link between the episodes explicit, and suggests that, as a result of his ethical epiphany, Judah is designated to be the progenitor of kings. Drawing extensively from midrash, this chapter explores the role that Tamar plays in mending the seam in Jacob's family, torn apart by fraternal schism, with a scarlet thread of continuity prescient of the royal line.

In the fourth chapter, 'Weaving the Messianic Light', I segue into the history of the Judean monarchy in a close reading of the three stories that constitute the background to the lineage of David—Genesis 19 (Lot's daughters), Genesis 38 (Judah and Tamar), and the book of Ruth. By subverting familial, legal and social norms, these women play a critical role in overcoming 'dichotomies, contradictions, and suppressions' (Mieke Bal) imbedded in the cultural context of the Hebrew Bible, especially manifest in the tension between endogamy (marriage within the clan) and exogamy (marriage outside the clan). The Hebrew verbs concerned with 'knowing' (*yd'* and *nkr*)—both in the figurative sense, as sexual knowledge, and in the normative sense, referring to consciousness or recognition—serve as *Leitwörter,* highlighting the thematic development of the female ruse. Read diachronically, these terms serve as markers in the transition from inchoate, unconscious knowledge to ethical recognition of the other, a move that is key to understanding the redemptive arc of biblical history.

As a sequel to the origins of the monarchy, I explore the background to the succession narrative in a close character study of three of David's wives—Michal, Abigail and Bathsheba (Chapters 6, 7 and 8). I frame these stories in terms of the use of promises and oaths, 'speech acts' (J.L. Austin's term), which the vying kings, Saul and David, both deploy in the early history of the monarchy (Chapter 5). These performative utterances not only bolster confidence in the political sphere but also serve as a litmus test for either divine sanction or approbation. In this reading, I follow the epithets attached to these three women as they are torn between men of power—either father and husband, or husband and king—David being the ultimate arbiter of their alliance. 'Uriah's wife' (Bathsheba), for example, is forced to betray her husband in submitting to the king's desire (2 Sam. 11.4). While she seems to play a submissive role in the passion play, her power comes to the fore in negotiating the inauguration of her son, Solomon, as successor to the throne (1 Kgs 1). There she invokes an oath that the king had supposedly made to her (though there is no prior record of it in the biblical text), and he responds, swearing on oath (again?) to set up Solomon, their son, as the next Judean monarch. Her name, Bathsheba, then takes on a new meaning as 'woman of oath [*bat-shevu'ah*]'. In all these stories, there is an underlying theme of dual loyalty, where women play a critical role in allying *with* or distancing themselves *from* authority, sometimes suffering tragic consequences. Do these women thereby voice a critique of the Davidic monarchy or reinforce its hegemony? The women are moved (Michal) or move themselves (Abigail and Bathsheba) across the king's chessboard in the adjudication of promises and oaths, testifying to the divine presence in history.

In the final chapter, 'Passing Strange: Gender Crossing in the Story of Joseph and Esther', I explore the dynamic analogies between these two narratives of exile at the end of book of Genesis and in the scroll of Esther. As feminine figures, both Joseph and Esther conceal their identities in the imperial court for the sake of their people's salvation. I show how the art of discretion or deceit, as a feminine mode of subterfuge, is not bound to the second sex; it is engendered, but not biologically determined. As orphans, beautiful strangers, the quintessential 'other' (Hebrew or Jew), Joseph and Esther rise to prominence in the foreign court. As they traverse this alien terrain, they gradually transcend their feminine traits. Moving from the status of *object* (the projection of others' desire and ire), to being *abject* (invisible or lacking agency in the harem or in prison), they finally surface as *subjects*, full agents in determining their own fate. Yet, as Esther sheds her 'feminine' persona in revealing herself as a Jew, Joseph becomes more 'masculine' behind the Egyptian mask, until it cracks upon confronting the specter of his father's bereaved face. In both these tales of Jew or Hebrew in the Diaspora, God is conspicuously absent. No revelation. No prophecy. No miraculous intervention. Yet the divine hand is palpable beneath the mask of the Egyptian viceroy and the crown of the Persian queen, as Joseph and Esther negotiate their own visibility and invisibility.

Introduction

On Method (or Madness)

I approach the Hebrew Bible in its final form as sacred literature that speaks across time and cultural context to the present reader. Though the insights of higher biblical criticism are informative, they have little sway over this reading of the text, for I am primarily interested in the *inter-text*, in the way each narrative speaks to another across the spectrum of the twenty-four books of the Bible. That is, the biblical text in its final form generates a meaning that is unique to us, and lost when subject to the scissor-cut-and-paste of source criticism. This 'holistic' or 'final form' study engages in the creative decisions and craftsmanship of the final redactor, before the text was sealed in its final canonical form.

The historical context and the authors' agenda underlying the sources are important, but the strands chafe against one another in generative ways. A Moabite woman becomes the great-grandmother of King David. How odd from the perspective of the Deuteronomist, where her nation is much maligned! The genealogies (*toledot*), characteristic of 'all those begats', were generated by P (the priestly source), yet they grind to a halt in the face of matriarchal barrenness. Why? To make way for J, the source that features the personal God of the Hebrews, Yhwh? There is something in the syncopation, in the rhythm of the written text as received, that summons us as *Miqra'*[11] to listen to the words and the silences that resonate around them, to read between the lines so 'fraught with background'.[12] The biblical text is both sparing and porous; the characters are so richly flawed and flailing. And the redactor, like God, wields the proverbial pen in judgment as he condemns and forgives. So Solomon, the son of David and Bathsheba, emblematic of a broken wholeness, conceived in the wake of the king's heinous sins of murder and adultery, becomes the successor to the throne. Only a great author could convince us of this choice! We nod our consent. It makes sense. It must be part of the method (or madness) of the providential plan. It aligns with our reading of the Bible as great literature, and the peculiar genius of the redactor in depicting the background and vicissitudes of the Judean monarchy.

In gesturing toward another story, each narrative, every character, is given a potential afterlife. Judy Klistner has identified many of these patterns as 'subversive sequels'. Like classic rabbinic midrash, she reads significance into the resonances between key words and phrases, allusions

---

11. The term for sacred Scripture, *Miqra'* in Hebrew, is derived from the verb *qr'*, meaning 'to call, to summon, to speak out loud'.

12. This is Erich Auerbach's now proverbial phrase, from 'Odyseus' Scar', *Mimesis: The Representation of Reality in Western Literature* (trans. Willard Trask; Garden City, NY: Doubleday, 1957), p. 9.

and parallel structures across disparate biblical stories, from Noah's dove to Jonah's prophecy, from the Tower of Babel to the midwives of Egypt. I, too, read midrashically into the *hereditary* sequels of the stories and impute an intention to the redactor's hand. My focus, primarily, is on the study of character and psychological transformation across generations. As a student of the midrashic tradition and a long-term disciple of Avivah Zornberg, I have absorbed rabbinic hermeneutics inexorably. It is a creative interpretive strategy, highly attuned to ironic gaps, verbal repetitions, even puns across the *Miqra'*, that empowers us to build a bridge from the world of the Bible, encrusted in ancient Mesopotamian legend and law, to the world of the reader. As Martin Buber eloquently wrote, 'I, the reader, the hearer, the human person, perceive through Scripture the voice that speaks from the origin toward the goal—this moment, my moment, mortal and eternal at once'.[13] The rabbis, of course, wrote commentary from within their own historical context, whether it be Palestine in late antiquity or medieval France in the wake of the Crusades.[14] I appropriate many of their exegetical insights, drawing from the profound resonances they heard between the lines. My goal, however, is quite different. The bridge between worlds must be longer and higher, for the waters that rush between their banks are deeper, wider and more treacherous to cross. I not only translate from the historical and social context of the Bible to the contemporary feminist reader, critical of its patriarchal machinations, but I cross discourses, from the creative world of rabbinic readings to modern literary scholarship.

Most importantly, I am interested in how God as a character of the Hebrew Bible can be read into the inter-textual resonances. God works through the feminine ruse to redeem people, political power, even the law over the course of biblical history. Like Buber and Rosenzweig, who were very much concerned with the redactor's 'theological project', I am interested in how the final form of the text *generates* the presence (or absence) of the divine. In retroactive justification of their translation of the Bible into German, Rosenzweig wrote:

> For us [the Hebrew Bible] is the work of a single mind. We do not know who this mind was; we cannot believe that it was Moses. We name that mind among ourselves by the abbreviation with which the Higher Criti-

---

13. Martin Buber, 'People Today and the Jewish Bible', in *Scripture and Translation* (trans. Lawrence Rosenwald with Everett Fox; Bloomington, IN: Indiana University Press, 1994), p. 8.

14. Whether the rabbis of classic rabbinic texts (second to seventh century CE), believed that this was the original meaning that *inhered* in the biblical text is a moot point. They did not make the same distinction between plain or contextual meaning, *peshat,* and creative or homiletical meaning, *derash,* as we moderns do. Rashi (1040–1105 CE) is heir to this beautiful naïveté.

cism of the Bible indicates its presumed final redactor of the text: R. We, however, take this R to stand not for redactor but for *rabbenu*. For whoever he was, and whatever text lay before him, he is our teacher, and his theology is our teaching.[15]

I too impute a revelatory role to the redactor. In continually receiving the *Word* as a gift, *Matan Torah*, I am empowered to learn anew from R, the redactor as *rabbenu*, though, for me, our rabbi may very well be a woman.

---

15. Franz Rosenzweig, 'The Unity of the Bible: A Position Paper vis-à-vis Orthodoxy and Liberalism', in *Scripture and Translation*, p. 23. I am grateful to my brilliant student, Jordan Schuster, for pointing out this source to me.

1

READING REBEKAH UNVEILED

> That is no country for old men. The young
> In one another's arms, birds in the trees—
> Those dying generations—at their song,
> The salmon-falls, the mackerel-crowded seas,
> Fish, flesh, or fowl, commend all summer long
> Whatever is begotten, born, and dies.
> Caught in that sensual music all neglect
> Monuments of unageing intellect.
>
> W.B. Yeats, 'Sailing to Byzantium'

Preamble

Oscillations between continuity and discontinuity, rupture and reconciliation, characterize the patriarchal narratives in the book of Genesis. The second of the matriarchs, Rebekah, is first introduced to the reader at one such transitional point, following the Binding of Isaac. Eight sons are born to Abraham's brother, Nahor; one begets a daughter destined to become Isaac's bride (Gen. 22.20-24). How auspicious! After the banishment of Ishmael, his first son, and the near sacrifice of his beloved younger son, Isaac, the biblical narrative recounts the potential for continuity within the family clan.[1] Though the story of Isaac and Rebekah opens with a promise of life through lineage, it is overshadowed by the specter of death; Sarah's demise follows this birth announcement (23.1-2). Isaac mourns his mother three long, dark years,[2] until he meets his bride from Paddan-aram: 'Then Isaac brought her into the tent of Sarah, his mother. He took Rebekah and

---

1. Rashi suggests that the passage (Gen. 22.20-24) signals an important postscript to the trauma of the *'Aqedah*. He implies that the biblical narrative speaks to the patriarch directly. According to Rashi's midrashic source, 'Abraham was troubled by doubts, saying to himself, "Had he (Isaac) died at Mount Moriah, would he not have died childless?" ... And so the Holy One, blessed be He, told him: "Don't worry, Isaac's bride has already been born, for Milcah has also borne children..."' (*Gen. R.* 57.3).

2. This is according to rabbinic tradition. See the reconstruction of the chronology in n. 11.

she became his wife and he loved her. Thus Isaac was comforted after his mother' (24.67). This is the first recorded love between husband and wife in the Bible. Yet this love is thwarted by barrenness, covert plotting, twins enthralled in rivalry that is spurred by the discrepancy between the parents' perceptions; the mother favors the chosen of God, Jacob, while the father favors the shunted one, Esau.

In this chapter, I explore the tensions within the drama of Isaac and Rebekah's family life, and highlight the discrepancy between their respective visions. How does Rebekah come to know more than her husband—he who, as a holy offering to God, had been bound for sacrifice on his father's altar? While the children are still *in utero*, she alone is privy to the divine oracle that 'the elder shall serve the younger' (Gen. 25.23), and she goes on to act on that knowledge, *beyond her husband's ken*. Why was Isaac not told that prophecy, either by his wife or by God directly? Was it because he was marked by trauma that would trail into his paternal relationship with his own sons? Perhaps. Most striking to the reader is that the prime mover behind the scenes is the mother, not the seemingly passive father. In this chapter, I foreground the role Rebekah plays in putting forward Jacob as the son of promise. She resorts to deceit, or (at least) fails to disclose the truth to her husband on no less than three occasions. I trace this pattern in their relationship back to their first meeting, where Isaac, returning from the fields of Beer-laḥai-roi, sees camels in the distance, while she sees *him*, falls off her camel, and (after ascertaining his identity) veils herself. This veiling sets the precedent for dissembling, an art that Rebekah masters and passes on to Jacob, her favorite son. To understand the meanderings of this argument, I begin with a rather long digression into the word *toledot*—signifying either genealogy or story—which opens the Isaac–Rebekah drama (and the Torah reading of that week), and proves to be a key *Leitwort* in the book of Genesis.

The Problem of Toledot

The overriding concern in the book of Genesis is the transition from one generation of males to the next, signaled by the key word *toledot* (lit. 'begetting'). The term *toledot,* variously translated as 'genealogy, generations, line, descendants', or 'lineage', derives from the root *yld*—'to generate, to give birth', or 'to beget'. It is always found in the plural, most often preceded by a demonstrative pronoun: *'eleh toledot*, 'these are the descendants of . . .' Further, it appears at ten significant points in the book of Genesis, each time marking off a distinct narrative cycle: (1) the heavens and the earth (Gen. 2.4); (2) Adam (5.1); (3) Noah (6.9); (4) Noah's sons (10.1); (5) Shem (11.10); (6) Terah (11.27); (7) Ishmael (25.12); (8) Isaac (25.19); (9) Esau (twice, 36.1, 9); and (10) Jacob (37.2). In addition, there are two addenda to the *toledot* series, accounting for the election of the levitical clan

(Num. 3.1) and the lineage of the Davidic monarchy (Ruth 4.18). With the exception of the 'generations of the heaven and the earth' (Gen. 2.4),³ the expression gestures *forward* to the descendants that follow the paternal line. In Genesis 10 (the descendants of Noah, known as the 'Table of Nations') and 11.10-26 (the descendants of Shem), the pattern opens with the naming of the father and his age at the birth of his firstborn, and trails off into a summation of the years he had lived *after* the next in line, perhaps with a bi-line about his other (inconsequential and unnamed) offspring: 'These are the begettings [*toledot*] of Shem. When Shem was one hundred years old, he became the father of Arpachshad two years after the flood; and Shem lived after the birth of Arpachshad five hundred years, and had other sons and daughters . . .' (Gen. 11.10-11). And so forth, from Arpaschshad to Shelah to Eber to Peleg, until we arrive at the genealogy of Terah. In these delineations of *toledot*, it is as if the birth of the next generation implied the death of the previous one; the son metaphorically brings about the demise of the father, who will then also 'die' when his son is born. These lists constitute, essentially, an anti-narrative, a refusal to tell the story about 'all those dying generations'.⁴

By contrast, the patriarchal narrative cycles open with a formula that defies the formulaic: *toledot* Terah (11.27), Isaac (25.19), and Jacob (37.2). The prior *toledot* are, for the most part, merely lists, while the *toledot* associated with the three patriarchs introduce a story line, generated by a thwarted genealogy. Most notable is the absence of *toledot Avraham*. The designated 'father of many nations' does not have his own line; rather, his genealogy is subsumed under the lineage of his father, Terah. This is peculiar to each of the three series introducing the patriarchs in Genesis: *toledot Terah* introduces the Abraham saga (11.27–25.11); *toledot Yitzḥaq* introduces the Jacob saga (25.19–35.29); and *toledot Ya'aqov* introduces the saga of Joseph and

---

3. Either this phrase is analeptic and concludes the first creation story (Gen. 1.1–2.4a) or it is proleptic, introducing the creation of humankind (Gen. 2.4b–4.26). Most Bible scholars see the *toledot* series as integral to the P (Priestly) source, and thus part of the first creation narrative. Jan Fokkelman, however, suggests that they are linking devices, like 'headers', and the creation of the human may be read as a combination of 'the heavens' (the breath of God) and 'the earth' ('dust of the ground') in Gen. 2.7. See the discussion in Jan P. Fokkelman, 'Genesis', in *The Literary Guide to the Bible* (ed. Robert Alter and Frank Kermode; Cambridge, MA: Belknap Press, 1987), pp. 41-42.

Noah's *toledot* (Gen. 6.9), like the three *toledot* introducing the patriarchal narratives, is similarly anomalous in that it does not mention his descendants but rather launches into a character description. One could argue that this is also a thwarted genealogy, a *toledot* that modulates into story, since continuity, the passage from father to son, is interrupted by the flood.

4. William Butler Yeats, 'Sailing to Byzantium'.

his brothers (37.2–50.26).[5] Furthermore, the simple progression from father to son is subject to disequilibrium,[6] an obstruction in the process of establishing the rightful heir. Consider the first of the major patriarchal cycles. The obstacle is introduced in the form of a barren wife, Sarah (Gen. 11.30), and is complicated by Abraham taking a second wife to generate a male heir. In the second cycle (Isaac's lineage), Isaac has only *one* wife, Rebekah, who is also barren. When that obstacle is overcome, it is the birth of twins that complicates the progression, prompting the question: Who should be the rightful heir to the birthright, Jacob or Esau? On what basis is the chosen son selected? True to the pattern in Genesis, the law of primogeniture is reversed, and the younger son is chosen. In the third cycle, Jacob is duped into marrying two sisters (accompanied by their maidservants), and obstacles abound, including whether all twelve sons will be included in the covenant, how that is achieved, and who gains supremacy over the other brothers. Will it be the firstborn son of the beloved wife (Joseph, son of Rachel), who rules them in his own lifetime according to his dreams, or Judah (the fourth born), who will become the progenitor of kings? Women are critical in all these stories of thwarted genealogy, and, in the end, they determine who is chosen and why.

Let us consider the opening of the Jacob cycle, introduced as *toledot Yitzhaq*: 'Now these are the begettings [*toledot*] of Isaac, son of Abraham; Abraham begot [*holid 'et*] Isaac' (Gen. 25.19).[7] Why does the verse not lead directly into 'And Isaac was forty years old when he *begot* Jacob and Esau' (v. 26)? Instead of a list of his sons (as in the genealogy of Ishmael or Esau), the verse redundantly asserts that Isaac is *the son of* Abraham,

---

5. I owe this insight on the *toledot* series to Joseph Blenkinsopp, *The Pentateuch* (New York: Doubleday, 1992), pp. 98-100. Jan Fokkelman, likewise, points to this pattern ('Genesis', p. 41).

6. I base these insights on the work of Naomi Steinberg, 'The Genealogical Framework of the Family Stories in Genesis', *Semeia* 46 (1989), pp. 41-50. She adopted the concept of the dynamics of 'equilibrium' and 'disequilibrium' within narrative from Tzevetan Todorov, *The Poetics of Prose* (Ithaca, NY: Cornell University Press, 1977). Edmund Leach, on the other hand, suggests that the simple progression of *toledot* is interrupted because of the complications in close kin endogamy. According to Leach, continuity can be achieved only through a breach in the rules of incest (*Genesis as Myth and Other Essays* [London: Jonathan Cape, 1969], pp. 21-22 n. 61).

7. Based on Everett Fox's translation, *The Five Books of Moses* (New York: Schocken, 1993), p. 115. The NJPS, interestingly, translates *toledot* here as 'story': 'This is the story of Isaac'. The NRSV, similarly, translates *toledot* in Gen. 37.2 as 'story': 'This is the story of the family of Jacob'. While *toledot* can imply both lineage and story (or history) in postbiblical Hebrew, I choose to be consistent in my translation of these key terms, to show how 'genealogy' modulates into 'story' by deviations from the expected path of 'begats'.

begotten by Abraham. The line, rather than thrusting forward toward the next generation, turns back on itself, like the Serpent Ouroboros swallowing its tail; it is a tautological, reflexive statement. Indeed, there is something eerily static about the Isaac cycle, as if the life of this patriarch is propped between the stature of Abraham, the first of the Israelite patriarchs, and the breadth of Jacob, his son.

Rashi (Rabbi Shlomo Yitzḥaqi, d. 1104), the great medieval Jewish exegete, commenting on Gen. 25.19, suggests that the redundancy addresses Isaac's potentially disputed paternity since his conception, announced in Gen. 21.1, follows the story of Sarah's abduction by Abimelech, king of Gerar (Gen. 20.1-18). According to Rashi's midrashic source, the 'scoffers in that generation' noted that Abraham's wife had been barren for decades and only conceived after the Canaanite king took her 'as his wife'. The biblical assertion of divine intervention on behalf of the old beauty and her centenarian husband (21.1) did not quell their snickering. So God concocted an ancient form of DNA testing, chiseling the features of Isaac's face into a mirror image of Abraham so that all would affirm that 'Abraham begot Isaac' (25.19).[8] Rashi's comment, here on 25.19, seems oddly misplaced in the context of *toledot Yitzḥaq*; it should be found, rather, in the episode of Isaac's birth and weaning (ch. 21). The midrashic sources deploying this motif, 'the image of the father's face', are based on a conflation between the passage concerned with Isaac's conception, his birth, and his weaning (Gen. 21.2, 7) and the opening verse of *toledot Yitzḥaq* (Gen. 25.19); the same motif surfaces in relation to Jacob and Joseph, albeit with a different

---

8. *Gen. R.* 53.6 on Gen. 21.1 (ed. Theodor-Albeck p. 561; hereafter, page references to *Genesis Rabbah* will refer to the following edition: *Genesis [Bereshit] Rabbah* [ed. H. Albeck and J. Theodor; 3 vols.; Berlin: Bi-defus Ts. H. Itskovski, 1912–31; reprint, Jerusalem: Wharmann, 1965]). This is characteristic of what James Kugel calls an 'exegetical motif' that can 'travel' from one biblical verse to another, where it may not have explanatory value on the verse at hand (fourth and fifth theses of his 'Nine Theses', in *In Potiphar's House* [Cambridge, MA: Harvard University Press, 1994], pp. 66-73 and 251-56). Rashi, on Gen. 25.19, uses the term *qlaster panav* [portrait of his face] but the midrash (*Gen. R.* 53.6 and *Tanḥ. Toledot* 1) uses the term *'iqonin* (image) from the Greek *eikonion*, meaning countenance. The midrash deploys this same motif in another context. In the Jacob–Joseph cycle, the father and son are likened to each other (*Gen. R.* 84.6, 8), based on the verse: 'And Jacob loved Joseph more than all his sons, because he was to him the son of his old age [*ben zqunim*]' (Gen. 37.3). The midrash implies a play on words between *zqunim* [old age] and *ziv 'iqonin* [the splendor of his countenance]. Similarly, Isaac is called the 'son of [Abraham's] old age [*ben li-zqunav*]' (Gen. 21.2), that is, 'the-son-in-the-image-of-the-father [*ziv iqonin shelo, domeh lo*]' (*Gen. R.* 53.6)—but the play on words is lost in the midrash on *toledot* (Gen. 25.19). On the likeness between Isaac and Abraham, see *b. B. Metz.* 87a; *b. Sanh.* 107b, *Gen. R.* 53.6, 9.

exegetical hook.[9] Yet, on another level, the rabbis may be subtly gesturing at the anxiety of paternity that lies curled around the root of each story of thwarted genealogy.

The unequivocal assertion of Abraham's fathering of Isaac points us in another direction. Instead of launching into a list of Isaac's descendants (as in Ishmael's and Esau's *toledot*), the focus is shifted from the question of sons to the identity of the father. Earlier, I noted that the genealogy of Abraham (*toledot Avraham*) is conspicuously absent from Genesis; his saga is subsumed under *toledot* Terah. In the story that follows *toledot Yitzḥaq*, focus is placed on the next generation, with the birth of Esau and Jacob, Isaac's twins. The conundrum revolves around *who* will be chosen for the covenantal blessing. Perhaps this is the *toledot Avraham* that is missing from the list of ten *toledot* in Genesis. Isaac serves merely as the bridge between Abraham, the first of the patriarchs, and Jacob, the third. In the words of Everett Fox, Isaac 'functions in Genesis as a classic second generation—that is, as a transmitter and stabilizing force, rather than as an active participant in the process of building the people'. After a mere two chapters, 'he fades out of the text entirely, only to die several chapters and many years later'.[10] Though Isaac is designated by his own genealogy, *toledot Yitzḥaq* is essentially Abraham's, and functions as the segue into the Jacob saga. Rather than a list of begats, a nonstory, or a refusal to tell about 'all those dying generations', *toledot* modulates into narrative as we are privy to a *very complicated* transition from father to son or, rather, from grandfather to grandson. Rebekah plays a key role in that transition.

Barrenness, Prayer, Conception and Crisis

At the age of forty, Isaac marries Rebekah; we are not told her age (Gen. 25.20).[11] A barren period of two decades passes,[12] but no maidservant is procured. In contrast to Abraham and Jacob, who willingly conceive sons by

---

9. In *Gen. R.* 84.6, 8 based on the word *zqunim* in Gen. 37.3. See the discussion in Chapter 9 n. 41.

10. Fox, *Five Books of Moses,* p. 111.

11. According to Rashi, Rebekah was three at the time of her marriage, because her birth (Gen. 22.23) was announced immediately following the *'Aqedah* (Rashi on Gen. 25.2). According to this sequence, Sarah died at the age of 127 (Gen. 23.1) as a result of the *'Aqedah* (when Isaac must have been 37) and the mother-substitute is then born. In the biblical text, Isaac is finally comforted from the death of his mother three years later, at the age of 40, upon his marriage to Rebekah (Gen. 25.20). Of course, her conjectured age of 3 is completely incongruent with her behavior at the well (Genesis 24). Rashi draws on *Seder 'Olam Rabbah.* 1. An alternative manuscript tradition more reasonably deems Rebekah to be 14 at her marriage (*S. 'Ol. R.* 1).

12. We are told that Isaac is 60 when the twins are born (Gen. 25.26).

a 'rival wife' rather than remain childless, Isaac does not acquire a second wife to Rebekah.[13] Instead, there is an appeal to God: 'And Isaac prayed to Yhwh in the presence of his wife, for she was barren, and Yhwh granted his prayer: Rebekah, his wife, conceived' (v. 21). He is the first man of whom it is said that he loved his wife (v. 67), and he is the only one to entreat God on her behalf when she is deemed, by the narrative, to be barren. Furthermore, of all the narratives concerning barren women—Sarah, Rachel, Hannah, the woman of Shunam and Samson's mother—God here responds *uniquely* to the husband's prayer in granting Rebekah conception.

Despite this effective appeal to God and the seeming synergy between husband and wife, Isaac's relationship with Rebekah is fraught with lack of communication and later duplicity on her part. Signs of a rift surface when she initiates contact with God during her pregnancy. It is, strikingly, 'the only biblical pregnancy'.[14] Predominately, biblical narratives are marked by the seamless 'she conceived and gave birth [*va-tahar va-teled*]'. But complications in gestation, as Avivah Zornberg suggests, prompt her to become 'the first biblical character . . . to go in quest of God'.[15]

> But the children struggled together within her womb [*be-qirbah*],
> So she said: 'If this is so, why do I exist [*lamah zeh 'anokhi*]?'
> And she went to inquire of Yhwh (Gen. 25.23).[16]

Rebekah experiences something unusual during her pregnancy: an intrauterine conflict, though she may not yet know that she carries twins. This struggle in the womb suggests that the rivalry over the birthright begins *in utero* and serves as a foreshadowing of the events that will ensue—complications in acquiring the birthright and blessing.[17] For Rebekah, it entails a

---

13. Robert Alter has characterized the recurrent pattern of the barren wife in terms of the near-ubiquitous annunciation scene: Sarah (Genesis 18), Rachel (Genesis 29–30), Hannah (1 Samuel 1–2), and Samson's mother (Judges 13), the Shunammite (2 Kings 4). The 'divine revelation', for Rebekah, happens after the conception. See the discussion in Robert Alter, 'How Convention Helps Us Read', *Prooftexts*, 3 (1983), pp. 115-30, and Rachel Adelman, 'On Laughter and Re-membering', in *Nashim* 8 (2004), pp. 230-44.

14. Avivah Zornberg, 'Her Own Foreigner', in *The Murmuring Deep* (New York: Schocken Books, 2009), p. 208.

15. Zornberg, *Murmuring Deep*, p. 208.

16. All translations of primary texts are the author's unless otherwise indicated.

17. See Hos. 12.4, and the discussion in Nahum Sarna, *Understanding Genesis* (New York: Schocken Books, 1966), pp. 182-83. See also Harold Ginsberg, 'Hosea's Ephraim, More Fool Than Knave: A New Interpretation of Hosea 12.1-14', *JBL* 80 (1961), pp. 339-47 (342). An explanation of the difference between the status of birthright [*bekhorah*, lit. firstborn status, or primogeniture], and blessing [*brakhah*] is in order here. The former refers to the principle that the firstborn is favored in some way. According to Deut. 21.15-17, he inherits a double portion. This is the privilege, presumably, that Esau 'sells' to Jacob (Gen. 25.29-34). The obvious question is: how can one sell one's birth-

keen sense of the gap between the outward 'smoothness' of her belly's skin and the inner tumult.

Given the intensity of her experience, why does she not first appeal to her husband, Isaac, before turning to God, as Sarah confronted Abraham in the case of Hagar (21.9-10), or as Rachel appealed to Jacob in distress over her own barrenness (30.1)? Classic rabbinic commentary reflects an uneasiness over Rebekah's direct consultation of God. Rashi, for example, suggests that she went to Shem's House of Study.[18] Perhaps the rabbis are uncomfortable with her direct appeal because of the consequences—she comes to know *more* than her husband about the divine plan. Her tone

---

right? Surely the firstborn status is decided by nature! Yet, according to the Hebrew Bible, it seems to be 'transferable'. Consider the displacement of Reuben by Joseph (or, rather, by Joseph's two sons, Ephraim and Manasseh, in Gen. 48.5 and 49.3; cf. 1 Chron. 5.1). For a summary of the significance of birthright in the Hebrew Bible and ancient Mesopotamia, see Sarna, *Understanding Genesis*, pp. 184-87. The blessing, on the other hand, is not necessarily linked to firstborn status. Rather, it refers to the patriarchal blessing that God first granted to Abraham—the promise of land (*'eretz*, specifically the land of Canaan) and the promise of descendants (*zer'a*, lit. seed)—Gen. 12.7; 13.15; 15.18; 17.8; 22.17-18 (God to Abraham); 21.12 (Abraham indirectly to Isaac at God's behest); 26.3-4 (God to Isaac); 28.3-4 (Isaac to Jacob); 28.13-14; and 35.11-12 (God to Jacob; cf. 48.4). Menachem Leibtag points out that Isaac never intended to give the patriarchal blessing of 'chosenness' (what he calls *beḥirah*) to Esau, but, rather, meant to bless him with prosperity and supremacy over his brother(s) (as in Gen. 27.28-29; see http://www.tanach.org/breishit/toldot/toldots1.htm). He argues that Isaac intended to bless both children, the first blessing (intended for Esau) to do with prosperity and power, while Abraham's blessing was reserved for Jacob. However, it is clear that in Rebekah's eyes (according to the divine sanction she is granted at the outset as well as retroactively), the birthright and the blessing are intertwined, based on the promise that 'the elder shall serve the younger'. Precisely because the blessing of the hybrid heir holds and is not turned into a curse (27.33), Isaac is willing to grant Jacob the patriarchal blessing of chosenness (*beḥirah*). It could also be that Esau has disqualified himself from chosenness through his marriage to Hittite women, in breaching the taboo against endogamy (27.46; cf. 26.34-35). See Michael Fishbane, *Text and Texture* (New York: Schocken Books, 1979), pp. 48-49.

18. Rebekah had gone to the 'Beit Midrash of Shem' (Rashi on Gen. 25.23, based on *Ag. Ber.* 73; cf. *Gen. R.* 63.6, p. 684). In this reading, Rebekah is not granted an unmediated relationship with the divine. Surprisingly, the rabbis identify Sarah as the only matriarch who hears God's words directly (albeit by eavesdropping, mediated through an angel; cf. Gen. 18.15). 'In the words of R. Yehuda bar Simon and R. Yochanan, in the name of R. Elazar bar Shimon: "The Holy One, blessed be He, would never converse with a woman out of necessity except with that righteous woman (i.e. Sarah), and then only indirectly"' (*Gen. R.* 63.7, p. 684, and the list of parallels there). Furthermore, despite the prophecy to which Rebekah is privy, she is not included in the list of seven prophetesses (*b. Meg.* 14a-b). See my discussion, later, on Gen. 27.41-42 (and the reference to *Gen. R.* 67.9 n. 47).

implies urgency: *lamah zeh 'anokhi* (lit. 'why this me?', or 'why is this happening to me?'). Ibn Ezra suggests that she consults other women, and, when they deny having had such an experience in pregnancy, she feels compelled to appeal to God: 'Then why am I beset with an unusual pregnancy?' Rebekah's question is essentially of a 'feminine nature'—the gynecological sort—which her husband cannot address. Rashi, on the other hand, understands her question as arising from a profound perplexity, a sense of purpose undermined—'If the pain of this pregnancy is so great, why did I pray for and desire conception so fervently?' Perhaps she does not appeal to Isaac because of the unusual nature of her discomfort. The meaning must come from the divine source.

Avivah Zornberg, drawing on Ramban's reading, understands Rebekah's appeal as an existential crisis—'Why I?'—a quest for meaning as to why she exists in the world altogether. Her *cris de coeur* is comparable to Job's lament: 'Why did I not die at birth, expire as I came forth from the womb?' (Job 3.10). 'Why did you let me come out of the womb? Better had I expired before any eye saw me, had I been as though I never was, had I been carried from the womb to the grave' (Job 10.18-19). In surveying the use of the interrogative 'why [*lamah*]', Zornberg suggests that it often opens a rhetorical question: '*Why* did Sarah laugh?' (Gen. 18.13); '*Why* did You bring us up out of Egypt to die in the desert?' (Exod. 17.3); 'My God, my God! *Why* have you forsaken me?' (Ps. 22.2); and '*Why* do you hide your face?' (Ps. 44.25; Job 13.24).[19] That is, if read rhetorically, Rebekah's question implies that it would have been better had she never been born. She is not simply asking, then, 'why this is happening to me', but expresses a death wish, even in the throes of the intensity of her vital, pregnant self. Unlike Job, however, who wishes the womb had been his tomb, Rebekah, in Zornberg's words, '*is* the womb, the belly, the entrails. She not only questions her natal condition, but *is* the body in which human life uncannily originates'.[20] In that state, she is keenly aware of the simultaneous 'presence and absence of meaning', the will to undo it all in the very act of gestation.

Does God's answer reassure her that there is meaning behind the severe pangs of her pregnancy and the angst it engenders?

The Divine Oracle

And Yhwh said to her:
'Two nations—in your womb,
Two peoples from your belly shall be divided,

---

19. Zornberg, *Murmuring Deep*, p. 220.
20. Zornberg, *Murmuring Deep*, p. 215.

[One] people over the [other] people shall prevail,
And the elder shall serve the younger [*ve-rav ya'avod tza'ir*]' (Gen. 25.23).

The oracle, as a poem, reveals the future gradually, as layers of knowledge peeled away. First there are twins who will emerge as two separate nations. As two peoples, they will be divided, but not peaceably. Rule, one over the other, and servitude, one to the other, will ensue. Suspense is only relieved in the last line—the younger brother, as a nation, shall rule over the elder. Is this meant to reassure Rebekah with regard to her anxiety? Does it answer her existential quest for meaning? It certainly explains the struggle in her womb. The rivalry between the brothers over the birthright is prenatal. But a terrible ambiguity is implied by this oracle. In Biblical Hebrew, it is not clear what the subject or the direct object of the verb, *ya'avod*, might be. Most translations and interpretations assume 'the elder will serve the younger', because it justifies the election of Jacob (*qua* Israel) over Esau (*qua* Edom) and the course of the biblical narrative that ensues. The younger will eventually bargain his older brother out of the birthright and usurp the patriarchal blessing; these acts of manipulation are seemingly divinely sanctioned. But one could render the Hebrew syntax as opening with the direct object and concluding with the subject: 'The elder—the younger will serve'.[21] This second reading has vast implications for the

---

21. For example, the direct object and subject are reversed in Job 14.19, *'avanim shaḥaqu mayim* [lit. 'stones—waters erode', or waters erode away stones]. Driver understands the 'rule of the younger over the older' unambiguously to refer to historical context—'Edom was subjugated by David (2 Sam. 8.12-14), and remained subject to Judah for nearly 130 years (cf. Gen. 27.40)' (S.R. Driver, *The Book of Genesis: With Introduction and Notes* [London: Methuen, 2nd edn, 1904], pp. 245-46). Likewise, Hermann Gunkel assumes no ambiguity in the syntax (*Genesis* [Macon, GA: Mercer University Press, 3rd edn, 1997], p. 289); see also Gordon Wenham, *Genesis 16–50* (Dallas, TX: Word Books, 1994), pp. 175-76, and Claus Westermann, *Genesis: A Commentary* (Minneapolis, MN: Augsburg Publishing House, 1985), pp. 12-36. Isaac, however, later modifies the oracle and blessing (27.29) in the promise he salvages for Esau (27.40). The midrash takes this even further, and suggests that '*rav ya'avod tza'ir*' assumes a new meaning when Jacob identifies Esau as his 'lord' [*'adon*] or 'master' [*rav*], referring to himself as his 'servant' [*'avadekha*] (Gen. 32.5; 33.13). Here the younger adopts an obsequious tone toward the elder upon his return to Canaan. According to the midrash, God then swears: 'By my life, it shall be according to your words; he shall rule over you in this world and you shall rule over him in the world to come' (*PRE* 37; see also *Gen. R.* 63.7, p. 686: 'If he [Jacob/Israel] is worthy he [Esau/Edom] will be subservient; if not, not'). Clearly the author of the midrash is aware of the discrepancy between the divine oracle and historical reality, imaginatively inverting the plain meaning of God's original decree. In his commentary on Genesis (*Da'at Mikra*), Yehuda Kiel suggests that the ambiguity allows for a double reading: 'the elder shall serve the younger [*rav ya'avod tza'ir*] or 'the older will be served by the younger' [(*'et*) *ha-rav, ya'avod tza'ir*], based on the Netziv, R. Naftali Tzvi Yehuda Berlin, on Gen. 25.23; Yehuda Kiel, *Sefer Breshit*

role of human initiative in unraveling the plot. Just as Macbeth brought on his own inimitable fate in heeding the witches' ominous greeting, 'All hail Macbeth, that shalt be king hereafter',[22] Jacob and his mother take an active role in the fulfillment of the oracle. In doing so, they both suffer tragic consequences. A shadow was cast upon Macbeth's fate—he would wear a 'fruitless crown' on his head and carry 'a barren sceptre' in his grip, 'thence to be wrench'd with an unlineal hand, no son of [his] succeeding',[23] while Banquo, according to the witches' harping, would 'get kings, though [he] be none'.[24] Similarly, a shadow is cast over Jacob's fate. Esau would continue to be a contender for supremacy all of Jacob's life. Indeed Isaac, as compensation to the older son for the usurped blessing, intones these ominous words: 'By your sword you shall live, and you shall serve your brother; but when you break loose, you shall break his yoke from your neck' (Gen. 27.40). The fraternal struggle for supremacy continues (by extension) throughout Jewish history: 'the elder—the younger will serve' at certain periods in the rise and fall of civilizations. Edom/Rome (*qua* Esau), for a period, would rule over the Jews; Christianity would presume to supersede Judaism.[25] Perhaps the fulfillment of the oracle is fraught precisely because 'the best laid plans of mice and men' are at odds with God's plan. Throughout the Bible, a tension persists between outward expectations and internal or hidden criteria of chosenness. What sets Rebekah apart from Isaac is her insight into the discrepancy between the outer norms (the election of the firstborn) and the inner truth of the divine plan. She also exemplifies the difficulty in externalizing that inner, divine truth as embodied in her intimate, womb-bound knowledge found in the tumult within her belly [*be-qirbah*, Gen. 25.22]. In fact, her name, *Rivqah*, can be read as an anagram of the Hebrew term *qirbah*, meaning 'her innards'.[26]

(3 vols.; Jerusalem: Mosad ha-Rav Ḳuḳ, 1997–2003), p. 225. Which brother rules will depend on historical circumstances.

22. William Shakespeare, *Macbeth* I.iii.50.

23. *Macbeth* I.iii.67.

24. *Macbeth* III.i.61-63.

25. Esau/Edom, in rabbinic literature, is symbolically identified with Rome and Christendom. See Alan Segal, *Rebecca's Children: Judaism and Christianity in the Roman World* (Cambridge, MA: Harvard University Press, 1986), and Gerson Cohen, 'Esau as Symbol in Early Medieval Thought', in *Jewish Medieval and Renaissance Studies* (ed. Alexander Altmann; Cambridge, MA: Harvard University Press, 1967), pp. 19-48. For a more recent treatment, see Mireille Hadas-Lebel, 'Jacob et Esaü ou Israël et Rome dans le Talmud et le Midrash', *Réforme, humanisme, renaissance* 101 (1984), pp. 369-92; and, most recently, Israel Yuval, *Two Nations in your Womb: Perception of Jews and Christians in Late Antiquity and the Middle Ages* (trans. Barbara Harshav and Jonathan Chipman; Berkeley, CA: University of California Press, 2006).

26. This is based on Zornberg's insight, *Murmuring Deep*, p. 219.

The tension between God's (internal) plot, as forwarded by women, and the 'best laid plans' of men is exemplified by the near-ubiquitous biblical motif of the overturning of primogeniture. Jacob's displacement of Esau is the paragon example of the usurpation of the right of the firstborn by the younger son. In Deut. 21.15-17, it is stated explicitly that the firstborn shall inherit a double portion, even if he is the son of the 'despised wife'.[27] Yet, as Robert Alter points out, 'the first-born [sons] very often seem to be losers in Genesis by the very condition of their birth'.[28] Isaac is selected, while Ishmael is excluded from the covenant of Abraham, and Jacob acquires the birthright and blessing, displacing Esau. This process of selection does not hinge on merit; Jacob, after all, is chosen by God *in utero*.[29] The recurrent theme illustrates a broader theological principle, in which divine election is set at odds with legal or social norms. Over the course of these narratives of selection, two perspectives are set in high relief, as Meir Sternberg argues: 'one oriented to internal and the other to external givens, norms, and probabilities'.[30] In the Jacob–Esau conundrum, Rebekah is privy to that internal principle, like God, 'who sees not as mortals see; they see through the eyes, but God looks to the heart' (1 Sam. 16.7). She alone is given insight into the divine plan, in response to her query about the tumult in her womb. Isaac, on the other hand, in favoring Esau, sees only as mortals see, although, ironically, he is purblind.

The struggle of the twins in the womb continues into the birth scene:

> The first came out red, all his body like a hairy mantle; so they named him Esau. Afterward his brother came out, with his hand gripping Esau's heel ['*eqev*]; so he named him Jacob [*Ya'aqov*] (Gen. 25.25-26).

Their emergence from the birth canal implies rivalry between the two infants. Intentionality is imputed to Jacob in the 'race for first place', as the

---

27. This principle, that the firstborn receives the double portion, is paralleled in Assyrian, Hittite and Nuzi documents of the ancient Near East. See the discussion in Sarna, *Understanding Genesis*, pp. 184-87, and his reference to the secondary literature, p. 190 n. 22. For a discussion of the principle in Jewish sources, see Jon D. Levenson, *The Death and Resurrection of the Beloved Son* (New Haven, CT: Yale University Press, 1993), pp. 55-60.

28. Robert Alter, *The Art of Biblical Narrative* (New York: Basic Books, 1981), p. 6.

29. Paul in his epistle to the Romans makes this acute observation (Rom. 9.10-11). In addition to Isaac/Ishmael and Jacob/Esau, there are many more examples: Cain and Abel (Gen. 4.3-5), Reuben's displacement by both Joseph and Judah (Gen. 49.3; cf. 1 Chron. 5.1), Zerah and Perez (Gen. 38.27-30), Manasseh and Ephraim (48.12), and the choice of David, the eighth of Jesse's sons, as king (1 Samuel 16). For a study of this typology, see Roger Syrén, *The Forsaken First-Born: A Study of a Recurrent Motif in the Patriarchal Narratives* (Sheffield: JSOT Press, 1993).

30. Meir Sternberg, *The Poetics of Biblical Narrative* (Bloomington, IN: Indiana University Press, 1985), p. 99.

verse in Hosea implies: 'In the womb he [Jacob] tried to supplant [*'aqav*] his brother' (Hos. 12.4).[31] Though he loses the race, the victor in the conflict has already been determined by God. Accordingly, Jacob is named 'Heel-Holder'.[32] What he does as a newborn, in hand-to-heel combat, he will eventually do as a more conscious, sentient adult when he sells Esau the bowl of lentil stew, that 'red, red stuff', for the sake of the birthright (25.29-34). And following his mother's cue, he will steal the blessing intended for the firstborn—the blessing that would grant him sovereignty, so that he would 'become lord over his brothers' (27.29), and 'they would serve him' (v. 37). When he returns after hunting and preparing the game, too late to receive the blessing of supremacy, Esau gives Jacob, 'Heel-Holder', a new meaning to his name: 'Is he not rightly named Jacob? For he has supplanted me [*ya'aqveni*][33] these two times. He took away my birthright; and look, now he has taken away my blessing' (27.36).[34] In usurping the position of firstborn, mother and son play an active role. Jacob is named for that act of supplanting; it is a name he must, in the end, overcome.

Jacob, as the quintessential supplanter, and Rebekah, his mother, play a peculiar role not only in interpreting the oracle unambiguously in his favor—'the *older* shall serve the *younger*'—but also in guaranteeing that it is fulfilled. One must note, however, that Rebekah is not involved in his naming, with the pejorative overtones that *Ya'aqov*, 'heel-grabber' and 'supplanter', connote. Esau is named by both parents: 'the first one came out ruddy . . . so *they* named [*va-yiqr'u*] him Esau' (25.25); while Jacob seems to be have been named by his father: '*he* named [*va-yiqra'*] him Jacob' (v. 26).[35] Judy Klitsner suggests that the asymmetry in naming the

---

31. The original Hebrew reads '*ba-beten 'aqav 'et 'ahiv*'; 'he took his brother by the heel' (RSV, KJV on Hos. 12.3; v. 4 in MT), or 'he tried to supplant his brother' (NJPS and NRSV). This is clearly a play on the etiology of Jacob's name, *Ya'aqov*. Hosea seems to imply a criticism of Jacob's 'clutching' at the heel as an attempt to supplant his brother. See Yair Zakovitch's discussion, *An Introduction to Inner-Biblical Interpretation* (Even Yehudah: Rekhes, 1992), pp. 13-15.

32. Fox, *Five Books of Moses*, p. 115. The heel, of course, is associated with lowly status and unscrupulous behavior—hence the English expression 'he's a real heel' (i.e. low-life). The connotation carries over, in Hebrew, from the curse of the primordial serpent: 'he [i.e. man] will strike your head, and you will strike his heel [*'aqev*]' (Gen. 3.15).

33. From the root *'qb*, it is roughly synonymous with the verb *rmh*—to act cunningly or deceitfully (see BDB entry 7344, p. 784).

34. The same negative connotation to the name *Ya'aqov* is found in Jeremiah, clearly alluding to the Jacob/Esau narrative: 'And put no trust in any brother; for every brother is a supplanter/deceiver [*'aqov ya'aqov*] . . .' (Jer. 9.3). See Zakovitch, *Inner-Biblical Interpretation*, pp. 14-15.

35. Rashi makes this observation: 'they all named him Esau . . .' whereas either God or Isaac names Jacob (Rashi on Gen. 25.25-26). Many English translations, however,

twins is yet another hint 'of the growing chasm between husband and wife' with regard to their children.[36] 'Isaac loved Esau, for [he hunted] game for his mouth',[37] while she 'loved Jacob' (v. 28)—apparently unconditionally; no explanation is given. But the reader, privileged along with the omniscient narrator, fills in the gap: Rebekah alone knows that Jacob must be the chosen son. Perhaps she does not engage in the naming of Jacob because she does not consider him a 'supplanter', a 'heel-grabber', or a 'usurper' at all, but rather the true heir to the right of the firstborn.

Drawing on Lionel Trilling's analysis of the historical movement in literature and philosophy from the admiration of 'sincerity' to that of 'authenticity', Avivah Zornberg traces the trajectory of Jacob's life in terms of his development into a more complex character.[38] He is transformed from a simple or sincere man ['*ish tam*, in Gen. 25.27] into one who will act in 'authenticity' as a result of his dissembling and trickery. In donning the mask as he stands before his blind father, he claims: 'I am Esau, your firstborn ['*anokhi Esav bkhorekha*]' (27.19). Rashi reads Jacob's statement as 'true' (the patriarch, surely, would not lie!) by splicing the statement: '*I* ['*anokhi*] am the one who is bringing you food, [but] Esau he is your firstborn [*Esav bkhorekha*]'.[39] By clever exegetical gymnastics, Jacob's deception is undermined. Yet, on another level, he does not *really* lie because he has become the firstborn, having acquired this status from his brother in exchange for a dish of stew. Nevertheless, at the level of plain meaning, a gap remains between the speaker, who *thinks* one thing, and the listener, who hears another. This is the essence of dramatic irony. In fact, the term *irony* derives from the Greek word for dissimulation, *eironia,* a kind of mock modesty, when one says less than one thinks. At that moment, as Jacob assumes the ironic posture, he represents a truth that lives in the gap

---

don't pick up on this discrepancy in the MT and, rather, amend the latter phrase to 'they called him Jacob' (NJPS; cf. Robert Alter, *Genesis* [New York: Norton, 1996], p. 128; Fox, *Five Books of Moses,* p. 115). Interestingly, the LXX follows the tradition of maternal naming in Genesis: she names both Esau and Jacob, though different verbs are used: *eponomazō* and *kaleō* respectively.

36. See Judy Klitsner, *Subversive Sequels in the Bible* (Philadelphia, PA: Jewish Publication Society, 2009), pp. 144-45.

37. The rabbis understand the possessive pronoun 'in his mouth [*ba-piv*]' to refer not to Isaac, but to Esau, 'who knew how to trap and to deceive his father with his mouth' (Rashi on Gen. 25.28; *Tanḥ. Toledot* 8; *Gen. R.* 63.10, p. 694).

38. See the discussion in Avivah Zornberg, *The Beginning of Desire: Reflections on Genesis* (New York: Doubleday, 1996), pp. 144-79.

39. In Rashi's source, the '*anokhi* [I am]' is identified differently: '*anokhi*—I am the one destined to receive the Ten Commandments' (*Gen. R.* 68.18, p. 730). This is a play on the opening term, '*anokhi*, of the Decalogue, Exod. 20.2 and Deut. 5.6: 'I am ['*anokhi*] Yhwh, your God who brought you out of Egypt'. See Zornberg, *Beginning of Desire,* p. 402 n. 73.

between the speaker and his interlocutor, according to Zornberg, 'a kind of truth, a truth of authenticity, rather than of sincerity'.[40] Jacob learns this art of dissembling, the art of masks, from his mother.

The Widening Rift

The rift between Isaac and Rebekah begins from the moment that the divine oracle introduces a discrepancy between their perspectives. It widens when Isaac, as a blind, old man, resolves to bless his son Esau, not knowing how soon he will die (Gen. 27.1-2).[41] Rebekah is sidelined from the process of bestowing the blessing. She merely *overhears* Isaac asking Esau to hunt for game and to prepare savory food for him to eat so that he might bless the heir-apparent before he dies (v. 3). Accordingly, the question has perplexed many scholars as to why Rebekah never told her husband, at that point, of the oracle that 'the elder shall serve younger' (25.23). She might have drawn her husband aside with the words: 'But, dear, you are mistaken. It is Jacob who should be the heir to the covenantal blessing'.

Perhaps in response to being shunted, she amends her husband's words when she reports them to Jacob, the 'true' heir: 'I heard your father say to your brother, Esau, "Bring me game, and prepare for me savory food to eat, that I may bless you *in* the presence of *Yhwh* before I die"' (vv. 6-7). She invokes the presence of God, the Tetragrammaton; this blessing is going to come from a place on High.[42] She then assures Jacob when he expresses anxiety that his father may curse him if he discovers that he has been cheated: 'Let your curse be upon me, my son . . .' (Gen. 27.13). Thrice she urges *her son* to listen to her words (*shma' be-qoli*, vv. 8, 13, 43). By contrast, Sarah appealed to Abraham directly to banish 'that slave woman and her son' when she saw Ishmael 'sporting [*metzaḥeq*]' (21.9-10).[43] As Klitsner points

---

40. Zornberg, *Beginning of Desire*, p. 172.

41. According to the biblical account, Isaac lived on to the age of 180 (Gen. 35.27-28). Jacob was later reunited with his father after his long sojourn in Haran (22 years) and buried him in Kiriath-arba (Hebron). That is, despite Isaac's consciousness of his imminent death, he lives several decades after the blessing of his sons. His lifespan extends even beyond the other patriarchs, Abraham and Jacob. According to classic rabbinic exegesis, Jacob was 63 when he stole the blessing; so Isaac must have been 123 (see Rashi on Gen. 28.9; *b. Meg.* 16b-17a).

42. Meir Sternberg points out the discrepancy between Isaac's words to Esau and how Rebekah reports the speech to Jacob, but does not draw any conclusions from this (*Poetics of Biblical Narrative*, pp. 391-93).

43. The term *metzaḥeq* in Gen. 21.9—playing, sporting, mocking, or laughing—in the piel usually takes a direct object, but here we are left wondering what exactly Ishmael had done and to whom that warranted banishment. Some translations add the explanatory gloss: 'with her son, Isaac' (NRSV based on the LXX). The text is clearly playing on Isaac's name (lit. 'he will laugh'). See the discussion in Levenson, *The Death*

out, God endorsed Sarah's harsh decision in a direct speech to Abraham: 'Whatever Sarah says to you, listen to her voice [*shma' be-qolah*]' (Gen. 21.12).⁴⁴ Rebekah, instead of appealing to her husband to heed her words, charges Jacob to do so. 'To Rebekah's mind, Isaac, who holds firm to his own interpretation of his children's destinies, will not heed her voice. Her only chance to be heard is through her son.'⁴⁵

So, instead of direct confrontation, she uses stealth and boldly promises to assume Jacob's curse if things go awry. Those words of self-sacrifice become a prophecy self-fulfilled. Like Abraham in the *'Aqedah*, she 'sacrifices' the relationship with her beloved son to guarantee the patriarchal blessing. Though Jacob is not cursed (rather, the blessing is affirmed in retrospect, v. 33), he lives the rest of his life estranged from his family. When he finally returns home, after his sojourn in Haran (Paddan-aram), it is to be by his father's deathbed and eventually bury him (Gen. 35.28-29), not his mother.⁴⁶ Presumably, after Jacob is forced to flee from the murderous intentions of his brother, he never sees her again.

And it is at the behest of Rebekah that he is sent away. In yet another example of the matriarch's prophetic powers, 'she is told' that Esau plots to murder Jacob: 'Now Esau hated Jacob because of the blessing with which his father had blessed him, and Esau said to himself [*belibo*, lit., in his heart], "The days of mourning for my father are approaching; then I will kill my brother, Jacob." And *it was told* [*yugad*] to Rebekah . . .' (Gen. 27.41-42).⁴⁷ She adjures Jacob to 'listen to [her] voice' for a third time, in order to save himself by fleeing to her brother in Haran (vv. 42-43). Yet for her husband, she concocts a cover story, knowing he is already sympathetic with her on the question of Esau's Hittite wives, who were a source of 'bitterness of spirit to Isaac and Rebekah' (26.35). At this point, she again calls into question the meaning of her life: 'I loathe my life on account of those Hittite women; if Jacob should take a wife from the Hittite women such as these, one of the women of the land, what good will my life be to me [*lamah*

---

and Resurrection of the Beloved Son, p. 101. For a recent exegetical and historical discussion, see David J. Zucker, 'What Sarah Saw: Envisioning Genesis 21.9-10', *JQR* 36 (2008), pp. 54-62. 'We may also be invited', as Alter suggests, 'to construe it as "Isaac-ing-it,"—that is, Sarah sees Ishmael presuming to play the role of Isaac, child of laughter, presuming to be the legitimate heir' (Alter, *Genesis*, p. 78).

44. Klitsner, *Subversive Sequels*, p. 145.

45. Klitsner, *Subversive Sequels*, p. 146.

46. Rashi notes on Gen. 35.29 that Isaac lives on for another twelve years after Jacob's return to Canaan, invoking the principle 'there is no set chronological order to the Torah'.

47. Based on this verse, the midrash identifies the matriarch as a prophet (*Gen. R.* 67.9, p. 765; *Yal. Shimoni* Gen. 116; *Midr. Teh.* 42; *Eccl. R.* 60.4), though she is not included in the list of seven prophetesses in *b. Meg.* 14a.

li ḥayyim, lit., why life for me]?' (27.46). But this time her plaintive 'why' [*lamah*] is directed to her husband, not to God. And this time Isaac picks up the clue and takes the rudder to steer the narrative on track by sending Jacob to Paddan-aram, to Rebekah's relatives, in order to find an acceptable wife. At that moment, he bestows upon the 'true' heir the patriarchal 'blessing of Abraham' (28.1-5). All's well that ends well; or so it seems. Remaining behind, bereft of her beloved son, Rebekah becomes the recipient of a displaced curse.[48] Given the consequences that this sacrifice entails, why does she resort to deception?

Esther Fuchs argues that the biblical trope of feminine deceit and divine endorsement reinforces the patriarchal hierarchy and the stereotype of women as powerless. 'The fact is that Rebekah deceives Isaac not because she is a devious wife but because legally she is inferior and subordinate to Isaac. Within biblical patriarchy, the institute of primogeniture and parental blessings applied strictly to males. Mothers could not give blessings to their children any more than daughters could receive them. . . . Although the narrative presents the woman as a strong-willed character, who outsmarts her husband and acts out her wishes, Rebekah is in fact as underprivileged as her son Jacob.'[49] Fuchs makes a cogent point, but it does not stand up to comparative scrutiny. Sarah has no compunction about correcting her husband's perception, while Rebekah does. Furthermore, God's endorsement of Rebekah's insight is indirect, unlike the story of Ishmael's banishment. Yet we know that God ultimately affirms Rebekah's manipulation of events, not only through the prophecy itself, but, also, because Isaac ratifies the blessing of the hybrid heir (Jacob *qua* Esau) in retrospect. When Esau returns from the hunt and confronts his father with the truth, the patriarch does not withdraw his words, nor does he curse Jacob. Rather, seized with very violent trembling, he declares: 'I blessed him; he shall again [*gam*] be blessed!' (27.33). What comes by feminine wile is endorsed by the patriarch himself, in the end, as heaven sent.

Yet why does God endorse the indirect route, and not encourage Isaac to follow Rebekah's insight at the outset? The patriarch *loves* the wrong son. Isaac chooses Esau to be blessed and is never corrected or rebuked for his bad judgment (though God twice 'corrects' Abraham with regard to the displaced Ishmael, informing him that Isaac would be the sole heir to the

---

48. Her tragic end is associated with a displaced weeping that is linked to the burial of her nursemaid, Deborah, at *'alon-bakhut* (lit. 'oak of weeping', or 'weeping for the other' in the midrashic reading, Rashi on Gen. 35.8). See Zornberg's complex discussion of this passage in *Murmuring Deep*, pp. 228-31.

49. Fuchs, 'Who Is Hiding the Truth?', p. 138. With respect to Jacob, perhaps Fuchs is referring to the fact that Esau is firstborn and loved by his father because he brought him game (Gen. 25.28), while Jacob as the second born, seems weaker; he is 'a simple or plain man [*ish tam*], dweller of tents' (v. 27).

patriarchal covenant; cf. 17.18-21 and 21.12). In his intention to bless Esau, Isaac would have overtly contradicted the prophecy, 'the elder shall serve the younger' (25.23). Instead the dissembler, Jacob, is the recipient of the words: 'Be lord over your brothers, and may your mother's sons bow down to you' (27.29), resonant with the oracle Rebekah received. It is true that this blessing does not necessarily guarantee the passing on of the patriarchal covenant, since neither the promise of land nor of seed is mentioned in this first blessing (27.28-29). Yet this blessing, I maintain, sets the son up for receiving the second—the patriarchal covenant, including the promise of land (*'eretz*, specifically Canaan) and of descendants (*zera'*, lit., seed) (28.3-4).[50] Only after the blessing intended for Esau is stolen does Isaac realize that Jacob 'shall again be blessed [*gam barukh yihyeh*]' (27.33).[51] Ironically, the mask reveals the deeper truth and prompts Isaac to 'tell the truth', bestowing Abraham's blessing upon Jacob. This knowledge comes to Isaac only through hindsight. Neither Rebekah nor God can enlighten him directly for he lacks initial insight as well as physical sight. The old patriarch is blind, 'his eyes darkened from seeing' (27.1), perhaps, as Rashi wryly remarks, 'so that Jacob should take the blessing'.[52] God, it seems, is in cahoots with the dissemblers.

Ramban, drawing on early mystical ideas, gestures at why Isaac could not know, consciously, whom he was blessing. In his commentary, he argues that Rebekah resorted to deceit and did not tell her husband about the prophecy (Gen. 25.23)

> out of a sense of decorum and modesty, for when 'she went to inquire of God' (Gen. 25.22), it was without Isaac's permission. Alternatively [she may have assumed he knew], saying to herself, 'I don't need to relate a prophecy to a prophet for Isaac is greater than the one who told me'.[53] She then did not want to recount: 'I was told, in the name of God, before I gave birth . . .' for she thought that as a result of his [i.e. Isaac's] *love for him* [i.e. Esau, being the favored son], he would not bless Jacob (consciously),

---

50. See n. 17.
51. The NJPS renders this phrase as 'now he must remain blessed!'; NRSV: 'yes, and blessed he shall be!' Most translations imply that the term *gam* here places stress on a particular word, reinforcing the present status of Jacob as irrevocably blessed—*gam* as 'even' or 'yea' (cf. Exod. 4.9; Num. 22.33; 2 Sam. 17.10; Jer. 2.33; Ps. 132.12; Prov. 14.13). This reading implies that though Jacob took the blessing against Isaac's conscious will, 'even so he will remain blessed'. Yet the verb *yihiyeh* is in the imperfect (implying, perhaps, the future tense), and the Hebrew *gam* may denote 'in addition, also, moreover' (cf. Gen. 3.6; 3.22; 4.4). So the term *gam* [also] may be proleptic, anticipating the second blessing of the Abrahamic covenant which Jacob will receive (Gen. 28.3-4). See BDB entry 1571, pp. 168-69.
52. See Rashi's third opinion in his comment on Gen. 27.1.
53. This is consonant with Rashi's understanding that Rebekah consulted Shem's House of Study (see n. 18).

but would give his will over to Heaven. And she knew that, as a result, Jacob would be blessed with a whole heart and willing soul. Alternatively, she might have wished Jacob to earn the 'blessing of might' that Isaac intended to give Esau. '(For Yhwh is a God of knowledge), and by him actions are weighed' (1 Sam. 2.3).[54]

According to Ramban, it was necessary to deceive Isaac for the blessing to be given over to the powers of Heaven, since divine knowledge is beyond human ken.[55] That is, Rebekah uses subterfuge in order to guarantee that the blessing would come from God. Mortals cannot know the inscrutable ways of the divine; only after being duped do they come to realize their limited perspective. In this reading, the blessing must be filtered through the patriarch's love of his son Esau (whose identity Jacob assumes). Blessing entails a suspension of the conscious will through a deeply sensual, even erotic experience. Isaac listens intently to his voice (27.21), feels his arms, drinks the wine, and eats the game brought to him. Yet only after kissing Jacob, inspired by the scent of the animal skins, does he break into blessing: 'Ah, the smell of my son is like the smell of a field that Yhwh has blessed . . .' (Gen. 27.27). Although Isaac does not really recognize who stands before him (v. 23), the voice being 'the voice of Jacob, the hands the hands of Esau' (v. 22), Jacob remains, after the fact, unequivocally blessed (v. 33). For the blind man, it is the love for his son and the experience of synesthesia—hearing, taste, touch and smell—that inspire blessing, despite the dissonance of reason.[56]

Yet Ramban's argument, that there must be a suspension of Isaac's conscious will, leaves one primary player out of the picture. What of Rebekah? Does she know that Isaac must give over the blessing in this way? Perhaps this is precisely what she implies when she adds the phrase to Isaac's original words, 'so that [your father] might bless you [Jacob *qua* Esau] *in the presence of* Yhwh' (v. 7). Was Rebekah privy to esoteric understanding? Or did she resort to devious means because she was powerless to realign her husband's intentions directly? Ramban claims that she was an agent of God's will, and couches her motivation in terms of feminine modesty and the false assumption that Isaac must have known, for he was 'a greater prophet than the one who told' her. When she finds out that her husband was not privy to her insight, it is too late to correct him. Still the question

---

54. Ramban's commentary on Gen. 27.4, author's trans..

55. Similarly Naḥmanides argues that this is the reason Isaac trembled violently upon realizing he had blessed Jacob and not Esau, affirming rather than nullifying the blessing. He comments, 'Or it may be that the expression "and shall again be blessed" means "against my will, since it is impossible for me to transfer the blessing from him." From the moment he blessed him, Isaac knew by the Holy Spirit that his blessings indeed rested upon Jacob. This then is the reason for his violent trembling for he knew that his beloved son Esau had lost his blessing forever' (Ramban on Gen. 27.33, author's trans.).

56. See the discussion in Zornberg, *Beginning of Desire*, pp. 169-79.

remains: why was their communication so *oblique*? Why was this strong, resourceful woman so intimidated by her husband? Rav Naftali Zvi Yehuda Berlin (otherwise known as the Netziv of Volozhin, 1816–1989) suggests that the communication gap between husband and wife can be traced back to their first meeting.

The Veiling of Rebekah

> Now Isaac was coming from the approach to Beer-laḥai-roi [lit. Well-of-the-Living-One Who-Sees-Me] for he was living in the Negeb. And Isaac went out to meditate[57] in the field at the turn of the evening (Gen. 24.62-63a).

The passage opens with explicit geographical markers: Isaac's chosen desert-dwelling place, the Negeb, and the approach to Beer-laḥai-roi. The latter recalls the scene of Hagar's first flight from the punitive hand of her mistress, Sarah. There an angel appeared to her by a spring (*'ayin ha-mayim*, lit., 'eye of water'), urging her to return. 'And she called Yhwh who spoke to her, "You are El-roi" [lit. God-Who-Sees-Me], by which she meant, "Have I not gone on seeing after he saw me!" Therefore the well was called Beer-laḥai-roi [Well-of-the-Living-One-Who-Sees-Me] . . .' (Gen. 16.13-14a). As an etiological narrative, the naming of the well expresses Hagar's exultant sense of having survived the hierophany, what Eliade defines as 'an irruption of the sacred' in space.[58] The sacred loci of hierophany are marked by images of opening. Here the scene takes place by a spring, an 'eye of water'—metonymic for the divine eye that sees her. The seeing God, *El-roi*, is identified in her experience as the One-who-sustains life, *El-ḥai*, in the naming of the well. This experience of asymmetry between the one *who sees and grants life,* and the one *who is seen and survives* is repeated again in Isaac's life in the trauma of his binding at Mt Moriah, named also for divine sight, 'Yhwh will see/provide [*yir'eh*]' (Gen. 22.14, echoing Abraham's words, 'God will see to/provide for himself [*yir'eh lo*] the sheep for

---

57. Alter and Fox render *la-suaḥ be-sadeh* as 'to stroll in the field' (Alter, *Genesis*, p. 122, and Fox, *Five Books of Moses*, p. 107), but both admit that the Hebrew here is obscure. I have adopted the rabbinic understanding that Isaac was engaged in some kind of prayer, the verb *la-suaḥ* based on the nominative, *siaḥ*—complaint, musing, or prayer (Ps. 102.1; 1 Kgs 18.27; Prov. 23.29; Job 23.2; BDB entry 9421, p. 967). See also Rashi on Gen. 24.63 and *Gen. R.* 60.14. According to the sages, Isaac set the precedent for the late afternoon prayer, *Minḥah* (b. Ber. 26b; b. 'Avod. Zar. 7b; y. Ber. 4.1; and *Gen. R.* 68.9, pp. 778-79).

58. Mircea Eliade, *The Sacred and the Profane* (New York: Harcourt Brace, 1959), p. 26. Manoah (father of Samson) also expressed this fear that he might die after his encounter with the angel of God (Judg. 13.20).

the burnt offering' (v. 8).[59] Both Hagar and Isaac experience a direct revelation—one on the threshold between sky and earth, bound to the mountain altar, and the other on the threshold between water and earth, at a life-spring in the ground. They have both been seen and have survived the sighting.

When Isaac first sees Rebekah, he is returning from Beer-lahai-roi, perhaps a place he frequents for prayer or meditation.[60] It is the first time the reader has seen Isaac center-stage since the traumatic scene of his binding, from which Abraham returned *alone* to his two servants, going on with them to Beer-sheba (Gen. 22.19). We invoke the famous question: what happened to Isaac? Since the *'Aqedah,* he has been discussed by the patriarch and his servant in negotiating a match from Paddan-aram, but he himself has been conspicuously absent—until now, this moment of first meeting:

> He raised his eyes and saw, and, behold, camels were coming! Rebekah raised her eyes and saw Isaac, and she fell [*va-tippol*] from her camel. And she said to the servant, 'Who is that man over there [*ha-lazeh*] walking through the field toward us?' The servant said, 'That is my master'. And so she took *the* veil [*ha-tza'if*] and covered herself. And the servant recounted to Isaac all the things he had done. And Isaac brought her into the tent of Sarah, his mother. And took Rebekah and she became his wife. And he loved her. And Isaac was consoled after [the death of] his mother (Gen. 24.63b–67).

Unlike 'Some Enchanted Evening', in which the hero's eyes meet the gaze of his beloved 'across a crowded room', the first meeting between Isaac and Rebekah reads like the opening of a comedy of errors. Melancholic, the patriarch is cast in the long shadows of early evening, in a meditative stroll, lost in his desert-dwelling mind. She is maudlin, the smell of camels in her nostrils, and the grit of sand in her hair, fingers and toes. There is no love at first sight. Their eyes *do not meet*. For he, marked by early myopia, sees the camels in the distance while she sees him, and falls [*va-tippol*] from her camel. Most translations render the Hebrew *va-tippol* as the genteel 'and she alighted'—as if she were elegantly riding sidesaddle like a lady riding a horse. Yet how would a woman, unassisted, lightly descend from a camel, a height of ten feet from the ground, without ignominy? No, she falls. Brushing the desert sand off, she rises and asks the servant to identify 'that man' over there walking toward them. When she realizes he is the one she is destined to marry, she veils herself, sealing the asymmetry of their first sight with a piece of cloth.

---

59. Isaac's blindness is strangely associated with the trauma of the *'Aqedah*. See Rashi on 27.1, and the discussion in Zornberg, *Beginning of Desire,* pp. 155-58.

60. In the end, Isaac settles there after the burial of his father, Abraham (Gen. 25.11).

Why does she fall from the camel? What does she see in Isaac that alarms her, sets her off balance? And why does she then veil herself?[61] The nineteenth-century commentator Rav Naftali Zvi Berlin of Volozhin suggests that, upon seeing this man deeply engaged in prayer 'like a terrifying angel of God',[62] she falls from her camel, filled with awe, though she does not know who he is. When she points to him, inquiring after his identity, she refers to him with the unusual demonstrative pronoun *ha-lazeh* ('that one there'). According to the Netziv, the expression refers to a man who is threatening, and suggests both the distance of space and awe. The sons of Jacob point to Joseph, as he approaches from a distance, with the same expression: 'And they saw him from afar. . . . And they said to one another, "Here comes that there dream-master [*ba'al ha-ḥalomot ha-lazeh*]!"' (Gen. 37.18-19).[63] In fear and trembling, she points at him as if he is *wholly other*, shrouded in another world.[64] The Netziv comments:

> 'And so she took the veil and covered herself' (v. 66)—out of a deep sense of shame and fear, as if she thought she was unworthy to be his wife. And from that moment onward, fear was imprinted in her heart. And she was not with Isaac as Sarah was with Abraham, and Rachel was with Jacob, for when they had an issue [with their husbands] they were not ashamed to speak directly to them. Whereas this was not the case with Rebekah. [This meeting] then serves as an introduction to the next story, in Parashat Toledot, where Isaac and Rebekah had a difference of opinion. Rebekah did not have the courage to present her thoughts to Isaac to discuss, though she knew the truth that Esau only had 'the hunt in his mouth' (Gen. 25.18).[65] And so, at the moment of [Isaac's] blessing, God had intentions that the blessings would come precisely in this way to Jacob [i.e. through deception]. . . . If Rebekah had been with her husband as Sarah and Rachel

---

61. Most commentators commend Rebekah for her modesty in veiling herself. Even Leila Leah Bronner comments, 'Thus the betrothed Rebecca covers herself upon first sight of her intended husband' ('From Veil to Wig: Jewish Women's Hair Coverings', *Judaism* 42 [1993], p. 466). She argues, however, that veiling was not necessarily a sign of the transition from maidenhood to the married state, though the ancient Mesopotamian sources suggest otherwise (as we shall discuss).

62. Based on the image in *Midr. Teh.* 90.18: 'she saw that his hand was extended in prayer [*yado shetuḥa be-tefilah*]' (cf. *Gen. R.* 60.14, p. 655; *Yal. Shimoni* Gen. 109). See n. 57.

63. Cf. *Gen. R.* 60.14. According to this midrash, the expression *ha-lazeh* is an allusion to another (*pilsono*), an angel that walked by Joseph's side.

64. The *Yal. Shimoni* Gen. 109 suggests that she sees him 'returning from the Garden of Eden', resurrected from the dead after the Binding of Isaac (cf. *Midr. ha-Gadol* on Gen. 22.19). See also *PRE* 31, where it is said that proof for the quickening of the dead in the Torah derives from the revival of Isaac after the *'Aqedah*. In that passage, Isaac is associated with the second benediction of the *'Amidah*. See the discussion in Shalom Spiegel, *The Last Trial* (New York: Schocken Books, 1969), pp. 5 and 28-37.

65. See n. 37.

were with theirs, events would not have unfolded in this way. From the beginning, all things are under divine providence—Rebekah arrived at that precise moment and, as a result, became alarmed (at the sight of him), so that later events would transpire according to the divine will.

This moment is prescient of the gap between husband and wife that would hold from that first meeting onward. Like the Ramban, the Netziv characterizes Rebekah as shrouded by her own modesty, becoming a mere pawn in the divine game where the main players—Isaac, Jacob and Esau—wrangle over blessing and birthright. Yet how could this woman, who had been so strong, forthright and hospitable at the well with the servant, now be seized with such fear and trembling? She was absolutely sure of her own destiny in joining Abraham's family back in Haran. With her one-word consent, she allayed the fears that the servant had expressed to Abraham before he left: 'Perhaps the woman may not be willing to follow me [*lalekhet 'aḥarai*] to this land' (Gen. 24.5). When her father and brother, Bethuel and Laban, asked her whether she was willing to go, she answered simply: 'I will go ['*elekh*]' (v. 58), echoing God's command to Abraham—'Go forth [*lekh lekha* . . .]' (Gen. 12.1). While Abraham did so at the behest of God, Rebekah did so of her own free will. Furthermore, the blessing she received from her father and brother, 'May your descendants inherit the gates of their foes' (24.60), echoes God's blessing to Abraham after the trial of the binding of Isaac (22.17). In leaving her family's home with this blessing and guaranteeing the future of the promised seed, she becomes the true 'daughter of Abraham'.

Yet, as Tikva Frymer-Kensky points out, she seems to lose her sense of autonomy when she marries. 'She who was so assertive and decisive in her meeting with the servant and in her discussions at home now turns into a wife. She who left Mesopotamia as an autonomous person turned into a betrothed woman "taken" by the servant and is now "taken" into her husband's domain. As soon as Isaac enters the scene, she veils herself.'[66] Nevertheless, Rebekah is Isaac's match. As Bethuel's daughter, she (like Isaac) is doubly of the lineage of Terah. Isaac's parents, Sarah and Abraham, may indeed have been related. The patriarch tells Abimelech that Sarah, in a sense, is really his 'sister', being the 'daughter of his father' (Gen. 20.12).[67]

---

66. Frymer-Kensky, *Reading the Women of the Bible*, p. 15.
67. Sarah may, in fact, have been Terah's granddaughter, Iscah (cf. Gen. 11.29)—hence Abraham's niece, daughter of Haran, his brother. Of the list of forbidden sexual relations in Leviticus 18 and 20, this is the only 'incestuous' one that is not condemned. Leach notes that the pattern of *toledot* is interrupted, in the patriarchal narratives, by the 'advantages of close kin endogamy'. Consistently, Abraham, Isaac, and Jacob all marry into *toledot Terah*. Leach suggests that the continuity in lineage is achieved through a breach in the rules of incest, which is why the *toledot* series are complicated in the patriarchal narratives. See n. 6.

Rebekah's grandparents are also both from that line. Milcah (daughter of Haran, son of Terah) and Nahor (son of Terah) are mother and father to Bethuel, Rebekah's father (11.29; 22.20-24).[68] Both Isaac and Rebekah, then, form the unbroken link between father and grandson, between Terah's descendants [*toledot Terah*] and Isaac's, which involves the transfer of the covenant from Abraham to Jacob. As I suggested earlier, *toledot Yitzhaq* is really a displaced *toledot Avraham*, guaranteed by Rebekah's agency. Frymer-Kensky suggests that while Isaac is promised land and progeny (Gen. 26.3-4), the process of inheritance entails a passage 'from Abraham to Rivka to Jacob and to the people of Israel. Her decisiveness, her strong will and her embrace of her destiny make her a strong active link between Abraham and Jacob.'[69] The genealogy of Isaac passes to Jacob through Rebekah, who acts as Abraham's proxy.

Accordingly, the veiling in this scene of first meeting is not necessarily a sign of modesty, fear or shame, but rather a sign of power that goes underground, turns inward and allies with the indirect ways of the divine will. We now turn to the reverberations that Rebekah's veiling has had upon the 'Jewish way in love and marriage'.[70]

Does the Veil Open the Interior Eye?[71]

The most intimate moment of a traditional Jewish wedding occurs at the *badeken*, when the groom veils the bride before she is escorted to the wedding canopy (*huppah*).[72] Rabbinic lore links the tradition to this scene of

---

68. See the analysis of the genealogy and the explanation of the wife-sister motif in Frymer-Kensky, *Reading the Women of the Bible*, pp. 5-7 and 12. See also Susan Niditch, *Underdogs and Tricksters* (San Francisco: Harper & Row, 1987), pp. 26-69.

69. Frymer-Kensky, *Reading the Women of the Bible*, p. 14.

70. Rabbinic tradition associates the veiling of the bride in the *badeken* ritual with Rebekah's veiling (Maharal, *Hilkhot Nissu'in*, cited in Maurice Lamm, *The Jewish Way in Love and Marriage* [San Francisco: Harper & Row, 1980], pp. 207-209, 256). After the veiling, it is even customary to recite the blessing that Rebekah's father and brother gave her: 'Our sister, may you become thousands of myriads. May your descendants inherit the gates of their foes' (Gen. 24.60); see Lamm, *Jewish Way in Love and Marriage*, p. 128.

71. I have adapted this line from Eve Grubin's poem 'Modesty', from her collection *Morning Prayer* (Riverdale-on-Hudson, NY: Sheep Meadow Press, 2005), p. 55. The original line reads, 'Does the head covering open/the interior eye?'

72. The term *badeken* derives from the Yiddish, meaning 'to cover', not, as one might suppose, from the Hebrew root *badaq* ('to check, verify'). According to some rabbinic authorities, the veiling has the force of law, identified as the bridal canopy [*huppah*] itself (Tosafot on *b. Yoma* 13b, s.v. *le-hadeh*; *Even ha-'Ezer* on 55.1, in *Hagah: Helkat Mehoqeq* 55.9; *Tashbetz* 463—sources in Aryeh Kaplan, *Made in Heaven: A Jewish Wedding Guide* [New York: Moznaim, 1983], p. 126 n. 21; and Lamm, *The Jew-*

Rebekah's veiling, though the custom, widespread in the ancient Near East, predates the biblical period.[73] It is a symbolic act, a gesture by which the groom claims his bride as exclusively his own. As he veils her, he is saying, you are uniquely mine; I give you the gift of being wholly-in-yourself, in intimacy with me alone. At that moment, she is drawn away from the public eye, into a private realm where the features of her face are blurred—her mouth a red crescent moon, her eyes but a flicker of light under the lace.[74] He veils her in public so that he might unveil her privately in the consummation of their marriage.[75] In the traditional ceremony, she is unveiled after the blessings have been sung, the veil lifted and the cup of wine brought to her lips. Symbolically, however, the real unveiling occurs in the *heder yihud* (the private room to which the couple is taken after the ceremony). The veil then is metonymic for virginity; the unveiling for its loss.[76]

ish Way in Love and Marriage, p. 256). The emphasis, in the ritual, is not on the verification of the bride's identity—she is covered (or bedecked) by the groom in order to be uncovered later in privacy. Only later in Jewish tradition did the ritual acquire a secondary significance of checking the identity of the woman under the veil, attributed to the duping of Jacob by Laban, when he passes Leah off as Rachel under the wedding canopy (see Kaplan, *Made in Heaven*, p. 127).

73. The tradition of veiling of the bride may be related to the expression *hinuma* in the Mishnah and Talmud: 'If there are witnesses that she went out *behinuma*, and with her head uncovered, then her marriage contract [*ketubah*] is worth two hundred [*zuz*]'—i.e. indicative that she was a virgin at her wedding (*m. Ket.* 2.1; *b. Ket.* 17b). The *hinuma* was either a bed or couch (derived from the Greek *hymenaios*), shaped like an oven (wide at the base and narrow at the top) and draped with myrtles, or it was a scarf, under which the bride dozed [*menamnemet*] (Rashi on *b. Ket.* 17b, and Jastrow 1926: p. 348). Michael Satlow, however, identifies the *hinuma* with hymns sung to the bride, in *The Jewish Marriage in Antiquity* (Princeton, NJ: Princeton University Press, 2001), pp. 171, 335.

74. In most traditional, contemporary Jewish weddings, the veil is made up of gauzy material, but in some Chassidic circles an opaque veil is used, which completely obscures the bride's face (Kaplan, *The Jewish Way in Love and Marriage*, p. 127).

75. See Matitiahu Tsevat, 'The Husband Veils a Wife', *Jewish Chautauqua Society* 17 (1975), pp. 235-40. As Jack Sasson points out, 'Near Eastern testimony . . . does suggest that in many cultures brides may have been veiled, by a husband or his proxy, a nonverbal act that may be read symbolically (possession by a groom) or metaphorically (a hymen, to be broken by a groom)', in 'The Servant's Tale: How Rebekah Found a Spouse', *JNES* 65 (2006), p. 241.

76. If it is the bride's second marriage, the *badeken* ritual need not be done (Lamm, *The Jewish Way in Love and Marriage*, p. 238). Other scholars have argued that the act of 'covering the head' (signifying the *huppah*) in the *badeken* has apotropaic powers as a sign of sorrow; the Hebrew expression 'to cover one's head [*lehafot ro'sh*]', in the Bible, is a sign of shame or mourning (see 2 Sam. 15.30; Jer. 14.3, 4; Est. 6.12 and 7.8). According to Jacob Lauterbach, the heads of both the bride and the groom were covered with black-and-white cloth (*Orhot Hayyim*, R. Aaron ha-Kohen II [Berlin, 1902], p. 67; *Kolbo Hilkhot Ishut* [Venice, 1547], p. 87a) or with a *tallit* (R. Eleazar of Worms, *Rokeah*

In the ancient Near East, the veiling of the bride was part of the betrothal ceremony. In Akkadian, the bride on her wedding day is called *kullatu kutumtu*, 'the veiled bride'; and the term for bride, *kallatu*, is interchangeable with *pussumtu*, 'the veiled one',[77] suggesting that she was presented to her husband already veiled. Various passages in the Hebrew Bible also testify to the ancient custom of veiling a young woman betrothed in marriage.[78] There are two principle biblical terms for a veil worn by young women: *tzammah*,[79] a piece of cloth that covered the face, and *tza'if*[80], a cloth wrapped around the face. In Karel van der Toorn's thorough study of ancient Near Eastern sources, he argues that veiling served as a symbol of appurtenance, although, for the most part, it did not usually coincide with the wedding ceremony. Rather, it may have taken place at the ceremony of betrothal as 'an act of designating the bride as exclusive to the groom and his family. . . . The Babylonian bride would normally be veiled before the wedding. As soon as she was betrothed, a girl was veiled. There is no reason, then, to disbelieve the description of the Babylonian virgin in Isa.

---

353 [Cremona, 1557], p. 64a). He argues that the custom was originally a means of 'hiding' the bride and groom, and thus protecting them from the harm of demons. Alternatively, the function of the veil was to fool the demons by making them believe that the betrothed couple was in mourning and therefore not to be envied. This is consonant with the tradition, recorded in the Talmud, of placing ash on the groom's head (*b. B. Bat.* 60b; see comments in Jacob Z. Lauterbach 'The Ceremony of Breaking a Glass at Weddings', *HUCA* 2 (1925), pp. 351-80, esp. 356-60. However, this understanding of the significance of veiling is very distant from the biblical context.

77. Nahum Sarna, *The JPS Torah Commentary: Genesis* (Philadelphia: Jewish Publication Society, 1989), pp. 162 and 336 n. 25. He cites the following primary sources: Middle Assyrian laws A, pars. 40, 41 (*ANET*, p. 183); see also Tsevat, 'The Husband Veils a Wife', pp. 235-40.

78. See the thorough discussion in Karel van der Toorn, 'The Significance of the Veil in the Ancient Near East', in *Pomegranates and Golden Bells: Studies in Biblical, Jewish, and Near Eastern Ritual, Law, and Literature in Honor of Jacob Milgrom* (ed. David P. Wright, David Noel Freedman and Avi Hurvitz; Winona Lake, IN: Eisenbrauns, 1995), pp. 327-39.

79. Isa. 47.2-3; Cant. 4.1, 3; 6.7 (*HALOT*, pp. 967-68 and 974). This understanding of *tzammah* is supported by the LXX on Isa. 47.2, translated as *katakalumma*, and as *siopesis* in Cant. 4.1, 3; 6.7. Another term for veil, *ra'alah* (Isa. 3.19), refers to ornamental scarves, standard attire for wealthy women. In Exodus, the term *masveh* is used for the veil of Moses, which covers his face when he descended from Sinai with the second tablets (Exod. 34.33-35).

80. Gen. 24.65; 38.14, 19. The first citation is from Rebekah's veiling; the second from Tamar's. Van der Toorn argues that Tamar's veiling does not signify betrothal here. Rather, she puts off 'the garments of her widowhood' and 'wraps herself in a veil (*tza'if*)' (Gen. 38.14) in order to make herself unrecognizable to her father-in-law ('The Significance of the Veil in the Ancient Near East', p. 330). I will discuss this veiling in Chapter 3.

47.1-3 nor is there anything unusual in the fact that Rebekah and Leah were veiled when they met their husbands for the wedding night.'[81] Accordingly, the veil could have served as (a) a symbol of social standing; (b) as a token of chastity; (c) and as a means of subtly accentuating feminine beauty.

However, Rebekah's behavior in the scene of first sighting, at Beer-laḥai-roi, is unusual in that she veils *herself*.[82] A unique bride, she is the one setting the boundary between her private and public face. Jack Sasson points out that 'as in the Mari [sources], Rebekah's veiling would signal betrothal, the actual marriage not occurring until Isaac makes her his wife. If so, what about the timing of the act? Why is Rebekah not veiled in Haran by the servant... why did Isaac not veil his bride in the fields of Beer-laḥai-roi...?'[83] Why does she only choose to cover up after her first sight of 'that man' and the identification of him, by the servant, as her husband? Ironically, rather than a symbol of the exclusive right of the groom to the bride, here the veiling signifies the murmurs of Rebekah's independence. In drawing the scarf down over her face, she maintains the asymmetry of sight at their first meeting: he 'raised his eyes and saw' camels coming; 'Rebekah raised her eyes and saw Isaac' (Gen. 24.63-64). The scarf, perhaps made of a gauzy material, porous to light and air, allows her to *continue* seeing the other while her face is obscured to him. It establishes a dynamic of hide-and-seek: you can't see me, yet I can see you. The veiling anticipates the three acts in which Rebekah strikes out on her own, beyond the purview of her husband: consulting God over the tumult in her belly, disguising Jacob as Esau to be blessed by the blind patriarch, and concocting a cover story as to why the blessed son must now leave for Paddan-aram. Call it duplicitous. Call it subterfuge. Call it feminine wile. In any case, the veiling appropriates a ubiquitous symbol of patriarchal power—the groom's unilateral *taking* of the bride as his own—and transforms it into a symbol of her autonomy. The veil gives her the gift of privacy, the ability to know an inner world wholly her own, free from the roving view of the outside world and free of social norms. It opens the interior eye. And through the gauze, the blurring of lines, a crack of light breaks through. In the words of Leonard Cohen, 'There is a crack, a crack in everything. That's how the light gets in.'[84]

---

81. Van der Toorn, 'The Significance of the Veil in the Ancient Near East', p. 336.
82. Sasson, 'The Servant's Tale', pp. 241-65.
83. Sasson, 'The Servant's Tale', p. 264.
84. Lyrics to Leonard Cohen's 'Anthem', http://www.azlyrics.com/lyrics/leonardcohen/anthem.html.

2

THE COLLUSION OF SISTERS: A STUDY IN THE LEAH–RACHEL–JACOB TRIANGLE

> All happy families are alike, but every unhappy family is unhappy in a different way.
>
> Leo Tolstoy, *Anna Karenina*

Preamble: On the Merits and Limits of Masks

In an illustrated children's version of the book of Genesis, I once saw a picture that remains etched in my memory: Jacob's arms, as they embraced the great stone just before he rolled it off the well at Haran, were dressed in goatskins. The narrative tells us that it would require the strength of several men to 'roll the stone from the mouth of the well' (Gen. 29.3, 8). Yet Jacob, when he saw Rachel, stepped forward and single-handedly rolled the stone from the mouth of the well and watered the sheep (v. 10). He then kissed Rachel, raised his voice and wept. One might conjecture that it was his passion that inspired this supernatural power, but the illustrator implied that it was his guise that imbued him with strength. No longer the 'simple', 'smooth' man, Jacob had fused the goatskins, which his mother had laid on his bare arms and the nape of his neck, onto his identity. In wearing the mock hairy mantle in which his brother was born, he *became* Esau, the he-man hunter, the Marlboro man. We, the readers, are aware that Jacob learned the art of dissembling, the art of masks, from his mother. Just as Rebekah drew a veil over her face, forging a gap between the outwardly seen and inward-seeing, so Jacob, dressed in goatskins, presented a fissure between the outer and inner man. Now exiled to Haran, in flight from the consequences of his (and Rebekah's) hoax, his life becomes complicated by thwarted love in a marriage split between sisters, the beloved wife barren and the despised one prodigiously fruitful and multiplying. And the justice stone rolls into the next generation in the irruption of near-fratricidal rivalry between the brothers. Indeed the trickster is tricked. The mask Jacob wore is mirrored back to him in the house of Laban. Is the man behind the mask thus transformed?

Through a series of inter-textual clues, Laban's ruse can be read as divine comeuppance for Jacob's deception of his father. On Jacob's wedding night, Laban substitutes Leah, the older sister of tender eyes, for the beloved younger daughter, Rachel. After that wedding night, in response to Jacob's outrage in the morning, Laban quips, 'It is not done thus in our place to give the younger before the firstborn' (29.26). It is as if he were implying: in your own land you may presume to get away with substituting the younger for the elder, but not here! The biblical narrative subtly implies that Jacob's unwitting marriage to Leah is just deserts for manipulating Esau into selling the birthright and then substituting himself, the younger brother, for the older at the scene of the blessing. By hinting at the principle of measure-for-measure, does the biblical text cast a moral judgement on Jacob's deception of his father? Is that original ruse sanctioned or condoned? In the midrashic narrative, Laban the Aramean [*ha-'arami*] is whimsically referred to as 'the deceiver [*ha-rama'i*]', though Rebekah (of the same land) is called a righteous woman, a 'lily among the thorns'.[1] While Rebekah is condoned, the rabbis are equivocal about both Jacob's and Laban's deception. The consequences are certainly good—the marriage to two sisters (and their two slave girls), who collectively birth twelve sons to the patriarch who become the tribes of Israel. Nevertheless, Jacob feels wronged.

According to Nahum Sarna, 'retributive justice is not the only motif. Just as Jacob's succession to the birthright was divinely ordained . . . so Jacob's unintended marriage to Leah is seen as the working of providence, for from this unplanned union issued Levi and Judah, whose offspring shared spiritual and temporal hegemony in Israel through the two great institutions of the biblical period, the priesthood and the Davidic monarchy'.[2] Furthermore, Jacob is the first of the three patriarchs to establish all twelve sons under the rubric of the covenant. He, *Ya'aqov* [Heel-holder], is renamed *Yisrael* [God-makes-straight],[3] and becomes the eponymous ancestor of the Israelite people. Unlike the patriarchs Abraham and Isaac, Jacob is never forced to exclude any one of his sons from the covenant. Is this a result of

---

1. See *Gen. R.* 63.4, pp. 680-81, based on Cant. 2.2.
2. Sarna, *Understanding Genesis*, p. 195.
3. The literal etiology of the renaming is linked to the scene of Jacob's wrestling match: 'Your name shall no longer be Jacob, but Israel, for you have striven [*sarita, srh*] with God (or divine beings) and men, and have prevailed' (Gen. 32.29). Yisrael properly means 'God strives', not 'he strives with God'. But one could vocalize the name as *yisher-el* [*yshr*, lit. 'God makes straight']—connected with the synonym for Israel, *yeshurun* (Jeshurun) in Deut. 32.15; 33.5, 26; and Isa. 44.2. 'The change of name would express the transformation of character from deviousness to moral rectitude' (Sarna, *JPS Torah Commentary: Genesis*, p. 405).

personal transformation? Does the man behind the mask regain his integrity? Is the dis-integration between the inner and outer man somehow made whole? Avivah Zornberg has explored Jacob's psychological development in terms of the transformation from a 'sincere' or 'simple man' (*'ish tam*) to an authentic, complex one.[4] Although my argument is very much influenced by her reading, I focus more on the role of the women in generating integrity for the House of Israel—the band of brothers that become the twelve tribes of Israel, representative of the patriarch himself.

I argue that only through the collusion of sisters is the House of Israel made whole. Following the thread of divine retribution, as teased out by the midrashic corpus, I suggest that his dubious marriage to Rachel and Leah, despite being an incestuous union,[5] redeems Jacob from complete degeneration into a double life. So the book of Leviticus inveighs: 'Do not marry a woman as a rival [*litzror*][6] to her sister and uncover her nakedness in the other's lifetime' (Lev. 18.18). Paradoxically, because Jacob is entangled in a life of sororal tension, he emerges whole as Israel, and the twelve tribes can be born and can remain under the rubric of the covenant as one nation. I trace the trajectory of these two themes—Jacob's comeuppance and the achievement of integrity for the next generation—through Midrash Aggadah, which lends the women voices as agents of the divine plan. According to midrash, Leah *chooses* Jacob, 'the righteous man', over his boorish brother, Esau, and (in cahoots with her sister and father), deceives Jacob on the wedding night in a classic case of 'the bedtrick'. Like Jacob, she rejects the assumptions of birth order (elder-for-elder, younger-for-younger), but, in contrast to him, she is driven by moral considerations. For this, Leah is rewarded

---

4. See Zornberg, *Beginning of Desire*, pp. 216-42; and *Murmuring Deep*, pp. 267-96.

5. I do not mean to assert an anachronism that the patriarchs observed the laws of forbidden sexual relations—simply that what is later deemed taboo is abrogated here. The motif of incest is nearly ubiquitous in the biblical female ruse. Almost all of the 'bedtricks' in the Hebrew Bible, especially those leading toward the messianic line, breach the boundary between the permissible and forbidden relations: Lot's daughters (Genesis 19), Judah and Tamar (Genesis 38), Ruth and Boaz (Ruth 3–4), and David and Bathsheba (2 Samuel 11). We will address this antinomian trend in later chapters. At this point, I wish to point out that the chimera of incest raises its head early in the patriarchal narratives as well. Rabbinic literature, of course, reads the forbidden relations to two sisters as problematic for Jacob, although the sources address the question sparingly—see *b. Pes.* 119b; *Eliyahu R.* 6; *Yal. Shimoni* Gen. 93 and 117; and *Midr. Yashar* Toledot 43a-b.

6. Baruch Levine comments, 'The Hebrew *li-tsror* reflects the noun, tsarah, rival wife, which, in turn, derives from the verb *tsrr*, "to assail, attack"' (B. Levine, *The JPS Torah Commentary: Leviticus* [Philadelphia: Jewish Publication Society, 1989], p. 92). In the prophetic literature, the rival wife (*tsarah*) is deployed as a metaphor for idolatry. We will discuss these allusions when we come to the passage in Jeremiah 31.

with the firstborn son. Rachel, too, mirrors Jacob, the deceiver, but she turns against her beloved and allies with her sister in a dire act of self-sacrifice. In so doing, she also stands on higher moral ground than her husband. In my analysis, I begin with a close reading of the biblical text, probing the gaps that remain, and then go on to explore how midrash, as 'narrative expansion', fills in these gaps while addressing broader thematic and ethical issues.

In the House of Laban

Jacob first encounters his beloved at a well, a favorite setting for biblical betrothal scenes.[7] Rather than romantic heroism or a test of character,[8] the bride-seeking scene here is framed explicitly in terms of familial relations, as Jacob follows the behest of his mother and father to find a wife from his uncle's house.[9] The focus, then, is on endogamy; Jacob will ally himself with the Terah clan through a marriage, as it turns out, to his two cousins. We are told, again and again, that Laban is 'his mother's brother'; he will also prove to be Rebekah's sibling in the art of deceit. In the opening scene, both the narrator and the shepherds inform us that the heavy stone on the mouth of the well cannot be removed by one man alone (vv. 3 and 8)—a formidable obstacle to watering the sheep, prescient of obstacles to come. In the midst of Jacob's asking after the well-being of 'Laban, the son of Nahor', the shepherds announce the arrival of his daughter: 'And there is his daughter Rachel coming with the flock' (Gen. 29.6). The narrative then focuses on what Jacob sees and does:

> When Jacob saw Rachel, *daughter of Laban his mother's brother*, with the flocks of *Laban, his mother's brother*, he stepped forward and rolled the stone from the mouth of the well and watered [*va-yashq*] the sheep of *Laban his mother's brother*. And Jacob kissed [*va-yishaq*] Rachel, raised his voice, and wept (vv. 10-11).

Note that, at this point, Rachel is *not* presented as 'shapely and beautiful'; the reader is told of her good looks only later when she is introduced again alongside her sister (v. 17).

This is not Hollywood's love at first sight, the romantic meeting of eyes 'across a crowded room'. Despite his heroic strength in rolling the stone off the mouth of the well, reverberant with erotic prowess, the emphasis here is on domesticity and familial relations. Jacob's watering of Laban's flocks

---

7. Alter, *Biblical Narrative*, pp. 52-58.
8. As in the scene of Abraham's servant's search for a bride (Gen. 24.10-28) or Moses' encounter with Jethro's daughters (Exod. 2.15-21).
9. As we discussed in the last chapter, there are two motivations for Jacob's flight: to flee from the murderous wrath of his brother (as advocated by Rebekah, Gen. 27.43-45), and to find a wife from Paddan-aram, as advocated by both parents (Gen. 27.46; 28.1-3).

[*va-yashq*] is parallel to the kiss he bestows upon Rachel [*va-yishaq*]. Her name evokes the ewe (*reḥelim,* pl. female sheep) that Jacob will shepherd as Laban's servant (Gen. 31.38; 32.15). Both the watering and the kiss, weighty with care, firmly establish a sense of relationship and responsibility. Jacob's strength in rolling the heavy stone from the well and watering the sheep echo his own mother's alacrity and generosity toward Abraham's servant at the well (Gen. 24.10-28). While Rebekah was unaware that she was being tested as to whether she was worthy to become Isaac's wife, or, more precisely, Abraham's daughter-in-law, Jacob is fully conscious that the flocks are his uncle's and he wants to prove his metal. His identity as kin is the first thing he tells Rachel about himself, and she then runs with the news to her father (v. 12). As Fokkelman suggests, 'blood relationship is what gives Jacob joy, strength and security. Marriage and love are a small, integrated part of this family-world, and are out of order now.'[10] Perhaps it is this very desire to establish himself as family that prompts him to break into tears. The cry, while born of his yearning for wholeness, echoes the recent rift in his own family when Esau, hearing of the stolen blessing, burst into wild and bitter crying (27.34). It also foreshadows the rift to come: that his union with Rachel will be thwarted on the first marriage night. Rashi comments on the reason for Jacob's tears: 'He foresaw . . . that she would not be buried with him' (on Gen. 29.11).[11] Eros and Thanatos merge at that moment, for Rachel, in life as in death, will be displaced by her sister. While she arouses Jacob's desire for integrity and the yearning for wholeness through family, the fulfillment will, in many ways, remain suspended.

Jacob is betrayed on the basis of those kinship relations. Laban seems to embrace him in familial loyalty—'surely you are my bone and my flesh' (v. 14)—and asks Jacob to name his own wages. Yet, in accepting Jacob's service of seven years of labor as a bride price for his daughter, Laban undermines those family ties. In his own words, 'It is better that I give her to you than give her to any other man' (v. 19), so why demand a bride price at all?[12] Laban further inadvertently subverts the original oracle, 'And the older shall serve the younger [*ve-rav ya'avod tza'ir*]' (25.23).[13] Jacob,

---

10. Jan Fokkelman, *Narrative Art in Genesis: Specimens of Stylistic and Structural Analysis* (Sheffield: JSOT Press, 2nd edn, 1991), pp. 124-25.

11. Based on *Gen. R.* 70.12, p. 812.

12. Sarna points out that in offering to pay him—'Are you my kinsman that you should serve me for nothing?'—Laban actually displaces Jacob from the position of family member: 'a member of the household does not receive payment for his services... Jacob has the status of an indentured laborer working to pay off the bride-price' (Sarna, *JPS Torah Commentary: Genesis*, p. 204).

13. The same root, *'bd*, repeated in the oracle and Isaac's blessing to Jacob (Gen. 25.23; 27.29, 37, 40), appears repeatedly in relation to Jacob's service to Laban (29.15, 18, 20, and 27).

to whom the promise of mastery was given, ends up laboring like a slave for his uncle. After Laban dupes him into a marriage to the older sister, once the initial bride price is paid in seven years of slave labor, he ekes out yet another seven years of labor for Rachel, and then Jacob works for another six, while Laban changes his wages 'ten times' (31.7, 41). At first, Jacob's seven years seem but 'a few days [*yamim ahadim*] because of his love for [Rachel]' (v. 20), echoing his mother's promise, 'Stay with [Laban, my brother] a while [*yamim ahadim*], until your brother's fury subsides' (27.44). Yet neither Esau's desire for revenge nor Laban's desire for slave labor lasts 'a few days' or even a few years.[14] They roll into over twenty years of terrible hardship for Jacob. Rebekah's hope that her beloved son would soon return is thwarted, at either end, by the vengeance of her older son and by the greed of her own brother.

Two Brides for Two Brothers

Laban's daughters are only introduced fully in the midst of finagling over wages after Jacob has been ensconced within his uncle's household for a month. He has just been asked what he would like to earn for his labor, when the narrative interjects:

> Now Laban had two daughters; the name of the older [*ha-gdolah*] was Leah, and the name of the younger [*ha-qtanah*] was Rachel. And the eyes of Leah were weak/tender [*rakot*] while Rachel was shapely and beautiful [*yfat to'ar vi-yfat mar'eh*]. Jacob loved Rachel; so he answered, 'I will serve you seven years for Rachel, your daughter, the younger one [*ha-qtanah*]' (Gen. 29.16-18).

The description of the two sisters echoes the initial description of Esau and Jacob. Esau is born bizarrely flawed—furry and ruddy all over, as though covered with a hairy mantle—and becomes a hunter, a man of the field, while Jacob, the 'smooth man' ['*ish halaq*] (27.11), is 'simple/blameless' [*tam*], a dweller of tents (25.25-27). Likewise, the two daughters are presented in contrast: Leah's weak/tender eyes point to a disfigurement while the beauty of Rachel is obviously laudatory.[15] The pairing of Laban's daughters in terms of the elder/younger [*gdolah–qtanah*] reverberates with

---

14. The term 'days'– *yamim* in Hebrew– may be an expression for years or time in general.

15. In Gen. 29.17, the term *rakot* to describe Leah's eyes has variously been translated as 'weak' (RSV, NJPS, as well as the LXX), 'tender' (KJV; Alter, *Genesis*, p. 153), 'delicate' (Fox, *Five Books of Moses*, p. 137), and 'lovely' (*Targ. Onq.* NRSV). Sarna suggests that her eyes 'lack luster' (*JPS Torah Commentary: Genesis*, pp. 204, 365 n. 8; for 'lustrous eyes' as a sign of beauty, see 1 Sam. 16.12; Cant. 4.1, 9). I favor 'weak' or 'tender' as a trait that mars her looks, in contrast to Rachel's beauty.

the narrative's reference to Rebekah's older and younger sons [*ha-gdolah/ ha-qtanah*] (27.15, 42). Although the difference between Esau and Jacob is congenital (they are clearly not identical twins!), Leah and Rachel grow into their differences, according to midrashic intimations. Leah's eyes *become* weak/tender as a result of weeping in her refusal to be paired with Esau.[16] As in the Broadway musical *Seven Brides for Seven Brothers*, the midrash picks up on the biblical parallel—Esau is to Jacob as Leah is to Rachel. And just as Jacob subverts the birth order in buying Esau's birthright and stealing his blessing, Leah subverts the alignment by posing as her sister on the wedding night.

After seven years of service, Jacob demands his reward, rather crudely: 'Give me my wife, for my days are fulfilled, so that I might come into her' (29.21).[17] Yet, in his urgency, he auspiciously does not name the bride!

> Laban then gathered all the people of the place and made a feast. And it was in the evening [*va-yehi va-'erev*], that he took his daughter Leah and brought her to him; and he [Jacob] came into her.... In the morning [*va-yehi va-boqer*], look: it is Leah![18] So he said to Laban, 'What is this that you have done to me? Was it not for Rachel that I served you! Why did you deceive me [*rimmitani*]?'[19] Laban said, 'Such is not done in our place to give the younger [*ha-qtanah*] before the firstborn [*ha-bkhirah*]' (Gen. 29.22-23, 25-26).

---

16. See *Gen. R.* 70.16, pp. 815-16, and the various parallels; see n. 29. We will discuss this midrashic tradition in detail later.

17. The expression, in Hebrew, *va-yav'o 'eleiha* [he came into her], will be reiterated in the Judah and Tamar episode (Gen. 38.16, 18).

18. The copula is missing in the Hebrew; if it were simple narrative past it would be written, '*va-tehi* Leah'—with the conversive-waw and the imperfect form—so, I suggest, the absence of the copula conveys present tense. It is as if Leah sustained the identity of Rachel, on some other plane, for the duration of that night.

19. Here, Laban draws on the same root (*rmh*) embedded in Isaac's explanation to Esau: 'Your brother came in deceit [*be-mirmah*] and took your blessing...' (27.35). The intertextual resonance, again, points to the workings of divine retribution (see Levinson, 'Dialogical Reading', p. 514; Fokkelman, *Narrative Art in Genesis*, pp. 123-41; Ilana Pardes, *Countertraditions in the Bible: A Feminist Approach* [Cambridge, MA: Harvard University Press, 1992], pp. 60-78). As Levinson points out, 'this could be a further example of what Sternberg has called the Bible's penchant for foolproof composition' (Sternberg, *Poetics of Biblical Narrative*, pp. 48-56). Deceit will reverberate, as a kind of family trait in later biblical stories of deception, betrayed loyalty and rivalry. The brothers 'speak deceitfully [*be-mirmah*]' to Shechem and Hamor in plotting revenge for the rape of their sister (34.13). The witch of Endor will use Jacob's very words in rebuking King Saul, 'why have you deceived me [*lamah rimitani*]?' (1 Sam. 28.12), just as Saul accused Michal, his daughter of deceit, in allowing David, her husband and father's arch-rival, to escape (1 Sam. 19.17).

2. *The Collusion of Sisters* 45

This is the moment of supreme dramatic irony, in which, this time, the older sister displaces the younger, just as Jacob, the younger, displaced his older brother, claiming in the presence of his father, 'I am Esau, your firstborn [*bkhorekha*]' (27.19). As Robert Alter notes, '[Laban's] perfectly natural reference to "our place" has the effect of touching a nerve of guilty consciousness in Jacob, who in *his* place acted to put the younger before the firstborn. The effect is reinforced by Laban's referring to Leah not as the elder but as the firstborn (*bkhirah*)'.[20]

But the question that continues to haunt the reader is how Jacob could be so supremely duped! The switch is enabled by the descent of darkness: 'And it was in the evening [*vayehi va-'erev*]' (v. 23). Epiphany dawns with the morning, *boqer* (v. 25), evoking the move from chaos to order in creation: 'And it was evening and it was morning [*va-yehi 'erev va-yehi voqer*]' for the first day, the second day, the third day and so forth (Gen. 1.5, 8ff.). Night blurs the boundaries between the sisters, the distinction between 'tender eyes' and the 'shapely and beautiful' lost in Jacob's dark night of groping. Likewise, Isaac's eyes were 'darkened from seeing' (27.1). Just as the goatskins on the arms and the nape of the neck transformed Jacob's identity so that he could stand before his blind father claiming to be Esau (27.19), so Leah, in the dark, assumed the identity of 'Rachel, [Laban's] daughter, the younger one' (29.18). The biblical text suggests that the revelation of the bride's identity was a total surprise to Jacob: 'In the morning, look: it is Leah!' (Gen. 29.25). Rashi comments, 'But at night, it was *not* Leah because Rachel had given her the [identifying] signs . . .'[21] He draws on a midrashic tradition where the sisters *collude* in deceiving Jacob through an exchange of signs on the wedding night so that Leah would not be shamed—a tradition we will explore in depth later. It is this 'semiotic ruse'[22] that enables Leah to *become* Rachel by night.

The exchange of identities in the bedtrick here mirrors the bedside scene when Jacob stood before Isaac, his blind father, claiming to be Esau. But where the act of blessing is infused with sensual exchange—listening, tasting, drinking, kissing, smelling and touch (27.18-29)—the description of the wedding night is highly restrained. Zvi Jagendorf points out that there is a sharp irony to the reticence in the text:

> In the episode of the stolen blessing (Genesis 27) which is as fully sensual and as detailed as the wedding night is modest and laconic the same ten-

---

20. Alter, *Genesis*, p. 155.
21. Rashi on Gen. 29.25, most likely drawing on *b. Meg.* 13b, which we will later discuss in detail.
22. Levinson, 'Dialogical Reading', p. 515.

sions are at play. . . . Sensual knowledge has turned out to be the opposite of true knowledge.[23]

The conundrum, then, is how Jacob is duped by the mask of sensory perception presented to him—the feel of the bride's skin, her hair, her scent (all that the biblical text does not make explicit). 'He, to borrow Isabella's phrase from *Measure for Measure*, is "Most ignorant of what he's most assur'd"—his intimate sexual purpose'.[24] While Jagendorf identifies erotic desire as the blinding force behind that night of deception, the midrashic narrative conjures complicity between the sisters, the exchange of identities willingly conferred.

The act of deception engenders, for the reader, the 'hermeneutic chromosome',[25] and reveals a deeper truth in the couple's merging—the mysterious workings of the divine through the woman's body. Leah possesses greater awareness, through sexual knowledge and conception, than Jacob. In the words of the midrash, 'There are those whose partner comes to them [*zivugo ba' 'etzlo*] and those who go toward their partner'.[26] In truth, Jacob gets both the spouse who comes to him (Leah) and the one toward whom he goes (Rachel). He fulfills both destinies in choosing Rachel and in being chosen by Leah. By imputing agency to Leah, the midrash alludes to the transformative power behind their encounter precisely because it is beyond his conscious knowledge. It is this unwitting fate that is at the core of Jacob's change.

Leah as Mirror

The midrashic sources explain how Laban was able to dupe Jacob effectively, who, after seven years in his uncle's household, presumably knew the sisters (and their differences). In the last chapter, I intimated that Leah may have been wearing a veil just as Rebekah wore a veil as a symbol of her betrothal. As a result, he could not distinguish her features. The marriage took place after sundown, perhaps on a moonless night. With the feasting, there may have been a great deal of intoxicating drink. Yet how could Rachel and Leah have been forced to comply with their father's plan? Was Rachel tied up? Leah bribed?

---

23. Zvi Jagendorf, '"In the morning, behold it was Leah"; Genesis and the Reversal of Sexual Knowledge', *Prooftexts* 4 (1984), p. 190.

24. Jagendorf, 'Genesis and the Reversal of Sexual Knowledge', p. 190.

25. Sandra Budick's term. See n. 10 in the Introduction.

26. Author's translation of *Gen. R.* 68.3, p. 771. The midrash ascribes the 'passive' position to Isaac, citing Gen. 24.64, while Jacob went out in pursuit of his spouse (Gen. 29.1). See the discussion in Zornberg, *Murmuring Deep*, pp. 279-80.

The discussion in the Babylonian Talmud not only attributes agency to the women in duping Jacob but praises them for doing so. In *Baba Bathra*, the discussion centers on the displacement of the firstborn: why did the right of the firstborn go to Rachel's son, Joseph? As it says, 'Ephraim and Manasseh shall be to me like Reuben and Shimon' (Gen. 48.5; cf. v. 22; 49.22-26). Consonant with the biblical text, the Talmud suggests that the right of the firstborn is *not* a given; rather, it is overruled by a combination of merit, divine election and feminine will. The rabbis imply that the process of selection is *prenatal* (as in the case of Jacob and Esau), determined by the respective merits of the women. The son may fail (as Reuben does in 'defiling his father's bed' by lying with Bilhah; cf. Gen. 35.22 and 1 Chron. 5.1), or the father may override the choice (as Jacob did in favoring Joseph). God, according to the aggadah, makes *his* choice according the merits of the women:

> The birthright should have come from Rachel, as it is written, 'These are the generations of Jacob, Joseph . . .' (Gen. 37.2), but Leah took precedence over her in [God's] compassion [*kidamta be-raḥamim*]. [However], on account of the discretion, which was characteristic of Rachel, the Holy One Blessed be He restored [the birthright] to her [i.e. Rachel]. Why [initially] did Leah take precedence in [God's] compassion?[27] 'And Leah had tender eyes' (29.17). . . . Rav said: Her eyes were indeed actually tender, but that was no disgrace to her but to her credit; for at the crossroads she heard people saying: 'Rebekah has two sons, and Laban has two daughters; the elder daughter should be married to the elder son, and the younger daughter to the younger son'. And she sat at the crossroads and inquired: 'How does the elder son conduct himself?' 'He is a wicked man, a highway robber'. 'How does the younger man conduct himself?' 'A simple man, dwelling in tents' (Gen. 25.27).[28] And she wept until her eyelashes dropped off. As it is written, 'And God saw that Leah was despised . . .' [That is] the Holy One blessed be He saw that Esau's conduct was despised by Leah, and so He opened her womb (*b. B. Bat.* 123a).[29]

---

27. The Talmud, at this point, has established that the mother-of-the-firstborn status was transferred to Rachel. Thus, the discussion now turns to why God opened Leah's womb first.

28. Note that the Talmud does not quote directly with reference to Esau. His wickedness is read into the biblical narrative, based on the description of him being a 'man of the hunt' and having the taste of the 'hunt in his mouth' (Gen. 25.27-28), whereas the description of Jacob is a direct quote. This demonization of Esau is consistent in rabbinic texts.

29. This draws considerably from Zornberg's translation in *Murmuring Deep*, p. 282, with some modification. In *Genesis Rabbah*, on 29.18, the deception is at Leah's initiative: 'Why were her eyes tender? Because she cried, saying, 'May it be his will, that my lot not fall with Esau, the wicked'. Said R. Huna: Powerful is the prayer that cancels the edict; not only that—she preceded her sister (in marriage)' (*Gen. R.* 70.16,

At first, the right of the firstborn [*bekhorah*] is vested in Rachel's son. Because Jacob's genealogy [*toledot Ya'aqov*] begins with Joseph, the aggadah presumes that Joseph is considered his firstborn (Gen. 37.2).[30] The right of the firstborn then shifts to Leah, because she resisted the fate of being paired with Esau. But it is returned to Rachel, on account of her modesty or, rather, sense of discretion, since she was willing to selflessly give the signs over to her sister on the wedding night and *keep the secret*. The question of who took precedence over whom in God's compassion [*kidamta be-raḥamim*] suggests a play on words—*raḥamim* resonant with the term for womb, *reḥem*. Who 'wins' the fertility race, the first to conceive in the womb, will depend both upon the woman's initiative and her self-sacrifice in arousing divine compassion. The rivalry of the sisters is thus transformed from competition for the one righteous husband, Jacob, into selection according to divine favor. In the biblical text, it is not Jacob's seed that 'opens the womb' but God: 'When Yhwh saw that Leah was despised [*senu'ah*], he opened her womb; but Rachel was barren' (Gen. 29.31).[31] Later, 'God remembered Rachel, and God *heard* her and opened her womb' (30.22). The displacement of Rachel by Leah from the position of first wife, then, occurs in the cosmic sphere as well as in the marital domain. She who is the beloved one becomes the 'second wife' and conceives last; Leah,

pp. 817-19); see the parallels in *Yal. Shimoni* Gen. 125, *Tanḥ. VaYetzei* 4; *Tanḥ.* (ed. Buber) *VaYetzei* 11; *Ag. Ber.* (ed. Buber) 49; *Midr. Teh.* 55.4.

30. Better prooftexts for the selection of Joseph as firstborn can be found in the biblical text (see Gen. 48.4-5, 21), but the Talmud links his chosenness to the overarching theme of genealogy [*toledot*]. The peculiar detail in Jacob's *toledot* is that none of his other sons are mentioned. We will speak about the rupture of Jacob's lineage that begins with this verse—'Joseph, being seventeen years old . . .' (Gen. 37.2), which leads to near fratricide, Joseph's sale into slavery, and the journey of the clan down to Egypt in later chapters.

31. The description of Leah as 'despised' reverberates with the passage in Deuteronomy in which a man marries two wives. If the firstborn of his loins is not the son of the beloved wife, but of the 'despised wife' [*ha-snu'ah*], 'he is not permitted to treat the son of the loved [*ha-'ahuvah*] as the firstborn in preference to the son of the despised [*ha-snu'ah*], who is the firstborn. He must acknowledge as firstborn the son of the one who is despised [*ha-snu'ah*], giving him a double portion of all that he has; since he is the first issue of his virility, the right of the firstborn is his' (Deut. 21.16-17). Yet Jacob contravenes this deuteronomistic principle by favoring the son of the beloved wife over Leah's firstborn. One way of reading the rabbinic text, then, is as a 'corrective' alignment with the fate of Jacob's sons. Despite the favoritism of Joseph, the biblical narrative does not affirm the patriarch's choice of the son of the beloved wife over his brothers in the long term. As Robert Alter observes, this displacement of the firstborn is not sustained: 'For while Joseph, next to the youngest of the sons, will eventually rule over his brothers in his own lifetime as splendidly as he has dreamed, it is Judah, the fourthborn [of Leah], who will be the progenitor of the kings of Israel' (Alter, *Biblical Narrative*, p. 6).

who is 'despised' of man, becomes 'beloved' in God's compassion and conceives first.

In her comparative folklore study *The Bedtrick,* Wendy Doniger characterizes the pattern of 'switching the brides on the wedding night' as the 'Lovely and Loathly Ladies', where 'the older/uglier sister pretends to be young and beautiful (a Lovely Lady), while she forces the younger/prettier sister to hide her beauty (like a Loathly Lady)'.[32] According to the midrash, what transforms Leah from being the 'Loathly one [*ha-snu'ah*]' into a 'Lovely Lady' is her beauty within—her desire to marry Jacob rather than Esau. In a creative play on words, the midrash transforms Leah from the passive position of being 'despised' to an active role in despising Esau's conduct. She reverses her fate precisely at the locus where it is declared—at the crossroads—and decides to take 'the road less traveled', against the fate of birth order. The people proclaimed, 'Leah is for Esau as Rachel is for Jacob' (two brides for two brothers). But Leah is determined to flout convention and expectations and collude in Laban's trickery by marrying herself off to the younger son. While Laban touts local convention—here 'they do not give the younger before the firstborn' (v. 26)—in order to eke out another seven years of labor from Jacob, Leah allies with Jacob in overturning primogeniture; she *chooses* him, the younger brother, on ethical grounds. Laban is Lucifer to Leah's Beatrice. In the end, it accounts for the reversal of her role, as Doniger suggests: 'Leah is really the Loathly Lady; she appears to be ugly but is in fact beautiful—that is fertile . . . the Hebrew Bible, reversing the superficial value of the folk structure, expands upon its more complex underlying agenda, the tension between beauty and fertility, desire and duty'.[33] Her passionate resistance leads Leah to shed her eyelashes in weeping, and God rewards Leah for sacrificing her outer beauty by opening up her womb, allowing the Loathly to be transformed into the Lovely Lady. This is what Doniger calls the 'double-cross-back'[34]: a counterseduction, but here the master plotter with whom Leah is allied in retribution for Jacob's earlier betrayal of his father and brother is none other than God.

In an alternative midrash, Leah is the one to answer Jacob's fearsome accusation directed, in the biblical text, at Laban: 'What is this that you have done to me? Was it not for Rachel that I served you! Why did you deceive me [*rimmitani*]?' (Gen. 29.25).

> All that night he called her 'Rachel', and she responded to him.
> In the morning, 'Look: it is Leah!'
> He said: 'Why you deceiver, daughter of a deceiver [*ramait'a bat ram'ai*]!'

32. Doniger, *Bedtrick,* p. 160.
33. Doniger, *Bedtrick,* p.162.
34. Doniger, *Bedtrick,* p. 29.

And she said: 'Is there a teacher[35] without students? Did your father not call you Esau, and you answered him? So too you called me and I answered you' (*Gen. R.* 70.19).[36]

Phrased as a rhetorical question, Leah's retort is laced with searing irony: 'Is there a teacher without students?' The midrash implies that she has learned the art of deception from him. But the ability to deceive depends on a response to a *call*: 'Did your father not call you Esau, and you answered him. So too you called me and I answered you'. In this imaginary dialogue, Leah mysteriously drops Rachel's name. Perhaps the midrash is reticent here about Leah's claim on her sister's identity; there's an implied silence that revolves around the question of voice, which cannot be disguised. As I will later show, another midrashic tradition conjectures a call and response, but it is Rachel's, not Leah's, voice. In this midrash, Jacob now faces Leah as a mirror of himself and resists the reflection. Zornberg comments on the verse 'And God saw that Leah was hated' (Gen. 29.31):

> Faced with his own image in Leah's impersonation, Jacob hates her. He hates her, of course, for not being Rachel, for depriving him of Rachel. But more subtly, he hates her for revealing himself to himself. This is a hatred that perhaps only God can discern. Perhaps he behaves with perfect propriety to Leah as his wife. Perhaps he is genuinely unaware of his own hatred. But God sees his real aversion to his own complexity, his own unobservable self. A simple coherent self has cracked up and he does not know himself.[37]

The question lingers as to why he never divorces her and continues bearing children by her year after year. Perhaps it is because, on some level, he acknowledges that as the 'partner who comes to him [*zivugo ba' 'etzlo*]', with all the rancor and resentment that an unwitting marital union entails, Leah may restore him to wholeness, to integrity in the end.

In the meantime, her sense of being despised reverberates into the next generation. The naming of her sons, again and again, reflects Leah's yearning for her husband's elusive love and her gratitude for divine recompense (v. 30). She names the first Reuben [*Re'u-ven*, lit., 'See, a son!'] 'For Yhwh has seen my affliction so now my husband will love me' (v. 32); the second, Shimon: 'Yhwh has heard [*shama'*] that I was hated' (v. 33); the third,

---

35. The term here, in Aramaic, is *sapar* (or *sopher* in some manuscripts), which may mean 'barber', or in other versions 'teacher' or 'scribe'. The idea is that just as one cannot learn to shave or cut hair by doing so to oneself, but must witness how it is done to another, so a student learns from his teacher by example (Alter, *Genesis*, p. 155; see also Albeck's comment on *Gen. R.* 70.19, p. 819 n.1). I have chosen to simplify the image, given the gendered nature of the profession (Leah could not very well liken herself to a 'barber').

36. Author's translation of *Gen. R.* 70.19, p. 819. Compare *Tanḥ. Va-Yetzei* 4.

37. Zornberg, *Murmuring Deep*, p. 288.

Levi: 'Now this time, my husband will be joined to me [*yillaveh 'ishi 'elai*]' (v. 34); and the fourth, Judah [*Yehudah*]: 'This time I will give thanks to Yhwh!' (v. 35). Three stages of wishful awareness—seeing, hearing, joining—are followed by a sense of reconciliation. When Leah finally expresses gratitude that God has compensated her for being the despised wife, she ceases to bear children—for this is the fourth son, the one who will ultimately become the progenitor of kings. In the language of the Talmud, the position of Leah as taking precedence in God's compassion [*kidamta be-raḥamim*] is thus fulfilled. But, in her lifetime, Rachel holds the position of the beloved woman, in some ways the sole wife in Jacob's world,[38] despite being displaced by her sister.

Rachel as Mirror

In *Countertraditions in the Bible,* Ilana Pardes identifies Rachel as the mirror of Jacob; both are compelled to surmount the 'tyranny of time in their respective struggles against their precursors, Leah and Esau. To overcome priority means to overcome nature, to replace a concept from the natural order with one from the spiritual sphere.'[39] Likewise, Jan Fokkelman systematically traces the parallels between the lives of Jacob and Rachel. Jacob's choice of Rachel is consistent with his rebellion against biological priority. Because he is the younger son destined for supremacy, he favors the young sister 'on the grounds of his destiny ("big serves little"); he had given priority to the "Jacoba" of the two sisters, Rachel'.[40] But as Pardes suggests, in naming her 'Jacoba' rather than calling Jacob 'Rachel-el' or some other masculinized form of 'Rachel', Fokkelman 'foregrounds the role of gender in the dissymmetry between the trajectory of their lives'.[41] Jacob usurps, chooses, couples and conceives sons while Rachel *is chosen, is usurped and is deemed barren*. 'Jacob's plot is the main plot, while Rachel's narrative is the subplot'.[42] The difference between their lots, however, does not solely hinge upon the hierarchy of power and gender relations, nor does the dichotomy between the 'natural' and 'spiritual' sphere line up in their respective lives, as Pardes would have it. Rather, the dissymmetry hinges precisely upon the blurring of those spheres in the lives of biblical women, whose destiny is tied inexorably to their fertility and the divine plan.

---

38. The most obvious account of this is in Judah's great speech before the supposed viceroy of Egypt (Joseph) where, in paraphrasing Jacob's words, the fourth son born of Jacob and Leah's union acknowledges, in his father's words: 'As you know, my wife [i.e. Rachel] bore me two sons . . .' (Gen. 44.27).
39. Pardes, *Countertraditions*, p. 60.
40. Fokkelman, *Narrative Art in Genesis*, pp. 131, 135.
41. Pardes, *Countertraditions*, p. 61.
42. Pardes, *Countertraditions*, p. 61.

God is all but absent in determining the direction of Rachel's life—in contrast to her male counterpart. Jacob usurps the blessing in accord with the original divine oracle (Gen. 25.23) and that blessing holds (27.33); his blind old father accedes to its power, despite the ambiguity of his son's identity at the time of the blessing. No such divine blessing or prophecy graces the life of Rachel. Although she, as Jacob's choice, must 'overcome' the priority of her older sister, she does not succeed due to her father's ruse, and no divine intervention rights that wrong. She is thus tragically, compelled to share her husband with her sister. Jacob, on the other hand, fully displaces his brother as the recipient of the patriarchal covenant. Thus, Rachel mirrors Jacob in birth order, yet, unlike him, does not maintain her position as the effective *supplanter*.

In fact, Rachel is the one who is displaced, and the biblical narrative does not reinstate her. Rather than affirm the 'overturn of primogeniture' (for the women), the inverse takes place: 'When Yhwh saw that Leah was despised [*snu'ah*], he opened her womb; but Rachel was barren [*'aqarah*]' (Gen. 29.31). God intervenes to guarantee that Leah is the one who will bear the firstborn. In the unraveling of the plot, both sisters become on-going rivals for love and fertility—the former granted by the husband, the latter bestowed by God. As the midrash wryly comments, '*'aqarah—'iqar ha-bayit* [the barren one is the principal woman of the house, i.e., the most beloved one]'.[43] The older sister takes hold of the privilege of *biological* first place while the other maintains priority in her husband's heart. Yet, in the end, Leah is buried in the ancestral grave, in the cave of Machpelah, and Jacob will ask to lie by her side there (49.31). As Pardes points out, 'this is Leah's ultimate triumph'.[44] The narrative trajectory seems to affirm the displacement of Rachel, and herein lies the tragedy of her life.

Yet God *does* intervene to show Rachel favor in her afterlife, with her propitious burial on the road to and from exile (Gen. 35.16-19; 48.7; and Jer. 31.15-16 [MT]).[45] Perhaps this defines Rachel's priority within the 'spiritual sphere'—at least in the collective imagination of the Jewish people—from Jeremiah to the moving commentary of Chassidei Ashkenaz.[46] Over

---

43. Author's translation of *Gen. R.* 71.2, p. 823.
44. Pardes, *Countertraditions*, p. 74.
45. This is not wholly accurate; the text states that 'God [*'Elohim*] remembered Rachel, and heard her, and opened her womb' (Gen. 30.22).
46. The matriarch, Rachel, is associated with the mystical concept of 'raising up the sparks' of the Jews who are forced to live under foreign rule in the Diaspora. 'This is the secret of why Israel is fated to be enslaved by all the nations of the world. In order that she [*knesset Yisrael*, identified with Rachel] may uplift those sparks which have also fallen among them.... And therefore it was necessary that Israel should be scattered to the four winds in order to lift up everything' (*Sefer ha-Likkutim*, in Gershom Scholem, *Major Trends in Jewish Mysticism* [New York: Schocken Books, 1954], p. 284). On the

the course of history, Rachel is transformed from the daughter, displaced in the biblical narrative, to the matriarch of the lost tribes of Israel within the collective rabbinic imagination. She becomes the mother of children of the Diaspora—from Joseph, who rises to prominence in Pharaoh's palace, to the ten northern tribes sent into exile by the Assyrians in 722 BCE and to Esther and Mordecai in the court of the Persian king Ahasuerus. As such, she becomes the symbol of *knesset Yisrael*, the principle of cohesion for a dispersed people.[47] How do the sages transform the life of Rachel from the biblical daughter-sister-wife to the nation's matriarch of aggadic lore?

The Distaff of Silence

The interpretive tradition on the displacement of Rachel hinges on the following question: how was Jacob so effectively duped on the wedding night? The mysterious 'exchange of signs' is recounted in many versions throughout the aggadic tradition, but the clearest lens for our discussion is found in the Babylonian tractate *Megillah*,[48] as it hinges on the trace Rachel leaves her descendants in the Diaspora. The opening question concerns the origin of Esther's discretion about her identity (Est. 2.20); her silence is deemed to be a genetic attribute of Rachel's children:

> R. Eliezer said: What is the meaning of the verse 'He does not withdraw His eyes from the righteous' (Job 36.7). As a reward for the discretion/modesty [*tzni'ut*] that Rachel demonstrated, she merited that Saul would be descended from her,[49] and as a reward for his discretion, Esther descended from him.

---

dispersal of the divine sparks, see Scholem's comment on p. 261. Martin Buber points out that the Jews of Safed participated in the 'rites of Rachel, where he mourned, participated, and became one with the exiled portion of the deity, and the rites of Leah, where through mystical exercises and contemplation he transformed his body into a chariot to lift on high the exiled fragments' (Martin Buber, *Hasidism and Modern Man* [New York: Horizon Press, 1966], pp. 7-8; 187-89; cf. Gershom Scholem, *On the Kabbalah and its Symbolism* [New York: Schocken Books, 1965], pp. 148-50).

47. Zornberg, *Beginning of Desire*, p. 305.
48. The parallel to this passage in found in *b. B. Bat.* 123a; we discussed a selection from this Talmudic passage on the origin of Leah's tender eyes earlier, which accounted for why the firstborn [*bekhor*] came from her. The focus, in this selection, is on the deception on the wedding night. See Joshua Levinson's brilliant analysis of the parallel passage in *Baba Bathra* ('Dialogical Reading', pp. 513-20). I borrow extensively from his insights.
49. Saul is associated with discretion in not revealing that he had privately been anointed king by the prophet Samuel: 'But about the matter of the kingship, of which Samuel had spoken, he did not tell him [*l'o higid lo*] anything' (1 Sam. 10.16). Modesty [*tzni'ut*] is manifest, in the case of Saul and Esther, in not telling the truth about their identity—for the queen that she was Jew; for Saul that he was king. Mordecai and

> What discretion did Rachel exhibit? It is written, 'And Jacob told Rachel that he was the brother of her father' (Gen. 29.12). Now was he [really] the brother of her father? Was he not the son of her father's sister [Rebekah]?[50]
> Rather, he said to her: Will you marry me?
> She said: Yes. But my father is a deceiver, and you cannot prevail against him.[51]
> He said to her: I am his brother in deceit.
> She asked him: Are the righteous permitted to act deceitfully?
> He answered: Yes, 'With the pure you show yourself pure, and with the crooked you show yourself perverse' (2 Sam. 22.27).
> He asked: What deception [is he planning]?
> She answered: I have a sister who is older than me, and he will not marry me off before her.
> [To prevent this, Jacob] gave her [i.e. Rachel] signs.
> When night descended, she said: Now my sister will be shamed, and she gave her these [signs], as it is written: 'In the morning, look: it is Leah!' (29.25). Does this imply that until then it had not been Leah? Rather, through the signs that Rachel gave to Leah, [Jacob] did not know until then. Therefore, she was rewarded, and Saul [the first king of Israel] descended from her. And what discretion did Saul show? 'But about the matter of the kingship, of which Samuel had spoken, he did not tell [*lo' higid*] him anything' (1 Sam. 10.16). And, as a reward, Esther descended from him. Rabbi Elazar said: The Holy One bestows greatness upon a person, and decrees so for his sons and grandson until the end of all the generations, as it is said, 'but with kings upon the throne he sets them forever, and they are exalted' (Job. 36.7) (*b. Meg.* 13b, author's trans.).

The homiletical passage opens with Rabbi Eliezer's teaching, based on Job 36.7, 'He [God] will not turn his eyes away from a righteous person . . . ,' and concludes with 'but with kings upon the throne he sets them forever, and they are exalted'. The 'distant verse' (from the Writings, *ketuvim*), taken from Elihu's speech defending the principle of retributive justice, is deployed to illustrate how the reward of the righteous may be delayed. For example, the merit of the matriarch was only recompensed centuries later upon the secret inauguration of Saul into kingship and the ascent of Esther to the Persian throne. Because of her discretion [*tzni'ut*] in passing

---

Esther, who was his niece, were both descended from Kish, of the tribe of Benjamin, Rachel's second son (Est. 2.5-7; 1 Sam. 9.1-2).

50. The commentary is based on the redundancy in the verse 'And Jacob told Rachel that he was her father's brother [*ki 'aḥi 'aviha h'u*] and that he was Rebekah's son' (Gen. 29.12). While the term 'brother' [*'aḥ*] connotes kinsman (cf. Gen. 13.8), Jacob also introduces himself as Rebekah's son. The Talmud then understands the phrase 'brother of her father' (v. 12) figuratively, as 'brother in deception' (see the Maharsha's commentary on *b. B. Bat.* 123a).

51. An allusion, perhaps, to Jacob's wrestling with 'the man/angel' whom he could not overcome (Gen. 32.25).

the secret signs to her sister, Rachel merited royal descendants who would likewise keep mum. But the virtue of discretion hinges on who withholds the secret from whom. Is Jacob or Laban to be deceived? At first, Rachel colludes with Jacob in undermining her father's plot to switch the brides; the secret signs were to be withheld from Laban and Leah. Since Jacob is Laban's 'brother in deception', the plan is to outwit the primary deceiver. Through the exchange of signs—a key held in the hand, a tug of the right earlobe, a word whispered, or the exchange of a crumpled note—Laban's ruse planned for the wedding would be thwarted. Yet, in the end, Rachel is discriminating about whom she chooses to withhold the secret from, favoring her sister over her husband. This is the crux of the midrashic drama; it hinges on the question as to why one deception trumps another. Measure for measure, Rachel reflects Jacob's own deception in a double irony: the deceiver who plots to deceive has his own ruse turned against him.

The question the matriarch raises, in conversation with Jacob, is one that resonates throughout the entire Jacob saga: 'Are the righteous permitted to act deceitfully?' Jacob's answer is glib; it rolls off his tongue in the form of a quotation from King David's swan song: 'And with the crooked you show yourself perverse' (2 Sam. 22.27).[52] In his readiness to deceive Laban, he does not prevaricate, although he expresses qualms about Rebekah's plot to dupe his father in the biblical account: 'Perhaps my father will feel me, and I shall seem to be mocking him, and bring a curse on myself and not a blessing' (Gen. 27.12). However, his hesitation is based on the risk of getting caught; he is pragmatic. Rachel, on the other hand, questions the deception on ethical grounds. She chooses to deceive the deceiver, Jacob (who acknowledges that he is Laban's 'brother in deceit'), not for herself, but for the sake of *another*. At her own expense, she dupes her future husband and thereby shows him up for the heel [*'eqev*] that he is. In Esau's own words, 'Was he, then, named Jacob that he might supplant me [*ya'aqveni*] these two times?' (Gen. 27.36).[53] Thus she becomes a means of divine retribution. In Joshua Levinson's reading of this midrash, she is both his 'sister in trick-

---

52. With regard to this quotation, Levinson remarks on the ironic reading of the verse that precedes this one: 'With the loyal you show yourself loyal; with the blameless [*tam*] you show yourself blameless' (2 Sam. 22.26). Jacob, once described as blameless [*tam*] (Gen. 25.27) in the biblical narrative, has lost that character trait, for now he is shrewd, having learned the principle of being 'perverse' with the 'crooked' (Levinson, 'Dialogical Reading', p. 515 n. 19).

53. The second etiology for his name alludes to the two times that Jacob, the 'heel-grabber' at birth, later manipulated himself into first place—in buying the birthright from his famished brother (Gen. 25.27-34) and in stealing the blessing from his blind father.

ery and ... the source of his downfall'.[54] In my reading, she is the mirror that facilitates his psychological transformation.

Jacob's pat answer, justifying his deception, clearly does not reassure Rachel, for there is another issue at stake: the shame she would cause her sister on the wedding night were Jacob to denounce Leah if she did not possess the secret signs. The midrash suggests that it is her sense of discretion/modesty [*tzni'ut*] that prompts this act of self-sacrifice. In Hebrew, the term *tzni'ut* is commonly translated as 'modesty', a trait, according to the rabbis, that is particularly praiseworthy in women. But it also connotes secrecy, privacy and hiddenness [*tzni'ah*], as in the midrashic reading of the verse in Isaiah: '"Remove your veil [*gali tzamatekh*] (strip off your robe, uncover your legs, and pass through the rivers)" (Isa. 47.2)—remove your modesty [*tzni'utekh*], this refers to the king [that is, God] who is kept behind seven screens'.[55] Similarly, God speaks to Moses in the privacy of the Tent of Meeting, shrouded by a cloud of divine veiling.[56] *Tzni'ut* is associated with erotic desire, with allusions to veiling and unveiling, restraint and chastity. What Rachel holds at bay is consummation with her husband, conceding to become the second wife, the *speculum of the other woman*. Ostensibly, the midrash frames the moral value in terms of anxiety over causing the other disgrace. Better that she remain hidden, withheld from her husband, than expose her sister to the burning consequences of disclosure that night.

In contrast to normative patriarchal society, where women are the tokens of exchange passed from man to man and father to son-in-law, here the sisters collude in exchanging the husband. In the biblical narrative, the drama is expressed most poignantly by the maternal naming of sons, where the rivalry (rather than collusion) between the sisters is emphasized. While the midrash suggests that she willingly displaced herself for her sister at her own initiative, Rachel is driven to despair as she watches her sister conceive, grow big with child and bear through the years, while she remains barren: 'When Rachel saw that she had borne Jacob no children, she became jealous of her sister, and Rachel said to Jacob, "Give me children, or I shall die"' (Gen. 30.1). As Michael Fishbane points out, 'The strife between Rachel and Leah is summed up in one poignant remark by Rachel, given as the etymology for the name "Naphthali", Jacob's son through her concubine Bilhah: "I have struggled mightily [*naftulei 'Elohim niftalti*] with my sister and have prevailed" (30.8). With this expression, Rachel's situation ironi-

---

54. Levinson, 'Dialogical Reading', p. 516.

55. *Cant. R.* 3.2 on the verse 'Upon my bed at night I sought him whom my soul loves; I sought him, but found him not; I called him, but he gave no answer' (Cant. 3.1). In the midrash, it is God (the king in the parable), who is asked to reveal himself where, through an ingenious play on words, 'the veil [*tzamatekh*]' becomes metonymic for 'modesty [*tzni'utekh*]'.

56. *Num. R.* 1.3.

cally recalls that of her husband, Jacob, who "strove with *'Elohim* and man and prevailed" (Gen. 32.29)'.[57] The tension reaches a peak in negotiations over the mandrakes (*duda'im*, 'love apples'), when Rachel exchanges with Leah a night with her husband for the plant that could serve either as an aphrodisiac or a fertility potion.[58] In the *only* conversation between Leah and Rachel recorded in the biblical narrative, we hear the rancor of their rivalry:

> Rachel said to Leah, 'Please give me some of your son's mandrakes'.
> But she said to her, 'Was it not enough for you to take away my man [*'ishi*], that you would also take my son's mandrakes?' Rachel replied, 'I promise, he shall lie with you tonight, in return for your son's mandrakes' (Gen. 30.14-15).

Leah then greets Jacob in the field, demanding, 'You must come in to me; for I have clearly hired you [*sakhor sekhartikha*] with my son's mandrakes' (Gen. 30.16). And her fifth son, Issachar, is named for this exchange.[59] Jacob, who hired himself out as *sakhir* for the bride price (Gen. 29.15; cf. 30.28 and 31.7-8, 41), is now the husband/stud, 'hired' out in negotiations between the sisters. The patriarch, who twice displaces his brother (Gen. 27.36) in buying the birthright and stealing the blessing is twice displaced in the collusion and rivalry between sisters—first on the wedding night, according to midrash, and then in the exchange for mandrakes, in the biblical narrative. Jacob seems to acquiesce passively to the women's manipulations over who should be his bedmate that night, whether sister or slave girl.

---

57. Fishbane, *Text and Texture*, p. 57.

58. Fox suggests the translation 'love-apples' for *duda'im* (*The Five Books of Moses*, p. 141), based on a play on the Hebrew—*dodim* ('love', pl. abstract noun), as in Ezek. 16.8; 23.17; and Prov. 7.18. In Song of Songs, the two are closely associated: 'There I will give my love [*dodai*] to you/The mandrakes [*duda'im*] exuding their fragrance... my beloved (*dodi*)' (Cant. 7.13-14). The plant has been identified as *Mandragora officinarum*, which grows wild in the fields. It has small yellow fruit, which exude a strong, heady smell, and the root, shaped like a homunculus, may have given rise to the folklore tradition associating it with aphrodisiac powers. Sarna points out that 'Aphrodite, the Greek goddess of love, beauty, and sex, was given the epithet *he-mandragoriti* [Lady of the Mandrake]' (Sarna, *JPS Torah Commentary: Genesis*, p. 209).

59. The biblical text is reticent about alluding to Jacob directly as 'hire' (*sakhar*) in the conception of Issachar. Leah attributes the birth of this son to a reward or wage (*sakhar*) for having given her slave girl to her husband (Gen. 30.18). Rashbam, however, noting the doubling of the letter sin, connects the naming both to the episode of Zilpah (30.10-14) and the exchange of the mandrakes for a night with Jacob. Fokkelman suggests that, in naming Issachar as a reward for giving Jacob over to 'my handmaid' (ambiguously referred to as *shifḥati*), Leah inadvertently refers to herself, the true sexual 'reward' for the conception of this son. The allusion to *sakhar*, however, 'taints the patriarch', who in Laban's house is reduced to a 'man of wages [*'ish-sakhar*], someone who must be hired to make his wife a mother, and a wage-earner' (*Narrative Art in Genesis*, p. 138).

Twice, both Rachel and Leah present their slave girls to be bedded, conceive and give birth on their knees. Bilhah and Zilpah then each bear him two sons: Dan (Justice) and Naphtali (Struggle); Gad (Fortune) and Asher (Happiness), respectively named according to the sororal rivalry (Gen. 30.3-13). As Levinson notes, 'We may have here a glimpse of a subversive counterdiscourse, where men are objects passed between women to further their own personal interests'.[60]

The midrash, however, lends Jacob's passivity and the sisters' wiles a higher hand, transforming the rivalry into cooperation, even collusion. Rather than viewing Jacob as a *male* fantasy of prowess, proving his virility through sexual mastery over two sisters,[61] the midrash challenges this surface reading. Jacob is morally trumped by the woman he loves because Rachel's motivation is neither for personal gain nor for national goals, 'but is', as Levinson points out, 'rather, motivated by an intensely personal and moral concern'.[62] The woman deceives the man for the benefit of *another* woman and even receives the narrator's approval. Whether competitive or cooperative, the women's interest also serves the divine plot by establishing the *communitas* of Israel (the birth of the twelve sons of Jacob/tribes of Israel). The midrash does not necessarily 'rub against the grain of [biblical] history' but, rather, highlights voices and shapes that remain inchoate in the biblical text: the search for wholeness in a life fractured by deceit and dual loyalty, and the yearning for unity for a nation divided by tribal affinities.

The Demise of the Matriarch

After the birth of Joseph, the next window into the sisters' world reveals a conversation between Jacob, Rachel and Leah, who are retreating in haste from Paddan-aram. Detailing the continued abuse at the hands of Laban, Jacob tells them of a dream in which God appeared to him, to account for yet another 'semiotic ruse': the secrets of genetic breeding for the 'streaked, speckled and mottled' goats in order to better maximize his earnings (31.11-

---

60. Levinson, 'Dialogical Reading', p. 518.
61. See Lori Lefkovitz's discussion in 'Leah behind the Veil: Sex with Sisters from the Bible through Woody Allen', *In Scripture: The First Stories of Jewish Sexual Identities* (Lanham, MD: Rowman & Littlefield, 2010), pp. 65-84.
62. Levinson, 'Dialogical Reading', p. 518. He suggests that there is only one other story in the Bible where a woman deceives a man for the benefit of another woman—in the book of Ruth—probably referring to the 'seduction' scene at the threshing floor (ch. 3). In a permutation on the theme, Michal and Jonathan both deceive their father, King Saul, in protecting David, ultimately at their own expense, with Michal as potential mother and Jonathan as heir to the throne (1 Samuel 18). On the parallels between Rachel and Michal see Alter, *Biblical Narrative*, pp. 114-30. We will compare the two episodes, again, in the chapter on Michal.

13). There is no such dream recorded in the biblical narrative; rather, it is Jacob's own negotiations over his wages (*sakhar*), while working for Laban, and his wily ways with black sheep and speckled and spotted goats, that increase and strengthen his flocks over the years. Having claimed the streaked goats and dark sheep that would be born for himself, he placed rods before the watering troughs as they mated in a bizarre Lamarckian process of selection (Gen. 30.25-43). With respect to Jacob's accumulation of wealth, the sons respond, 'Jacob has taken all that was our father's; he has gained all this wealth from what belonged to our father' (31.1). But the sisters, seeing themselves as 'strangers' [*nokhriyyot*] in their father's house, portray their father as having 'sold' them and 'devoured' all their money (v. 15). In unison,[63] they ally with Jacob against Laban (as Michal, wife of King David, will do against *her* father, Saul, the first monarch of Israel). God and Jacob, along with Leah and Rachel, form an alliance in this ruse against Laban. Tragically, however, the daughters' betrayal of their father entails a sacrifice as the plot is played out.

The term 'steal' (*gnb*) constitutes the *Leitwört* in the narrative of their getaway. In the biblical text, the narrator informs the reader:

> Now Laban had gone to shear his sheep, and Rachel stole her father's household gods [*va-tignov Raḥel et ha-teraphim*]. And Jacob *stole away* the heart of Laban the Aramean [*va-yignov Ya'aqov et-lev Lavan ha-'arami*], in that he did not tell him that he intended to flee (Gen. 31.19-20).

An exact parallel is made between Rachel stealing the idols and Jacob 'stealing away' the heart/mind of Laban. Most translations render the phrase '*va-yignov Ya'aqov et-lev Lavan*' as 'And Jacob deceived Laban', which dampens the overtones of the verb, *gnb*.[64] The narrative here focuses on Laban, focalizing on *his* subjective experience of being swindled as Jacob sneaks away by night with all his wives, children, servants and livestock. When the older man catches up with Jacob, he rails at him with the same words, saying, 'What have you done? You have deceived me [lit. you have stolen my heart/mind, *va-tignov 'et levavi*], and carried away my daughters like captives of the sword' (v. 26). One wonders whether Laban is concerned with the loss of his daughters and their children, or whether it is in fact the stolen idols (*teraphim*) that cause him distress (v. 19). He ends his litany of accusations with the words 'But why did you steal [*ganavta*] my

---

63. 'Then Rachel and Leah answered [*va-ta'an*] and said [*va-toma'rna*] to him . . .' (Gen. 31.14). The first verb, *ve-ta'an*, is actually in the singular, which suggests that Rachel takes the lead here. Both Ilana Pardes (*Countertraditions*, p. 70) and Fuchs ('"For I Have the Way of Women"', p. 73) make this suggestion.

64. The passage in Leviticus makes the parallels between stealing [*gnb*], deception [*kḥsh*], and lying [*shqr*] explicit: 'You shall not steal; you shall not deal deceitfully; and you shall not lie to one another' (Lev. 19.11).

gods?' (v. 31), implying that his motive is less than paternal. It is the pursuit of his gods among Jacob's belongings that provides the impetus for the confrontation. We hear no sweet parting words between father and daughters in Gilead, as we had heard from Rebekah's father, Bethuel, when she left for the land of Canaan (Gen. 24.50-60).

We are not told the matriarch's motive for stealing the idols. Perhaps she is concerned that the *teraphim,* as oracular devices, would whisper their whereabouts.[65] Given the historical context, she may be following ancient Mesopotamian custom in taking the household gods with her.[66] According to rabbinic tradition, she wished to purge her father's house of idolatry.[67] Esther Fuchs, however, argues that the narrative is deliberately opaque with regard to Rachel's motive. 'By fully explaining Jacob's motives for stealing away from Laban, and by clarifying that—unlike Rachel's deception—this move was strategically necessary (Gen. 31.31), the narrator removes any doubt we might entertain about Jacob's moral reformation'.[68] Her deception, by contrast, is sullied by ambiguity, whereas he appears morally upright. The argument from absence, however, is flawed, since motive is often unstated in biblical narrative and does not necessarily malign the character. I suggest that her reason for stealing the idols is actually irrelevant to the plot. Rather, it is allusions to past and future deceptions that are of significance here.

Jacob, in utter certitude that none of his servants or family members would have stolen the idols, invites his uncle to conduct a thorough search, declaring, 'With whomever you find your gods, that person shall not live' (Gen. 31.32). In a dramatic aside, the narrator alerts us: 'But Jacob did not know that Rachel had stolen them'. Echoing the scene of the stolen blessing, Jacob's father-in-law feels all around Rachel's tent, groping [*mshsh*] like a blind man (31.34; cf. 37). But he recoils from her seat, where she has hidden the *teraphim* under the camel's saddle, for she claims to have 'the way of women [*derekh nashim*]' (v. 35). Just as Isaac, Jacob's blind father, felt his arms [*mshsh*] covered in goat's skins, and was fooled, declaring them to be 'the hands of Esau' (Gen. 27.22), Laban feels [*mshsh*] all around her tent but does not find the idols. The father *does not* touch his daughter as father touched son, bound as he is by the taboo of menstruation.[69] As Fokkelman

---

65. According to Zech. 10.2, teraphim do speak. See the discussion in Moshe Greenberg, 'Another Look at Rachel's Theft of the Teraphim', *JBL* 81 (1962), pp. 239, 247 n. 3.

66. Greenberg, 'Teraphim', pp. 239-48. See also the discussions in E.A. Speiser, *Genesis: Introduction, Translation, and Notes* (AB, 1; Garden City, NY: Doubleday, 1964), pp. 248-51; and Pardes, *Countertraditions*, p. 70.

67. See *Gen. R.* 74.5, p. 863, and *Tanḥ. VaYetzei* 12.

68. Fuchs, 'For I Have the Way of Women', p. 77.

69. Mieke Bal points out that Rachel's claim to have 'the way of women' is ambiguous—does it refer to menstruation or feminine wiles? 'For the taboo [of menstruation]

points out, 'Here Jacob's uncle is retrieving his own "truth", feeling, frisking, house-searching, and now a trick of Jacoba's [i.e. Rachel's] renders this search in vain. Thus Jacob can retain the blessing and leave with his most precious "asset."'[70] Is this 'asset' his beloved Rachel (*Jacoba*)? If so, the patriarch does not emerge triumphant this time. True, both deceptions succeed. Jacob emerges 'blessed', and his father never rescinds the blessing. Similarly, Laban never finds the idols. The latter trick is not without dire consequences, however. Stealing Laban's *lev* [heart/mind], whether this refers to his idols or daughters, is followed by the forfeit of a life.

We, as readers, know more than the dramatis personae and, like the midrash, come to acknowledge the ironic import of the patriarch's words: 'With whomever you find your gods, that person shall not live' (31.32). With fear and trembling, we sense that Jacob may have just, inadvertently, sentenced his beloved wife to death:

> Why did Rachel die first (i.e. before Leah)? . . . According to Rabbi Yossi, Rachel died only as a result of the patriarch's curse, as it says, 'With whomever you find your gods, that person shall not live' (Gen. 31.32), and it was so, 'as a great error that proceeds from the ruler' (cf. Eccl. 10.5), [for it says] 'And Rachel stole the household idols . . .' (Gen. 31.19; cf. v. 32), [and] 'Then Rachel died . . .' (35.19) (*Gen. R.* 74.4).[71]

Quid pro quo, the very next scene involving the matriarch recounts her death. Jacob has just left Bethel, where he buried all the 'alien gods' (were the *teraphim* included?), and set up an altar to God in fulfillment of his vow (35.1-4; cf. 28.20-22). They were some distance short of Ephrath, when Rachel went into hard labor. Benjamin was born at this borderland and doubly named there 'son-of-my-sorrow' [*ben-'oni*] according to Rachel, and 'son-of-the-right-hand' according to Jacob (35.18). His birth can be understood as a fulfillment of Rachel's own demand upon naming Joseph: 'May God add another son to me [*yosif li ben 'aher*]' (30.24), as the midwife affirmed, 'Have no fear, for it is *another* boy for you' (35.17). Yet her

---

is itself semiotic in nature, interpreting the blood as a symptom of bodily impurity, in its turn a symptom of female inferiority, in its turn a deceptive symptom of female deceptiveness' ('Tricky Thematics', p. 151; see also the discussion in Fuchs, 'For I Have the Way of Women', pp. 78-79).

70. Fokkelman, *Narrative Art in Genesis*, p. 170. See also the discussions in Fishbane, *Text and Texture*, p. 56; and Pardes, *Countertraditions*, pp. 70-72.

71. Author's translation of *Gen. R.* 74.4, p. 861. Jacob is subsequently haunted by her death, perhaps as a result of his troubled conscience. Nahmanides on Gen. 48.7 suggests that he adopts Ephraim and Manasseh as his own sons in response to his qualms of conscience, because he was forced to bury Rachel hurriedly on the way and not in the ancestral cave of Machpelah (Ramban *ad loc.*). On the other hand, Hayyim ben Moses ibn Attar (in his commentary *Or haḥayyim, ad loc.*), suggests Jacob inadvertently caused her death.

death is also the tragic realization of Jacob's ominous words: with whomever Laban might find his gods, 'that person shall not live' (31.32), though the *teraphim* were never found. The patriarch who 'stole the heart' of Laban suffers inexorably when his own heart is stolen from him upon the death of Rachel. His beloved son, Joseph, will then be 'stolen' and sold into slavery in Egypt,[72] and Benjamin will later be framed by the so-called 'Egyptian' viceroy for 'stealing' the goblet of divination.[73] Stealing the heart/mind—whether idols or daughters, brothers or sons—reverberates across the generations.

The rivalry between the brothers, including the near fratricide and the 'stealing' of Joseph to be sold into slavery, are indirect results of the tragic loss of the mother. Where both Rebekah and Sarah play a formative role in determining the future of their sons, Rachel is conspicuously absent. Sarah urges the patriarch to exclude Ishmael and Hagar from the inheritance, despite Abraham's misgivings, and God endorses her: 'Listen to her voice, for it is through Isaac that offspring shall be named for you' (Gen. 21.12). Likewise, Rebekah alone is privy to the promise that Jacob, the younger, will have supremacy over his brother (Gen. 25.23). It is *she* who undermines the father's choice in order to bring about the divine will. Rachel, however, is absent, and as a consequence no one tempers Jacob's decision when he confers the cloak on his son. There is no mother to affirm its significance or to guarantee the peaceable fulfillment of Joseph's dreams.

As Tikva Frymer-Kensky points out:

> Rachel's premature death has great consequences for Jacob's family. She is not there to guide her young son Joseph as the children grow up, or to mediate between him and his brothers. Leah does not fill Sarah's or Rivka's position in the family. Either she is too busy managing a household with thirteen children, or she also dies at some point. Without Rachel's presence, Jacob cannot ensure their transition to the next generation. As the stories of Genesis show, nobody orchestrates their marital contracts, and the stresses between Jacob and his grown sons and among the brothers

---

72. Joseph, in recounting his sale into slavery while he is in jail, reiterates the verb *gnb* in the emphatic form: 'For in fact I was stolen [*gunov gunavti*] out of the land of the Hebrews' (Gen. 40.15).

73. In defending themselves against the accusation, the brothers echo their own father: 'Why does my lord say such things? Far be it from your servants to do anything of the kind! Here we brought back to you from the land of Canaan the money that we found in the mouths of our bags. How then could we have stolen [*nignov*] any silver or gold from your master's house! Whichever of your servants it is found with shall die; the rest of us, moreover, shall become slaves to my lord' (Gen. 44.7-9). Benjamin does not die, although the goblet was found in his sack; whereas Rachel (his mother) does die, although the idols were never found under her camel's saddle.

threaten to destroy the family. When nobody rocks the cradle, nobody rules the world.[74]

Yet Rachel is not wholly absent. Jacob marked her grave with a pillar, 'which is there to this day' (Gen. 35.20). It is 'on the way' (v. 19; cf. Gen. 48.7), situated on the border between the promised home and exile.[75] The matriarch negotiates that boundary between the land of Israel and Diaspora in her afterlife. She is the moon in eclipse in the patriarchal period, eerily absent despite the second dream, where 'the sun, the moon and eleven stars bowed' to Joseph (37.9). On the basis of the spurious presence of the moon, as symbolic of his mother who was no longer alive, Jacob rejects the significance of the dream (v. 10), but he 'kept the matter in mind' (v. 11). We, too, must keep the matter in mind and explore the dark side of the moon. What role does Rachel play in negotiating unity for her children, despite divisiveness between the tribes and, ultimately, despite their dispersion? How does she come to signify the mother of all twelve sons, the code word for the united people, *Knesset Yisrael* (lit. 'the gathering of Israel')?

Rachel on the Verge

I would like to explore one last midrash on the alliance of the sisters in duplicity against Jacob. This *petiḥta* (or proem)[76] from *Lamentations Rabbah* opens with a discussion of a passage in Isaiah: 'My Lord God of Hosts summoned on that day to weeping and lamenting, to baldness and girding

---

74. Frymer-Kensky, *Reading the Women of the Bible*, p. 23.

75. The site of Rachel's tomb, 'on the way to Ephrata, that is Bethlehem' (Gen. 35.16, 19 and 48.7) is a controversial topic. According to 1 Sam. 10.2, her tomb is in the tribal territory of Benjamin, and in the Jeremiah passage, her cry is heard from Ramah. While the Genesis text locates her gravesite in Bethlehem, south of Jerusalem (in Judah's territory), the later texts point north of Jerusalem, implying that 'on the road' may refer to the passage the Jewish people take as they are banished from their homeland under the Assyrian (or perhaps Babylonian) exile (Jer. 31.15-17). See Zecharia Kallai, 'Rachel's Tomb: A Historiographical Review', in *Studies in Biblical Historiography and Geography* (Frankfurt am Main: Peter Lang, 2011), pp. 142-49. Rashi (on Gen. 48.7) suggests that she was never buried in the land of Israel at all, but rather on the border (based on Jer. 31.15, and the rabbinic tradition). He reads the location of her grave in the light of the Jeremiah passage and later midrashic sources. Ramban, on the other hand, argues that she was buried 'within the land of Israel' (in the territory of Benjamin), and 'on the road there' (Gen. 48.7) should be understood in temporal rather than spatial terms. As Zornberg points out, 'Rachel is buried at the point of contact with the future passage of her children' (*Beginning of Desire*, p. 414 n. 43).

76. See Pinchas Mandel's article, 'On Patah and the Petihah: A New Study', in *Higayon L'Yona: New Aspects in the Study of Midrash, Aggaah and Piyut, in Honor of Professor Yona Fraenkel* (ed. Y. Elbaum, G. Hasan-Roken and J. Levinson; Jerusalem: Magnes, 2007), pp. 49-82.

with sackcloth' (Isa. 22.12).[77] This verse is concerned with God's reaction to the sacking and destruction of Jerusalem at the hands of the Babylonians in 586 BCE. God calls on Jeremiah to comfort him and to arouse his compassion for his children. The prophet summons the patriarchs, Abraham, Isaac and Jacob from the cave of the Machpelah, as well as Moses, to plead the cause of his people. Each argues his case: Abraham on the basis of his willingness to bind his son on the altar; Isaac because he went willingly to slaughter; Jacob in subjecting himself to exile in Laban's house; and Moses, the faithful shepherd, because he led the people for forty years through the desert. But only when the matriarch Rachel leaps, of her own accord, from her grave to intercede on behalf of the people does God relent and promise that they will one day return. She is, quintessentially, Rachel *'Imenu*, 'our matriarch', at this moment in claiming all of Israel as her children. She spontaneously jumps from the grave, on the border between homeland and exile, where, according to parallel midrashic sources, she was buried for this very purpose:[78]

> At that moment, Rachel leapt before the Holy-One-blessed-be-He, and said: 'Lord of the Universe, you know that Jacob, your servant, loved me exceedingly, and toiled for my father on my behalf for seven years. And at the end of the seven years, when the time of my marriage arrived, my father advised that my sister should replace me, and I suffered greatly when his plot became known to me. And I informed my husband and gave him a sign that he might distinguish between my sister and me, and my father would be unable to replace me. Later, I regretted [what I had done] and suppressed my desire, and took pity on my sister so that she would not be shamed. In the evening they substituted me for my sister [to be] with my husband, and I gave my sister all the signs I had agreed upon with my husband, so that he would believe she was Rachel. Even more than that, I went under the bed upon which he lay with my sister, and when he spoke to her and she remained silent, I made all the answers so that he would not recognize my sister's voice. I was gracious; I was not jealous and spared her shame and dishonor. If I, only flesh and blood, dust and ashes, was not jealous of my rival [*tzarah*] and spared her shame and dishonor, why should you, the everlasting and compassionate King, be jealous of idolatry, which is insubstantial, and exile my children who were slain by the sword, and let their enemies do with them what they wish?'

---

77. Solomon Buber, in his edition of *Lamentations Rabbah*, argues that the last section of the proem may have been inserted from a much later midrashic work, which he could not identify (ed. Buber, *Lam. R.* 24, 14a.36-14b.11). In a verbal communication with Galit Hasan-Rokem, Pinchas Mandel confirmed this view (see Hasan-Rokem, *The Web of Life: Folklore and Midrash in Rabbinic Literature* [Stanford, CA: Stanford University Press, 2000], p. 232 n. 48).

78. Gen. 35.17-19, and Rashi on Gen. 48.7. Rashi draws on the *Pes. R.* 3; other parallel sources include: *Gen. R.* 82.10, p. 988), *Yal. Shimoni* Gen. 136, *Eliyahu R.* 28 (ed. Ish Shalom).

2. *The Collusion of Sisters*

> Forthwith, the mercy of the Holy-One-blessed-be-He was stirred, and He said, 'For your sake, Rachel, I will restore Israel to their place'. And so it is written: 'Thus said Yhwh: A cry is heard in Ramah—wailing, bitter weeping—Rachel weeping for her children. She refuses to be comforted for her children, who are not' (Jer. 31.15). And it is written: 'Thus said Yhwh: Restrain your voice from weeping, your eyes from shedding tears; for there is a reward for your labor—declares Yhwh' (v. 16). And it is written: 'They shall return from the enemy's land. And there is hope for your future—declares Yhwh: Your children shall return to their country' (vv. 16-17) (*Lam. R. petiḥta* 24).[79]

Rachel's testimony is extremely personal, intimate and painful. She has sacrificed her own desire, even betrayed her husband, out of loyalty to her sister—to spare Leah from shame and dishonor. Rachel's claim is based on an *a fortiori* argument: I, a mere mortal, put up with a *real* rival wife [*tzarah*] of flesh and blood, and you, who are a living, compassionate king had merely to tolerate your people's worship of idols, made of wood and stone, also called *tzarah*, which have no substance to them.[80] How much more so should you forgive the Israelites! The tradition about the exchange of the signs, just before the wedding night, is familiar. But the intimate scene of the first night, in the bridal chamber, adds a new twist. All that night, Rachel lay under the bed, projecting her voice like a ventriloquist in order to collude with her father's ruse, obscuring her sister's identity. The midrash, perhaps, tries to account for how, all that night, Jacob did not know it was *not* Rachel, and only 'When morning came, look: it is Leah!' (Gen. 29.25). That night, she *had been* Rachel, for it was *her* voice to which Jacob responded, the erotic depth of the woman as she resonated, vicariously, while he made love to Leah. This is a fascinating reversal of the original betrayal of Isaac, who declares, in a state of bewilderment before the hybrid heir: 'The voice is the voice of Jacob but the hands are the hands of Esau' (Gen. 27.22). In absolute ironic reversal, it is now the skin, breasts, hair and mouth of the older sister that Jacob feels over the course of that night: 'the hands are the hands of Leah', but 'the voice is the voice of Rachel'. Not the eyes but the

---

79. This translation is roughly based on Galit Hasan-Rokem's rendition in *The Web of Life*, pp. 126-27.
80. The rival wife or vexer, *tzarah*, appears in 1 Sam. 1.6 (BDB entry 8374, p. 865) and in the verb form, 'to make a [sister] a rival wife' (Lev. 18.18) (BDB entry 8375, p. 865). As *tzar* or *tzror*, it refers to an enemy or foe (BDB entry 8373, p. 864), as in Amos 3.11; Gen. 14.20; Num. 10.9; 24.8; Deut. 32.27; 33.7, and so forth. With reference to God, it becomes a euphemism for idolatry in rabbinic literature. See the discussion of the Maharal's commentary on Rashi (Gen. 48.7) in Zornberg, *Beginning of Desire*, pp. 212-14.

voice is the 'window to the soul', as the Talmud states: 'the woman's voice is her nakedness [*'ervah*]' (*b. Ber.* 24a).[81]

The other aspect of Rachel's voice lies in its power to compel God's promise to return *her* children; all twelve tribes are covered by her maternal wings. While God adjured Abraham to hear Sarah's voice in the patriarchal narrative, it is now Rachel's voice, in the prophetic afterlife, to which God responds: 'A *voice* is heard in Ramah, lamentation and bitter weeping. Rachel is weeping for her children because they are no more [*ki 'einenu*]' (Jer. 31.15). She, like Jacob (Gen. 37.35), refuses to be comforted for her children who, although absent (perhaps presumed dead), may yet return alive from exile, as Joseph 'who was not' would be reunited with his father. God reassures her, through the prophet Jeremiah: 'Restrain your voice from weeping, your eyes from shedding tears; for there is a reward for your labor ... they shall return from the enemy's land' (Jer. 31.16). Even in the silent interstices of Rachel's pain, God hears her, at first, when she finally conceives after years of barrenness, although there is no explicit mention of her prayer: 'Now God remembered Rachel; God *heard* her and opened her womb' (Gen. 30.22);[82] the second, according to Jeremiah, when she pleads for the return of the exiled children of Israel. According to Galit Hasan-Rokem, the power of woman's voice is conveyed through the lament; it is very personal, very intimate. 'This personal concern, together with the erotic energy of the love for her sister and her beloved that suffused Rachel's waiting, represent the strength required to shift the balance from condemnation to mercy. Love, in its most human and tender variation, rather than the zealous love of God expressed in the willingness to sacrifice a son, bears the power of redemption.'[83]

In this final scene, the rabbis transform Rachel's tragic death, on the border between exile and homeland, into a redemptive message. As David Stern observes, 'in an ironic reversal of *imitatio dei* that we might call *imitatio hominis*', or *imitatio gynaikos,* rather, 'it is the model of *human* behavior to which God now turns. By submitting to Rachel's example, to her acknowledgment of her own jealousy, God is now able to acknowledge his jealousy, and is able to extend mercy to Israel.'[84] This is a remarkable reading of the midrash, in which God follows the woman's lead. She teaches him what compassion entails, *raḥamim* resonant with womb [*reḥem*].

---

81. I owe this insight to Galit Hasan-Rokem: 'But it is actually in this impressive picture of lovemaking through the voice (confirming as it were, the rabbinic saying that "a woman's voice is her sexual organ" . . . that the female voice finds its typical avenue for self-expression in the midrashic text', in *The Web of Life*, p. 129.

82. I owe this insight to my friend and chavruta, Bracha Rosenberg.

83. Hasan-Rokem, *The Web of Life*, p. 128.

84. David Stern, *Midrash and Theory: Ancient Jewish Exegesis and Contemporary Literary Studies* (Evanston, IL: Northwestern University Press, 1996), p. 85.

In the midrashic tradition, transforming the tension between sisters from rivalry to collusion, the rabbis convey their own desire for return—both for the return of the children of Israel in repentance to their homeland and for God's return. Despite divisiveness and exile, the matriarch effects the reconciliation of the brothers, as a united people, upon the return of the tribes to the land. Longing to respond to the mortal summons, the Divine Presence answers her call: 'They shall return from the enemy's land. . . . Your children shall return to their country' (Jer. 31.16-17). Presumably God, too, would return to dwell in their midst. From the well to the grave, from *eros* to *thanatos,* Rachel's repeated deferral uniquely speaks to divine yearning. In her lifetime, she colludes with her sister as an agent of Jacob's transformation, for, in covert 'penance' for displacing his own brother, he never rejects Leah, but, rather, acknowledges all his children under the rubric of the patriarchal covenant. Buried tragically on the border, displaced by her sister who lies beside her husband in the ancestral grave, Rachel also embodies a unique power in her afterlife. No maternal voice ruled in her lifetime to soften the blows of rivalry between brothers. Indeed no hand 'rocked the cradle', but the matriarch's voice, fraught with deferred love and maternal longing, moves the seemingly distant God to promise their reunion in history.

3

OF VEILS, GOATS, AND SEALING RINGS, OF GUARANTORS AND KINGS: THE STORY OF JUDAH AND TAMAR

> 'The time has come', the author said,
> 'To talk of many things.
> Of veils, and goats, and sealing rings,
> Of guarantors and kings.'
> Adapted from Lewis Carroll's 'The Walrus and the Carpenter', in *Through the Looking-Glass and What Alice Found There*, 1872

Preamble: The Bridge between Rebekah and Tamar

'Probably never—or never up till then—did a woman love and desire a man so entirely apart from his own sake and so entirely for the sake of an idea as Tamar loved Judah'.[1] This is how Thomas Mann opens his retelling of Genesis 38. The biblical story, though more sparing than the novelist's rendition, nevertheless leaves the reader with the striking impression of Tamar's heroism. Married off to the eldest son of Judah but soon widowed and left childless by him, she is coupled to the second son and bereft again at his death. After years of desperately waiting for the third son to grow up, she poses as a harlot by the side of the road in order to seduce Judah, her father-in-law, heedless of the taboos on incest and sexual depravity. By the roadside she conceives twin sons by Judah. One of whom, Perez, will spawn the Davidic line. Not born into the Israelite people and against all odds, she risks everything—biological, social and legal censure—to become the grand matriarch of the monarchy.

The novelist portrays her as a disciple of Jacob, the old patriarch, and explains her audacity in terms of a will to 'interpolate' herself into history: 'She was bent on pushing herself into the great history and she did it with amazing strength of purpose . . . for it was by seduction that Tamar shoved

---

1. Thomas Mann, *Joseph and his Brothers:* Vol. 4. *Joseph the Provider* (trans. H.T. Lower Porter; London: Sphere Books, 1968), p. 243.

herself into the great history of which this is an episode. She played the temptress and whored by the way, that she might not be shut out; she abased herself recklessly to be exalted. . . .'[2] Whether Tamar's courage stemmed from her love of an *idea*, as Thomas Mann suggests, or from her own maternal clamoring, the biblical story does not say. Whatever the motives, the narrative is one of the most compelling accounts of female heroism in Genesis. Further, it is deeply transformative for both Judah and the whole Jacob clan. Tamar risks her life in posing as a prostitute at the entrance to Enaim, duping her father-in-law into conceiving a child (actually twins), unbeknown to him. As will be shown, she not only guarantees the much-sought-after promise of continuity (*toledot*) but also prompts an ethical epiphany within Judah that enables him to become the progenitor of kings. After she veils herself in the act of seduction, a discrepancy emerges between the biological *knowing* of woman and the oblivion of man. Through the female ruse, a 'method' she shares with the other matriarchs—Rebekah, Rachel and Leah—Tamar inserts herself into the patriarchal history and, in effect, determines the heir for the chosen line.

But deception has its casualties. The original 'cover story' in the Jacob and Joseph saga set up a chain of events of tragic dimensions in the book of Genesis. As I argued in the first chapter, Rebekah's veiling after first seeing Isaac impels her *not* to tell her husband about the prophecy of the younger son's chosen status. She then dresses Jacob in goatskins as he steals Esau's blessing. *Quid pro quo,* Laban dupes Jacob on his wedding night where, presumably Leah too wears a veil.[3] And the patriarch's own sons deceive him as they present Joseph's ornamented tunic dipped in goat's blood. Judah, Jacob's son, is then deceived by the veiled Tamar, who offers her services as a harlot in exchange for a promised goat. The wife of Potiphar, in the next scene, uses Joseph's garment as her alibi, in the false accusation of rape. The saga is replete with veils, goats and garments, all deployed in these acts of deception. Yet it is the veiling of women that presents the most evocative parallel between the fabulae.[4]

The midrash draws out the resonances:

> There were two women who covered themselves with veils and bore twins: Rebekah and Tamar: Rebekah—'so she took the veil [*ha-tza'if*] and covered herself [*va-titkas*]' (Gen. 24.65) and so too Tamar—'covered her face with a veil [*va-takhas ba-tza'if*] . . .' (Gen. 38.14) (*Gen. R.* 60.15).[5]

---

2. Mann, *Joseph the Provider*, p. 227.
3. See the discussion in Chapter 1 nn. 72-79.
4. For a thorough analysis of the parallels between Rebekah and Tamar's veiling as a motif in the birth of twins, see Sharon Roubach, '"Two who donned the veil": The Image of Twins in the Bible', *Beit Mikra* 50 (2004), pp. 366-90 (Heb.).
5. Author's translation of *Gen. R.* 60.15, p. 656; cf. *Gen. R.* 85.7, p. 1040.

It is as if the twins are born of the woman's duplicity—the split between what is known, *internally* to the woman and what is known to the man and accepted in terms of external norms. Unlike the other episodes of the 'female ruse', however, Tamar's act of deception is transformed, in retrospect, upon her 'unveiling', for Judah will recognize her righteousness and come to align himself with the divine plan. As a result, he becomes the ancestor of the messianic dynasty established by David, whom God sees, 'not as mortals see; they look on the outward appearance, but Yhwh looks into the heart' (1 Sam. 16.7). Tamar interpolates herself into the patriarchal history by *seeing into the heart*.

The Descent of Judah

The narrative of Judah and Tamar (Gen. 38) is bracketed by the stories of Joseph's sale into slavery (Gen. 37) and his escapades in the House of Potiphar (Gen. 39), where it seems to interrupt the flow of the Joseph saga.[6] Rather than understanding the tale of Tamar as an interruption, I adjure the reader to draw the threads of the narratives together; this story begins the process of mending the seam rent by the brothers when they sold Joseph into slavery. Rabbinic tradition, along with literary scholars concerned with the canonical text in its final form, assume the integrity of the biblical narrative and suggest that Judah's descent 'from the presence of his brothers' (38.2), his assimilation among the Canaanites, and his eventual entanglement with Tamar are all significant incidents for the advancement of the plot.[7] It tells

---

6. There is widespread consensus among Bible scholars that the Judah and Tamar story was introduced into the Joseph narrative by a later editorial hand, and that it has no intrinsic connection to the broader Joseph saga. Speiser, for example, attributes it to the J-source, providing the etiological narrative for the ancestors of the tribe of Judah (Gen. 38.27-30). See the discussion in Speiser, *Genesis*, pp. 299-300; Claus Westermann, *Genesis 37–50* (Minneapolis, MN: Augsburg, 1986), p. 49; Walter Brueggemann, *Genesis* (Atlanta, GA: John Knox Press, 1982), pp. 307-308; and Bruce Vawter, *On Genesis: A New Reading* (Garden City, NY: Doubleday, 1977), p. 390.

7. Robert Alter, for example, pointed to various parallels between the Joseph and Judah stories—their respective 'descents', the use of the Hebrew phrase *haker na'*, 'articles of attire' used for deception, the role of the goat [*seir 'izim*], which provided the blood to stain Joseph's tunic, and the goat [*gedi 'izim*], promised to Tamar), and sexual seduction initiated by a woman—in the case of Judah, successfully, in the case of Joseph and Potiphar's wife, thwarted (Alter, *Biblical Narrative*, pp. 6-10). To this impressive list, Jon Levenson adds the anxiety of losing another son (Judah's fear of losing Shelah; Jacob's fear of losing Benjamin) and the emergence of the younger son as leader of the kingdom—both Joseph and Judah become the progenitors of kings (Levenson, *The Death and Resurrection of the Beloved Son*, pp. 157-62). For a criticism of these literary readings, see James Kugel's 'Appendix 1: Apologetics and Bible Criticism Lite'

us how the nefarious Judah, who initiated the scheme to sell his brother into slavery, became the hero who offered himself instead of Benjamin as surety for his brother (Gen. 43.9; 44.32-34). The veiled daughter-in-law, Tamar, is the agent of Judah's moral redemption and transformation. She does this by deploying the classic 'bedtrick', ironically the means by which man, in this case Judah, comes to really know himself, acknowledge his responsibility, and thus rises to become the progenitor of kings.

There are ostensibly three levels of reading Tamar's agency in the context of the larger biblical narrative. (1) First and foremost, she is the agent of her own life; she refuses to accept the fate of the childless widow, taking charge of her own procreativity through the seduction at the crossroads, and thereby assures her own continuity in the chain of *toledot* (genealogy). (2) She is the agent of Judah's ethical epiphany, in forcing him to acknowledge his neglect of her and, inadvertently, the bereavement he had caused his own father, Jacob; she thereby heals the breach in continuity for Israel that the sale of Joseph engendered. (3) She is the agent of God, insofar as she advances the divine plan of 'weaving the messianic light'[8] through a principle that defies social and legal norms. All three levels—the proximate goal of procreation, the broader ethical transformation, and the divine antinomian mode—are causally linked and resonant with one another.

Genesis 38 opens with a movement of descent: 'And it came to pass at that time, that Judah went down [*va-yered Yehuda*] from his brothers, and turned in to a certain Adullamite, whose name was Hirah' (Gen. 38.1). The verb 'go down [*yrd*]' is echoed again in the opening of the next chapter: 'When Joseph was taken down [*hurad*] to Egypt, a certain Egyptian, Potiphar, a courtier of Pharaoh and his chief steward, bought him from the Ishmaelites who had brought him down [*horiduhu*] there' (Gen. 39.1). This later verse marks a resumptive repetition, reasserting what we were told at the end of ch. 37. Commenting on the parallels between the passages, *Genesis Rabbah* poses the question: why does the chapter about Judah and Tamar interrupt the two stories about Joseph—the sale into slavery and the attempted seduction by the wife of Potiphar?

> R. Le'azar said: so as to connect a descent with a descent [Joseph's with Judah's]. R. Yochanan said: in order to connect 'please recognize [*haker na'*]' (Gen. 37.32) to the same expression, 'please recognize [*haker na'*]' (Gen. 38.25). R. Samuel bar Nahman said: so as to connect the story of Tamar to the story of the wife of Potiphar (*Gen. R.* 85.1).[9]

(responding to *How to Read the Bible: A Guide to Scripture, Then and Now* [New York: Free Press, 2007]; http://jameskugel.com/read.php), pp. 25-29.
   8. This is my phrase, based on *Gen. R.* 85.1, to be discussed later. See n. 53.
   9. Author's translation of *Gen. R.* 85.1, pp. 1030-31.

Three parallels between the two plots are listed: a descent, an act of recognition and a seduction. According to the midrash, the lives of the two brothers are inextricably bound together, represented by the verb 'go down [*yrd*]', understood as a descent into exile or assimilation. Judah, however, goes willingly: 'Judah went down [*va-yered Yehuda*]' into a self-imposed exile among the Canaanites while Joseph went unwillingly; he 'was brought down to Egypt [*ve-Yosef hurad mitzrayma*]' and sold into slavery. According to another midrash on the opening verse, 'And Judah went down from his brothers' (Gen. 38.1); the brothers *all* disbanded, fearing that if they were found together their crime would surface—for when all ten are together, 'the deed (of debt) is bound to be exacted' (*Gen. R.* 85.2, p. 1033). And, in fact, the next time we hear of the assembly of these ten brothers (before the supposed Egyptian viceroy) trouble begins, memories surface, the collective conscience trembles (Gen. 42.21-22). But, at this point, they reject the pangs of conscience, which would inevitably be stirred when they were together. So the edict, which the old patriarch had uttered, 'Joseph is surely torn, torn apart [*tarof toraf Yosef*]' (Gen. 37.33), rends a seam through the whole family. In disbanding, 'going down', they deny conscience and shun the possibility of recognizing their own culpability mirrored in one another's faces.

Judah then attempts to mend that seam by occupying himself with marriage and procreation, the project of establishing a lineage (*toledot*) for himself. Yet he who plunged his father into bereavement at the loss of his favorite son will soon be bereaved of two sons in quick succession. Initially, Judah marries a Canaanite woman (clearly a discredited choice for the descendants of Abraham, Isaac and Jacob).[10] He soon fathers three sons. He marries his firstborn, Er,[11] off to Tamar, who, while named (in contrast to Judah's own wife), is of unknown stock. The first son dies by divine decree for he 'did evil in the eyes of Yhwh' (Gen. 38.7). The second, Onan,[12] unwilling to conceive a child in the name of his brother through levirate marriage to

---

10. See the injunction of Abraham to his servant in Gen. 24.3-4, and the disapproval of Esau's Hittite wives, Gen. 27.46 (cf. 26.34-35) and 28.1-2 and 8-9.

11. The name, *'Er*, may derive from the Hebrew root *'rh*—to be naked, bare—or from the root *'rr*—to be barren (as in Abraham's reference to his barren state: *anokhi holekh 'ariri* (Gen. 15.2; cf. *Targ. Ps.-J.* on Gen. 38.8). Frymer-Kensky points out the ironic implications of the naming: 'Er, whose name could have meant "the energetic one" (from *'ur*, "arise, awake"), instead does evil (*ra'*) and becomes "the one who has no issue" (from *'rr*, "be barren")' (*Reading the Women of the Bible*, p. 266).

12. The name Onan may be related to the root *'wn* meaning 'mourning' or 'misery' (cf. Gen. 35.18; Deut. 26.14). Frymer-Kensky comments, 'Onan, whose name could have meant "vigor" (from *'wn*, "manliness, vigor"), becomes instead "nothingness" (from *'awen*, "nothing")' (*Reading the Women of the Bible*, p. 266). And Shelah, lit.,

Tamar, the wife of the deceased, spills seed, and he too is expunged.[13] All has gone awry when the sons fail to cooperate with the project of procreation. Judah then sends Tamar back to her father in widow's garb with the false promise to give her to Shelah when he grows up, for 'he thought that he [the third son] too may die like his brothers' (Gen. 38.11). Blaming her, as a *femme fatale*, for the death of his two sons,[14] he sends her back to her father's house to live as a grass widow. Sending her away marks the first stage in a sequence of ethically dubious acts, what Meir Sternberg identifies as a series of 'deceptions and counter-deceptions'.[15]

Tamar Interpolates Herself into History

Initially, Judah treats her unconscionably. She, in essence, is the first *'agunah* (lit. 'chained woman') in Israelite history. Bound by a promise of marriage, she is powerless to initiate relations with another and thereby conceive, despite the onslaught of time through her procreative years. Years pass, perhaps even a decade, until she notes that her father-in-law's neglect is deliberate and she is compelled to take matters into her own hands.

'hers', that is, promised to Tamar, is born in Kezib, from *kzb*, meaning 'to deceive'—Judah's promise to Tamar is never fulfilled.

13. The laws of levirate marriage are outlined in Deut. 25.5-10. While this is clearly before the giving of 'the Law', it is well known from ancient Mesopotamian legal codes that some kind of quasi-levirate marriage was commonly practiced. According to Hittite laws (fourteenth–thirteenth century BCE), if a married man dies, 'his brother shall take his wife, then [if he dies] his father shall take her' (par. 193). That is, Judah could have performed the role of *levir* himself. See the discussion in Sarna, *JPS Torah Commentary: Genesis,* p. 248. See also Eryl W. Davies, 'Inheritance Rights and the Hebrew Levirate Marriage', *VT* 31 (1981), pp. 138-44, 257-69; and Raymond Westbrook, *Property and Family in Biblical Law* (Sheffield: JSOT Press, 1991). For a thorough study of levirate marriage in the Hebrew Bible and rabbinic corpus, see Dvora Weisberg, *Levirate Marriage and the Family in Ancient Judaism* (Hanover, NH: University Press of New England, 2009).

14. In 38.11, the narrator makes us privy to Judah's private thoughts. A similar assumption is made with regard to the 'oft-widowed bride, Sarah, daughter of Raguel', in the apocryphal book of Tobit (Tob. 3.7-17; 6.9–8.21); the woman is held culpable for the repeated deaths of her husbands. Mieke Bal draws the parallel between the story of Tamar and Judah and the episode of Joseph and Potiphar's wife (Genesis 39), and argues that ch. 38 of Genesis is placed there to warn the reader *not* to conclude unequivocally that women are lethal. She writes, 'While Rachel and Leah corrected the fault of the split between the two aspects of femininity [that is, sexuality and motherhood], Tamar corrects a more archaic fault against woman, which is even more destructive: the fault of being afraid of her, and of institutionalizing that fear, that *horror feminitatis*' (*Lethal Love* [Bloomington, IN: Indiana University Press, 1987], p. 86).

15. Sternberg, *Poetics of Biblical Narrative,* p. 165.

One cannot underestimate the risk Tamar assumes. If she conceives by another, according to the laws of levirate marriage, her illicit relations would be considered on par with adultery. The implied severity of the consequences are later reinforced in the narrative when Judah orders that Tamar be taken out and burned after discovering that she is pregnant (supposedly by 'harlotry') (Gen. 38.24).[16] Moreover, sexual relations between daughter and father-in-law are strictly forbidden according to the laws of incest (Lev. 18.10, 15).[17] Yet she breaks this taboo as well. Not only does she defy social and legal norms, but she risks her life in so doing.

In the meantime, Judah's Canaanite wife dies. Tamar is then told that her father-in-law is coming up to Timnah for the sheep-shearing.[18]

> So she took off her widow's garb, covered her face with a veil, and, wrapping herself up, sat down at the entrance to Enaim [*Petah 'Enaim*], which is on the road to Timnah; for she saw that Shelah was grown up, yet she had not been given to him as a wife.
> When Judah saw her, he took her for a harlot, for she had covered her face. So he turned aside to her by the road and said, 'Here, let me come into you'—for he did not know that she was his daughter-in-law.
> 'What', she asked, 'will you pay for coming into me?'
> He replied, 'I will send a kid from my flock'.
> But she said, 'Only if you leave a pledge until you have sent it'.
> And he said, 'What pledge shall I give you?'
> She replied, 'Your signet and cord, and the staff in your hand'. So he gave them to her and came into her, and she conceived by him. Then she went on her way. She took off her veil and again put on her widow's garb (Gen. 38.14-19).

---

16. In rabbinic terms, Tamar would be considered 'awaiting the *levir* [*shomeret yavam*]' and any relations outside that union would be considered adulterous, carrying with it the death penalty (see Lev. 20.10 and Deut. 22.22). See Sarna's comment on Gen. 38.24 (*JPS Torah Commentary: Genesis*, p. 269). According to *Genesis Rabbah*, Judah's reaction is so severe because Tamar is identified as the daughter of a priest (Shem), and, according to the levitical laws (anachronistically applied), any daughter of a priest who defiles herself through harlotry must be burned (*Gen. R.* 85.10; see also Lev. 21.9).

17. There is clearly a tension between the laws of levirate marriage and the incest taboo. Sexual relations between daughter and father-in-law, in pentateuchal legislation, are strictly forbidden (Lev. 18.10, 15); the violation of this taboo constitutes a capital offense (Lev. 20.12). Given this incident occurs prior to the giving of the law, it could be that this quasi-levirate case extends the responsibility to the father-in-law. See n. 13.

18. A time renowned for its drunken revelry; cf. 1 Sam. 25.2 and 36, and 2 Sam. 13.23-28. See James Kugel's comment, 'Judah and the Trial of Tamar', who connects Judah's possible drunken state to the exegetical tradition on Jacob's blessing (Gen. 49.11), in *The Ladder of Jacob* (Princeton, NJ: Princeton University Press, 2006), p. 173.

This scene takes place at the entrance to Enaim, perhaps at a crossroads,[19] marked by a spring or well.[20] The Hebrew place name *Petaḥ 'Enaim* (lit. 'opening of the eyes') is fraught with irony for this is the place where sight is obscured. Yet the name also connotes a double irony. Eventually there will a *re*-cognition of what took place there as the unmasking allows a deeper truth to emerge.

Tamar's actions are marked by four strong verbs in succession in v. 14: 'Then she shed her widow's garb [*va-tasar*], covered her face with a veil [*va-takhas*], and wrapped herself up [*va-titalaf*] and sat [*va-teshev*] at the entrance to Enaim'. Her veiling is an unusual disguise; it usually signals the status of a married woman (as in the apocryphal book of Judith [10.2; 16.9]). Contrary to the custom of the harlot's pose, Tamar uses a veil to conceal her face.[21] Before recognition comes deception; before *na'* can be spoken, there is an initial *mis*-recognition. Great emphasis is placed on the man *not knowing*: 'And Judah took her for a harlot for she had covered her face' (v. 15), and 'he did not know that she was his daughter-in-law' (v. 16). While he knows her carnally, he does not *recognize* her. She, on the other hand, knows him, both literally and figuratively, and in this way brings him to ethical recognition.[22] Following the sexual act (which, we are told, resulted in the much-sought-for conception), Tamar once again donned her widow's garb, with four emphatic verbs, the inverse of v. 14:

---

19. The Aramaic *Targum Neofiti* and the Syriac Peshitta, in fact, omit the proper name of the place, designating it instead 'at the crossroads' (Peshitta and *Targ. Neof.* on Gen. 38.24, 21; cf. the Latin Vulgate *in bivio itineris* (Martin McNamara [ed. and trans.], *The Aramaic Bible Targum*, vol. 2 [Collegeville, MN: Liturgical Press, 1994], p. 175 n. 10).

20. The term *'ayn* in Hebrew means 'spring', 'the eye of the earth', so literally *Petaḥ 'Enaim* means 'entrance to two springs/eyes'.

21. Frymer-Kensky points out that, in Middle Assyrian laws, only married women were allowed to veil themselves and prostitutes were explicitly forbidden to do so (*Reading the Women of the Bible*, p. 270). See John R. Huddleston, 'Unveiling the Versions: The Tactics of Tamar in Genesis 38:15', *Journal of Hebrew Studies* 3: article 7 (2001) http://www.arts.ualberta.ca/JHS/Articles/article_19.htm. The rabbis were certainly perplexed by Tamar's gesture and read the 'veiling of Tamar' as an unveiling. Contrary to the plain meaning, Tamar had consistently covered her face while she lived in her father-in-law's household and only at Enaim did she uncover her face: 'One must accustom oneself to the look upon one's wife's sisters and relatives ... how do we know? From the story of Judah and Tamar' (*Gen. R.* 85.8, p. 1041; *b. Meg.* 10b; cf. *Targ. Neof.* and *Targ.Ps.-J.* on Gen. 38.15).

22. Jagendorf, 'Genesis and the Reversal of Sexual Knowledge', pp. 191-92. On Judah's moral transformation in terms of Aristotle's narrative theory of *anagnorisis* (recognition), see the discussion in Rachel Adelman, 'Ethical Epiphany in the Story of Judah and Tamar', in *Recognition and Modes of Knowledge: Anagnorisis from Antiquity to Contemporary Theory* (ed. Teresa Russo; Edmonton: University of Alberta Press, 2013), pp. 51-76.

'She arose [*va-taqom*] and went on her way [*va-telekh*]. She took off her veil [*va-tasar*] and again put on her widow's garb [*va-tilbash*]' (v. 19). The scarf and widow's garb are symbolic counterpoints in negotiating the transition from harlot to widow, from a private, masked identity to a social role, from *mis*-recognition to public disclosure.

Of Veils, Goats, and Sealing Rings

The pledge, of course, is pivotal to the plot. At Enaim, in lieu of payment, Tamar demands a guarantee or pledge—Judah's 'signet, cord and staff' (v. 18). Her demand is tantamount to asking for his car keys, driver's license and credit card, all marked indelibly with his identity. The promised payment—a kid (goat) [*gdi 'izim*] from the flock evokes an association with the goat [*se'ir 'izim*] (Gen. 37.31), slaughtered to stain the ornamented tunic in lieu of Joseph's blood, and the goatskins ['*orot gdayei ha-'izim*] used to disguise Jacob as Esau (27.16). While the pledge stands in lieu of the goat to eventually *reveal* the truth, in the Jacob and Joseph stories, the goats serve to *conceal* the truth.

Likewise, Joseph's ornamented tunic, stained with goat's blood, would seem to act as a means of disclosure but, in fact, facilitates a *mis*-recognition. The blood-stained garment serves as the 'cover story' for the sale of Joseph into slavery: 'Then they took Joseph's tunic, slaughtered a kid and dipped the tunic in the blood. They had the ornamented tunic taken to their father, and they said, "We found this. Please recognize this [*haker na'*]; is it your son's tunic or not?" He recognized it [*va-yakirah*], and said, "My son's tunic! A savage beast devoured him! Joseph is surely torn, torn apart"' (Gen. 37.31-33). The tunic accounts for Joseph's absence and conjectured death. It diverts the grieving father from the truth about his beloved son's true fate—sold ignominiously into slavery in Egypt.

Similarly, in the story of Joseph's escapade with the wife of Potiphar, clothing serves as false testimony. The young man's garment is torn from him by Mrs Potiphar as he flees her lascivious grasp. She then uses the garment as her alibi, both with the servants and with her husband: 'She kept his garment [*bigdo*] beside her, until his master came home. Then she told him the same story, saying, "The Hebrew slave whom you brought into our house came to me to play with me; but when I screamed at the top of my voice, he left his garment [*bigdo*] with me and fled outside"' (Gen. 39.16-18). The Hebrew term referring to Joseph's garment, *beged*, is generic for clothing, though a pun may well be intended, with the resonant *biggud* (betrayal). Clothing (*beged*) in the Joseph saga serves as betrayal (*biggud*), false testimony; the tunic and garment cover for heinous acts—the sale of Joseph into slavery and the married woman's attempted seduction of the handsome Hebrew slave, whom she later frames with rape. Desdemona's handkerchief, in Shakespeare's *Othello*, is likewise used by Iago to rouse the Moor's jealousy, the 'green-eyed monster which doth mock the meat it feeds on' (3.3), instigating the tragic murder. In the two scenes in the Joseph story, the act of *mis*-recognition hinges on the leitmotif of clothing—a blood-stained tunic and a garment.

By contrast, in the Judah and Tamar episode, the promised goat is the catalyst for the *uncover story* in failing to fulfill its role as payment for services conferred. It is the signet, cord and staff, rather, that testify to truth and lead to recognition by serving as a substitute, a pledge ('*eravon*) for the payment that was never conferred. It is this substitution that effects the reversal. Where one would expect the pledge to prompt payment, instead it impels the revelation of identity and brings about an ethical epiphany and confession from their owner. As the 'private eye' at *Petaḥ 'Enaim* ('opening of the eyes'), the tokens serve as testimony to the disguise and uncovering enacted there.

Reversal and Recognition—haker na'

An attempt to pay the debt and reclaim the pledge is made as Judah's friend, Hirah, set out to search for the harlot who sat at the entrance to Enaim but she is not to be found. 'He inquired of the people of that town, "Where is the cult prostitute [*qdeshah*],[23] the one at Enaim, by the road?" But they said, "There has been no cult prostitute here"' (Gen. 38.21). Judah is then left with the goat, his tokens of identity unredeemed. He expresses anxiety lest he 'become a laughingstock' if he were to pursue the matter further (v. 22). The turning point arrives, when . . .

> About three months later, Judah was told, 'Your daughter-in-law Tamar has played the harlot; in fact, she is with child by harlotry'. 'Bring her out', said Judah, 'and let her be burned'. As she was being brought out, she sent [*shalḥah*] to her father-in-law, saying: 'I am pregnant by the man to whom these belong'. And then she said [*va-to'mer*], 'Please discern/recognize [*haker na'*] these; whose signet and cord and staff are these?'

---

23. The term 'sacred prostitute [*qdeshah*]' (vv. 21 [2x], 22), as opposed to the earlier term 'harlot [*zonah*]' (v. 15), is used by Hira, perhaps, to elevate Judah's sexual liaison with the woman. In ancient Mesopotamia, the cult prostitute, 'hierodule', was attached to the temple rather than to a family, and was able to control her own sexuality (see the discussion in Frymer-Kensky, *Reading the Women of the Bible*, pp. 271, 422-23). The dramatic effect for the reader, however, is to implicate Judah, ironically, with yet another 'sin' in his assimilating among the Canaanites—the idolatrous association with temple prostitution (cf. Deut. 23.18 and Hos. 4.14). For a discussion of the difference between *zonah* and *qdeshah*, see Phyllis Bird, 'To Play the Harlot', in *Gender and Difference in Ancient Israel* (ed. Peggy L. Day; Minneapolis, MN: Augsburg Press, 1989), pp. 84-88.

Judah recognized them, and said, 'She is more in the right than I [*tzadqah mimeni*], inasmuch as I did not give her to my son Shelah'. And he did not know her again (Gen. 38.24-26).

This scene marks the pivotal point, the moment of reversal, where the tokens that *should have* been procured for payment instead reveal the true identity of the protagonists. The scene signifies the best of the complex plots, according to Aristotle's *Poetics,* wherein reversal and recognition coincide. The drama is heightened by irony (with the reader privy to knowledge withheld from the players themselves), and is intensified by the element of surprise. But the course of events does not hinge on plot alone dictated by necessity or probability (as Aristotle would have it), but by a critical shift in moral consciousness on the part of Judah. Based on scant clues in the biblical text, the rabbinic sources amplify the degree of pivot, the about-face, that Tamar demands of her father-in-law.

Tamar's gesture, at that moment, allows Judah to either deny the identity of the tokens or, conversely, to acknowledge them as his own, for, as the text says, 'she sent [*shalḥah*] to her father-in-law' (v. 25). Did she send a message or the tokens themselves? The biblical text is ambiguous. Furthermore, the words she relays are addressed in the third person, 'I am pregnant by the man to whom these belong', which indicates no direct confrontation. Only later does she address him face to face, according to the midrashic reading, after he had already acknowledged the signs in private. This is borne out by the shift from third to second person, implied by the latter part of her speech: 'Please discern/recognize [*haker na'*] these . . .' (v. 25). The Talmud enigmatically explains her action by drawing on a moral aphorism: 'Better to cast oneself into a fiery furnace rather than put someone else to shame [*'al yalbin pnei ḥavero be-rabim*, lit., do not blanch the face of one's friend in public].[24] Whence do we know this? From Tamar' (*b. Sot.* 10b).[25] That is,

---

24. The Hebrew expression *'al yalbin pnei ḥavero be-rabim* [lit. do not blanch the face of one's friend in public] seems to contradict the physiological phenomenon of shame, which usually entails the reddening of the face. A similar aphorism is found in *m. 'Av.* 3.11, attributed to Rabbi Elazar ha-Moda'i: 'He who shames another [*ha-malbin pnei ḥavero*, lit., blanches the face his friend] in public renounces the covenant of Abraham our forefather'. However, many manuscripts point to an alternative version of the aphorism: 'he who reddens the face of another [*ha-ma'adim pnei ḥavero*] . . .' See S. Sharvit, *Tractate Avoth through the Ages* (Jerusalem: Bialik Institute, 2004), p. 133 (Heb.).

25. Other midrashic parallels include *ARN B* 38, *b. Ket.* 67b, *b. Sot.* 10b. See also the parallel in the pseudepigraph *T. Jud.* 12.5-6: 'Judah said: Not knowing what she had done, I wished to kill her but she privately sent me the pledges and put me to shame [or, rather, did not put me to shame—Kugel's emendation]. And when she was taken out she sent word to her father-in-law, "The man to whom these belong is the one by whom I am pregnant". And she said, "Recognize whose these are, the signet and the cord and the

she *privately* sent him the tokens to spare him embarrassment, risking her life at the stake. In another version of this aggadic passage, the martyrdom implied by this aphorism is made explicit: 'since she [Tamar] was set on fire [*mutzet*, punning on the term *mutze't*, 'brought out', in Gen. 38.25] yet still she did not shame him in public' (*b. Ber.* 43b).[26] She saves him 'face', both literally and figuratively, in choosing death rather than commiting a metaphorical murder. Is the Talmud being hyperbolically literal or is there a figurative dimension to the passage? If literal, the aggadah implies that Tamar already feels the scorching fire at her feet before Judah finally admits to his fault. According to the aphorism, it is 'better to cast oneself into a fiery furnace rather than put someone else to shame'; the external burning takes ethical precedence over one internally generated in another.[27]

On another level, the Talmudic passage evokes a range of poetic imagery; the blanching of Judah's face in shame, or the rush of blood under his skin,

---

staff". Then Judah recognized them'. See the discussion in Kugel, 'Judah and the Trial of Tamar', pp. 180-82.

26. Based on Kugel's reading, 'Judah and the Trial of Tamar', p. 182. The continuation of the Talmudic passage makes the link between 'the fiery furnace' and Tamar's burning at the stake even more explicit: 'Judah who sanctified the heavenly Name in public [through confession] merited that the whole of his name should be called after the Name of the Holy One blessed be He. When he confessed and said, "She is more righteous than I", a voice issued forth and said, "You rescued Tamar and her two sons from the fire. By your life, I will rescue through your merit three of your descendants from the fire." Who are they? Hananiah, Mishael and Azariah' (*b. Sot.* 10b). Another passage in the Talmud states an opinion, in the name of R. Nahman b. Yitzhak, that 'anyone who shames another in public, it is as though he shed blood [*shofekh damim*]' (*b. B. Metz.* 58b; cf. *Midr. haGadol* on Gen. 38.25 and *Yal. Shimoni* 145). Not shaming another is then tantamount to not committing bloodshed, and is therefore a means of sanctifying the [divine] name [*qiddush ha-shem*]. This principle adjures that one should be martyred rather than commit the three cardinal sins (murder, idolatry and illicit sexual relations) under duress. In the *Targum Neofiti* (an ancient Aramaic paraphrastic translation of the Pentateuch), the central motif is the sanctification of the [divine] name, according to Esther Menn (*Judah and Tamar [Genesis 38] in Ancient Jewish Exegesis: Studies in Literary Form and Hermeneutic* [Leiden: Brill, 1997], pp. 214-87). Both Tamar and Judah do so—she by not shaming him, he by sparing her death-by-fire—and therefore they merit 'three just men in the Valley of Dura'—Hananiah, Mishael and Azariah. Their descendants become exemplars of martyrdom for the sake of 'sanctifying the name' [*qiddush ha-shem*] (cf. Dan. 1.6; 3.14-27; cf. *b. Pes.* 53b; *b. Sanh.* 93a; and *b. Sot.* 10b).

27. The overlapping images of burning in fire and burning in shame constitute a central motif in *Targum Neofiti*. In response to Tamar's presentation of the tokens, 'Judah immediately stood upon his feet and said: "I beg of you brothers, and men of my father's house, listen to me: It is better for me to burn in this world, with extinguishable fire, that I may not be burned in the world to come whose fire is inextinguishable. It is better for me to blush in this world that is a passing world, so that I may not blush before my just fathers in the world to come' (*Targ. Neof.* on Gen. 38.25; McNamara, *The Aramaic Bible*, p. 177).

is replaced by the blistering of her own skin from the fiery furnace. Emmanuel Levinas, the modern French philosopher, explains this ethical gesture as an act of substitution, 'the possibility of putting oneself in the place of the other, which refers to the transference from the "by the other" into a "for the other."'[28] In a relation of substitution, one may go so far as to give one's very life for the other. In the same essay, Levinas describes the ethics of responsibility in highly physical terms, in which, through responsibility, 'as one assigned or elected from the outside, assigned as irreplaceable, the subject is accused in its skin, too tight for its skin. . . . The irremissible guilt with regard to the neighbour is like a Nessus tunic my skin would be'.[29] The image of the mythical poisoned shirt is most telling. Hercules accidentally donned that 'intolerable shirt of flame', daubed in the tainted blood of the centaur, Nessus, and was compelled, by the burning of his skin, to throw himself on the funeral pyre—'consumed by either fire or fire'.[30] In Levinas's terms, it is the substitution of one's skin for the *other's* that characterizes the ultimate sacrifice, a 'responsibility, for which I am summoned as someone irreplaceable . . . as being-in-one's-skin, having-the-other-in-one's-skin'.[31]

In a metonymic reading of the aggadic passage, Tamar's anticipation of Judah's burning skin compels her to sacrifice herself, substituting her own skin for his skin on the funeral pyre—'to be redeemed from fire by fire'. The self is bound in responsibility for the other through physical awareness of the other's pain. Levinas writes, 'In the exposure to wounds and outrages, in the feeling proper to responsibility, the oneself is provoked as irreplaceable, as devoted to the others, without being able to resign, and thus as incarnated in order to offer itself, to suffer and to give'.[32] The Talmudic passage lends us a graphic image of the ethical act of substitution, comparable to the Nessus tunic. But it goes even further insofar as Tamar *would have* thrown herself into the fiery furnace to save the other, Judah, from shame, from the burning skin of his face. It is this ultimate compassion, the transference of a 'by the other' into a 'for the other', that makes Levinas's ethical imperative such a compelling means of understanding this aggadic passage. Tamar was saved from the funeral pyre because Judah responded to her sacrifice with

28. Emmanuel Levinas, 'Substitution', in *The Levinas Reader* (ed. Seán Hand; Oxford: Blackwell Publishers, 1989), p. 107.

29. Levinas, 'Substitution', pp. 95, 99.

30. T.S. Eliot alludes to the tunic of Nessus in 'Little Gidding', the last section of the Four Quartets: 'The only hope, or else despair/ Lies in the choice of pyre of pyre—/ To be redeemed from fire by fire./ Who then devised the torment? Love./ Love is the unfamiliar Name/ Behind the hands that wove/ The intolerable shirt of flame/ Which human power cannot remove./ We only live, only suspire/ Consumed by either fire or fire' (IV, lines 5-14).

31. Levinas, 'Substitution', p. 104.

32. Levinas, 'Substitution', p. 105.

a recognition of responsibility. Her gesture of 'substitution' then becomes a model for Judah himself.

Tamar is saved from conflagration by Judah's admission of responsibility. The rabbinic sages conjecture the presence of a court at that moment. This is implied by the language of verdict, 'take her out and let her be burned' (v. 24).[33] The judges, however, remain invisible with a silent role in the biblical text, which the midrash makes explicit as divine adjudication. In the hearing, there are two stages to her defense: first, she *sends* the pledge (*shalḥah*), the signet, cord and staff, and then she appeals (*va-to'mer*) to Judah directly to examine or recognize (*haker na'*) the tokens. She allows Judah (in privacy) to either deny their identity or, conversely, to claim them as his own. In this way, she enables him to make the shift toward acknowledging his responsibility without shame. When she appeals to Judah directly to discern/recognize [*haker na'*], she echoes the very words the brothers had addressed to their father, Jacob. This phrase, according to the midrash, is delivered *quid pro quo*: 'The Holy One, blessed be He, said to Judah: you said "please recognize [*haker na'*]" to your father, by your life, Tamar will say "please recognize [*haker na'*]" to you!' (*Gen. R.* 85.11).[34] The midrash implies a *double entendre* for Judah and a concomitant demand for a twofold *re*-cognition—to retrospectively acknowledge the bereavement of his own father at the presentation of the bloodied cloak and to recognize his responsibility toward Tamar. He does so with respect to his daughter-in-law, in admitting that he had neglected her by not giving her to his son Shelah (Gen. 38.26). With respect to his father, he will enact a *reversal* of his previous role, as the one who had initiated the sale of Joseph into slavery (Gen. 37.26-27), by standing as surety on behalf of Benjamin (Gen. 43.9 and 44.32).[35]

Judah's declaration in response—*tzadqah mimeni*—can similarly be read on multiple levels. At first glance, *mimeni* is read as a comparative: 'she is *more* in the right than me'. But how can justification be compared? Either one is vindicated or not. This leads to a splicing of the phrase, with an implied ellipsis. In the Aramaic translation, *mimeni* is read as causative: '*tzadqah*—she is right', and '*mimeni*—from me she is pregnant' (*Targ. Onq.* on Gen. 38.26).[36] In this second reading, she is vindicated, and Judah acknowledges his paternity. In a third reading, the rabbinic sages sug-

---

33. James Kugel, 'Judah and the Trial of Tamar', pp. 169-184.
34. *Gen. R.* 85.11, p. 1045. Other midrashic sources point to this parallel as well: *Gen. R.* 85.1, as discussed earlier (ed. Theodor-Albeck, p. 1031); *b. Sot.* 10b and *b. Ber.* 43b.
35. Frymer-Kensky makes exactly this point in *Reading the Women of the Bible*, p. 275.
36. This splitting of the phrase is also found in the *Targ. Neof.* (on Gen. 38.26), as well as the *T. Jud.* 12.6. Though the actual divine utterance is missing in the latter, it is

gest that a divine voice intervened as a kind of *deus ex machina.* Judah affirms Tamar's innocence, and God affirms Judah's paternity—'from me [*mimeni*]', because of Me (with a capital M) she conceived; it was all part of the divine plot. 'God said, "You testify about what happened in public and I will testify to what happened in private"' (*Gen. R.* 85.12).[37] The midrash makes the question of Judah's dubious knowledge of paternity explicit. God intercedes precisely where Judah's capacity for knowledge is limited.

As Zvi Jagendorf has pointed out, the reversal of carnal knowing— where 'sensual knowledge' (by which man *knows* a woman) turns out to be the opposite of 'true knowledge' (where she knows him)—hinges upon the woman's initiative.[38] The drama suggests that the hidden nature of conception evokes an anxiety over paternity, generating the 'hermeneutic chromosome', where the gap in the text invites the interpreter to step into the father's seeding. The midrash shifts the locus of 'knowing' from the woman onto God in attributing knowledge to divine omniscience. It does so, however, not as a means of *undermining* female privilege but, rather, to imply a synergy between the two. The insight of maternity, engendered at conception and in pregnancy, lies at the core of the alliance between God and women. For the men, the significance of the deception comes only in hindsight. Isaac realizes that the true 'blessed son', chosen for the patriarchal covenant, must be Jacob *only after* he has been duped, and Judah only admits to his responsibility to Tamar (and his father) after the seduction. So the 'best laid plans' of man go astray, until woman intervenes in subterfuge.

Of Guarantors and Kings

What impact does this incident have upon character development in the greater saga of Joseph and his brothers? The very next encounter with Judah in the biblical text entails the ethical act of 'substitution', standing as surety for another. This concept is represented by the key term *'arev,* the root of the same Hebrew word used for the pledge [*'eravon, 'rb*] Tamar had exacted of Judah. Two years into the seven years of famine, Canaan is sorely hit. The brothers have gone to Egypt for food and returned already once, with an edict from the alleged Egyptian viceroy not to return without their youngest brother, Benjamin. When hunger strikes again, Jacob refuses to comply, fearing he will be bereaved yet again of a beloved son (of the

---

paraphrased by Judah, who refrains from killing Tamar when he realizes that what has happened 'was from the Lord' (Menn, *Judah and Tamar*, p. 355).

37. Kugel suggests that the rabbis understood this to be a court scene, and God intervenes to issue the final edict. See the detailed discussion on the variant interpretations of *tzadqah mimeni* in Kugel, 'Judah and the Trial of Tamar', pp. 169-84.

38. Jagendorf, 'Genesis and the Reversal of Sexual Knowledge', pp. 189-90.

beloved wife) as he was with Joseph. Reuben fails to convince him. Judah, however, speaks up:

> And Judah said to Israel his father, 'Send the boy with me, and we will arise and go, that we may live and not die, both we and you and also our little ones. I will be surety for him ['*a'ervenu*]; of my hand you shall require him. If I do not bring him back to you and set him before you, then let me bear the blame for ever; for if we had not delayed, we would now have returned twice' (Gen. 43.8-10 NRSV).

The promise Judah makes here will determine the role he plays before the supposed Egyptian viceroy, where he pleads to be taken as a slave instead of his brother, Benjamin, falsely accused of theft. Standing before the apparently impassive man, Judah pleads,

> 'For your servant became surety ['*arav*] for the boy to my father, saying, "If I do not bring him back to you, then I will bear the blame in the sight of my father all my life." Now therefore, please let your servant remain as a slave to my lord in place of the boy; and let the boy go back with his brothers. For how can I go back to my father if the boy is not with me? I fear to see the suffering that would come upon my father' (Gen. 44.32-34 NRSV).

At this point Judah finally rectifies the tragedy he had brought on his father, when (along with his brothers) he deceived Jacob with the bloodied cloak. Having experienced the bereavement of his own two sons, he faces the imminence of yet a second loss to his father. In stepping up as guarantor, at this point, he rises to the status of a true leader. The return of Jacob's two sons, Joseph and Benjamin, is comparable to the two sons (twins) whom Judah gains 'back' through Tamar. One of those twins, Perez, significantly becomes the father to the Davidic lineage.[39] With an interesting twist, the pledge Tamar had exacted of Judah shows him the principle of standing as a surety for another. Just as the pledge—the signet, cord and staff—disclosed Judah's paternity, so too Judah, as a human pledge for his brother, catalyzes the revelation of Joseph's identity and, ultimately, the reunion between father and son. Tamar risked her life in doing so. Judah rose to the call and went on to act on the very same principle of 'substitution' in serving as surety for his brother, willing to throw himself 'into the fiery furnace' of slavery in Egypt to save another.[40]

The rabbis ask by what merit was Judah singled out as the progenitor of the Davidic lineage (cf. Gen. 49.10)?[41] The Tosefta answers, 'Because

---

39. Cf. Gen. 38.29; 49.10; Ruth 4.18-22; and 1 Chron. 2.3-15.
40. Metaphorically, Egypt is identified as the 'iron furnace' or 'iron-smelter' [*kur ha-barzel*], from which the Israelites, as God's people, were drawn (Deut. 4.20; 1 Kgs 8.51; Jer. 11.4).
41. In an alternative midrash, the following speculations on Judah's merit as progenitor of the monarchy were made: 'Was it because he had saved Joseph from murder

he acknowledged Tamar [*hodeh be-Tamar*]' (*t. Ber.* 4.17).[42] The term *hodeh* may refer to the recognition of his sin and confession for neglecting her—*hodeh* as *hitvadeh* (confession)—when he declared, 'she is more righteous than I' (Gen. 38.26). It could equally refer to his recognition of paternity through her, *hodeh* as an act of public acknowledgment. It is, in fact, imbedded in Judah's very name. As Leah declared upon his birth, '"This time I will praise/thank [*'odeh*] Yhwh." Therefore she named him Judah [Yehuda]' (Gen. 29.35). The broadest understanding of the Hebrew verb *hodeh*, however, implies recognition of truth (either through praise or acknowledgment of debt). The term implies a re-evaluation of the past, parallel to the English '*re*-cognition' and the Greek '*ana-gnorisis*' (the recovery of lost knowledge)—a concept embedded in Judah's very name, *Yehuda*.

Beyond the human dimension, the term *hodeh* implies the recognition of the Ultimate Other—God's presence in the private interstices of the human encounter, 'an optical instrument to the divine' in Levinas's words.[43] The seeming 'ontological absence' of God modulates into an 'ethical presence' between individuals.[44] According to the rabbinic sources, God acts through human interplay in plotting Judah and Tamar's union, in confirming the source of the conception and in catching 'the conscience of the king'. But, on the surface level of the text, God is absent, concealed in the crannies of the human conscience as it surfaces in the face-to-face encounter.

---

in suggesting the sale into slavery (cf. Gen. 37.26)? Or because he had acknowledged the righteousness of Tamar (cf. Gen. 38.26)? Or because he had served as guarantor for Benjamin (cf. 44.33)? In all three cases, one finds the 'guarantor' [*'arev*, that is, Judah] is liable to pay' (*Mek. Ish., BeShallaḥ*, 5 [106]). See also *Sifre Deut.* 405; *y. Sot.* 1,4).

42. The root of *hodeh* (*ydh*), has a fairly broad semantic range: 'to praise' (cf. Ps. 45.18; 49.19; Job 40.14), also in Gen. 49.8 (a play on the name Yehuda), and Gen. 29.35 (as the etymology of Judah's name); 'to thank in prayer', as in Neh. 11.17; 12.24; 1 Chron. 16.4; 23.30; and 'to confess' (primarily in the hitpael), as in Lev. 5.5; 16.21; 26.40; Num. 5.7; and Dan. 9.20 (*HALOT*). In rabbinic literature, it takes on a formal, legalistic meaning as a declaration in court, acknowledging one's debt to another—*hoda'at ba'al din*, as in *b. B. Metz.* 3b (see Jastrow, p. 337).

43. Emmanuel Levinas, *Difficile liberté* (Paris: Edition Albin Michel, 1963), p. 187, cited in Susan Handelman, *Fragments of Redemption* (Bloomington, IN: Indiana University Press, 1991), p. 270. I believe the original quote reads, 'Ethics is an optic, such that everything I know of God and everything I can hear of His word and reasonably say to Him must find an ethical expression', in Levinas's essay 'A Religion for Adults', in *Difficult Freedom* (trans. S. Hand; Baltimore, MD: Johns Hopkins University Press, 1990), p.16.

44. Susan Handelman, 'Facing the Other: Levinas, Perelman, and Rosenzweig', in *Divine Aporia: Postmodern Conversations about the Other* (ed. John C. Hawley; Lewisburg, PA: Bucknell University Press, 2000), p. 276.

Unnatural Birth

Throughout this chapter, midrash has served not only as a literary tool to tease out the parallel plots, motifs and key terms but also as an answer to the theological question: how is God in cahoots with the women? Let us return to the relationship between veiling and the womb of 'double sewing'.[45] The parturition of twins, for both Rebekah and Tamar, are oddly similar. Both entail a breach birth, with the hand emerging before the head, which has no corroboration in the laws of human natural birth.[46] At Rebekah's delivery, 'The first one came out red, his whole body like a hairy mantle, so they named him Esau/Rough-One.[47] Afterward his brother came out, with his hand gripping Esau's heel so he named him Jacob/Heel-Holder' (Gen. 25.25-26).[48] As Tamar labored, the first put his hand out, to which the midwife tied a crimson thread (so he was called Zerah)[49] and the second came out, head and shoulders ahead, so the midwife named him Perez: 'What a breach you have made for yourself [*mah paratzta peretz*]!' (Gen. 38.29).[50]

---

45. I borrow the expression from Sophocles' tragedy *Oedipus the King*: 'this mother's womb, this field of double sowing whence I sprang, and where I sowed my own children' (lines 1256-58) (*Sophocles I* [trans. and ed. David Grene and Richard Lattimore; Chicago: University of Chicago Press, 3rd edn, 2013], p. 132).

46. Yair Zakovitch and Avigdor Shinan argue that the description of the birth of Jacob and Esau, in their struggle for firstborn status, informs our reading of Zerah's and Perez's birth (Y. Zakovitch and A. Shinan, *Ma'aseh Yehuda ve-Tamar: Breshit 39 ba-Mikra, ba-targumim ha'atikim uva-sifrut ha-Yehudit* [Jerusalem: Mifalei ha-meḥqar shel ha-makhon le-mada'ei ha-yahadut, 1992], pp. 13-15 [Heb.]). This type of breach, however, is not a realistic description of birth. The suggestion that the hand emerges first is based, rather, on the agricultural experience of men with domestic animals such as horses, camels and donkeys, where the hooves emerge first. Eran Viezel asserts that 'there is no evidence in medical records of births in which a baby emerges with its arms extended forwards'. In a human breech birth, the baby's buttocks emerge first; whereas 'in a birth in the "transverse lie" position (0.3% incidence), the head of the baby curves away from the exit of the birth canal until its neck breaks' (Eran Viezel, 'The Influence of Realia on Biblical Depictions of Childbirth', *VT* 61 [2011], p. 687). In these cases, one of the hands may emerge first, but the baby is no longer alive at that point.

47. The etiological significance for the name Esau is not made explicit. One could read '*esav* as 'completed [*'asui*]', the hairy mantle on his infant form suggesting a bizarre manly appearance. According to Rashi, 'They all called him *'Esav* because he was made and finished [covered as he was] by hair as though much older' (Gen. 25.25). Fox, on the other hand, suggests that Esau's name derives from the Arabic *'athaya*, 'rough one' (Fox, *Five Books of Moses*, p. 115 n. 25).

48. Adapted from Fox's translation, *Five Books of Moses*, p. 115.

49. BDB entry 272 and 273, p. 280.

50. The term 'breach' [*prtz*] connotes an outburst of water (cf. 2 Sam. 5.20; 1 Chron. 14.11), or, as in this case, to 'burst forth from water' (i.e. the womb). It also suggests the making of a breach in a wall (cf. Amos 4.3; 1 Kgs 11.27; Neh. 6.1; Ps. 144.14; Job 30.14). In the figurative sense, it implies the act of intercession—'to stand in the breach'

Biologically, Zerah is born 'breach', in opening the womb with his hand, though the break [*pritzah*] is attributed to Perez as the first to emerge whole. Intentionality is inferred to both the infants—Jacob and Perez; the 'race for first place', both try to supplant their brother.⁵¹

On a deeper level, however, it is the mothers who initiate the breach in the norm; they take the circuitous route, and their veils, as masks, enable the ruse to ensue. God's plan, in overriding the right of the firstborn, is thus ensured—Jacob supplants Esau as heir to the patriarchal covenant just as Judah supplants Reuben in becoming the progenitor of the Davidic line.⁵² The Davidic kingship emerges from the lineage of Perez (Ruth 4.18-22). And Jacob's blessing to Judah ('the tribe') is replete with regnal imagery: the obeisance of brothers, the lion crouching ready to pounce, the scepter and the staff, and the gifts and obedience he will command (Gen. 49.8-10). But most significantly, the name Perez signifies a spontaneous breach of boundaries, alluding to the rupture of those social norms that Tamar so audaciously defied. Perhaps Perez, conceived by his parents at the crossroads, is infused with his mother's courage through some strange Lamarckian notion of 'inherited characteristics'. As ancestor to David, he represents the pursuit of an internal truth against the grain of external norms.

This is how God 'sees', not with the eyes but with the heart. As the midrash wryly comments on the opening line of this biblical episode, 'While the tribes were occupied with the sale of Joseph, Jacob with sackcloth and fasting, Judah with taking a wife, the Holy One, blessed be He, was creating the light of the messianic kingship' (*Gen. R.* 85.1).⁵³ The midrash highlights the irony; it is precisely through Judah's clumsy attempts to establish continuity [*toledot*]—thwarted by his sons and realigned through Tamar's deception—that the Davidic line is established. God plants the seeds of the messianic light in the private interstices of the face-to-face encounter, against the grain of conscious human knowledge and will. Yet again, 'the

---

(cf. Ezek. 13.5). But it can also mean, conversely, an outburst of God's wrath (2 Sam. 6.8; 1 Chron. 13.11; Job 16.14; Judg. 21.15). See BDB entry 7877. Most telling, in terms of the role of leader, is the verse from Micah: 'He who opens the breach [*ha-poretz*] will go up before them; they will break through [*partzu*] and pass the gate, going out by it. Their king will pass on before them, the Lord at their head' (Mic. 2.13). Tamar and Judah, as the progenitors of kings, figuratively 'open the breach' and 'break through', so that 'their king will pass on before' them (cf. *Gen. R.* 85.13, p. 1049).

51. As the verse in Hosea implies, 'In the womb he [Jacob] tried to supplant ['*aqav*] his brother' (Hos. 12.4, NJPS), rendered 'he took his brother by the heel' (RSV, KJV on Hos. 12.3). This is a pejorative play on the etiology of Jacob's name, *Ya'aqov* (from '*eqev*, 'heel'). Hosea seems to imply a criticism of Jacob's 'clutching' at the heel in his attempt to supplant his brother. See Zakovitz and Shinan, *Ma'aseh Yehuda ve-Tamar*, pp. 13-15.

52. Cf. Gen. 38.29; 49.10; Ruth 4.18-22; and 1 Chron. 2.3-15.

53. *Gen. R.* 85.1, p. 1030.

best-schemes o' mice an' men gang aft agley'. The woman, as the vanguard of the divine, steers the course of patriarchal history.

The narratives that constitute the critical background to the making of the Davidic dynasty all share the theme of *peretz*, a radical breach in social norms. The maternal ancestor of David, Ruth the Moabite, is the descendant of yet another 'bedtrick'—the seduction of Lot by his daughters, engendering the eponymous ancestor, Moab (lit. 'of the father'). Ruth herself will also engage in a near bedtrick at the threshing floor. In making the alliance between God and the duplicity of the women explicit, I read between the lines of the biblical text, *lifnim mishurat hadin*, to find a subjective space *within* the line of law. In the next chapter, we will explore, in greater detail, this seemingly antinomian trend in the narratives concerned with the background to the Davidic dynasty.

ADDENDUM: THE SIGNET, CORD AND STAFF[54]

Three more items were created at twilight on the sixth day—the signet, cord and staff, bound together 'like a threefold thread not readily broken' (Eccl. 4.12). The staff served as a divining rod, their travel guide. The signet ring indicated when to stop and when to move on. The cord gave voice to qualms of conscience, as it says, 'Tell them to make fringes on the corners of their garments throughout their generations and to put a blue cord on the fringe at each corner . . . so that, when you see it, you will remember all the LORD's commandments and do them, and not follow the lust of your own heart and your own eyes' (Num. 15.38-39).

The time came for their debut on the stage of human history. The three were destined to be sold in a flea market to a man named Judah, son of Jacob. He admired the bdellium, lapis lazuli, and gold engraved into the handle of the staff, carved of almond wood. He was amazed by the bright colors of the two threads woven into one cord—blue and crimson. He fondled the form engraved on the signet ring—two cherubs entwined in each other. And the ring fit his finger perfectly. Immediately, he paid twenty pieces of silver for them without haggling.

Years passed for them with Judah. Years of loveless marriage, the outrageous pangs of pregnancy, birth and rearing children. Years of barrenness and blindness, of sin and disillusionment.

---

54. This piece was originally written in Hebrew as a 'modern midrash' in the context of a seminar on the book of Ruth at Beit Midrash Elul, Jerusalem, in 2011.

Years of fertility and bereavement—the death of his wife and two sons. The signet, cord and staff then turned to one another: 'When will the redemption begin? Come, let us deal shrewdly with him!' in order to draw Judah out of the pit.

Following these words, Judah went out to the sheep-shearing festivities with the threesome-not-readily-broken, a week after his wife had been buried. (He did not refuse comfort in mourning.) He came to a feast in a tent where they poured wine like water, until 'He washed his garment in wine, his robe in blood of grapes, his eyes darker than wine, and his teeth whiter than milk' (Gen. 49.11-12). At twilight, Judah left on his way with the threesome, his heart joyous (though his feet were not so steady). The staff led them to a crossroads at Petaḥ Enayim, and, there he raised his eyes and, lo, he saw a prostitute sitting by the road. In truth it was Tamar, his daughter-in-law, but he failed to recognize her since she had covered her face with a veil. She, on the other hand, knew him well!

She called out, 'Judah! Judah!' And the signet ring signaled him to stop.

'Here I am', he answered. 'Let me come into you'.

'What will you give me if I let you?'

'A kid from my flock. What shall I give you as a pledge?'

'Your signet, staff and cord [*ptilkha*] that is in your hand' (Gen. 38.18).

And yet the cord did not slap him in the face, as a reminder 'not to follow the lust of his own heart'. Instead, as Judah and Tamar became entangled in each other, the cord split into two threads.

Three months later, when they took Tamar out to be burnt at the stake, she presented the threesome to Judah in order to save herself, saying, 'By the man to whom these belong, I am with child. . . . Please recognize whose these are—the signet, cords [*ve-ha-ptilim*] and staff' (Gen. 38.25). She did not say 'cord [*ptil*]' but 'cords [*ptilim*]'. Of course, Judah recognized the threesome that was now about to be broken up, and saved Tamar and his two sons in her womb from the fiery furnace. What did he do with the signet, cords and staff? The signet ring he bequeathed to the line of the Davidic monarchy, the staff to Aaron, the high priest, but Tamar kept the cords for herself.

One of the threads was appointed for the conscience, the other for ruminations of the heart—the blue for pure thoughts, the crimson for desire of the eyes. The blue was given to Perez, to distinguish between the colors of white and blue at the break of dawn, for blue is like the sea, and the sea is like the Heavens, and the Heavens are like the Throne of Glory. And the crimson thread was given to Zerah, for crimson is like the red of Edom, like the red of the earth, which opened its mouth to swallow a brother's blood. The thread was tied around his wrist, as the midwife said, 'What a breach you have made for yourself!' Therefore he was named Perez. Afterward his brother came out, on whose hand was the crimson thread; he was named Zerah' (Gen. 38.29-30).

Tamar took the blue thread and wove it into her veil, the one she had used to cover her face. And a wind carried off the crimson thread from the hills of Judah to Rahab, the Canaanite prostitute in Jericho, where her dwelling was in the city wall (Josh. 2.15). That is the very crimson cord Rahab would suspend from that wall, and she came to dwell in the midst of Israel (Josh. 6.25). Tamar passed the scarf with the blue thread on to Serah bat Asher (who spanned the generations), and Serah bat Asher passed it on to Naomi. Before Ruth went down to the threshing floor, Naomi adorned her with the veil, embroidered with the blue thread of conscience.

After what happened (or did not happen) at the threshing floor, Ruth spread out the veil, and Boaz measured out six seeds of barley, as it is written: 'And he said, "Hold out the veil you are wearing". She held it while he measured out six measures of barley . . .' (Ruth 3.15).

There would be a day that the signet, cords and staff would meet again. But were I to tell you when, this would be the end of my tale. So read on, dear reader, read on . . .

4

Weaving the Messianic Light: Law and Narrative in the Making of the Davidic Dynasty*

> 'Everyone strives to reach the Law', says the man, 'so how does it happen that for these many years no one but myself has ever begged for admittance?' The doorkeeper recognizes that the man has reached his end, and, to let his failing senses catch the words, roars in his ear: 'No one else could ever be admitted here, since this gate was made only for you. I am now going to shut it.'
>
> Franz Kafka, 'Before the Law'

Preamble

The book of Ruth[1] reads like a pastoral romance, replete with images of reapers in late spring, poignant blessings from friends and neighbors, as well as acts of loving kindness between relations. It concludes with a classic 'happy ending', the union of Boaz and Ruth and the birth of their child, a devoutly desired heir, who becomes the grandfather of King David, the founder of the Judean monarchy. Despite the idyll, various hints in the text compel us to look back to darker shadows in the book of Genesis—to the origins of the Moabite people (in ch. 19) and the story of Tamar's seduction of Judah (in ch. 38). These earlier narratives adumbrate the book of Ruth, eclipsed by the threat of extinction, disguise and drunken oblivion, incest and the conniving conception of children. In unfurling the scroll alongside the Genesis narratives, I show how the *Megillah* redeems these problematic stories of deception that lie curled like worm-rot around the roots of the Davidic monarchy. In the long days of the harvest season, Ruth, the eponymous heroine of this pristine romance, not only shrinks those past shadows, but also deepens the subtlety of shade.

---

* An earlier version of this chapter was published as 'Seduction and Recognition in the Story of Judah and Tamar and the Book of Ruth', *Nashim* 23 (2012), pp. 87-109.

1. Also known as *Megillat Ruth*, 'the Scroll of Ruth', in the Jewish tradition.

There are three clues that prompt us to return to these narratives in Genesis. The first appears toward the end of the story. All the people and elders at the gate bear witness to the union of Ruth and Boaz, and spontaneously launch into blessing:

> 'We are witnesses. May Yhwh make the woman who is coming into your house like Rachel and Leah, who together built up the house of Israel. May you produce children in Ephrathah and bestow a name in Bethlehem; and, through the children that Yhwh will give you by this young woman, may your house be like the house of Perez, whom Tamar bore to Judah' (Ruth 4.11-12).

The voice of the citizens resonates like a Greek chorus, revealing the normative, collective perspective on the drama. Here the town's people allude to two foundational narratives in the patriarchal history in the process of legitimizing Ruth. As in Sophocles' dramas, the Greek chorus reveals essential background to the plot, which had remained only covert until the pivotal point. Yet unlike a Greek tragedy, the background here reinforces the sense of redemption rather than inevitable doom in the dénouement. The reader senses no chagrin on the part of Boaz upon receiving such a blessing from the citizens, though problematic sexual liaisons underlie the narratives of all three women named—Rachel, Leah and Tamar. The first story entails the switching of the brides, the elder for the more beloved younger sister on Jacob's wedding night; as a result, these two sisters, Rachel and Leah, 'built up the house of Israel'. The second allusion here is to Tamar who, disguised as a whore by the crossroads, seduces her father-in-law, Judah. She consequently gives birth to twins, one of whom was Perez, 'whom Tamar bore to Judah'. In blessing Ruth to emulate these female founders of the Israelite nation, our heroine is presented as an honorary 'fifth matriarch'.[2]

The second clue, elaborating on this latter reference, can be found in the coda on the genealogy of Perez [*toledot Peretz*] (vv. 18-22).[3] Why is he singled out as having his own *toledot*, with an auspicious count of ten generations from Perez to David, founder of the messianic dynasty? Perez,

---

2. This idea was suggested by Yitzhak Peleg in an oral presentation, 'Why Did Ruth the Moabitess Not Raise her Child?', delivered at the World Congress of Jewish Studies (WCJS, July 31, 2013).

3. The term *toledot* is a central organizing principle for the book of Genesis. There are ten generations from Adam to Noah (Genesis 5), and ten from Noah to Abraham (Genesis 10–11, 'The Table of Nations'). The term *toledot* is deployed 11 times (though 10 are implied): 'heaven and earth' (Gen. 2.4); Adam (5.1); Noah (6.9); the sons of Noah (10.1), Shem (11.10), Terah (11.27), Ishmael (25.12), Isaac (25.19), Esau (36.1, 9), and Jacob (37.2). There are two *toledot* outside the book of Genesis: in Num. 3.1 (concerned with the levitical clan) and Ruth 4.18. Both should be considered addenda to Genesis—one with regard to the priesthood and the other with regard to the kingship (*toledot* Perez). See my discussion of *toledot* in Chapter 1.

son of Judah and Tamar, never appears as an active character in the Hebrew Bible at all, except in his peculiar birth scene (discussed in the previous chapter). *Peretz* connotes *pritzut*, breaking through, bursting across boundaries or limits, for he was born through a breach birth. He is named by the midwife as he comes out ahead of his twin brother: 'What a breach you have made for yourself [*mah paratzta peretz*]!' (Gen. 38.29).[4] More significantly, his name alludes to the transgression his mother initiated, in breaching the strict adherence to law, or, rather, in forging a fissure within its line. This name is a crystallization of the central theme of redemption in the book of Ruth—how life finds a way despite the seeming strictures of law.

The third hint is found in the continual reference to the heroine as 'Ruth, the Moabite'.[5] Moab, the eponymous ancestor of that nation, was conceived by yet another female ruse when, after the destruction of Sodom, Lot's daughters made their father drunk and had sexual relations with him. By continually referring to Ruth's Moabite origins, the text urges us to re-examine the taboo against inter-marriage with that nation. According to Deuteronomy, 'No Ammonite or Moabite may enter the congregation of Yhwh; none of their descendants, even in the tenth generation, shall ever enter into the congregation of Yhwh' (Deut. 23.4; cf. Neh. 13.1). Unlike the Moabite people who did not meet the Israelites with food and water on their journey out of Egypt and hired Balaam to curse them (Deut. 23.5), and then yoked the Israelite men to the idolatry of Baal Peor through ritual fornication (Num. 25.1-9), Ruth 'the Moabite' behaves scrupulously. A source of blessing not curse, she acts out of *ḥesed*, loyal toward her mother-in-law in facilitating the redemption of Naomi's land, even bearing her a child. The rabbis introduce a qualification to the law; it is forbidden to intermarry with Moabite and Ammonite men, but the women are permissible.[6] It is Ruth, as

---

4. On the significance of the root *prtz* see Chapter 3 n. 50. Frymer-Kensky points out that the term *peretz*, lit., 'breakthrough', is a word frequently associated with the story of David, who named Baʿal Peratzim saying, 'YHWH broke through [*paratz*] my enemies as water breaks through a dam' (2 Sam. 5.20-22), also naming the place Peretz Uzzah, where YHWH 'broke through against Uzzah' (2 Sam. 6.8) (*Reading the Women of the Bible*, p. 278). The term can also connote transgression of the law (cf. Hos. 4.2).

5. Over the course of the *Megillah*, her status as Moabite is mentioned no less than seven times: Ruth 1.4 (indirectly); 1.22; 2.2, 6, 21; 4.5, 10.

6. In the Mishnah, the biblical verse is understood to be gender specific: 'An Ammonite or a Moabite [man] is forbidden [in marriage to Israelite women] and forbidden for all time, but their women are permitted [to Israelite men] forthwith' (*m. Yeb.* 8.3; *b. Yeb.* 77a; *Pes. R.* 42 and various parallels). The rabbinic justification for this ruling is based on the premise that it is not customary for women to go out and greet strangers with food and water, invoking the following verse: 'the honor of the king's daughter is inward [*kol kevudah bat melekh penimah*]' (Ps. 45.14; see *Ruth R.* 4.6). This, of course, belies the biblical context, where it seems that this is precisely what women do in the Bible—greet

the embodiment of all that is atypical of the Moabite in the Hebrew Bible, who makes the Moabite women acceptable according to rabbinic law.

Biblical scholars claim that the book of Ruth was written precisely for this reason—to clear the stain of incest, seduction and inhospitality associated with the Moabite nation and linked to the Davidic dynasty along the matrilineal line. Ruth presents an exception, the necessity for a reinterpretation of the law. Though set in the time of the judges (Ruth 1.1),[7] the composition most likely dates to a much later period.[8] Edward Campbell argues that Ruth was most likely composed in the early monarchic period (950–700 BCE), perhaps as a means of justifying the Davidic line following Solomon's succession to the throne.[9] Yair Zakovitch, on the other hand, suggests that it was composed as a polemic directed at the edict against Judean intermarriage with foreign wives [*nashim nokhriot*] during the heyday of Ezra and Nehemia in the fifth century BCE.[10] Whether the book of Ruth serves to bolster the Davidic dynasty, as Campbell argues, or serves as a diatribe against a purely genetic definition of Judaism and a defense of women who cleave (as outsiders) to the Israelite people and become 'naturalized citizens', the implications are similar: Ruth is to David's credit as his great-grandmother.

---

men with water at a well—especially in the betrothal-type scene. See Robert Alter, 'Biblical Type-Scenes and the Uses of Convention', in *Biblical Narrative*, pp. 47-62.

7. In the Hebrew Bible, the *Megillah* is positioned in the Writings (*Ketuvim*), among the other four scrolls associated with the liturgical calendar. The Septuagint and Christian canon places it according to its supposed historical context and setting, following the book of Judges (*Shoftim*) and before the books of Samuel. In this position, it accounts for the transition from the anarchy at the end of the period of the judges to the establishment of the monarchy. On the relationship between the books of Ruth and Judges, in general, and the contrast with the story of the concubine of Gibeah, see Yael Ziegler's discussion in *Ruth: From Alienation to Monarchy* (Jerusalem: Koren/Maggid, 2015), pp. 27-58.

8. For an overview of the scholarship on the dating of Ruth, see Jack M. Sasson, *Ruth: A New Translation with a Philological Commentary and a Formalist-Folklorist Interpretation* (Sheffield: Sheffield Academic Press, 2nd edn, 1989), pp. 240-52. For the dating of Ruth based on linguistic evidence, see F.W. Bush, *Ruth/Esther* (WBC, 9; Dallas, TX: Word Books, 1996), pp. 18-30; and Z. Zevit, 'Dating Ruth: Legal, Linguistic and Historical Observations', *ZAW* 117 (2005), pp. 574-600.

9. See Edward Campbell, *Ruth* (AB, 7; New York: Doubleday, 1975), pp. 23-28.

10. Yair Zakovitch, *Ruth: Introduction and Commentary* (Tel Aviv: Am Oved–Magnes, 1990), pp. 19-20, 24 (Heb.). For a critique of this view and its rejection by various scholars, see Roland E. Murphy, *Wisdom Literature: Job, Proverbs, Ruth, Canticles, and Esther* (Forms of Old Testament Literature, 13; Grand Rapids, MI: Eerdmans, 1981), pp. 86-87. See the thorough review of the literature in Edward Greenstein, 'Reading Strategies in the Book of Ruth', in *Women in the Hebrew Bible* (ed. Alice Bach; London: Routledge, 1999), pp. 211-31. See also the discussion in Frymer-Kensky, 'Outsider Women', in *Reading the Women of the Bible*, pp. 283-91.

I will not join the fray of biblical scholarly debate over who wrote the book of Ruth, when, or why, but engage, rather, in a synchronic reading, highlighting the inter-textual resonances between biblical stories that set the tension between narrative and law in high relief. The question is how we situate these stories within the final redacted corpus of the Hebrew Bible—which includes both a normative body of laws and a collection of stories that rub against their grain?[11] Is there an attempt here to right the wrong, to redeem the previous episodes in Genesis through the story of Ruth, as Harold Fisch claims in his seminal essay 'Ruth and the Structure of Covenant History'?[12] My claim is that Ruth, especially in the near-seduction scene at the granary, radically transforms our understanding of the seemingly opprobrious behavior of her ancestresses. It belongs to a larger biblical theme on the discrepancy between the expression of divine will and law.

All three clues in the book of Ruth linking us back to the foundational narratives in Genesis—references to Moab, Rachel and Leah, and Perez (of Judah and Tamar)—allude to a 'bedtrick'. In the pivotal scene, the woman seduces the male protagonist (unbeknown to him) in the context of an incestuous or quasi-incestuous union (at least in two of these stories). The man knows the woman, *carnally,* though he is oblivious as to her identity; she, on the other hand, is the true *knower.* Zvi Jagendorf describes the paradox thus:

> A man may know a woman (physically)—as Adam knew his wife, Eve (Gen. 4.1)—and [yet] be mistaken about her identity. He may even know

---

11. Here I presume that these three narratives are integrated into the final redaction of the Hebrew Bible, alongside the laws of Deuteronomy (on levirate marriage, Deut. 25.5-6, and the exclusion of the Moabite, Deut. 23.4-5), as well as the list of sexually forbidden relations (Leviticus 18 and 20). Given the scope of this work, I will not engage in a critique of source criticism, but rather present a literary reading of the text as an integral whole with the assumption that its final form is intentional and artful. My concern is not with the Bible's composition but with its canonical reception by the modern reader, preserving the contradictory and multivocal nature of the text.

12. Harold Fisch, 'Ruth and the Structure of Covenant History', *VT* 32 (1982), pp. 425-37. For further discussion of the relationship between these three narratives, see Frymer-Kensky, *Reading the Women of the Bible,* in particular her three chapters on 'royal origins', pp. 238-77; Phyllis Trible, 'A Human Comedy', in *God and the Rhetoric of Sexuality* (Philadelphia, PA: Fortress Press, 1978), pp. 166-99; Mieke Bal, 'One Woman, Many Men, and the Dialectic of Chronology', and 'Heroism and Proper Names, or the Fruits of Analogy', in *Lethal Love,* pp. 68-88 and 89-103; Susan Niditch, 'The Wronged Woman Righted: An Analysis of Genesis 38', *HTR* 72 (1979), pp. 143-49; Johanna Bos, 'Out of the Shadows: Genesis 38; Judges 4:17-22; Ruth 3', in *Reasoning with the Foxes: Female Wit in a World of Male Power* (ed. Cheryl Exum and Johanna W.H. Van Wijk-Bos; Semeia, 42; Atlanta, GA: Scholars Press, 1988), pp. 37-67; and Ellen van Wolde, 'Texts in Dialogue with Texts: Intertextuality in the Ruth and Tamar Dialogues', *BI* 5 (1997), pp. 1-28.

her carnally without any awareness whatsoever. (Think of the drunken Lot with his daughters.) On the other hand, a woman being possessed in sex, apparently the object, may yet be the subject; the only possessor of the volatile element of awareness. She may *know* the man that *mis-takes* her.[13]

What happens in the book of Ruth, however, is an act of recognition that displaces the potential seduction at the granary to the town gates (Ruth 4.1), the gates of the law, the site of adjudication.[14] There Ruth enters the community of God, the man fully conscious, the marriage consummated, presumably after the wedding. Only then is the chosen seed conceived with all I's dotted and T's crossed—fully legitimate, legally certified. Does *Megillat Ruth* thereby really affirm conformity to the law or shift its line? As Jacob Licht contends, the story 'endeavors to show how the apparently reprehensible female ancestor has been absorbed into the thoroughly respectable family of Boaz in a perfectly proper way, and for irreproachable reasons'.[15] Perfectly proper? Well, not quite! Ruth too transgresses norms, both as a Moabite and a potential seductress.

In comparing these seduction scenes, from the hill caves overlooking Zoar to the entrance of Enaim and to the granary in Bethlehem, I focus on the use of the verbs 'to know' [*yd'*] and 'to recognize/acknowledge' [*nkr*]— the movement from 'knowing', or rather 'not knowing', to 'recognition' over the narrative arc of these three stories. The use of the former verb, *yd'*, is consistently marked by a double entendre, an irony where women are 'in the know' about identity while men 'know' only through the flesh. The latter, *nkr*, supplements or complements the verb *yd'*, as it entails both recognition in a face-to-face encounter and acknowledgment at the level of conscience. The act of recognition allows a gap between self and other, the presence of two separate beings as subjects, whereas *yd'*, at least in the sexual sense, collapses them.[16] The play between these verbs is key to the

---

13. Jagendorf, 'Genesis and the Reversal of Sexual Knowledge', p. 188.
14. For a discussion of the town's gate as the traditional site of public justice, see Bernard Levinson, *Legal Revision and Religious Renewal in Ancient Israel* (New York: Cambridge University Press, 2008), pp. 37-38.
15. Jacob Licht, *Storytelling in the Bible* (Jerusalem: Magnes Press, 1978), p. 125 (Heb.), quoted in Greenstein, 'Reading Strategies', p. 226 n. 41.
16. For this use of the verb 'to know [*yd'*]', see BDB entry 3819 (p. 395), definition 3: 'to *know a person* carnally, of sexual intercourse' (cf. Gen. 4.1, 17, 24; 24.16; 38.26; 1 Sam. 1.19; 1 Kgs 1.4, in which King David did *not* know Abishag); to refer to a woman who either has 'known' or 'not known' man (sexually), see Gen. 19.8; Num. 31.16, 18, 35; and Judg. 11.39 and 21.11. With regard to the intended act of 'sodomy', see Gen. 19.5 and Judg. 19.22; and the gang rape of the concubine of Gibeah, Judg. 19.25. On the verb 'to regard, recognize [*nkr*]', primarily in the hiphil, see BDB entry 6136 (p. 648), especially as it traverses episodes of misrecognition/recognition in the Jacob, Judah, Joseph and Ruth narratives: Gen. 27.23; 31.32; 37.32 and 33; 38.25 and 26; Gen. 42.7-8 (3x, to be discussed in Chapter 9); and Ruth 2.10, 19 and 3.14. The lexicon, however,

central theme of redemption in *Megillat Ruth*. The question is how her story stays within the lines of the seemingly 'perfectly proper' while remaining risqué, challenging us to look beyond the norms of Judean society to find room at the gates of the law for anomaly.[17]

Ḥesed—On the Fissure between Nomos and Narrative

The coda on David's lineage notwithstanding, the rabbis were perplexed by *Megillat Ruth*. What is the purpose of this scroll? It teaches us nothing about law; it does not further the Israelite history in recounting political intrigues between prophet, judge, priest or king; and God is conspicuously absent (though often invoked in blessings to kith and kin). In the words of R. Ze'ira,

> This scroll [of Ruth] tells us nothing of purity or of impurity, of prohibition or permission. For what purpose then was it written? To teach how great is the reward of those who do deeds of kindness [*le-gomlei ḥasadim*].[18]

Indeed, the theme of *ḥesed* is predominant throughout the book of Ruth. The term itself appears at three critical junctures in the story—often translated as 'loving kindness, faithfulness or mercy'. It has been compared to the Greek term *agape* or the Latin *caritas* (from which the term 'charity' is derived) and is often misconstrued as a 'pure', 'selfless' love grounded in

---

does not acknowledge the paradoxical relationship between the hiphil form of the verb *nkr*, 'to recognize', with respect to the hithpael, meaning 'to make oneself strange' (as in Gen. 42.7; 1 Kgs 14.5-6; BDB entry 6143, p. 649), and the adjective form, *nokhri/iya*, 'stranger, alien' (BDB entry 6142, p. 649), which we will discuss later.

17. Ruth Kaniel Kara-Ivanov, similarly, engages in a deep-level reading of these narratives, primarily through the lens of rabbinic literature and the Zohar. See her dissertation, *Motherhood and Seduction in the Myth of David's Messianic Dynasty: The Hebrew Bible, Rabbinic Literature and the Zoharic Corpus* (PhD diss., Hebrew University of Jerusalem, 2010) (Heb.). On the analysis of Lot's daughters, see her article 'Seed from Another Place: Transformation of the Account of Lot's Daughters', in *Jerusalem Studies in Jewish Thought* 22 (2011), pp. 91-119 (Heb.), and '*Gedolah Averah Lishmah*—Mothers of the Davidic Dynasty, Feminine Seduction and the Development of Messianic Thought from Rabbinic Literature to Luzzatto', *Nashim* 24 (2013), pp. 27-52. She and I both focus on the subversive (yet divinely elected) acts of women in the making of the messianic dynasty, though my reading centers on the biblical text, while hers is on the rabbinic and later works, primarily the Zohar. With regard to the overarching movement from the daughters of Lot (overt incest) and Tamar (harlotry), to Ruth's near seduction of Boaz in the granary, Kara-Ivanov argues that the drama undergoes a 'softening' or 'sublimation' of the sexual encounter, whereas I suggest that there is an overt deferral and resolution at the 'gates of the city'. She emphasizes the antinomian trend in all three narratives, while I trace the movement toward redemption and recognition *within* the law.

18. *Ruth R.* 2.14.

giving without the expectation of return.[19] This is a love supposedly free of *eros*, not skewed by the magnetics of gender.

Rather than an expression of selfless, unconditional love, *ḥesed* suggests devotion or fidelity to commitment in the Hebrew Bible. Naomi first invokes the term when she turns to her daughters-in-law, Orpah and Ruth, to dissuade them from following her to Bethlehem: 'Turn back, each of you to her mother's house. May the LORD deal kindly with you [*ya'as Yhwh 'imakhem ḥesed*], as you have dealt with the dead and with me!' (Ruth 1.8). In this blessing, Naomi appeals to God to reward the young women, emulating their devotion to their husbands and her, their mother-in-law. Similarly when Boaz enters their lives, Naomi praises God, 'who has not failed in his kindness [*ḥesed*] to the living or to the dead' (2.20). She then identifies Boaz as the redeeming kinsman, the one who will enact God's providence for her in the world! Boaz will suggest the same idea when he turns to Ruth in praise: 'Be blessed of Yhwh, daughter! Your latest deed of kindness [*ḥesed*] is greater than the first . . .' (3.10). Here, Boaz alludes to Ruth's loyalty to her mother-in-law and her discretion in not following after the young men in the field (and, instead, demonstrating fidelity to him). In all these verses, God is invoked as the source of *ḥesed*, mirroring human acts of kindness in a mode of *imitatio hominis*. In the book of Ruth, *ḥesed* is about loyalty not unconditional love per se.[20]

---

19. This distinction between *eros* and *agape* was first articulated by the Lutheran theologian Anders Nygren (*Agape and Eros* [New York: Harper & Row, 1969]). The crux of his argument is that *eros* is acquisitive and self-serving, expressing a desire to enhance one's happiness or well-being by seeking something of value, while *agape*, associated with Christian love, is altruistic and unmotivated: giving without seeking anything in return. André LaCocque adopts this Christian understanding of love in *Ruth: A Continental Commentary* (trans. K.C. Hanson; Minneapolis, MN: Fortress Press, 2004). He claims that the term *ḥesed* 'is an opening on an interpretation of the Law that surpasses the letter' (p. 28). By projecting these charactcristics onto *ḥesed*, we perpetuate these false Christian theological tropes that juxtapose 'the law', as obligation or duty, and love as beyond law. This dichotomy is not borne out in the way *ḥesed* is deployed in the Hebrew Bible. My thoughts on this arise from a long, enduring conversation with my philosopher friend Simon May, author of *Love: A History* (New Haven, CT: Yale University Press, 2011).

20. As in 2 Sam. 9.7, where David, in kindness (*ḥesed*) invites Mephibosheth, Jonathan's one surviving son, to eat at the king's table for the remainder of his life in honor of his covenant with his beloved friend; and in 1 Kgs 2.7, David, at the end of his life, invites the sons of Barzillai the Gileadite to do the same as a reward for the loyalty/ kindness [*ḥesed*] of the old man toward him during the civil war. It sometimes connotes forgiveness, grouped along with other divine attributes (as in Exod. 34.6). With regard to God's actions, it most often entails upholding the covenant, as with Abraham (Mic. 7.20), with Moses and Israel (as in Deut. 7.9, 12; 1 Kgs 8.23; 2 Chron. 6.14; Neh. 1.5; 9.32), and with David and his dynasty (2 Sam. 7.15, and so forth). It often describes God's actions in rewarding future descendants or guaranteeing the promise of an heir

Yet it is not just a word with which to thresh the semantic field; *hesed* is also a predominant theme. Nowhere is this more highlighted than in Ruth's famous declaration of loyalty, perhaps the greatest love poem of the Hebrew Bible, oddly addressed by a young widow to her mother-in-law: 'For where you go, I will go [*ka'asher telkhi 'elekh*]; wherever you lodge, I will lodge; your people shall be my people, and your God my God . . .' (1.16-17). Ruth is moved by loyalty to follow Naomi to a land, to a people, to a God she has not known, literally to *go forth* [*hlkh*], just as Abraham followed the word of God: 'Go forth [*lekh lekha*] from your land, your kin, your father's house . . .' (Gen. 12.1). The human characteristic of *hesed* pervades Ruth's behavior, just as it did the first patriarch. As Tamar Cohn Eskenazi summarizes,

> When still in Moab, Naomi is the widow, the poor, and the stranger. In refusing to abandon Naomi, Ruth embodies *hesed* (1.8, 16-17). Ruth's loyalty to her mother-in-law inspires wealthy Boaz, who extends generosity toward Ruth, stretching himself beyond the call of duty (2.8-12). The domino effect continues: Naomi, enlivened by Ruth's success with Boaz, regains hope and takes responsibility for Ruth's welfare (3.1-4). At the threshing floor, Ruth draws Boaz toward his better self by urging him to undertake the role of redeemer (3.9-10). As a result, Boaz extends the circle of *hesed* into the public arena (4.1-10), linking redemption of the land to the redeemer's responsibility for the widows and their deceased husbands. Then, going even further beyond the redeemer's call of duty, he marries Ruth, taking the fullest responsibility for her. The circle of *hesed* reaches its fullness when the entire community blesses their union (4.11-12).

In Eskenazi's understanding, *hesed* is about going beyond the call of duty, beyond social expectations, and it reverberates outward from the individual to the community. Though Ruth acts in the absence of a divine call, her acts of *hesed* and the blessings invoking the term inspire the awareness of God's providence. It reflects the earthbound compassion of the divine gaze effected through human kindness, 'optical instruments of the divine'.[21] But this kindness, or loyalty rather, acquires a transcendent quality—not transcendent of the self but of the limits of law. It breaches or stretches, rather, the boundaries of obligation—relational and otherwise.

In his seminal essay 'Nomos and Narrative', Robert Cover contextualizes the normative world of law in relation to myth or foundational narratives: 'No set of legal institutions or prescriptions exists apart from the narratives that locate it and give it meaning. For every constitution there is an epic, for each Decalogue a scripture. Once understood in the context of the nar-

---

(cf. Gen. 24.12, 26; 32.11; Deut. 7.12; 1 Kgs 3.5; Ps. 62.13). See the essay by Tikva Frymer-Kensky, 'Hesed in the Bible', in *The JPS Bible Commentary: Ruth* (Philadelphia, PA: Jewish Publication Society, 2011), pp..xlviii-l.

21. This is Levinas's term, cited in Handelman, *Fragments of Redemption*, p. 270.

ratives that give it meaning, law becomes not merely a system of rules to be observed, but a world in which we live'.[22] To illustrate the dynamic between law and narrative, Cover draws on 'the precept of succession' (primogeniture) in Scripture, where the firstborn inherits a double portion from his father's estate, even if he is the son of the 'despised' (that is, less beloved) wife (Deut. 21.15-17). Yet so many of the narratives in Genesis seem to contradict this precept; primogeniture is almost ubiquitously overturned. In the final redacted version of the canon, the biblical narratives lie alongside the text in Deuteronomy in palpable tension. As Cover summarizes,

> These texts included: (1) the story of Cain and Abel, in which God accepts the sacrifice of Abel, the younger son, rather than that of Cain, the elder, and in which Seth, the third born, ultimately becomes the progenitor of the human race; (2) the story of Ishmael and Isaac, in which Ishmael, the first fruit of Abraham's loins, is cast out so that the birthright might pass to Isaac, the later son born of the preferred wife; (3) the story of Esau, the first-born son of Isaac, who is denied his birthright by the trickery of Jacob, his younger brother; and (4) the story of Joseph and his brothers, in which Joseph—a younger child of the preferred wife—is favored by his father, dreams of his own primacy, provokes retaliation, and comes to rule over his brothers in an improbable political ascendancy in another land.[23]

These foundational stories all point to an incommensurability between *nomos*, that is, legal custom, and the narratives concerned with the election of the chosen heir through a divinely endorsed destiny or grace. God deliberately sets up an 'alternity', challenges the *nomos* in order to demonstrate that the privileged position cannot be assumed by any natural law or normative practice, but is bestowed upon the 'chosen one' by divine election. As Cover avers, these foundational biblical narratives 'always retained their subversive force—the memory that divine destiny is not lawful'.[24] But, as he argues, this is *not* an antinomian phenomenon but characteristic, rather, of the foundational narratives of any culture or civilization in its formative

---

22. Robert Cover, 'The Supreme Court, 1082 Term—Foreword: Nomos and Narrative', *Harvard Law Review* 97.4 (1983), pp. 4-68. I am grateful to Avivah Zornberg for pointing me to this source. See her discussion of Cover in 'Law and Narrative in the Book of Ruth', in *Murmuring Deep*, pp. 348-50.

23. Cover, 'Nomos and Narrative', p. 20. To this impressive list, Cover adds the displacement of Aaron by Moses, the younger son, as leader of the exodus, and David, first of the Judean kings and the youngest of Jesse's sons. The narrative in 1 Samuel 16 highlights the surprise element, against normative expectations, in the selection of the king for anointing from among Jesse's sons. When Samuel assumes that it is Eliab, the firstborn, God adjures the prophet, 'Do not look on his appearance or on the height of his stature, because I have rejected him; for Yhwh does not see as mortals see; they look on the outward appearance, but Yhwh looks on the heart' (1 Sam. 16.7). It is precisely this divine principle that Cover insists on reading as the role redemption in law.

24. Cover, 'Nomos and Narrative', p. 24.

period. The Bible presumed a normative universe, where meaning making was bound by law yet 'required a well-honed sense of where the rule would end and why'.[25] In adopting Cover's model of the tension between *nomos* and narrative, we see Ruth not in antinomian terms but rather as reforming or, rather, transforming the interpretation of law. It is shaped by a redemptive arc that sets in relief the tension between the 'the "is" and the "ought", and the "what might be". . . . It presumes (1) the unredeemed character of reality as we know it, (2) the fundamentally different reality that should take its place, and (3) the replacement of the one with the other. The term "redemptive" also has the connotation of saving or freeing *persons,* not only "worlds" or understandings'.[26] We are compelled to return to origins, to stand, again, at Sinai while it quakes at our feet.

Using Robert Cover, we read the book of Ruth as a means of freeing not only the eponymous heroine from the seeming stricture of law but also as a way of redeeming the 'world' of biblical norms. Ay, there's the rub! According to the opinion of Rabbi Ze'ira, in the midrash, *ḥesed* really has nothing to do with law. Indeed, there is no direct allusion to laws concerned with purity and impurity or to prohibition or permission in the book of Ruth. Yet the story is fraught with implied social sanctions. All those who do acts of kindness [*gomlei ḥasadim*] in the *Megillah* rub against the grain of the law, and this is precisely why the story of Ruth is so very compelling. Consider the integration of Ruth the Moabite into the Judean fold. The reader is called to question the exclusion of the Moabites and ultimately the separation of Lot from Abraham—a separation that ends by grafting the old branch, which had been lopped off from the clan, back onto the Israelite tree.[27] As discussed earlier, many Bible critics understand this inclusion of Ruth 'the Moabite' as indicative of a tension between Ruth and the precept forbidding 'foreign women' (under Ezra and Nehemiah). But it is actually a much deeper thread that runs throughout the book of Ruth, made most explicit by the theme of illicit sexual relations in the background narratives from the book of Genesis leading to the Messianic dynasty.

In many other ways, the *Megillah* introduces alternative, or non-normative expressions of legal precepts from the Pentateuch. For example, the final chapter demonstrates a rather idiosyncratic understanding of levirate marriage, where the nearest kin is not the brother of the deceased but a distant relative.[28] At the 'gates of the law', Boaz proposes that the nearest

---

25. Cover, 'Nomos and Narrative', p. 22.
26. Cover, 'Nomos and Narrative', pp. 34-35.
27. I draw this metaphor both from the Talmud (*b. Yeb.* 63a) and Paul's epistle to the gentiles in Rom. 11.23-24. See n. 50.
28. See Deut. 25.5-10. Outside the book of Deuteronomy, the term for levirate marriage, *yibbum* [from the root *ybm*], is mentioned only in Gen. 38.8 and in Ruth 1.15. In the latter verse, Naomi refers to Orpah, Ruth's sister-in-law, as her *yebemet.* In *yibbum,*

kin, *Ploni 'Almoni* (Mr So-and-So),[29] redeem Naomi's lands, and at first he is willing (Ruth 4.5). But when Boaz insists that the nearest of kin must marry the widow of the deceased, Ruth 'the Moabite', in order to reclaim Elimelech's land, the anonymous redeemer refuses to fulfill the condition (v. 6). In *ad hoc* fashion, Boaz makes the redemption of land contingent on the 'redemption of seed',[30] although they are not intrinsically linked in other biblical passages.[31] Instead of retaining Naomi's lands, the inheritance

the brother or redeeming kinsman [*go'el*], raises seed through the widow of the deceased in order to guarantee an heir for his relative's land holding. In the *Megillah*, this precept is enacted for Naomi through Boaz's marriage to Ruth, the widow of Machlon. Boaz, however, is not Machlon's brother, nor is the child named after the deceased. The passage in Genesis 38, along with ancient Near Eastern texts, suggests that there are variations on levirate practice that do not conform to the strictures outlined in Deuteronomy. Though many biblical scholars reject the notion that the union of Ruth and Boaz is a form of levirate marriage (see the discussion in Eskenazi and Frymer-Kensky in *The JPS Bible Commentary: Ruth*, pp. xxxii-xxxviii), I maintain that this legal background is presumed and transformed in the service of the overall theme of redemption in the *Megillah*.

29. The text preserves the anonymity of the nearest of kin, called *Peloni 'Almoni* (Ruth 4.1), which, according to Sasson, is characteristic of the juristic verisimilitude of this passage; essentially the term alludes to his function as 'redeemer [*go'el*]' (3.12-13). On the parallel use of this 'obscuring' term, *ploni 'almoni*, see 1 Sam. 21.3; 2 Kgs 6.8 (both referring to place 'such-and-such'), 'to whoever it was [*la-palmoni*]' (Dan. 8.13), with reference to a person (Jack Sasson, 'Farewell to "Mr. So and So" (Ruth 4.1)?', in *Making a Difference: Essays on the Bible and Judaism in Honor of Tamara Cohn Eskenazi* (ed. David J.A. Clines, Kent Harold Richards and Jacob L. Wright; Sheffield: Sheffield Phoenix Press, 2012), pp. 251-56.

30. The term *go'el zer'a* (redeemer of seed) is never used in the Bible, but the concept behind it is implied in the precept associated with levirate marriage (Deut. 25.5-6). Ramban, on Gen. 38.8, explains that this 'secret of redemption' has the impetus to overcome the incest taboo. To reject the injunction to do the duty of the *levir* is a source of shame in the community, as implied by the ceremony of *halitzah* (lit. 'the loosening of the shoe', in Deut. 25.9-10, a variation of which is enacted in Ruth 4.7).

31. In the redemption of land, a near relative (*go'el*) comes to repossess, on behalf of his kin, a landholding that had been sold or dispossessed due to debt, enslavement, a period of exile and/or the absence of heirs (Lev. 25.23-28). For a detailed discussion of the *ad hoc* application of these precepts in the *Megillah*, see Adele Berlin, 'Legal Fiction: Levirate "cum" Land Redemption in Ruth', *Journal of Ancient Judaism* 1 (2010), pp. 3-18. Berlin argues that the innovations in the law do not reflect practice specific to a historical context nor do they reflect 'midrash', a new interpretation of the law, but indicate deliberately constructed 'legal fictions' that reflect a process of 'scripturalization'—the intertextual use of earlier biblical passages to give authorial weight to a later biblical work. According to Levinson, this is a form of 'conscious archaizing'—most clearly demonstrated by the narrator's comment on the legal ceremony conducted at the gates of the town: 'Thus formerly [*lefanim*] it was done in Israel in cases of redemption or exchange . . .' (Ruth 4.7). See the discussion in Levinson, *Legal Revision*, pp. 33-45.

would go the child born of this quasi-levirate union. As Bernard Levinson points out, the closer kin (who is disparaged as nameless) 'would disadvantage himself by purchasing the land that would paradoxically not increase his estate but rather transfer out of it'.[32]

Yet why, at first, does Peloni Almoni accept the role of redeemer when it relates to land but decline when Boaz links it to the obligation to marry Ruth 'the Moabite'? There is something in Ruth's status as Moabite that retains its stigma.[33] The nearest kin avows, 'I cannot redeem it for myself, lest I corrupt/mar my own inheritance [*pen 'ashḥit et naḥalati*] . . .' (Ruth 4.6). The verse echoes the refusal of Onan, Judah's second son, to raise seed in the name of his dead brother: 'And he spilled *it* [seed] on the ground [*ve-shiḥet 'artzah*], lest he give seed to his brother' (Gen. 38.9). Onan then dies by divine decree. Similarly, the book of Ruth condemns the foil to Boaz, Peloni Almoni, who, ironically, in fearing the 'corruption of his estate' [*shḥt*], refuses to 'raise seed in the name of the dead', and thus metaphorically spills seed, neglecting the call of redemption—that is, redemption in Cover's sense of the term, as expanding the normative understanding of law. Boaz is valorized for daring to do so. It is the barb of Ruth's Moabite status, as linked to the redemption of land via this quasi-levirate scheme, that Boaz gallantly transcends.

All three of the central characters—Naomi, Ruth and Boaz—in quiet, yet deeply heroic ways, defy social and legal norms, and in so doing, transform them. In Cover's conceptual scheme, *nomos* and narrative are not antithetical to each other but operate in dynamic tension. The principle of *ḥesed*, then, is not above or beyond the law but rather a mode of shifting the line; it grates even as it glistens.

The term *ḥesed* assumes a darker hue, however, against the background of the stories of the daughters of Lot and Tamar in Genesis. In an anomalous use of the word, *ḥesed* connotes the shame or reproach of incest in Leviticus: 'If a man takes his sister, a daughter of his father or a daughter of his mother, and sees her nakedness, and she sees his nakedness, it is a disgrace [*ḥesed*] . . .' (Lev. 20.17). Though the rules of philology discourage any connection between this usage of the term and the way it is deployed in

---

32. Levinson, *Legal Revision*, p. 38. Linking the role of the redeemer of land (*go'el 'adamah*), as outlined in Lev. 25.25-28, to that of the redeemer of seed in levirate marriage could compromise the inheritance for his own children. The land he redeems with his own money will pass to the child (Naomi's descendant), who is not his legal heir. See the discussion in Frymer-Kensky, *Reading the Women of the Bible*, p. 251, and Greenstein's detailed n. 112 in 'Reading Strategies', pp. 230-31.

33. This is Zakovitch's argument (*Ruth*, pp. 8-20 and 106-107). Mieke Bal goes even further and suggests that Mr. So-and-So assumed that, in acting as redeemer, he would be transgressing the law against intermarrying with the Moabites (Deut. 23.4) (*Lethal Love*, p. 81).

the book of Ruth,[34] the taboo of incest percolates below the surface in the foundational narratives in Genesis that serve as the backdrop to the Davidic dynasty. Tamar seduces her father-in-law, Judah, and they beget Perez, the ancestor of Boaz. Yet, according to the holiness code, sexual relations between daughter and father-in-law are strictly forbidden (Lev. 18.10, 15). Lot's daughters seduce him, and the elder bears a son, naming him Moab (lit. 'of the father'). Yet a verse in Leviticus states, 'You shall not uncover the nakedness of your father . . .' (Lev. 18.7).[35] The author of the book of Ruth would be well aware of these taboos in the union of Boaz of Judah and Ruth of Moab. Both David's paternal and maternal lineages are overcast by these shadowy sexual liaisons. The acts of *hesed* go beyond the letter of the law or, rather, shift its line in the *Megillah*, drawing from the alternative meaning of *hesed* as incest between brother and sister. It implies excess of intimacy, endogamy gone awry. Akin to worm-rot, it threatens to climb the root and infect the trunk, undermining the strength and stature of the tree unless an antidote to that rot, a powerful admixture of the same potential poison, could heal the root and save the branches from ruin. In the Abrahamic legacy, the worm-rot begins with a fetid drop in a cave overlooking the Jordan Valley all ablaze.

The Story of Lot's Daughters

The story of Lot's seduction by his daughters can be read etiologically as an account for why the nations of Moab and Ammon embody both a forbidden and a protected status. They cannot enter the community of Yhwh (Deut. 23.4), yet no war may be waged against them (Deut. 2.9, 19). According to Deuteronomy, they are proscribed, untouchable. Lot, Abraham's nephew

---

34. This meaning of *hesed* as 'shame, reproach, or disgrace' is also deployed in Prov. 14.34, and as a verb [piel] in Prov. 25.10, 'Lest he reproach you [*pen yehasedkha*] and expose you to shame'. The root may derive from the Aramaic *ḥisd'a*, meaning 'shame'. See BDB entry 3285.

35. While the formulation, in Hebrew, is in the second person masculine [*l'o tegaleh*], and so may be presumed to apply only to the son (and not the daughter), the verse introducing the list of forbidden sexual liaisons makes a general caveat against incest: 'None of you shall approach anyone near of kin to uncover nakedness: I am Yhwh' (Lev. 18.6; cf. 18.17). Frymer-Kensky points out that the absence of an explicit prohibition against incest with one's daughter suggests that 'the legal corpora were squeamish about reinforcing this taboo' (*Reading the Women of the Bible*, p. 261). I disagree with her analysis. The default position for address is always the male in the Pentateuch; it in no way implies that incest between father and daughter was not condemned. For a discussion of these incest laws, see S.F. Bigger, 'The Family Laws of Leviticus 18 and their Setting', *JBL* 98 (1979), pp. 187-93; Jonathan Ziskind, 'The Missing Daughter in Leviticus xviii', *VT* 46 (1996), pp. 125-30; and Tirzah Meacham, 'The Missing Daughter: Leviticus 18-20', *ZAW* 109 (1997), pp. 254-59.

and the patriarch of these two nations, belongs to the Terahide clan, yet his descendants are excluded from intermarrying with the Israelites. While the patriarchs all marry nieces or cousins within the Terahide clan, Lot's line becomes tainted. This moment of breaking off from the familial band begins with Lot's choice to settle by Sodom in the Jordan Valley, which was well watered 'like Yhwh's garden' (Gen. 13.10), though the people were 'evil and great sinners' against God (v. 13). He remains an outsider to them, and seemingly defies their custom of spurning the stranger, demonstrated when God sends down two messengers to 'see altogether whether they have done according to the outcry' (18.21). Lot's generosity, *hesed* toward the stranger, however, turns against itself—poisons the seed, so to speak, when it entails the sacrifice of daughters and the ultimate outcome: incest.

Sodom's heinousness hinges on the violation of the codes of hospitality, their complete disregard for *hesed*; the men of the city wish to violate rather than welcome the strangers in their midst. When the two divine messengers are taken in by Lot, all the men of Sodom form a collective mob, surround the house, and demand to 'know' the guests (19.5)—that is, they wish to sexually violate them, literally, 'to know them' in the biblical sense.[36] To stall them, Lot offers his two daughters, 'who have not known a man' (v. 8), though the men refuse to be placated by female substitutes and a dazzling light must intervene to save the guests and prevent the storming of the house. Were it not for this divine intervention, Lot's two virgin daughters might have been subject to the same fate as the concubine of Gibeah (Judges 19), thrust out the door to protect the male guest sequestered within, and then gang raped all night only to return to be dismembered as a call to arms in civil war.[37] Sodom later becomes associated with the 'sin' of homosexuality, but the deeper transgression revolves around the will to exclude and even harm the stranger. As Robert Alter observes, the behavior of the Sodomites is presented as a violation of civilized norms.[38] Later in the Hebrew Bible, Sodom and Gomorrah become a byword for absolute evil in a society that warrants wholesale destruction by God.[39]

---

36. In Hebrew, *neda'a 'otam*, from the root *yd'*. See n. 16.

37. For an analysis of this episode, see Phyllis Trible, 'An Unnamed Woman: The Extravagance of Violence: Judges 19:1-30', in *Texts of Terror* (Philadelphia, PA: Fortress Press, 1984), pp. 64-87; and Alice Bach, 'Rereading the Body Politic', in *Women in the Hebrew Bible* (ed. Alice Bach; London: Routledge, 1999), pp. 389-401. For an overview of the literature comparing Genesis 19 and Judges 19, see Frymer-Kensky, *Reading the Women of the Bible*, pp. 388-89 n. 124.

38. Robert Alter, 'Sodom as Nexus: The Web of Design in Biblical Narrative', in *The Book and the Text: The Bible and Literary Theory* (ed. Regina M. Schwartz; Oxford: Blackwell, 1990), p. 151.

39. Isa. 1.9-10; 3.9; 13.19; Jer. 23.14; 49.18; 50.40; Amos 4.11; Zeph. 2.9; and Lam. 4.6. Their sins include complete disregard for the needy, the rejection of *hesed*. In Ezek.

In their brilliant analysis of this episode, Ronald Hendel, Chana Kronfeld and Ilana Pardes comment,

> Lot's choice to offer his daughters to the men of Sodom involves a dangerous exchange. He chooses to value the rule of hospitality higher than his duty to protect his virgin daughters. In so doing, he preserves his home as host but is stained with shame as father. It would seem that—to Lot's eyes—his duty to other males is a higher value than his duty to his daughters. The hierarchy of power is such that daughters can be sacrificed in deference to male obligations. His speech makes the gender hierarchy clear; '... but to these men, do not do anything'. This is a heightened example of the inner contradictions of the patriarchal value systems which are exposed in a moment of crisis.[40]

Eventually Lot flees and survives with only these two virgin daughters in toe, his other daughters left behind (bound in marriage to mocking sons-in-law), while his wife is turned into the proverbial pillar of salt. That night of terror, with the threat of violation, expressed by the Sodomites' will 'to know' the other as an object of humiliation, is mirrored in the subsequent seduction in the cave. These same daughters, who might have been the victims of that violation, seduce their father, turning him into an object of *their knowing*. Is their seduction, *quid pro quo*, a strange mode of vengeance for offering them up as a substitute for the male guests? Or should it be understood as a desperate act of survivors? Within the metanarrative in Genesis, the episode tells of us of Moab's origins, in the traumatic wake of impending violence.

> Now Lot went up out of Zoar and settled in the hills with his two daughters, for he was afraid to stay in Zoar; so he lived in a cave with his two daughters. And the firstborn said to the younger, 'Our father is old, and there is not a man on earth to come in to us after the manner of all the earth. Come, let us make our father drink wine, and we will lie with him, so that we may cause seed to live by our father.' So they made their father drink wine that

---

16.49-50, their transgressions are attributed to pride and stinginess, unwilling to 'aid the poor and the needy'. In rabbinic lore, *midat Sedom* (the characteristics of Sodom) is associated with one who says, 'what is mine is mine and what is yours is yours' (*m. 'Av.* 5.10). In rabbinic literature, the halachic principle of *kofim 'al midat sedom* empowers the court to force the litigant *not* to be strict in adherence to his rights and, rather, act compassionately, according to the principles of *ḥesed* (*b. B. Bat.* 12b, 59a, 168a; *b. 'Eruv.* 49a; and *b. Ket.* 103a). For an overview of early exegesis on the sins of Sodom, see James Kugel, *The Bible as It Was* (Cambridge, MA: Harvard University Press, 1997), pp. 187-89. It is interesting that Ruth, who emerges out of this morass as a descendant of Moab (conceived in the shadow of Sodom's destruction), epitomizes the opposite traits and thus, by virtue, belongs to the Israelites.

40. Ronald Hendel, Chana Kronfeld and Ilana Pardes, 'Gender and Sexuality', in *Reading Genesis* (ed. Ronald Hendel; Berkeley, CA: University of California Press, 2010), p. 86.

night; and the firstborn went in, and lay with her father; he did not know her lying down or her getting up [*ve-lo' yad'a be-shikhvah u-ve-qumah*]. On the next day, the firstborn said to the younger, 'Look, I lay last night with my father; let us make him drink wine tonight also; then you go in and lie with him, so that we may cause seed to live by our father'. So they made their father drink wine that night also; and the younger rose, and lay with him; and he did not know her lying down or her getting up [*ve-lo' yad'a be-shikhvah u-ve-qumah*]. Thus both the daughters of Lot became pregnant by their father. The firstborn bore a son, and named him Moab; he is the ancestor of the Moabites to this day. The younger also bore a son and named him Ben-ammi; he is the ancestor of the Ammonites to this day (Gen. 19.30-38, author's trans.).

This scene follows the destruction of Sodom. Lot and his daughters witness the sky falling—sulphur and fire raining from heaven. Following the debacle, the daughters are infused with a sense of the utter destruction, in the wake of the Great Deluge of the Earth (Genesis 6–9). This must be the end of the world as they know it, for they say to themselves, 'there is not a man on earth to come in to us after the manner of all the world' (v. 31). They feel impelled to guarantee the continuity of humanity.[41] Judah's lineage, similarly, faces near extinction in Genesis 38, and the house of Elimelech is on the verge of demise until 'life finds a way' through Ruth. This threat of extinction propels the women into 'forbidden territory'; the daughters of Lot violate the incest taboo. As Frymer-Kensky points out, 'When the posterity of their house is in peril, these women act unconventionally, even contra-conventionally, to preserve it. Subverting one cultural norm, conventional sexual mores, they reinforce and support an even more primal principle, paternal lineage'.[42]

Though no overt censure is voiced in Genesis, the necessity of deceit implies how very fraught their act was. The cave, according to Hendel, Kronfeld and Pardes, 'serves as a metonymy of anti-culture, far from the comforts of home and civilization. A cave is a home for wild animals and Cyclops, where cultural norms do not apply'.[43] The women enter this dark, primitive space to reverse social norms and invert hierarchies of knowledge and power. Twice we are told that the drunken Lot did not know 'her lying down or her getting up [*ve-lo' yad'a be-shikhvah u-ve-qumah*]' (vv. 33, 35). Despite his carnal knowledge of them, they alone possess 'the volatile element of awareness'. In Jagendorf's words, they '*know* the man that *mis-takes* them'. The progeny born of this incestuous union are named

---

41. There is no way of knowing if their intent was the renewal of the entire human race, as *Gen. R.* 57.10 sees it, or just the perpetuation of their father's name, as Radak [R. David Kimchi on Gen. 19.31-32] believes.
42. Frymer-Kensky, *Reading the Women of the Bible*, p. 263.
43. Hendel, Kronfeld and Pardes, 'Gender and Sexuality', p. 87.

accordingly: Moab, born of the elder, meaning 'of the father' [*mi 'av*], and Ammon, born of the younger, meaning 'son of my [father's] kinsman'. Endogamy, marriage within the clan, has gone awry. No judgment is cast in this context, but later, it is precisely these two nations that, according to the passage in Deuteronomy, will 'never enter the congregation of Yhwh . . .' (Deut. 23.4).[44] 'The two nations, the devastation of the Dead Sea region, and the lone pillar of salt are reminders of the dangerous history of sexuality in Sodom, the antitype of civilization'.[45] Moab, as the progeny of Lot and his elder daughter, who had not known man, is born out of this morass. The famous descendant of this union, Ruth, will wrestle with these shadows both overtly, as an agent of *ḥesed,* and covertly, in transforming the sexually transgressive reputation of the Moabite.

Blessed or Engrafted

If we take a wide-angle lens to the scene, the story highlights the tension between endogamy and exogamy in the context of the patriarchal narratives. The legal prohibition in Deuteronomy gestures toward a taboo against mixing with peoples of incestuous origin. The law prohibiting Moabites and Ammonites from entering the 'congregation of Yhwh' even unto the tenth generation (Deut. 23.4), is immediately preceded by the same formula with respect to the 'bastard' [*mamzer*] conceived of an illicit union (v. 3). It is this covert sexual stigmatization with respect to Moab and Ammon that lingers across the generations. Furthermore, the explicit reason given for their forbidden status seems trumped up: 'because they did not meet you with food and water on your journey out of Egypt, and because they hired against you Balaam son of Beor, from Pethor of Mesopotamia, to curse you' (v. 4).[46] It runs against the grain of their protected status in Deut. 2.9 and 19. Perhaps the suppression of the incestuous origins of the Moabites and their association with the Baal Peor incident (Num. 25.1-9) stems from a positive stance to their ancestor Lot, who is of Abraham's stock, his nephew no less. He belongs to *toledot Teraḥ*, as all the wives of the patriarchs did—Sarah, Rebekah, Rachel and Leah. There is an implied mandate to marry within the clan in the patriarchal narratives. Brueggemann highlights the positive status that these two nations maintain: 'If Lot is saved because of Abraham (cf. 19.19),[47] then it is also true that Moab and Ammon are blessed because of

---

44. For a thorough analysis of thematic development of this motif in rabbinic literature and the Zohar, see the dissertation of Ruth Kaniel Kara-Ivanov, *Motherhood and Seduction in the Myth of David's Messianic Dynasty*, cited in n. 17.

45. Hendel, Kronfeld and Pardes, 'Gender and Sexuality', p. 90.

46. See my comment in n. 6.

47. Abraham also rescues Lot from captivity in the war between the four and five Canaanite kings (Genesis 14).

Abraham (cf. 12.3, 18.18)'.[48] Yet Lot is effectively excluded from the 'lot' of the Terahide clan through the prohibition against the Israelites intermarrying with these nations. It seems that the entanglement between father and daughters points to the danger of intramarriage, when endogamy becomes too intimate, to the point of incest, a blurring of boundaries too close to be condoned.

The rabbis articulate the tension between the inclusion and exclusion of Lot in a clever play on words:

> Rabbi Elazar said, What is meant when it is written, 'And all the families of the earth shall be blessed through him [*va-nivrehku vo*, i.e., *brk* through/ onto Abraham]' (Gen. 18.18). The Holy One, blessed be He, said to Abraham, 'I have two good shoots/blessings [*brakhot*] to graft [*lehavrikh*] onto you: Ruth the Moabitess and Naamah the Ammonitess' (*b. Yeb.* 63a, author's trans.).[49]

The context of the biblical quote informs the interpretation. God muses on why he should reveal his plan to wipe out Sodom to the patriarch Abraham. And the answer is that he will ultimately prove to be a source of blessing to the families of the earth. In that same biblical passage, the patriarch will plead with God not to destroy the innocent along with the wicked, perhaps understood as an appeal to spare Lot and his family. The rabbis use this verse to reflect on Lot's merits, accrued by way of his female descendants. He will be spared the fate of Sodom, along with his daughters. The rabbinic source identifies these 'survivors' ancestors of Moab and Ammon with the 'families of the earth' that are excluded from Abraham's covenantal relationship with God, though blessed through him [*vo*]. Against the plain sense of the verse, R. Elazar understands the preposition *vo* as signifying how these 'families of the earth' may serve as a blessing *to* Abraham, many generations down the line, once their descendants are grafted back in. We see an interesting dynamic, here, between exclusion in the short term and inclusion in the long term. The interpretation engages in a word play where blessing [*brkh*] is read as 'engrafting' (in the causative, hiphil form). The image of grafting a branch from a wild olive tree onto a cultivated one in order to strengthen the stock is familiar to us from the Pauline epistles (Rom. 11.23-24).[50] Whether or not the midrashic source was aware of the text from the

---

48. Brueggemann, *Genesis*, p. 177

49. Ruth, as Moabite, and Naamah, as Ammonite, are engrafted back onto the 'tree' of the Israelite people—Ruth as the ancestor of David (Ruth 4.18-22) and Naamah as wife of Solomon and mother of King Rehoboam (1 Kgs 14.21), who was in turn the ancestor of several praiseworthy Judean kings: Hezekiah, Asa and Jehoshaphat, as well as the prophet Isaiah.

50. 'And even those of Israel, if they do not persist in unbelief, will be grafted in, for God has the power to graft them in again. For if you have been cut from what is by nature a wild olive tree and grafted, contrary to nature, into a cultivated olive tree, how

New Testament, the same idea underlies the metaphor: that which was once excluded, lopped off from the chosen line, may be grafted back on. According to the midrash, this engrafting is done by exceptional women who prove themselves, contrary to their ethnic origins, as belonging to Abraham's line by virtue of merit rather than blood right.

The tension between 'virtue' and 'blood right' plays itself out over the nexus of endogamy/exogamy. Edmund Leach, drawing on the structural anthropology of Lévi-Strauss, has analyzed the biblical narratives leading up to Solomon's succession as 'offering a "mediation" between an insistence on the need for a pure Israelite ancestry and a recognition that there had been intermarriage with foreigners. The synthesis achieved by the story of Solomon is such that by a kind of dramatic trick the reader is persuaded that the second of these descriptions (exogamy), which is morally bad, exemplifies the first description (endogamy), which is morally good'.[51] He dates these counternarratives to the period of Ezra and Nehemiah and lists the sexually transgressive, foreign women in the line of the messianic dynasty as Tamar, Rahab, Ruth, Bathsheba (wife of Uriah) and Abigail (*sic*) (based on Mt. 1.2-16). Despite the plethora of errors in Leach's analysis—philological, factual and theological[52]—the suggestion that a fundamental tension between endogamy and exogamy informs these messianic texts is deeply insightful. The question of their inclusion/exclusion *does* hinge on incest—when endogamy becomes excessive and necessarily engenders taboo status. Paradoxically, it is by virtue of their sexually transgressive acts that Lot's daughters sew themselves back into the patriarchal line. I argue that the tension between the binary opposites of exogamy/endogamy is negotiated over the course of these three episodes, diachronically, where the excluded becomes included once again.

Judah and Tamar Revisited: From Knowing to Recognition

As in the stories of Lot's daughters and of Ruth, the threat of extinction overshadows the story of Judah and Tamar in Genesis 38. We discussed this episode at length in the previous chapter, but I'd like to revisit it as the centerpiece of the narrative triptych that constitutes the backdrop to the

much more will these natural branches be grafted back into their own olive tree' (Rom. 11.23-24 NRSV).

51. Leach, 'The Legitimacy of Solomon', in *Genesis as Myth*, p. 31. See Chapter 1 nn. 6 and 67.

52. The most egregious of his errors is his characterization of Judaism as insistent on being a 'pure race'. Further, he anachronistically identifies the daughters of Lot, in Genesis, as 'foreign women' and Tamar (of unknown ancestry) as 'pure-blooded'. For a thorough critique of his analysis, see J.A. Emerton, 'An Examination of a Recent Structuralist Interpretation of Genesis xxxviii', *VT* 26 (1976), pp. 79-98.

Davidic dynasty. Following the sale of Joseph into slavery (Gen. 37), Judah descends 'from the presence of his brothers' (38.2) and marries a Canaanite woman. The birth of three sons quickly follows, and he marries the firstborn, Er, off to Tamar—who, though named, is of unknown ancestry. Despite his hurried attempt to secure biological continuity, he soon faces the near extinction of his line. The first son does evil in the eyes of God, and 'Yhwh put him to death' (v. 7). The second, Onan, refuses to do the duty of the levir (*yabam*). 'Knowing that the seed would not count as his, [he] let it go to waste [*ve-shihet 'artzah*, lit., corrupted/spoiled it upon the earth] whenever he joined with his brother's wife, so as not to provide offspring for his brother' (v. 9). He too dies by divine decree. This same act of defiance is echoed by the words of Peloni Almoni at the city gates, when he declines to redeem Naomi's land and marry Ruth (4.6). Perhaps the same motive underlies his refusal; the property he would have inherited will first go to the son of the firstborn, Er, thus conceived.

In this drama, as in the stories of Lot's daughters, the motif of incest percolates just below the surface. As Leviticus adjures,

> You shall not uncover the nakedness of your daughter-in-law: she is your son's wife; you shall not uncover her nakedness. You shall not uncover the nakedness of your brother's wife; it is your brother's nakedness (Lev. 18.15-16; cf. 20.21 NRSV).

The principle of levirate marriage, *yibbum*, provides an exception to the rule. According to Deuteronomy, a man has an obligation to his widowed sister-in-law: 'When brothers dwell together and one of them dies and leaves no son, the wife of the deceased shall not be married to a stranger, outside the family. Her husband's brother shall unite with her: take her as his wife and perform the levir's duty [*va-yibbemah*]' (Deut. 25.5). But when Judah's first son, Er, dies and the second son, Onan, fails to do his duty as the levir, the next in line is not necessarily Shelah, the youngest, but Judah himself. As Nahum Sarna points out, in ancient Near Eastern sources, the father-in-law could even assume the role of the levir, *yabam*.[53] Here, redemption of the childless widow, by granting her seed in the name of the deceased, trumps the laws of incest.

Initially, Judah treats his widowed daughter-in-law, Tamar, unconscionably. Blaming her as a true *femme fatale* for the death of his two sons, he sends her back to her father's house to live as a grass widow, with a false promise to marry her to his third son, Shelah, when he gets older. Years pass, perhaps even a decade, during which time she notes that her father-in-law's neglect is deliberate. In the meantime, Judah's Canaanite wife dies, and Tamar is told that her father-in-law is coming up to Timnah for the

---

53. See Chapter 3 n. 13.

sheep-shearing. She decides to take matters into her own hands, but in so doing, she assumes a terrible risk. As a woman bound by promise to another man, illicit relations with another would be considered on par with adultery. The severity of the consequences are later confirmed when Judah, upon discovering she is pregnant, orders that she be taken out and burned (Gen. 38.24).

The seduction scene (Gen. 38.14-19), as discussed in Chapter 3, takes place at the entrance to Enaim—perhaps at a crossroads, marked by a spring or well. The Hebrew place name, *Petaḥ 'Enaim,* literally, the 'opening of the eyes', is fraught with irony, for this is the place where sight is veiled. Great emphasis is placed on Judah's *not knowing*: he 'took her for a harlot for she had covered her face' (v. 15), and 'he did not know that she was his daughter-in-law' (v. 16). As a result, Judah knows her carnally, though he does not *recognize* her; whereas she *knows* him, both literally and figuratively. She not only conceives in that one encounter but cleverly takes a 'pledge [*'eravon*]'—the signet, cord and staff—in lieu of the promised goat. These tokens will later prompt Judah's acknowledgment of his paternity.

The Act of Recognition—haker na'

An attempt to pay the promised goat and reclaim Judah's pledge is made as his friend, Hirah, sets out to search for the harlot who sat at the entrance to Enaim, but she is not to be found. Three months later, upon hearing that Tamar is pregnant, 'with child by harlotry [*li-znunim*, i.e., illicit relations]' (v. 24), her father-in-law orders her to be burned at the stake. The turning point arrives when she presents the three tokens: the signet, cord and staff:

> As she was being brought out, she sent [*shalḥah*] to her father-in-law, saying, 'I am pregnant by the man to whom these belong'. And then she said [*va-to'mer*], 'Please discern/recognize [*haker na'*] these, whose signet and cord and staff are these?' Judah recognized them, and said, 'She is more in the right than I [*tzadqah mimeni*], inasmuch as I did not give her to my son Shelah'. And he did not know her again [*leda'atah*] (Gen. 38.25-26, author's trans.).

This scene marks the crisis in the drama, the moment of reversal, where the tokens that *should have* been procured for payment instead serve to reveal the true identity of the protagonists. Tamar first *sends* [*shalḥah*] the signet, cord and staff—presumably presented to him in private—allowing Judah either to deny the identity of the tokens or to claim them as his own. She enables him to make the shift toward acknowledging his responsibility without shaming him. She then appeals [*va-to'mer*] to Judah directly to discern/recognize [*haker na'*], echoing the very words the brothers had addressed to their father, Jacob (Gen. 37.32-33). The resonance implies a *double entendre* for Judah, and a concomitant demand for a twofold *re*-cognition—to acknowledge retrospectively the bereavement of his own father at the presentation of the bloodied cloak, and to admit his responsibility toward Tamar. He does so with respect to Tamar by acknowledging that he had neglected her in not giving her to his son Shelah (Gen. 38.26). With respect to his father, he will enact a *reversal* of his previous role, when he stands as surety on behalf of Benjamin. Where once he betrayed his brother Joseph by suggesting that he be sold into slavery (Gen. 37.26-27), he later stands as a guarantor for the younger brother, Benjamin, to save him from enslavement (Gen. 43.9; 44.32). Judah places himself on the line, willing to take his brother's place as a substitute slave to the supposed Egyptian viceroy when Benjamin is framed with stealing the goblet. That is, Judah is transformed by Tamar's demand for righteousness, and comes to understand the ethical call to risk not only public ignominy but one's life for the sake of another.

This episode with Tamar ends with the rather blunt statement that Judah 'did not know her again [*leda'atah*]' (v. 26)—as if to imply that awareness of her identity, following the recognition, excluded the possibility of carnal knowledge.[54] Once the levir's duty has been completed and Judah becomes fully conscious of her identity as his daughter-in-law, the incest taboo holds sway.

Judah then earns the status of progenitor of the monarchy, anticipated in Jacob's final blessing to his son on his deathbed (Gen. 49.10) and the birth of Perez (38.29), whose genealogy concludes the book of Ruth. The rabbis ask, 'By what merit was Judah granted kingship? Because he acknowledged Tamar [*hodeh beTamar*]' (*t. Ber.* 4.17).[55] As discussed in the previous chapter, his words 'she is more righteous than I [*tzadqah mimeni*]' (v. 25) entail an acknowledgment, a recognition of his paternity and an admission of his guilt in neglecting to give her to Shelah. On another level, the term *hodeh* [*ydh*] implies the recognition of the role of the Ultimate Other—God's presence in the private interstices of the human encounter, 'the optical instrument to the divine'. Throughout these stories, God is absent in an overt way, but 'clearly', as Phyllis Trible points out, 'the human struggle itself is divine activity. ... As a whole, this [drama] suggests a theological interpretation of feminism: women working out their own salvation with fear and trembling, for it is God who works in them.'[56]

---

54. The rabbinic sages, however, suggest this verse is ambiguous—either he never 'knew' her again, or he never stopped [*lo'yasaf*] knowing her (see *b. Sot.* 10b).

55. See Chapter 3 n. 42.

56. Phyllis Trible, 'A Human Comedy', in *God and the Rhetoric of Sexuality*, pp. 195-96. This comment is based on her insights into the actions of Naomi and Ruth, but much of her feminist theological commentary on the book of Ruth can be applied to the drama of Judah and Tamar.

4. *Weaving the Messianic Light* 113

Naomi, Boaz and Ruth: Questions of Identity

The theme of recognition (or misrecognition) also appears throughout the book of Ruth. It can be traced through the deployment of the two terms for the Hebrew verb 'to know'—*nkr* and *yd'*—with their ironic double entendre, as well as four critical moments of recognition that punctuate the drama. When Naomi returns to Bethlehem with her Moabite daughter-in-law, the whole city is abuzz, and the women ask in astonishment: 'Can this be Naomi [*hazo't No'omi*]?' (Ruth 1.19). To which the older woman responds by renaming herself 'Mara', bitterness. 'Do not call me Naomi. Call me Mara, for Shaddai has deeply embittered me' (v. 20). Returning home, bereft of husband and sons, she no longer feels the pleasant [*na'im*] sweetness of life. At that moment, the loyal Ruth seems invisible by her side, as the key verb 'return' [*shwb*] concludes the chapter in the singular (v. 22). Yet this young woman, cast in shadow, occluded, emerges into the light through Boaz's act of recognition. He asks the reapers about Ruth's identity as he sees her gleaning in his fields: 'Whose girl is that [*lemi hana'arah hazo't*]?' (2.5). Later, during the harvest season, he is startled at night by her presence on the threshing floor, and asks, 'Who are you? [*mi 'at*]?' (3.8). Naomi poses the same question when Ruth returns early the next morning, in a greeting that mingles both intimacy and estrangement: 'Who are you, my daughter [*mi 'at biti*]?' (3.16). The identities of both Naomi and Ruth are in flux, poised for transformation in their own eyes and in the eyes of others. Naomi, after loss and impoverishment, moves from a position of tragic self-definition over the course of the drama toward a more expansive sense of self—to the point where she even nurses her own grandchild, who, in the woman's words, 'will renew her life and sustain her through old-age', the very child born to her by Ruth, her daughter-in-law, 'who has loved her and been better to her than seven sons' (4.15). Concomitantly, Ruth must shift out of her mother-in-law's shadow in transforming her own identity as a Moabite and stranger within the community. As a result, the contours of Naomi are sweetened, broadened and realigned.

By contrast, Boaz and his significance to Naomi's family are *known*. His identity as 'kinsman' and man of substance [*gibor ḥayil*] seems fixed, a Rock of Gibraltar. The term *moda'*, by which he is first introduced, open ch. 2 and derives from the root *yd'*:

> Now Naomi had a kinsman [*moda'*] on her husband's side, a prominent rich man [*gibor ḥayil*], of the family of Elimelech, whose name was Boaz (Ruth 2.1 NRSV).

Boaz is again referred to by Naomi as 'our relative [*moda'tenu*]' in 3.2. The term is a near *hapax legomenon*, appearing only once elsewhere in the

Hebrew Bible (Prov. 7.4),[57] where it is difficult to gauge its precise meaning. Here it assumes two possible forms: *moda'*, the *qere* (the vocalized form, as read aloud); or *meyuda'*, the *kethib*, the written form in the MT. Edward Campbell, in his commentary on Ruth, suggests that the *kethib* is to be preferred over the *qere* since it appears on six other occasions in the Bible, with the meaning of 'intimate friend, companion'.[58] He proposes translating *moda'* as 'covenant brother'. Boaz, then, is the kinsman, the known relative—*meyuda'*. On another level, he is the one who will bring about redemption through knowing/recognition.

As in the Judah and Tamar story, the verb *lahakir* [*nkr*], 'to acknowledge, discern, or recognize', plays a central role in the book of Ruth. In the first conversation between Boaz and Ruth, he adjures her to continue gleaning in his fields and remain close to the young women, for he has ordered the men not to harass her (2.8-9). She then 'falls on her face, bowing to the ground', and bursts forth with these astonishing words: 'Why have I found favor in your eyes, *that you acknowledge me, when I am a foreigner?*' [*lehakireni ve'anokhi nokhriyah*]' (v. 10). With a musical play on words, repeating the consonants nun and kaph, Ruth reveals a deeper resonance of meaning to the verb *lahakir*. A seeming oxymoron is embedded in the root *nkr*.[59] As we saw in the stories of Joseph and Judah, the verb generated from this root in the hiphil form means 'to recognize' or 'discern', yet the noun *nekhar* and the adjective *nokhri/nokhriyah*, based on the same root, connote foreign lands or an alien/foreign person. Ruth, at that moment, understands that Boaz, in acknowledging her, has seen beyond her status as stranger, beyond the Moabite taboo. This act of recognition is akin to what Walter Benjamin describes as friendship, the forging of a relationship with another who remains *other*. In his words, friendship 'does not abolish the distance between human beings but brings that distance to life'.[60]

This moment of recognition between Boaz and Ruth presents a contrast with carnal *knowing*, the merging of selves/bodies that sexual union entails. In this astonishing line, Ruth acknowledges that the self within her [*'anokhi*], as stranger [*nokhriyah*], has been embraced by an act of recognition [*lehakireni*], and through his kindness she is brought under the wings of the God of Israel. As Boaz avers,

---

57. 'Say to wisdom, "You are my sister", and call insight your intimate friend [*umoda' labinah tiqra*]' (Prov. 7.4 NRSV).
58. Campbell, *Ruth*, pp. 88–90, and also Sasson, *Ruth*, p. 39. On the term *meyuda'* (or the *qere*, *moda'*), as a nominal form of the verb *yd'*, see BDB entry 3829, p. 396.
59. Edward Greenstein, in 'Reading Strategies', p. 215, also points out the compelling play on the word 'foreigner' (*nkr*) embedded in this verse. See my philological comment in n. 16.
60. Walter Benjamin, 'Commentaries on Poems by Brecht', in *Understanding Brecht* (trans. Anna Bostock; London: Verso, 1983), p. 73.

> All that you have done for your mother-in-law since the death of your husband has been fully told me, and how you left your father and mother and your native land and came to a people that you did not know before. May Yhwh recompense you for what you have done, and a full reward be given you by Yhwh, the God of Israel, *under whose wings* [*taḥat kenafav*] *you have come to take refuge*! (Ruth 2.11-12, author's translation, emphasis added).

At the threshing floor, the tension between knowing and recognition reaches its apex. *Carpe noctem,* Naomi seizes the night, sending Ruth down to the threshing floor 'just around midnight' (3.8). This is a transformative time, when identities may shift in the dark, boundaries between self and other dissolve, and new identities form. Naomi tells Ruth that this very night Boaz will be winnowing barley at the granary—perhaps taking part in the harvest festival, associated with drinking and revelry. He, like Lot and Judah, may be inebriated (v. 7), his faculties of discernment blurred. The younger woman is to bathe, anoint herself, dress up, and go down to the threshing floor, but Naomi urges, 'Do not make yourself known to the man [*'al tivad'i la-'ish*] until he has finished eating and drinking' (v. 3). Ruth is to uncover his feet [*vegilit margelotav*] and lie down, and rely on what he will 'tell [her] to do' (v. 4). As with her predecessor, Tamar, the shift in Ruth's role, from gleaner in the fields in the public arena to seductress by night is negotiated by bathing, anointing and dressing up. Her visit to the threshing floor, in stealth, is fraught with the risk of ignominy and public shaming if her role as seductress should be exposed. As Boaz tells her, she must rise up early, 'before any man could recognize [*yakir*] another', for 'it must not be known [*'al yivada'*] that the woman came to the threshing floor' (v. 14). While Ruth is *not* to be known (that is, recognized, *nkr*) by any other man when she slinks away before dawn, Naomi's intention was that she be known [*yd'*] that night, carnally, by one man, Boaz, the known/knowing one [*moda'/meyuda'*].

According to her mother-in-law's instructions, Ruth is initially 'not to be known'—that is, recognized—by Boaz (v. 3), though Naomi sets the younger woman up for a seduction, or *carnal* knowing. Ruth must uncover his feet and lie down there, concealing her identity, though revealing, possibly, his nakedness. Much ink has been spilled over the phrase 'uncover his feet' as a euphemism for sexual relations.[61] Indubitably, as the verb 'lie down' [*shkhb*] connotes (deployed three times in v. 4 and twice in v. 7), Naomi is setting Ruth up for a 'bedtrick' in the mode of her predecessors Tamar and the daughters of Lot. Yet the scene is fraught with ambiguity as to who is

---

61. As in Isa 6.2, where two of the six wings of the seraphim are used to cover 'their feet'. See Zakovitch, *Ruth*, pp. 89–90. Campbell and Sasson, however, both concur that 'the storyteller meant to be ambiguous and hence provocative'; see Campbell, *Ruth*, p. 121; and Sasson, *Ruth*, pp. 69-71.

really directing the script, Naomi or Ruth, and whether relations between Boaz and the younger woman were actually consummated that night.

In this passage, there are two fascinating discrepancies between the *qere* and *kethib* (the oral and written tradition), shifts between first and second person that point to an alternative reading percolating just below the surface. Naomi tells Ruth to bathe, to anoint herself, to put on a dress, commanding, '[you] go down [*veyaradet*] to the threshing floor', according to the *qere*. The *kethib*, however, reads, '*I* will go down' [*veyardeti*, v. 4]. Likewise, Naomi tells her, according to the *qere*, to 'uncover his feet and lie down [*veshakhavt*]', but the *kethib* reads, '*I* will lie down' [*veshakhavti*, v. 4].[62] Does Naomi intend Ruth to take along her mother-in-law's shadow as she wraps herself up in her garments and descends to the threshing floor? Like Tamar, doffing the widow's garb, covering her face with a veil and wrapping herself up as a harlot to sit by the side of the road, is Ruth assuming an alternative identity, perhaps the identity of Naomi herself? Do these 'slips of the tongue' and 'pen' gesture at the older woman's desire to lie at the man's feet, to bear his child, to be the one who will redeem *herself* of widowhood and reclaim her lost lands? Perhaps an untold (even unconscious) story underlies these 'slips'; a liaison that began before the marriage of Naomi to Elimelech and the sojourn in Moab, involving the 'known/ knowing one [*moda'/meyuda'*]', Boaz. Perhaps he *had* known her, carnally or otherwise, but now that she is older, beyond her fertile years and impoverished, Naomi must live vicariously through the younger woman. It is Ruth who will fulfill her desire and in the end bear a child to Boaz, whom the older woman will take as her own, lay in her bosom and nurse (4.16).

Wendy Doniger evocatively suggests a resonance with yet another 'bedtrick' in the Genesis narratives—the duping of Jacob by the replacement of Leah, the elder sister, for Rachel, the younger one, on the wedding night (Gen. 29.23-26).[63] The names Rachel, Leah and Tamar are invoked

---

62. The additional yod in the second-person feminine singular perfect may reflect an archaic form of the verb (as in Jer. 2.33; 3.4; 4.19; and 31.21 (MT); see GKC §44h, p. 121), yet these unusual forms are included in a command sequence, not in the perfect case. The book of Ruth has other anomalous forms of verbal endings (as in the *-yn* ending, also in the context of instructions; see Ruth 2.8, 9; 3.4, 18), which, according to Mark S. Haughwout, reflect First Temple linguistic forms. See his analysis of Ruth 3.3, http://markhaughwout.com/Bible/Ruth_3_3.htm. This, however, may be a conscious means of archaizing, on the part of the author, as Berlin has argued with regard to the idiosyncratic interpretation of law in 'Legal Fiction', pp. 3-18. Brian Irwin, on the other hand, claims that the scribe (in the *kethib*) is deliberately removing Ruth from sexual implications and replacing her with Naomi. Thus Naomi says, 'I will go down' and 'I will lie' ('Removing Ruth: tiqqune sopherim in Ruth 3.3-4?', *JSOT* 32 [2008], pp. 331-38).

63. See the discussion in Doniger, *Bedtrick*, pp. 261-62. Mona DeKoven Fishbane calls the discrepancy between the *qere* and the *kethib* Naomi's 'slips of the tongue',

in the community's blessings of Boaz's marriage to Ruth at the town gate (Ruth 4.11-12), the 'gates of the law', the site of adjudication. Doniger suggests that Leah, Tamar and Ruth all collude with other women in levirate or pseudo-levirate marriages; 'each of the three women', she adds, 'pretends to be another woman in bed'. While Leah simulates Rachel, and Tamar dresses up as a harlot, it is Naomi's identity that Ruth assumes. When Boaz awakes with a start, it is the older woman whom he expects, according to Doniger, though he hopes for Ruth.[64]

Yet, what actually happens is *not* a bedtrick at all; no seduction takes place, but, rather, an act of recognition that *does not entail* the man knowing the woman, in the 'biblical' sense of the term:

> In the middle of the night, the man gave a start and pulled back—there was a woman lying at his feet! 'Who are you [*mi 'at*]?' he asked. And she replied, 'I am your handmaid, Ruth. Spread your robe/wing [*knafekha*] over your handmaid, for you are a redeeming kinsman [*ki go'el 'atah*]' (Ruth 3.8-9, author's trans.).

This is not the script that Naomi had in mind. For one, Boaz wakes up startled and asks to know the woman's name. His query stands in stark contrast to the seduction of the drunken Lot by his daughters, where he 'did not know her lying down or her getting up', and to Tamar's seduction of Judah, for 'she had covered her face' and 'he *did not know* that she was his daughter-in-law'. Boaz, in contrast to his male predecessors, wants to know the identity of the woman lying at his feet; he chooses recognition over carnal knowledge.

Ruth responds by saying her name (dropping the pejorative 'Moabite') and identifies herself as his handmaid.[65] She then tells him to spread his

---

which represent 'the conflation of identities in Naomi's mind'; see her article 'Ruth: Dilemmas of Loyalty and Connection', in *Reading Ruth: Contemporary Women Reclaim a Sacred Story* (ed. Judith Kates and Gail Reimer; New York: Ballantine, 1994), p. 303.

64. See Doniger, *Bedtrick*, pp. 259-60. Doniger cites Bal, *Lethal Love*, p. 78, but misrepresents her position. The story of Leah and Rachel has little to do with levirate marriage; Bal argues that its resonance has to do with the split between love (sexual desire) and fertility, which is 'corrected' by the bedtrick, while Tamar's seduction of Judah 'corrects' the more archaic fault—the fear of feminine power' (Bal, *Lethal Love*, pp. 84–87).

65. Previously she had asserted that she did not *even* have the status of his handmaid, *shifḥah* (2.13), whereas here she asserts, 'I am your maidservant [*'amatekha*]'. According to Sasson, the *shifḥah* belongs to the lowest rung of the social ladder. In using the term *'amatekha* (presumably of higher status), Ruth refers to herself 'as ranking among those females who might be taken by a freeman either as a concubine or as a wife' (Sasson, *Ruth*, p. 81).

robe, or his wing, over her.[66] This is the most striking and deeply resonant statement Ruth utters. She does not wait for him to tell her what to do, as her mother-in-law had instructed; instead, she tells *him* what to do. As Phyllis Trible points out, 'Ruth herself is in charge'.[67] Taking the very words Boaz had uttered in the fields with reference to God—'May Yhwh recompense you for what you have done, and a full reward be given you by Yhwh, the God of Israel, *under whose wings [kenafav] you have come to take refuge*' (Ruth 2.12, emphasis added)—she addresses them to Boaz: 'Spread *your* robe/wings [*knafekha*] over your handmaid' (3.9). This is no simple marriage proposal, as Rashi suggests. Rather, it is a request to be included within the covenantal community. In Ezekiel, to be brought under the wings of love implies both a marriage and an initiation into the covenant between God and his people: 'I passed by you again and looked on you; you were at the age for love. I spread the edge of my cloak/my wings [*knafai*] over you, and covered your nakedness: I pledged myself to you and entered into a covenant with you, says Yhwh God, and you became mine' (Ezek. 16.8). Ruth's invocation implies both the allegorical and the literal meaning underlying this image, hinting that Boaz's blessing to her—to be brought under the wings of the God of Israel—entails both marriage and covenantal inclusion. She then identifies his expansive role: 'You are a redeeming kinsman'. At the gates of the law, he takes on that responsibility by fusing both redemptive roles, of land and seed, by begetting through the widowed Ruth a child that Naomi will nurture.

---

66. The Hebrew term *kanaf* can mean the corner or skirt of a garment (cf. Num. 15.38; Ezek. 5.3), so that 'to uncover the *kanaf*' may assume sexual connotations (Deut. 23.1, and perhaps Ezek 16.8 in the figurative sense). Alternatively, the term refers to the wings of a bird, metaphorical for the caring presence of the divine being (cf. Exod. 19.4; Deut. 32.11; Zech. 5.9); see BDB, entry 4553, p. 489. According to Sasson, some of the Hebrew manuscripts record *knafeikha*, the plural form of the noun, in alluding to Boaz's words (3.9) (*Ruth*, p. 81). Zakovitch suggests that this allusion is quite deliberate on her part (*Ruth*, p. 93). I maintain, as does Judith Kates, that this expression deliberately merges marital relations with covenantal inclusion. Quoting David Hartman, she states that 'the God of Israel "relies on humans to embody [God's] designs and expectations in history because of [God's] uncompromising commitment to safeguard human freedom and integrity." The idea of covenant implies a sense of human "adequacy." . . . throughout Judaism, we encounter this crucial notion of the necessity for human cooperation in fulfilling divine purposes in history' (Judith A. Kates, 'Women at the Center: Ruth and Shavuot', in *Reading Ruth* [ed. Judith A. Kates and Gail Twersky Reimer; New York: Ballantine Books, 1994], pp. 189-98 [197]; David Hartman, *A Living Covenant: The innovative Spirit in Traditional Judaism* [New York: Free Press, 1985], p. 26). For a broader discussion of this paradigm in the contemporary context, see Nancy Cott, *Public Vows: A History of Marriage and the Nation* (Cambridge, MA: Harvard University Press, 2001).

67. Trible, 'A Human Comedy', in *God and the Rhetoric of Sexuality*, p. 184.

The encounter at the threshing floor ends with a significant 'gift of seed', but not one that might result in the conception of a child. Rather, before dawn, Boaz asks Ruth to spread out her shawl, and he measures out 'six barleys [*shesh se'orim*]' for her (3.15). The plain sense suggests that the six grains or measures of barley are meant as a gift that promises a contractual agreement, yet the symbolism resounds louder. In the Talmud, the following question is raised:

> Was it six grains or six bushels of barley? Would it have been the custom of Boaz to give only six grains? Yet six bushels would have been too much for one woman to carry! Instead, in these six grains he intimated to her that six descendants were to come from her, each blessed with six blessings: David, the Messiah, Daniel, Hananiah, Mishael and Azariah (*b. Sanh.* 93b).

The sages tease out the irony underlying the image; the six barley grains or bushels are, in fact, immeasurable, for they allude to the promise of the messianic dynasty that will arise from this couple, who did not plant a physical seed. Precisely because their encounter did *not* result in conception that night, this story becomes one of redemption. Instead of consummating relations of an illicit or deceptive nature, the two recognize each other, and Boaz then presents their case for public recognition by the gates of the law.

When Ruth returns home, Naomi is anxious to know what happened but, as noted, she asks a rather odd question: 'Who are you, my daughter [*mi 'at biti*]?' (3.16). Naomi's surprise in seemingly failing to recognize Ruth, here, contrasts with the women's alarm upon her return from Moab ('Is this Naomi?'), misshapen by tragedy into Mara (bitterness). The question now posed to Ruth resonates deeply with Boaz's earlier question, 'Who are you [*mi 'at*]?' (3.9), as Naomi strives to recognize the radiance in Ruth's face. The young woman answers her, supposedly quoting Boaz (though the text does not record him saying these words): 'He gave me these six [measures of] barley, saying to me, "Do not go back to your mother-in-law empty [*reiqam*]"' (3.17). She is echoing Naomi's original lament in answer to the Bethlehem women: 'I went away full, and God has brought me back empty [*reiqam*]' (1.21). How little it takes to turn from empty to full, from despair to hope: six grains of barley wrapped in a shawl! Eternity measured in a kernel of grain. Naomi's own contours are radically transformed by the daughter-in-law who recasts her shadow.

Conclusion

Harold Fisch outlined the structural parallels between the three narratives, showing that the function of the story of Ruth is to 'redeem' the previous episodes in the corpus.[68] All three stories involve the following motifs: descent (Lot, from Abraham, by settling in Sodom; Judah, from the presence of his brothers in Canaan; Elimelech, in leaving Bethlehem for Moab); disaster (the destruction of Sodom; the deaths of Judah's wife and two sons; the deaths of Naomi's husband and two sons); an *'agunah* theme (a chained or bereft woman—Lot's daughters, Tamar, Naomi/Ruth); and redemption through a *go'el* (a redeemer—Lot, Judah, Boaz). In terms of plot structure, all three stories entail a bedtrick, feasting (if not drunkenness), some kind of levirate union, and the conception of the much-sought-for progeny. I would like to add yet another parallel between the three stories as they develop along both the synchronic (time) and diachronic (motif/word-play/plot) axes, that of the increasing level of consciousness at the critical scene of seduction. Whereas Lot conceives in a state of total depravity, not knowing 'when she lay down and when she arose', and Judah does not know (yet *does know* carnally) his daughter-in-law, Tamar, only later *recognizing* her, Boaz is fully aware of the identity of the woman who dares to 'uncover his feet' at the threshing floor. What we have here is a movement from lesser to greater levels of awareness, and an increasing conformity to legal or normative propriety along the axis of time. Fisch writes,

> One is tempted to claim that the real value of the synchrony, i.e., the exhibition of the structural pattern which unites the stories, is in lighting up the social and moral differences between them in the diachronic scale.[69]

This, then, is the arc of redemption that links one seduction to the next.

As Fisch points out, the theme of redemption (*ge'ulah*) is central to the book of Ruth; the term *ga'al* is a *Leitwort*, appearing some twenty times. At the simplest level of meaning, the story has to do with the redemption of a parcel of land belonging to Elimelech and his dead sons (Ruth 4.3-4; cf. Lev. 25.25-28 and Jer. 32.6–8). Yet, in a rather *ad hoc* manner, the book also links the redemption of land to the redemption of seed through Boaz's quasi-levirate marriage to a widow left childless, Ruth (4.5ff.). It is precisely this unusual legal contingency that makes the anonymous Peloni Almoni, the closer kinsman holding the prior redemptive option, drop out of the real estate deal, perhaps because the stigma of 'Moabite' still clings to Ruth. Boaz, then, redeems the woman from her widowed state and her identity as stranger; in so doing, he also redeems Naomi's lands.

On another level, there will be a kind of redemption for the dead, through a quasi-levirate marriage, when Boaz acquires Mahlon's widow 'so as

---

68. Fisch, 'Ruth and the Structure of Covenant History', pp. 425-37. He summarizes the parallels in a 'synchronic' chart on pp. 430-31, which I adapted in Addendum 2, adding a ninth column, concerned with the dynamic transformation of knowledge/recognition over the course of the three narratives.

69. Fisch, 'Ruth and the Structure of Covenant History', p. 433.

to perpetuate the name of the deceased upon his estate' (4.10). One can also consider the newborn child a redeemer (*go'el*), insofar as he renews Naomi's life and puts an end to her sorrow and emptiness (4.14-16). Finally, Ruth and Boaz redeem the sexual 'transgressions' of their ancestors—the daughters of Lot, Judah and Tamar—in pursuing recognition before the law. As Fisch avers,

> 'Redemption' not only connotes the saving or freeing of persons or land, but also of worlds or understandings. . . . Ruth may be the redeemer of the unnamed ancestress who lay with her father in Gen. 19. Just as Boaz is the redeemer of his ancestor Judah who, in an only slightly more edifying fashion, 'went in' to the supposed prostitute at the crossroads leaving his seal, his cord, and his staff as a pledge. Boaz redeems that pledge.[70]

Fisch denotes three levels of understanding the word 'redeem': (1) the proximate meaning within the Hebrew Bible: to free another person from bondage, to preserve continuity for the deceased (through levirate marriage), or to release a parcel of land from debt; (2) the eschatological meaning: to improve upon the world by making it a better place through ethical action; and (3) the interpretive function: to 'free' our understanding of the world as we know it from the bondage of a prior normative universe. Similarly, Robert Cover understands this ultimate form of redemption as taking place within an 'eschatological schema that postulates (1) the unredeemed character of reality as we know it, (2) the fundamentally different reality that should take its place, and (3) the replacement of the one with the other'.[71] Redemption thus connotes not only the saving or freeing of *persons,* but also of 'worlds' or 'understandings'.

I would like to return to my opening question: Why does redemption entail, at least initially, a *breach* in the law (as the name for Tamar's son and Boaz's ancestor, Perez, suggests)? Why does the messianic line move from the drunken oblivion of an incestuous union in a cave to seeming harlotry by the roadside to near seduction on the threshing floor in Bethlehem? What is this narrative arc all about? Why does the force of life, of continuity, chafe against the line of law? And why are women the subversive agents who propel this life force forward? Ironically, while it is the men that uphold the law as authoritative, asserting the power of the licit, they are 'undone', seduced, by the illicit actions of women. The heroines, on the other hand, use their feminine power, specifically the illicit bedtrick, to become licit, to gain recognition within the normative world, both biologically and socially. Their seduction (or near seduction) establishes the possibility of continuity for them as mothers, thereby granting them social status and acceptance (at least for Tamar and Ruth) as they join the Israelite people.

70. Fisch, 'Ruth and the Structure of Covenant History', p. 436.
71. Cover, 'Nomos and Narrative', pp. 34-35.

I would like to answer the larger question about the relationship between law and narrative by way of a teaching from the Talmud. R. Yochanan makes an audacious claim about the cause of the destruction of Jerusalem in 70 CE, which led to nearly two thousand years of exile for the Jewish people.

> Jerusalem was destroyed . . . *only* because [the judges] based their judgments [strictly] upon biblical law, and did not go beyond the line of the law [*lo' 'avdu lifnim mishurat hadin*] (*b. B. Metz.* 30b).

That is, the sages were too strict in their interpretation of the law and failed to act compassionately in expounding it. By contrast, the process of redemption, which might have prevented the destruction, entails an opening up of the 'line' of the law to loving kindness (*ḥesed*). The translation 'beyond the line of the law' does not quite capture the meaning, since it presumes *either* mercy *or* law, grace *or* legality, compassion *or* justice—a hackneyed trope I do not intend to resurrect.

In truth, the Hebrew expression *lifnim mishurat hadin*—literally *within the line of the law*—gestures at a paradox, through an image of a geometric impossibility. How can a line have space within it? When law shifts, moved by the force of narrative to accommodate, in Cover's terms, 'the "is", the "ought", and the "what might be"'[72] of a contingent universe, a space within the line is created. The demands of the particular penetrate the line, open its two dimensions into three by forging a fissure, an inner world, *lifnim mishurat hadin,* a space within the law for change. Redemption is precisely about the struggle to expand the line of the law to include the contingencies of life, the particulars of 'dappled things . . . all things counter, original, spare, strange'.[73] By risking history, Lot's daughters, Tamar and Ruth come to forge that space within the line and redefine the normative world of the Hebrew Bible.

Addendum 1: David's Inheritance[74]

'Now he was ruddy, and had beautiful eyes, and was good-looking' (1 Sam. 16.12).

The more we try to ignore our roots, the more they restrain us like invisible shackles tied to our ankles. In order to loosen them or free their hold, we must come to acknowledge them, transforming the chain into a golden bond.

---

72. Cover, 'Nomos and Narrative', p. 34.
73. Gerard Manley Hopkins, 'Pied Beauty' (1918).
74. This piece was originally written in Hebrew as a modern midrash in the context of a seminar on the book of Ruth at Beit Midrash Elul, Jerusalem, in 2011.

4. *Weaving the Messianic Light*

Link by link, David wove together the stories of his roots—at first, they felt heavy like the shackles of prison, as it is said, 'Indeed I was born in iniquity' (Ps. 51.7).

In his beginning, there was a fetid drop in a cave, in the hill country of Seir, on the day God rained down sulfurous fire from heaven. And Lot drank wine and ate from the desire of his hands, not knowing when they lay down and when they rose. From the older daughter, Moab was born. Lot and his daughter gave to David his hands, and they were like the hands of Esau, 'ruddy [*'admoni*], his whole body like a hairy mantle' (Gen. 25.25), and of David it is written, 'Now he was ruddy [*'admoni*]' (1 Sam. 16.12).

From the house of Perez, whom Tamar bore to Judah, he received his 'beautiful eyes'. Judah did not know that she was his daughter-in-law, for she was wrapped in a veil at the entrance to Enaim. He recognized her only when she was sent to be burnt at the stake, as it says, 'Judah recognized, and said, "She is more righteous than I . . ."' (Gen. 38.26). His eyes were opened and he knew that he could not hide his face from her or from his creator. Those eyes he passed on to David.

And from Ruth and Boaz, he received his good looks—just as God looks into the heart of man, 'For the LORD does not see as mortals see; they look on the outward appearance, but the LORD looks into the heart' (1 Sam. 16.7). And in the middle of the night, a moonless night, wrapped in deep fog, Boaz asked her, 'Who are you?' 'Ruth, the foreigner from Moab, the lineage of *not knowing,* of drunken oblivion'. And Boaz *knew* Ruth, recognized her before any man could. This way of seeing, of being seeing—good looking—Ruth and Boaz passed on to David.

The chain, as a whole, can strengthen its weakest link, transforming the links into a golden bond. This is what David meant in his psalm, 'O Lord, I am your servant, your servant, the son of your maidservant; you have undone the cords that bound me' (Ps. 116.16).

Addendum 2: A Comparison of the Three Narratives[75]

I Descent	II Disaster	III *Agunah*-Theme / Abandonment	IV Redemption
Lot and Abraham separate (Gen. 13)	Destruction of Sodom and Gomorrah (Gen. 18)	Lot's two daughters are left without the prospect of acquiring men	The *go'el* is Lot himself
Judah descends from his brothers (38.1)	Deaths of Judah's wife and two sons, Er and Onan	Tamar bidden to remain a widow in her father's house	The *go'el* is Judah
Elimelech leaves Bethlehem for Moab	All the male members of the family die	Naomi's two daughters-in-law left widowed	The *go'el* is Boaz
This column expresses the tragic separation of families	This column expresses the resultant tragedy	This column expresses how the hope of the family is preserved in or by a woman/women	A near kinsman is made to express responsibility for the continuation of the family

V The Bedtrick	VI The Celebration	VII The Levirate Union	VIII The Issue	IX Knowing and Recognition
Lot is deceived into cohabiting with his daughters	Lot is made drunk with wine	Lot's two daughters conceive from their father	Moab and Ammon—the former is the ancestor of Ruth	Lot 'knows' his daughters in the carnal sense but does not know (i.e.) recognize them (Gen. 19.33, 35)
Tamar disguises herself as a prostitute (Gen. 38.12)	The sheepshearing festivity	Judah recognizes the justice of Tamar's claim	Perez and Zerah—the former is the ancestor of Boaz	Judah did *not* know that she was his daughter-in-law, but then he comes to *recognize* [*nkr*] her claim

75. Adapted from Fisch, 'Ruth and the Structure of Covenant History', pp. 430-31.

Ruth comes to the threshing-floor	The merry-making in connection with the barley feast	Boaz formally acquires the title to the property of his dead kinsman, including the possession of Ruth	Birth of Obed, the grandfather of King David	Boaz is not seduced, does not 'know' Ruth in the carnal sense, but recognizes her (Ruth 2.10, 3.9).
The woman takes the initiative	Temporary loss of order or self-control (emphasis on drunkenness)	The '*yibbum*' (levirate marriage) is enacted—where the incest taboo is overcome for the sake of continuity	All are, in a sense, 'from the father [= *Mo'av* as *mi-'av*]'	Along the diachronic scale, increasing consciousness; 'civilizing'

5

DAVID'S WIVES AS WOMEN OF OATH

An oath, an oath, I have an oath in heaven:
Shall I lay perjury upon my soul?
No, not for Venice.
                                    Shakespeare, *The Merchant of Venice* V.i

Preamble: The Question of Succession

As a sequel to the making of the Davidic dynasty (Chapter 4), this chapter introduces three women who play a pivotal role in determining the successor to the monarchy—Michal, Abigail and Bathsheba—the central figures for Chapters 6, 7 and 8 respectively. Once again, I take up the central question: how the chosen line is directed by the female ruse in life-affirming transgressive acts. But whereas the daughters of Lot, Tamar and Ruth engaged in sexual seduction, or near seduction, the 'transgression' on the part of David's wives extends beyond the body to the realm of language in oaths or promises, fragile testimonies vulnerable to being broken. Here I discuss the general character of these speech acts in the Hebrew Bible and the purpose of their betrayal in the relationship between David and his wives.

What role do women play in determining the successor to the Davidic monarchy? The king was a man loved by many, as suggested by an alternative pronunciation of his name—*David* as *dod* [lover]. Yet, unlike the male lover [*dod*] in Song of Songs, who was devoted to and loved by one woman—'I am my lover's and my lover is mine [*'ani le-dodi ve-dodi li*]'[1]—it is questionable whether David ever loved any of his wives.[2] Rather, love

---

1. Song 2.16, 6.3 and 7.8 (a variation thereof).
2. Although David is often the direct object of others' love: Saul (1 Sam. 16.21), Jonathan (1 Sam. 18.1, 3 and 20.17 [2x]), the tribes of Judah and Israel (1 Sam. 18.16), and, most poignantly, Michal (1 Sam. 18.20, 28), the warrior king is never the subject of the verb 'love' [*'hb*]. The one exception to this rule is found in the LXX's report on David's love of Amnon, his firstborn (2 Sam. 13.21); the MT only records David's anger. Because the king fails to punish Amnon for the rape of Tamar, his half-sister, David's

and marriage with the king were complicated by political motives. Given the number of women, their role in his life would play a decisive factor in determining which of his many sons would succeed him on the throne. In the biblical narrative, all three women—Michal, Abigail and Bathsheba—are torn between powerful men (either father and husband or husband and king). David is not only a rival pole; he becomes the one who ultimately determines the outcome of their alliance. What these three wives have in common is the binding power of the word in the form of a promise, oath or vow. Ironically, these verbal statements—enacted as declarations of commitment—also express a breach of faith. The language of oath sets the conflict of loyalties in high relief. Herein lies the female ruse peculiar to the Davidic monarchy.

For Michal, her dual loyalty is poignantly expressed in the epithets attached to her name—'Saul's daughter' or 'David's wife'. The demarcation highlights the rivalry between the curmudgeon king and her younger, more charismatic rival over the course of the drama.[3] She sets the precedent for our paradigm of 'women of oath', as she is promised to David in marriage and shuttles between her father, the rejected king, and her husband, the divinely chosen successor to the throne. Because she loves David (1 Sam. 18.20, 28), Michal replaces her older sister, Merab, who had been promised in matrimony to David as a reward for slaying, first, Goliath and subsequently the Philistines in battle.[4] While King Saul intended to use his daughter as a 'trap' to fell the young warrior in battle, David takes on the challenge in order to marry into the monarchy. Michal, not Merab, is given to David as his bride.

However, Michal's love for her father's rival only fans the flames of jealousy and paranoia for the incumbent king. So when Michal betrays

---

purported love for his son has fatal consequences. It devolves into fratricide and civil war. Absalom avenges his sister's violation by killing Amnon and then forcibly takes possession of the throne.

3. See David Clines, 'The Story of Michal, Wife of David, in its Sequential Unfolding', in *Telling Queen Michal's Story: An Experiment in Comparative Interpretation* (ed. David J.A. Clines and Tamara C. Eskenazi; Sheffield: Sheffield Academic Press, 1991), pp. 129-40; Edith Deen, 'King Saul's Daughter—David's First Wife', in Clines and Eskanazi (eds.), *Telling Queen Michal's Story,* pp. 141-44; and Hebert H. Lockyer, 'Michal', in Clines and Eskanazi (eds.), *Telling Queen Michal's Story,* pp. 227-28; and Lillian R. Klein, 'Michal, the Barren Wife', in *A Feminist Companion to Samuel and Kings* (ed. Athalya Brenner; Second series; Sheffield: Sheffield Academic Press, 2000), pp. 37-46.

4. See 1 Sam. 17.25 and 18.17, 22, and 25. When the time came to bestow the reward, Merab is mysteriously given to another man, Adriel, the Meholathite (1 Sam. 18.19). The replacement of the older by the younger sibling echoes the theme of the overturn of primogeniture in the Jacob and Esau story, and its feminine reversal, with Leah and Rachel (Gen. 29.23-26), in the sequel to the rivalry between sons.

her father to protect her husband (19.10-17), King Saul hands her over to another man in marriage (1 Sam. 25.44). Later she is reclaimed by David as he moves the capital to Jerusalem in a bid to unite the monarchy. Her role in securing continuity is essentially sealed by their last bitter repartee. Her fate? A barren scepter in her grip, no son of hers succeeding.[5]

Likewise Abigail allies herself, through oath, with David and his henchmen *against* her boorish husband, Nabal, a wealthy landowner in Carmel (1 Sam. 25). When the man refuses to feed David and his henchmen as recompense for 'protecting' the landowner's shepherds and flocks, David swears an oath to seek vengeance against Nabal and all the males of the household. Abigail, upon hearing his bloody intentions, secretly intercepts David on the path. Replete with gifts of drink and food, she persuades David with an eloquent speech, invoking a second oath, to restrain him from bloodshed. In doing so, she breaks faith with Nabal. Yet, while Abigail, after being widowed and marrying the future king of Israel, *does* become a mother of David's child (unlike Michal), she never sheds the epithet of 'Nabal's wife'. She too is wrenched with an unlineal hand, no son of hers succeeding.

Finally, and most infamously, Bathsheba, 'the wife of Uriah', is forced to betray her husband in submitting to David's desire. The consequences? Adultery. Uriah's murder. The death of the infant born of their adulterous union. And the tragic unraveling of King David's reign. Yet it is Bathsheba who bears Solomon, *the* successor to the throne. This is commensurate with the theme that the messianic line must emerge from a transgressive union, discussed in the last chapter. Bathsheba sews, like Lot's daughters, Tamar and Ruth, a life-giving thread after broken faith and heinous crimes in the dénouement to the David story. And it is she who guarantees Solomon's succession. In collusion with the prophet Nathan, she invokes an oath at the king's sickbed, which David had supposedly made to her (though no such words are recorded in the biblical narrative), guaranteeing the succession of the throne to her son (1 Kgs 1.13, 17). As a result, her name, Bathsheba, may be read with an alternative vocalization: 'woman of oath [*bat shevu'ah*]'.[6]

In these three stories of the king's wives, oaths or promises expressive of dual loyalty underpin the dialogue, highlighting the way women play a critical role in allying *with* or distancing themselves *from* male authority. They play the role of either pawn or queen upon the king's chess board in

---

5. I paraphrase from *Macbeth*: 'Upon my head they placed a fruitless crown/And put a barren scepter in my grip,/Thence to be wrenched with an unlineal hand,/No son of mine succeeding' (*Macbeth* III.i).

6. See the discussion in Moshe Garsiel, *Biblical Names: A Literary Study of Midrashic Derivations and Puns* (Ramat Gan: Bar-Ilan University Press, 1991), pp. 129-30.

determining the successor to the Judean lineage. Do these women thereby reinforce the hegemony of the Davidic monarchy or voice a critique of its power machinations?

The Oath as Speech Act

In my analysis of the role of oaths as counters in the semiotic play of power, I draw upon J.L. Austin's theory of speech acts.[7] An oath or vow belongs to that category of performative speech that 'gets something done', as in the marriage vow 'I do'.[8] In contrast to illocutions such as warnings or commands ('Thou shalt not . . . !' or 'Don't . . .') directed at another, the oath, vow or promise entails a commitment on the part of the speaker to his or her own performance of an action. Whereas promises, however, simply refer to a commitment to do or refrain from doing something in the future, an oath or vow calls upon a third party, a court of law or God, to bear witness to the speech act and serve (ultimately) as the arbiter of truth in its fulfillment. These speech acts create a binding reality that have both religious and political implications, redefining personal, social and legal boundaries. Before a justice of the peace, a couple vows even in a secular matrimonial ceremony, 'to have and to hold, to love and to cherish from this day forward, for better or for worse, for richer or for poorer, in sickness and in health'. In a modern court of law, the witness takes an oath 'to tell the truth, nothing but the truth so help me God' (putting his or her hand on the Bible). These are secular instantiations of speech acts, yet a religious phenomenology undergirds even these illocutions.

In breaking an oath or vow within the religious world, where the presence of God was invoked as witness, the speaker would bear the consequences as meted out by heaven. In the secular world, the court takes over the role of the arbiter of truth before the law. Perjury, which refers to lying under oath in court about truths with respect to past action, probes the line between these domains of sacred and profane. It presupposes a promise made to tell the truth (and nothing but the truth) in the future about what *had* been done

---

7. Austin argues against the positivist claim that language has truth value only as 'constative' (descriptive of some real or possible state of affairs). He suggests that many statements have value because they belong to that class of 'performatives', linguistic acts which get something done (J.L. Austin, *How to Do Things with Words* [Cambridge, MA: Harvard University Press, 1975]). See also John Searle, *Speech Acts: An Essay in the Philosophy of Language* (Cambridge: Cambridge University Press, 1969). For an application of Austin's theory to oaths in the Hebrew Bible, see Yael Ziegler, *Promises to Keep* (Leiden: Brill, 2008), pp. 29-30.

8. Or, at a Jewish wedding (in Hebrew): 'Behold, you are sanctified to me by the Law of Moses and Israel [*harei 'at mequdeshet li ke-dat Moshe ve-Yisrael*]'.

in the past. So President Clinton's transgression was *not* about his sexual relationship with Ms Lewinsky, despite the hubbub in the press, but about the violation of his oath to tell the truth in court. The appended words to the vow, 'so help me God', then must be understood as elliptical. In violating the oath, divine help may indeed be called upon when punishment is meted out by the court. In both the secular and religious arenas, whether God is invoked in the oath or one swears on the Bible in court or declares marriage vows before a justice of the peace, a higher authority is called upon as the ultimate witness to the truth.

Yet how is the test of truth borne out in the future within the world of the Hebrew Bible? Who adjudicates? For David's wives, their loyalties are divided between men, between father and husband, or husband and king. The promises or oaths delineate alliances, and therefore may be in conflict. As expressions of commitment in the court history, these speech acts may be corroborated on two levels—in drawing upon God as a witness to their truth and in determining whether (or how) they are fulfilled in the future (with God as the assumed 'author' and 'mover' of this history). That is, how they play out in the future, whether fulfilled or broken, will tell the reader about the alliances, the strength of the verbal bonds, and whether they meet with divine sanction.

Consider the role of the oath, for example, in Shakespeare's *Merchant of Venice*. Shylock commits himself on oath before the irascible (Jewish) law to exact a 'pound of flesh', which Antonio had promised on bond. Were Antonio to forfeit on his debt of 30,000 ducats, he would be in breach of the oath. As Shylock avers, 'An oath, an oath, I have an oath in heaven. Would I lay perjury upon my soul?' (*Merchant of Venice* IV.i.2169-71). That's why he refuses his money in open court. Shylock's oath commits him to claiming his bond; as Kerrigan points out, 'should he relent, he would stand guilty before a higher judge, God himself, of the crime of perjury'.[9] Shylock's conversion represents the consequences of relenting: 'His punishment for breaking the vow of faith turns out to be forced conversion to another one'.[10] The anti-Semitic legacy of the play juxtaposes Christian 'faith' and 'mercy' with the Jewish adherence to the 'letter of the law'. But the drama also exposes the hypocrisy of the Christian world that calls for so-called mercy. Through the careful deployment of the subplot (in Belmont), also woven with oath language and the concomitant exchange of rings, promises of

---

9. William Kerrigan, *Shakespeare's Promises* (Baltimore, MD: Johns Hopkins University Press, 1999), p. 133. See also the discussion in W.H. Auden, 'Brothers and Others', in *The Dyer's Hand and Other Essays* (London: Faber & Faber, 1963), pp. 218-37. Kerrigan does not make a distinction here between 'oath' and 'vow', whereas I do in the discussion that follows.

10. Kerrigan, *Shakespeare's Promises*, p. 135.

matrimony are made and carelessly breached. Swearing on oath, as distinct from simply making a promise, functions on the cusp between human social contracts and divine sanction and serves to expose commitments as either hallowed or hollow.

Before I explore the double bind imbedded in the oath in the biblical narrative, we must explore the terms and syntax characteristic of oath language in the Hebrew Bible. Two terms, *neder* and *shevu'ah*, are to be distinguished.[11] The latter is an oath proper. It is categorical. The former is associated with an 'If . . . then . . .' hypothetical formula and, like many promises, is conditional as in a promise of a dedication to God or a votive offering. Jacob, for example, vows [*ndr*] to set up a monument in Bethel *if* God takes care of him over the course of his sojourn (Gen. 28.20; 31.13). The chieftain Jephthah vows [*ndr*] to sacrifice anything (or anyone) that comes to greet him upon his return *if* he is successful in the battle against the Ammonites (Judg. 11.30-31). Hannah vows [*ndr*], *if* she conceives, to dedicate that child to God (1 Sam. 1.11).

Swearing on oath [*shb'*], though it may also entail a promise to do (or *not* to do) something in the future, usually implies a curse if abrogated. Joshua, for example, imposes an oath on the Israelites with respect to the booty in Jericho (Josh. 6.26), which entails an imprecation (a consequent curse) for anyone who violates that oath. When the Israelites fail in the battle against Ai, Joshua knows that the ban has been violated and draws lots (perhaps through the oracular device of the priestly breastplate) to determine the transgressor. Achan is found guilty, so that he and his family are stoned to death, and all that belongs to him is proscribed (7.24-25). Saul imposes an oath on the people not to eat meat, and he vows to sentence Jonathan to death for violating that oath (1 Sam. 14.24, 39). David had (supposedly) made an oath [*shevu'ah*] to establish Solomon as the heir to

---

11. Both terms are used in Numbers: 'When a man makes a vow [*neder*] to the LORD, or swears an oath [*shevu'ah*] to bind himself by a pledge, he shall not break his word; he shall do according to all that proceeds out of his mouth' (Num. 30.3 NRSV). In biblical literature, the *neder* often entails an offering to God, having fulfilled the protagonist's wish (as in Gen. 18.20; 31.13—Jacob at Bethel), whereas the *shevu'ah* implies negative consequences when it is *not* fulfilled (BDB entry 9660, 9664). In rabbinic literature, both speech acts (the vow or the oath) refer to a stringency one imposes on oneself not to enjoy something. According to the rabbis (as elaborated in tractate *Nedarim*), a *neder* (vow) is imposed on the object, and a *shevu'ah* (oath) concerns the person himself. So, for example, if one were to swear not to drink anymore (perhaps because one has an alcohol problem), the vow [*neder*] would concern the status of the object, the wine or liquor, whereas the oath [*shevu'ah*] would be incumbent on the person. For a very clear explanation on the rabbinic distinction between oath and vow, see the following article by Louis Jacobs, http://www.myjewishlearning.com/practices/Ethics/Talk_and_Gossip/Types_of_Speech/Vows_and_Oaths.shtml.

the throne (1 Kgs 1.13, 17). God commits himself on oath [*shb'*], as well, to fulfill the covenant with the patriarchs, in particular Abraham, by bringing the Israelites out of the house of bondage and granting them the Promised Land,[12] and in promising to establish a dynasty for David.[13] Though God is bound by an oath [*shb'*], not a vow [*ndr*], the divine is both the designated agent of delivery and the ultimate arbiter of whether the oath has been abrogated or fulfilled.

Underlying these promises of commitment lurks an anxiety about the loose nature of mortal agency within the social and sacred contract.[14] God is often invoked in order to bolster the role of human action in the public domain. As the plot unravels, the action may undermine the heroic intent of words. A vow or an oath may expose words as rash, with pernicious consequences. By way of example, when Jephthah vows to sacrifice anything (or anyone) that comes to greet him, tragically it turns out to be his only child, his daughter (Judg. 11.35). In opening [*yiftah*] his mouth, the hero (true to his name) hazards on oath and loses, despite his resounding victory in war. The unraveling of the fabula casts the judge/chieftain in tragic relief. Words may also counter words; later betrayals and alternative promises may effectively undermine the power of the vow or oath in the public and private domain. It is these fissures in loyalty that oaths and counteroaths conspicuously uncover. Just as the exchange of secret signs between Rachel and Leah, in the midrashic narrative, entails a semiotic ruse where the younger's empathy for her elder sister trumps loyalty to her husband under the wedding canopy,[15] oaths in the books of Samuel and Kings often express dual loyalty, bound by the ambiguity of language and by shifting positions within the power hierarchy. Ultimately, it is the presence or absence of God, as the plot unfolds in this theocentric history, which determines how the oath is fulfilled or undermined.

---

12. The term *shb'* is deployed in Deut. 7.8; 8.1, 18, perhaps harking back to the covenant between the pieces (Gen. 15.13-16).

13. Only in retrospect, as in the covenant with the patriarchs, is this characterized as a vow (*shb'*), in Ps. 132.11, alluding to 2 Sam. 7.12-16.

14. Ziegler, *Promises to Keep*, p. 30. Ziegler draws on the political philosophy of Thomas Hobbes (*Leviathan* [Indianapolis: Bobbs-Merrill, 1958], pp. 118-19), who argues that the only effective means of binding human beings to their commitments (on oath) is the fear of consequences—the source of the punishment may come from God or man. In the Hebrew Bible, the power of the oath to maintain order in civil society is contingent on a belief (a) in the power of language as binding; and (b) that God will punish those who do not act on their word. David Hume, on the other hand (*A Treatise of Human Nature* [Harmondsworth: Penguin, 1969], pp. 541-42, 568-77), suggests that the strength of human conventions and the potential loss of honor may be a sufficient deterrent in a civil society to breaking an oath.

15. Recounted in the midrashic tradition, as discussed in Chapter 2.

The Oath as a Test of Divine Sanction

One telling example is recounted in ch. 14 of 1 Samuel.[16] The king's oaths are pitted against a counteroath, illustrating the weakening of Saul's hold over the people and over Jonathan, his son, supposedly next in line for the throne.[17] An analysis of the grammar and complex power dynamics in these speech acts sets the precedent for our study. It is significant that this episode follows the prophet's rejection of Saul as founder of a royal lineage (1 Sam. 13.13-14). Just as Macbeth is driven mad by the witch's oracle, King Saul knows that he bears a fruitless crown on his head, and he, like the Scottish thane, is increasingly unhinged over the course of the story; his thoughts turn bloody, his reactions impetuous. The first indication of his impending madness is found in the oath that he imposes upon the troops in a battle against the Philistines: '"Cursed be anyone who eats food before it is evening and I have been avenged on my enemies." So none of the troops tasted food' (1 Sam. 14.24 NRSV).[18]

Saul has made an oath, not just a promise or even a vow. It is a rash one. His power is subsequently undermined in the narrative. First, Jonathan, not having heard the imprecation, tastes honey that he finds in the forest whereupon he is warned by the troops that he has abrogated his father's oath (vv. 26-29). He then denounces his father in response: 'See how my father has troubled [*'akhar*] the land . . .' (v. 29) for had the troops eaten, the slaughter of the Philistines would have been that much greater (v. 30).[19]

---

16. I am grateful to Yael Ziegler for pointing this out to me in conversation. See also the discussion of this passage in her book *Promises to Keep,* pp. 66-68.

17. Following this incident, we are given a list of Saul's progeny (1 Sam. 14.49), as if to say, ironically, 'Yet no son or daughter of his became heirs to the throne'. In the very next chapter, he is permanently deposed as king by the prophet Samuel (1 Sam. 15.22-23), though he continues to function as the monarch through the end of ch. 31 in 1 Samuel.

18. The term for the imposition of an oath here is *'lh*, which means 'to swear, curse' (as in Judg. 17.2; 1 Kgs 8.31; Hos. 4.2; and 10.4 (see BDB entry 529). Later, however, the king's imputed curse is referred to as a *shevu'ah* in 1 Sam. 14.26, and by the more ubiquitous root *shb'* in vv. 27 and 28. See also Gen. 24.8-9 and 41, where these terms again appear to be employed interchangeably.

19. The term here for 'troubled' [*'kr*] resonates with the story of Achan, who 'broke faith in regard to the devoted things', in abrogating the oath not to take of booty, which Joshua had imposed on the people in the conquest of Jericho (Josh. 7.1). Achan is subsequently stoned to death, as one 'who brought trouble [*'akhartanu*]' upon the nation, in an etiological account for the name of the Valley of Achor (vv. 24-25). Similarly, Jephthah insists that his vow is intractable (as though it were an oath), and accuses his daughter: 'You have brought me very low; you have become my troubler [*ve'okhri*]' (Judg. 11.35). And Ahab calls Elijah, 'the troubler [*'okher*] of Israel' (1 Kgs 18.17), perhaps for having imposed an oath that it would not rain except by his word (1 Kgs 17.1). The epithet 'troubler [*'oker*]' is often irrevocably tied to an oath—whether it refers to the one who

As a result of the fast, the men swoop down upon sheep and oxen taken as spoil, gorging themselves upon meat not ritually slaughtered, thus 'sinning against the Lord' in 'eating with the blood' (vv. 32-35). And finally, God responds to Saul's inquiry of the divine oracle before battle with silence (v. 37). Indeed, the absence of heavenly approval is palpable.

What is the function of an oath in the absence of divine sanction? In the tragic unraveling of this episode two more rash oaths are uttered by Saul that ostensibly sentence Jonathan to death. The people, in a counteroath, move to redeem him. When the divine oracle fails to answer Saul before the battle against the Philistines, the king surmises that the oath imposed on the troops must have been abrogated. So the king sets up a process of selecting the guilty party by lot,[20] ironically declaring another, more specific oath: '"For as Yhwh lives who saves Israel, even if it (the abrogation) is through my son Jonathan, he shall surely die!" But there was no one among all the people who answered him' (1 Sam. 14.39). Neither the troops nor Jonathan step forward, at this point, to reveal the guilty party.[21] An oracular device alone is used to discern the transgressor. When Saul and Jonathan are singled out and then Jonathan is taken by lot, prompting a confession, Saul utters yet a third rash oath: 'May God do so and even more; You shall surely die, Jonathan!' (v. 44).

Yael Ziegler notes that the usual formula would entail a conditional self-imprecation, which remains unstated here, 'May God do so *to me*' (that is, punish me with death or loss of all that is dear to me), 'and even more so', if I fail to follow through with this oath (that is, have Jonathan killed for

---

abrogated it (Achan), harshly imposed it (Saul and Elijah), or tragically was forced to fulfill its consequences (Jephthah's daughter).

20. The means by which the guilty party is selected is left open, though it implies the consultation of an oracle (perhaps through the priestly breastplate and/or the Urim and Thumim). This episode also resonates with the Joshua narrative, where Achan is entrapped, caught or taken by lot (the term *lqd* is deployed four times in Josh. 7.15-18) just as both Saul and Jonathan (1 Sam. 14.41) are taken by lot, and later Jonathan alone is selected (v. 42). The effect of these intertextual resonances is to read Saul's oath here as the *inverse* of Joshua's. The earlier oath is in line with God's will; the latter (Saul's) meets divine disapprobation, and results in the 'troubling' of the people, evoking a deferred death sentence that hovers over the king and his son, Jonathan.

21. As Achan confessed (Josh. 7.21-22), following the debacle at Jericho, affirming the authority of the oath, whereas Jonathan's so-called confession (v. 43) essentially undermines his father's oath by emphasizing how minor the transgression was: 'I tasted a little honey with the tip of the staff that was in my hand' (1 Sam. 14.43 NRSV). In the altercation over the lots, Jonathan does not invoke the excuse that he had not heard the oath in the first place, but rather declares (heroically), 'Here I am, I will die [*hineni 'amut*]' (v. 43).

transgression).²² The invocation normally conveys a strong measure of confidence, self-reliance and leadership on the part of the speaker, as if to say, 'I will take the brunt of the consequences if I fail to follow through'. Yet the indirect object, *li* [to me] is conspicuously absent here.²³ Ziegler suggests that the omission reflects 'Saul's inability to assume personal responsibility in leadership in the narrative. . . . This deficiency emerges as a key component . . . in which Saul's rejection by God is finalized (1 Sam. 15)'.²⁴ I would go further and suggest that the invocation of God's name, which, as a religious speech act, would normally affirm the depth of one's commitment, here only resonates with ontological absence. Saul hazards on oath and loses. On one level, Jonathan *should* meet the inimical fate of Achan or Jephthah's daughter. But because God is seemingly absent, human agency steps in to redeem the son.

The people intercept the king's fatal declaration with their own oath, 'Shall Jonathan die, who has accomplished this great victory in Israel? Far from it! As Yhwh lives, not one hair of his head shall fall to the ground; for he has worked with God today' (v. 45 NRSV). They then redeem him, and Jonathan is spared (at least) the immediate death sentence. The language of the people's oath reverberates with the earlier one, where Saul invoked the living God 'who saves Israel', in committing 'even his son' (were he to be found guilty) to die (v. 39). In trumping the earlier words, so fraught with tragic irony, the people inadvertently reassert the divine presence as compassionate and salvific. But in usurping the role of God and mitigating justice, they leave Saul exposed to the consequences, the implied imprecation of his own oath. That is, *he,* Saul, will surely die. Ironically, the oath, as a speech act 'that gets something done', rebounds and strikes the one who uttered those words. As the plot unravels, Saul's original intentions in the oath are undermined. Rather than demonstrating his commitment to the fulfillment of the oath *in the presence of* God, his language exposes, rather, *Deus absconditus*. The presence of divine justice is delayed as the conse-

---

22. In Hebrew, the oath opens with the formula 'May God do so to . . . and more so . . . [*ko ya'aseh 'Elohim/Yhwh l-* . . . *ve-koh yosif* . . .], as in 1 Sam. 3.17; 14.44; 20.13; 25.22; 2 Sam. 3.9; 19.14; 1 Kgs 2.23; 2 Kgs 6.31; Ruth 1.17; and 1 Kgs 19.2 and 20.10, though, in these last two examples, Jezebel and King Ben Hadad of Aram both deploy verbs in the plural since their gods are many: *ya'asun* . . . *yosifun*; Jezebel, like Saul, drops the personal pronoun, *li*. These words imply a curse of self-imprecation, originally intended as a deterrent against abrogating the oath (see the discussion in Ziegler, *Promises to Keep*, p. 37).

23. Ziegler points out that the Greek, Syriac and Vulgate translations all include the word *li* as part of the oath formula. Driver suggests that it is implied, given the context, and is only interpolated into the verse in these later interpretive traditions (Ziegler, *Promises to Keep*, p. 66).

24. Ziegler, *Promises to Keep*, p. 67.

quence, for Saul's rash oath is only later meted out upon Mt Gilboa in the first king's demise on the battlefield against the Philistines.

Herein lies the tragic moment, revealed through the power of the speech act in the unraveling of fate. As Paul Ricoeur avers,

> The tragic properly so called does not appear until the theme of predestination to evil . . . comes up against the theme of heroic greatness; fate must first feel the resistance of freedom, rebound (so to speak) from the hardness of the hero, and finally crush him, before the pre-eminently tragic emotion—*phobos*—can be born.[25]

By juxtaposing these oaths, the redactor underscores how the Saulide monarchy is undermined by both the absence of divine sanction and the political will of the people. It thus anticipates the people's choice of David, also divinely selected, as the one who will ultimately upstage Saul. Furthermore, the father–son bond is irrevocably broken, not only by the rejection of Saul but also by the father's near filicide. The breach between Saul and Jonathan is a chasm that yawns over the father's willing sacrifice. In the narrative, the heir apparent is now free from filial duty and lineal destiny to ally with his rival for the throne. Jonathan binds himself in loyalty to David through oath and pact (1 Sam. 18.3; 20.13-16; 23.16-18).[26]

Like Jonathan, Michal mirrors her brother's relationship with David through a series of promises, rather than oaths, made and broken by her father. As scholars have before me, I analyze the relationship between Michal and King David along gender lines, with an added theological dimension. The promise and their consequences reflect the shifting power dynamics between deity, people, king and successor to the throne. By invoking God in the implied imprecation, these religious speech acts dare pose the question, 'Is God in our midst or not?'[27] As the prime mover in this history, God will ultimately be the arbiter of the oath's outcome. Whether and how the consequences of the oath are borne out or undermined tests the power of human speech acts and ultimately serves as a litmus test for divine favor.

---

25. Paul Ricoeur, *The Symbolism of Evil* (New York: Harper & Row, 1967), p. 218. For an eloquent discussion of Saul as a tragic figure, see Cheryl Exum, 'Saul: The Hostility of God', in *Tragedy and Biblical Narrative: Arrows of the Almighty* (Cambridge: Cambridge University Press, 1992), pp. 116-52; and David Gunn, *The Fate of King Saul: An Interpretation of a Biblical Story* (Sheffield: JSOT Press, 1980).

26. See the discussion in Ziegler, *Promises to Keep*, pp. 71-72.

27. An allusion to Exod. 17.7.

6

MICHAL: THE KING'S DAUGHTER OR THE KING'S WIFE?

> Bassanio: *I swear to thee, even by thine own fair eyes,*
> *Wherein I see myself—*
> Portia: *Mark you but that!*
> *In both my eyes he doubly sees himself;*
> *In each eye, one: swear by your double self,*
> *And there's an oath of credit.*
>   Shakespeare, *The Merchant of Venice* V.i

Michal as a Liminal Figure

Michal inhabits liminal space, in Victor Turner's terms, 'betwixt and between assigned societal positions' in the biblical narrative.[1] Caught between the role she is born into as the 'daughter of the king [*bat Sha'ul*]' and the one she assumes as 'wife of the king [*'eshet David*]',[2] she navigates the treacherous terrain of power play in the king's court. It is important to note that she both chooses to be David's wife and is chosen for that role as a ploy. She is an agent of her own narrative but is also acted upon by the male protagonists. Along the diachronic axis, I trace the complex negotiations between the king and his rival in marrying into the monarchy and the shifting nature of Michal's agency (or lack thereof) in the palace. One promise is displaced by another in the negotiations between Saul and David over the bride price, which is analyzed within the larger theme of the female ruse peculiar to the Davidic narrative. Along the synchronic axis, in spatial terms, I examine Michal's position as the classic 'woman in the window' who negotiates her liminal role either in allying *with* David or *against* him, metaphorically in terms of the degrees to which she leans in or out of the sanctioned window frame.

---

   1. Victor Turner, *The Ritual Process: Structure and Anti-Structure* (Chicago: Aldine Publishing, 1969), p. 95.
   2. Alter, *Biblical Narrative*, p. 127.

Inauspiciously, Michal is introduced to us only after the first rejection of Saul and the debacle with the broken oaths in ch. 14:

> Now the sons of Saul were Jonathan, Ishvi, and Malchishua; and the names of his two daughters were these: the name of the firstborn was Merab, and the name of the younger, Michal (1 Sam. 14.49 NRSV).

Given the unhinged mind of King Saul and God's covert plans for the monarchy, the redactor, in placing the verse here, casts a shadow over this lineage as if to say, 'Here is the list of Saul's descendants, yet none of his progeny will assume the throne'.

Cheryl Exum has astutely pointed out the differences between brother and sister, as displaced heirs, in terms of their gender and agency.[3] Both Jonathan and Michal love David, and both betray their father in order to save him. The narrator informs us that 'the soul of Jonathan was bound to the soul of David [*niqsherah benefesh David*], and Jonathan loved him as his own soul [*kenafsho*]' (1 Sam. 18.1; cf. v. 3 NRSV).[4] Similarly, we are told twice that Michal loved David (vv. 20, 28). As Robert Alter points out, 'This love, twice stated here, is bound to have special salience because it is the only instance in all biblical narrative in which we are explicitly told that a woman loves a man'.[5] Yet Jonathan's love of David is reciprocated,[6] while Michal's love becomes subservient to Saul's murderous plot (vv. 17, 21) and the young hero's desire to marry into the monarchy (v. 26). Furthermore, Jonathan is valorized as a military hero in chs. 14 and 31, in anticipation of David's role at the army's helm. When David becomes a fugitive from Saul's wrath, Jonathan shuttles between court and field to prove fealty

---

3. Cheryl Exum, 'Michal: The Whole Story', in *Fragmented Women: Feminist (Sub) versions of Biblical Narratives* (Valley Forge, PA: Trinity Press International, 1993), pp. 42-60. See also Adele Berlin, *Poetics and Interpretation of Biblical Narrative* (Sheffield: Almond Press, 1983), pp. 24-25.

4. See also 1 Sam. 18.3 and 20.17. The Hebrew idiom *nafsho qeshurah benafsho* is used with respect to the father–son bond (as in Jacob's attachment to Benjamin in Gen. 44.30). The phrase suggests that he who loves is willing to substitute his life for the other. This is most poignantly expressed by Jonathan's dressing David up in his battle garb, sword and belt (1 Sam. 18.4)—as if David were now the true crown prince in his stead. This is an act of renunciation, the clothing metonymic for the person himself. Jan Fokkelman comments, 'He not only confirms his love by a ritual around a solemn oath, he finally also shows everything he feels and means in a gesture and a sign: he gives David his arms... Jonathan is transferring the title of champion to David; champion in the sense of the national hero who acts in the name of the Lord of Hosts and becomes the great liberator.... In the inter-regnum arising from Saul's failure in ch. 13, he [Jonathan] was only the temporary substitute for David, who still had to be found by the prophet, and now [Jonathan] withdraws' (Jan Fokkelman, *Narrative Art and Poetry in the Books of Samuel*. Vol. II: *The Crossing Fates* [Assen: Van Gorcum, 1986], p. 198).

5. Alter, *Biblical Narrative*, p. 118.

6. Cf. 1 Sam. 20.41.

to his friend (19.2-7 and ch. 20). And the prince dies a hero in battle, eulogized by the very man who supplants him: 'I grieve for you, my brother, Jonathan. Very dear you were to me. More wondrous your love to me than the love of women' (2 Sam. 1.26).[7] The displaced heir inhabits the classic masculine locus of a military hero in the public domain. Yet Jonathan's love is hyperfeminized, '*more* than the love of women', marked by the narrator as a total submersion of the self in the other, for he loved David as himself (1 Sam. 18.1, 3; cf. Lev. 19.18).[8]

Michal, on the other hand, is confined to the home, to the palace, to the private domain of women, her agency increasingly occluded. Looking out the window in her final scene, she sees her husband-king cavorting before the ark of the Lord as he escorts it into the capital. The omniscient narrator informs us that 'she despised him in her heart' (2 Sam. 6.16). She is then removed ignominiously from the biblical narrative after a bitter exchange with her husband. The reader is told, 'And Michal daughter of Saul had no child till her dying day' (v. 23). Where Jonathan's love surpasses the love of women, Michal's love meets the fate of the most maligned of women; she is left childless. What, in love, 'admits impediment, alters when it alteration finds',[9] turning Michal's love to hatred?

The Bride Price: Broken or Displaced Promises

As we explore Michal's role as an adjunct to David's meteoric rise to power, it is important to recall, as summarized in the previous chapter, how Saul sets marriage to the princess up as a deathtrap for his rival through a series of promises, which are then ignored, deferred, displaced or broken. Though not uttered as formal oaths, these promises still function as counters in the semiotic play of power. His words spin in a widening gyre where the falcon cannot hear the falconer. Michal, the promised princess, is also marked with fatality. After the private inauguration and David's appointment to the court as the king's minstrel (ch. 16), the young rival to Saul's throne first appears

---

7. Robert Alter's translation, *David Story* (New York: W.W. Norton, 1999), p. 200. The love between the friends is reinforced by the pact they make between themselves and their emotional parting (18.3; 20.14-17 and 41-42). In contrasting David's love for Jonathan and his feelings (or absence of feelings) for Michal, Berlin points out, 'David, then, seems to have related to Michal as to a man and to Jonathan as to a woman' (Berlin, *Poetics*, p. 25). I think the gender aspect of love is rather more complicated than this, concerned with the shifting boundaries of self and other.

8. On the wide range of love in the David story, from selfishness to self-love, from tenderness and recognition to masked aggression, see the discussion in Fokkelman, *The Crossing Fates*, pp. 196-97, as well as the discussion of Jonathan's absorption into David in n. 4 of this chapter.

9. A paraphrase of Shakespeare's Sonnet 116.

on the public scene bare of military regalia, merely his sling and stones in hand, daring to defeat Goliath, the indomitable giant of the Philistine camp. But he takes on the challenge with the ulterior motive of marrying into the monarchy. An Israelite first announces the reward: 'The king will greatly enrich the man who kills him, and will give him his daughter and make his family free in Israel' (1 Sam. 17.25 NRSV). David then verifies, twice, that such will be the reward for the slayer of Goliath, 'the uncircumcised Philistine' who defies 'the armies of the living God' (vv. 26-27, 30). As in the classic folktale pattern, the most unlikely candidate—a poor Hans (or Shlemiel), a mere shepherd boy—defeats the ogre or giant by virtue of his courage and wit, and thereby wins the hand of the princess. Yet, strangely, at the end of ch. 17 nothing comes of this incident. The fulfillment of the king's promise is deferred or simply ignored, perhaps because the youngest son of Jesse has yet to take on the role of leading the troops into the fray (18.1-16).

In the next chapter, David demonstrates that the Lord is with him (v. 15), earns the love of Jonathan, Judah and Israel (vv. 1, 3, 7, 16) and becomes, both literally and psychologically, the target of the king's enmity (vv. 10-11, 16). When Saul appoints him captain over a thousand (v. 13) in battling the Philistines, a second pretext for marrying into the monarchy is established, setting up a contrast between the motives of King Saul, his rival and the princess promised in marriage:

> Then Saul said to David 'Here is my elder daughter Merab; her I will give to you as a wife; only be valiant for me and fight Yhwh's battles'. And Saul said [to himself], 'Let not my hand be against him, but let the hand of the Philistines be against him'. David said to Saul, 'Who am I and who are my kin,[10] my father's family in Israel, that I should be son-in-law to the king?' And at the time when Saul's daughter Merab should have been given to David, she was given to Adriel the Meholathite as a wife. And Saul's daughter Michal loved David, and they told Saul, and the thing was pleasing in his eyes. Saul said [to himself], 'Let me give her to him that she may be a snare for him and that the hand of the Philistines may be against him'. Therefore Saul said to David, 'Through two [*bishtayim*] you can become my son-in-law'. Saul commanded his servants, 'Speak to David in private saying, 'See, the king is delighted with you, and all his servants love you; now then, become the king's son-in-law' (1 Sam. 18.17-22, author's trans.).

---

10. Literally, 'what is my life [*hayai*]', according to the vocalization of the MT. If, as Bar-Efrat argues, the term *hay* is indicative of family clans (as in the Arabic cognate), the text should be amended to *hayi* ['my kin'] (Bar-Efrat, *I Shmuel* [Tel Aviv: Am Oved, 1996], p. 242; see also Alter, *David Story*, p. 115). The obsequious tone David assumes is parallel to his self-deprecation after God promises him a dynasty: 'Who am I, my Lord Yhwh, and what is my house that you have brought me thus far?' (2 Sam. 7.18).

In this scene, the narrative deploys irony through various modes of verbal exchange—direct speech, indirect report or thoughts pronounced *sotto voce*. Marriage to the king's daughter did not follow the defeat of Goliath, as the king had declared, so another promise is invoked through Merab, 'the older daughter' (v. 17). Yet this promise, too, is broken when she is given away to another.[11] Pronounced at a stage whisper, we are told twice of Saul's ploy (vv. 17, 21). In loving David, Michal would serve as 'a snare to him' (v. 21). The promise of the king's daughter becomes the pretext for sending the warrior to his peril at the front (perhaps anticipating David's murder by proxy of Uriah). Saul's intentions are later corroborated by the narrator: 'Saul intended to bring about David's death at the hands of the Philistines' (v. 25). Yet, ironically, the very means by which the king plots his rival's downfall becomes the source of David's rising esteem in the eyes of others (v. 30).

According to Alter, Saul is portrayed as a 'Machiavellian schemer ... inclined to clumsy lunges rather than deft thrusts and perhaps for that reason not *political* enough to retain the throne'.[12] David's speech, on the other hand, is ambiguous and highly political. His declarations of humility are made in public—'Who am I and who are my kin . . . ?' (v. 18) and 'Do you think that becoming the son-in-law of a king is a light matter [*ha-neqallah*], when I am but a poor man of no consequence [*'ish-rash va-niqleh*]?' (v. 23). We wonder whether he indeed feels unworthy of marrying into the monarchy or whether he is trying to deflect attention away from his vaulting ambition. The reader is left to speculate about the intent behind the formally obsequious language, caught in the gap between the private person and the public man. While Saul is wholly transparent, David completely opaque, Michal is a 'sliver of transparency surrounded by darkness'.[13] The narrator informs us that 'Michal loved David' (vv. 20, echoed in v. 28), yet we are not told why.

Once Merab is given in marriage to another, Plan C ensues, and again we are privy to Saul's thoughts, preemptively this time; he will use his daughter's love as a snare. Ambiguously he proposes, 'Through two [*bishtayim*]

---

11. No explanation for Merab's marriage to another is given in the text—perhaps it was of her own volition that she married Adriel rather than David, or it was a bungled ruse on the part of her father. The displacement of the older by the younger sister inversely resonates with Laban's duping of Jacob and perhaps anticipates that Michal, too, will later be given to another (1 Sam. 25.44). The five sons of Merab, whom she bore to Adriel, were sacrificed upon the demand of the Gibeonites at David's orders (2 Sam. 21.8, the MT records 'the five sons of Michal', though this is clearly a textual error; the 'correct' or 'corrected' version is preserved in the LXX). This tragic episode effectively ends Saul's line of descendants.
12. Alter, *Biblical Narrative*, p. 118.
13. Alter, *Biblical Narrative*, p. 118.

you can become my son-in-law' (v. 21).[14] Rather than a glossing over the awkwardness of the Hebrew, I suggest that a triple entendre is intended.[15] At the simplest level, Saul promises David his *second* daughter, Michal, in lieu of the first. On another level, the king alludes to the two reasons he wishes David to become his son-in-law: because the 'king desires you' and 'all his servants love you' (v. 22). On yet a third level, Saul intends to bring David down by a 'second' feat (the head of Goliath being the first). Saul adjures his servants, 'Thus shall you say to David: "The king has no desire for any bride price except a hundred Philistine foreskins, to take vengeance against the king's enemies". And Saul devised to make David fall by the hand of the Philistines' (v. 25). At this point, we are given a clue as to David's intentions: 'And the thing was pleasing in David's eyes to become son-in-law to the king' (v. 26). He is not moved by love!

Saul puts David's masculinity on the line by demanding, as the bride price, a hundred Philistine foreskins, the 'scalped potency of the enemy'.[16] The foreskin symbolizes an abomination, circumcision the somatic sign of distinction for the male Israelite; to be defeated by the 'uncircumcised' is the ultimate reproach.[17] Saul's declaration that 'through two [*bishtayim*]' David may 'become [his] son-in-law' (v. 22) resounds with yet another layer of irony, anticipating David's later doubling of the bride price; he returns from battle, having killed two hundred Philistines and blithely counts out the skins before the king (v. 27).[18] As Fokkelman notes, 'With superior ease he pays double the (substitute) bride price for obtaining Michal, so that he is doubly assured of the hand of the princess and outdoes the king who had cunningly kept the other princess from him'.[19] Addressing the question as to why Saul set this particular task for David, Fokkelman comments,

> David earned the princess on the battlefield, but even before the king could give her in marriage the women of Israel sang their victory song and Saul

---

14. The Aramaic amends the phrase: 'through one of two [*behad'a min tartein*]' (*Targ. Jon.*); similarly: 'Thou shalt this day be my son-in-law through the one of the twain' (JPS, KJV); 'And Saul spoke to David *a second time*' (NRSV); 'You can be my son-in-law even now through the second one' (NJPS; Alter, *David Story*, p. 116); the Septuagint omits vv. 17-19 altogether.

15. Based on Alter, *David Story*, p. 116; and Fokkelman, *Crossing Fates*, pp. 241-42.

16. Fokkelman's apt term (*Crossing Fates*, p. 240).

17. David twice answers the challenge of Goliath by reference to his uncircumcised status as a reproach: 'What shall be done for the man who kills this Philistine, and takes away the *reproach* from Israel? For who is this *uncircumcised* Philistine that he should defy the armies of the living God?' (1 Sam. 17.26, 36; cf. 1 Sam. 31.4; 2 Sam. 1.20).

18. The Septuagint reads one hundred Philistines; cf. 2 Sam. 3.14.

19. Fokkelman, *Crossing Fates*, p. 241.

felt slighted, thinking that David had received the highest praise.[20] Beside himself with rage and jealousy he threw the phallic weapon in a desperate attempt once again to be the only loved one at the top. Now he continues destruction by incorporating into his strategy the woman, first hesitantly (Merab), and then clearly developed (Michal as the snare). He connects the elements wife and death in order to give David both.... The wish that David should kill 100 Philistines is thus a shift of his own tremendous aggression towards David. And it may be assumed that underlying this aggression is Saul's fear of David's potency (the hero is already celebrated by all women . . .).[21]

Where does this leave Michal? The very fact that the reader is twice told 'And Michal loved David' (vv. 20, 28), without any motivation given, suggests that she may operate independently of her father's machinations. Alter notes how the displacement of Merab by Michal, the older by the younger daughter, inversely resonates with Laban's ruse against Jacob.[22] While the deception of the patriarch was enabled by a night-time switch of the brides, the younger for the older in the infamous bedtrick, where the women served as mere pawns in their father's plot (at least in the biblical narrative), here the displacement of the older sister by the younger is done overtly, by way of a promise, a barter in broad daylight, wherein the motivations of the male parties are made explicit. The first promise, however, is broken, and this allows Michal to move center stage, both as a pawn in her father's ploy and a player in her own right. Leaving the reason for her love muted allows her independence as an agent in aligning herself against her father, but it also leaves Michal vulnerable to her husband's power play, her love open for a bitter turn. As Fokkelman suggests, 'The salutation to her love poses the question: how will Michal fare in the future at David's side? Will we hear that David returns her feelings?'[23]

The Woman in the Window

The next encounter with Michal follows alternating scenes of murderous and affectionate interactions between Saul and David, as the characters traverse the setting of palace, field and home. The vicissitudes of Saul's alternating aggression toward and affection for David are first mediated by Jonathan: 'And Saul urged *his son* and all his servants to kill David, but Jonathan *his son* greatly delighted in David [*hafetz bedavid me'od*]'

---

20. Referring to the song with which the women come out to greet them: 'Saul has struck down his thousands and David his tens of thousands' (1 Sam. 18.7).
21. Fokkelman, *Crossing Fates*, p. 245.
22. Alter, *David Story*, p. 117, and Fokkelman, *Narrative Art in Genesis,* p. 120.
23. Fokkelman, *Crossing Fates*, p. 243.

(1 Sam. 19.1).[24] The relational epithet, 'his son', highlights the tension between Jonathan's loyalty to his father and his protective feelings for his friend, anticipating Michal's shift of loyalty. Jonathan responds to his father's orders by staging a conversation in the field with his father, which David (in hiding) is meant to overhear, urging the king not to kill 'his servant' because he has been so successful in battle against the Philistines.

In response, Saul swears, 'As Yhwh lives, he (David) shall not be put to death' (1 Sam. 19.6 NRSV).[25] The grammar and the rhetorical thrust of the oath implies a curse of self-imprecation: By the life of God, may such and such a calamity befall me if so-and-so dies. As we pointed out earlier, Saul is prone to hazard on oath and fail, indicative of a fault line in his character and the absence of divine sanction. Just as an oath can later be undermined by another, reflecting shifting alliances in the power hierarchy, this king continually undermines his own promises, foreshadowing the final renunciation that David will exact of Saul in the cave at Ein Gedi (ch. 24) and in the Wilderness of Ziph (ch. 26). The oath highlights the widening gap between Saul's command of language as a binding force over his conscience and his erratic and violent outbursts against David.[26] As a speech act that 'gets something done', it also reverberates ironically back onto the king as he fatally pursues David; the implied curse puts Saul's own life increasingly on the line. As Alter points out, 'Saul's paranoia and uncontrolled outbursts manifest themselves in an intermittent cycle. He is amenable to the voice of reason and conscience, and vows in presumably good faith not to harm David, but further evidence of David's military brilliance will unleash another round of violent impulses. In consequence, through this sequence of the narrative, David oscillates between being a proscribed person and someone Saul expects to be a faithful member of his court.'[27]

That is until Michal takes sides—whereupon David flees the court permanently:

24. The stative verb $hfiz$ is usually associated with desire (not necessarily erotic), as Saul ironically avows, 'Look the king desires you and all his servants love you . . .' (1 Sam. 18.22).

25. Literally, in Hebrew, 'As Yhwh lives . . . if he dies ['*im yamut*]'. In this oath formula the curse, incumbent upon the one who utters the oath if he fails to follow through with the promise, remains unstated. It serves as a personal pledge *not* to act. The function of the oath, in this chapter, contrasts with Saul's resolve to uphold his oath even at the risk of Jonathan's life (1 Sam. 14.39, 44). Yael Zeigler points out that Saul's seeming lack of concern over the subsequent violation of his own oath here indicates a downward spiral in his moral character (*Promises to Keep*, pp. 175-76).

26. On a number of occasions, Saul thrusts his spear at David when the 'evil spirit of the Lord' overtakes him, and David successfully eludes it (1 Sam. 18.10-11 [2x] and 19.9-10). The king is finally driven to threaten even Jonathan, David's stand-in and protector (1 Sam. 20.33), which marks the final breach between father and son.

27. Alter, *David Story*, p. 118.

> And Saul sought to strike the spear through David into the wall but he slipped away from his presence and [Saul] struck the spear into the wall, and David fled and escaped that very night. Saul sent messengers to David's house to keep watch over him, planning to kill him in the morning. And Michal *his wife* [*'ishto*] told David saying, 'If you do not save your life tonight, tomorrow you will be killed'.
> So Michal let David down through the window [*be'ad ha-ḥalon*]; he went off, fled away and escaped.
> Then Michal took the household idol [*ha-teraphim*] and laid it on the bed; she put a net of goats' hair on its head, and covered it with the clothes.
> When Saul sent messengers to take David, she said, 'He is sick'.
> Then Saul sent the messengers to see David for themselves, saying, 'Bring him up to me in the bed, that I may kill him'.
> When the messengers came in, behold, the household idol was in the bed, with the net of goats' hair at its head.
> Saul said to Michal, 'Why have you deceived me like this, and let my enemy go, so that he has escaped?'
> Michal answered Saul, 'He said to me, "Let me go; why should I kill you?"'
> And (so) David fled and escaped . . . (1 Sam. 19.10-18).

In this scene at their home, Michal is identified unequivocally as 'his wife', in allying with David by enabling his escape. The dialogue between Michal and David is hurried and one-sided, perhaps to emphasize the rapid sequence of actions—'he went off, fled away and escaped'—but his silence also contributes to the narrative asymmetry in presenting their motives. As Alter points out, 'it continues the pattern of occluding David's inner responses that we observed in ch. 18. Michal is risking a great deal in order to save David. We have no idea about his feelings toward her as she does this.'[28] To elude the messengers, she uses the household idols [*teraphim*] as a makeshift figure in place of her husband's body in bed, claiming he is sick. The prop resonates with the Genesis story, in which a daughter allies with her husband against her father, and is inadvertently condemned to death by this act of deception. Rachel had stolen her father's idols [*teraphim*], unbeknown to Jacob (Gen. 31.19), and when Laban accuses Jacob of stealing his gods, Jacob pronounces an oath that, ironically, effectively acts as a death threat upon his beloved wife: '"Anyone with whom you find your gods shall not live . . ." And Jacob did not know that Rachel had stolen them' (v. 32). Though Laban never recovers his *teraphim,* Jacob's condemnation of the thief anticipates, poetically, the fatal consequences; soon after, Rachel dies prematurely in giving birth (35.17-18).[29] In both these scenes

---

28. Alter, *David Story*, p. 120.
29. Picking up on the dramatic irony, *Gen. R.* 74.4, p. 861, makes the causal link between Jacob's imprecation in Gen. 31.32 and Rachel's fate, 'And Rachel died . . .' (Gen. 35.19). See the discussion in Chapter 2 at n. 71.

of the *teraphim*, the woman renounces her allegiance to her father while caught in a tragic act of deception.[30]

In contrast to the Genesis narrative where Jacob inadvertently condemns Rachel to death, it is Michal's own words that anticipate her figurative death, what Cheryl Exum provocatively calls her 'literary murder'.[31] Saul, in outrage, accuses her, 'Why did you deceive [*lamah rimitani*]?', echoing Jacob's indignation after the night of the switched brides (Gen. 29.25). Yet, it is not the father-in-law but the daughter here who takes the lead in the ruse. As a cover, Michal presents herself as the potential victim of a threat: 'He said to me, "Let me go; why should I kill you [*'amitekh*]?"' (v. 17). As Exum points out, 'the last word of that account . . . reappears hauntingly in the last word of 2 Samuel 6: "[And Michal the daughter of Saul had no child] until the day of her death [*motah*]."'[32] Indeed her childlessness is a kind of death. But I disagree with Exum's claim that David's threat to kill Michal, in the end, is carried out. For one, there is no indication that any such threat was made. And the reason why she remains childless evocatively remains unstated.[33] Her invocation of a threat that David supposedly made must be read as an initial alliance *with* her husband in deceiving her father. But she is not invited to flee with David, nor does she stand up to Saul directly or feign shock at the discovery in the bed. So her father does not fall for the ruse. Her *own* words, then, ironically rebound against her, foreshadowing her death-in-life fate, which none of the dramatis personae consciously will.

More significantly, the portent of Michal's mortality in this scene concerns her role as a liminal figure. She is a woman betwixt and between social roles, the king's daughter and the king's wife, framed by the window through which David escapes and from which she will later gaze down upon him in scorn (*be'ad ha-ḥalon*, 1 Sam. 19.12; 2 Sam. 6.16). According to Don Seeman, the biblical window is 'deployed poetically to signify a threshold across which anxiety concerning the boundaries and integrity of kin groups plays out. . . . Narratives involving window motifs convey messages about the political and ideological oppositions between kin-based groups, including political regimes like the houses of David and of Saul.'[34]

There are three other biblical women whose allegiance of kinship is framed by the window, by the boundary between the inner and outer domains, defin-

---

30. Alter, *Biblical Narrative*, p. 120. For a literary comparison of the biblical figures Michal and Rachel, see Chaya ben Ayun, 'Between Michal and Rachel—Reflection of Misery', in *Beit Mikra: Journal for the Study of the Bible and its World* 48 (2003), pp. 289-301 (Heb.).

31. Exum, 'Michal: The Whole Story', p. 50.

32. Exum, 'Michal: The Whole Story', p. 50.

33. Alter, *Biblical Narrative*, p. 124.

34. Don Seeman, 'The Watcher at the Window: Cultural Poetics of a Biblical Motif', *Prooftexts* 24 (2004), p. 1.

ing the line between home, the feminine locus of privacy, and the masculine locus of the public arena, of shifting horizons, of freedom and escape. Yet Saul undermines that inner sanctum, commanding that the husband be delivered over even as he presumably lies sick in bed (19.15). When the home, metonymically represented by the bed, the site of conjugal relations, itself becomes threatened by the woman's position of dual loyalty, then there is nowhere to go except through a portal into liberty, crossing the boundary between inner 'safety' and outer freedom, through a back door, across a roof, or lowered from a window by a rope. So Rahab negotiates her betrayal of Jericho *through* the window [*be 'ad ha-ḥalon*], from which the spies escaped by a rope (Josh. 2.15) and where she ties the crimson cord (v. 21) to signal her allegiance and eventual rescue from the walls that come tumbling down. Similarly, the mother of Sisera, commander of the Canaanite army, peers out of the window [*be 'ad ha-ḥalon*], through the lattice, in anticipation of her son's return (Judg. 5.28). But her hopes that he will come laden with spoil, women and embroidered cloth, 'wombs [*raḥam raḥmatayim*]' and colorful woven goods '*riqmah . . . riqmatayim*' (v. 30), are ironically dashed on that windowsill; the reader knows that Sisera has been felled by a woman. His mother never crosses that threshold of hope into reality.

Jezebel is also divided in loyalty as she paints her eyes and adorns her head, and brazenly looks out the window [*be 'ad ha-ḥalon*] (2 Kgs 9.30). She prepares herself to ally with Jehu, the new king of Israel, murderer of her husband and sons, but she is quite literally dashed to her demise when she is thrown through that very same window and trampled to death by horses (v. 33). Despite her intentions, Jezebel does not cross sides, never traverses that liminal threshold alive, but remains confined to the supposedly 'safe', now endangered, feminine inner domain. The room bodes death; a tombstone invisibly frames the window into freedom.

So too Michal stands frozen in that inner space. In the earlier scene, she took sides as David's wife, enabling *his* escape. But as Saul's daughter, she could not travel through that window with her husband into freedom. Instead, she is relegated (once again) to a pawn. Following the list of David's wives (Ahinoam and Abigail) at the end of ch. 25, we are told that 'Saul had given his daughter Michal, David's wife, to Palti son of Laish, who was from Gallim' (1 Sam. 25.44). Again, she is identified here by the epithet 'David's wife', as if to demarcate the reason for the king's maneuver; her father intends to undermine that very relationship in response to his daughter's earlier betrayal. In her next scene, she is again shuttled between husbands as David, now king, moves to unite the tribes of Judah and Benjamin following the civil war:

> David also sent messengers to Ish-bosheth son of Saul, to say, 'Give me *my wife* [*'ishti*] Michal, whom I betrothed with one hundred Philistine foreskins'. So Ish-bosheth sent and had her taken away from *a man* [*'ish*],

from Paltiel son of Laish. *Her man* [*'ishah*] walked with her, walking and weeping as far as Bahurim; then Abner ordered him, 'Go, turn back', and he returned (2 Sam. 3.14-16, author's trans.).

The narrator sets up a contrast between David's proprietorial and political claim over Michal, whom he identifies as '*my wife* [*'ishti*]', and the emotional loyalty of Paltiel, identified first as 'a man [*'ish*]', and then as '*her* man [*'ishah*]'. Politically calculating and cold, the king crudely recalls his virile feat in marrying into the royal clan of Benjamin. Paltiel, by contrast, walks by her side, weeping all the way until he reaches the territorial boundary between Judah and Benjamin. We hear no conversation between Michal and David upon their reunion. Once again, she crosses sides, but not of her own volition.

In the next scene, we see Michal for the last time, again framed by a window:

> David whirled with all his might before Yhwh; David was girt with a linen ephod. Thus David and all the house of Israel brought up the ark of Yhwh with shouts and with blasts of the horn. As the ark of Yhwh came into the city of David, Michal daughter of Saul looked out of the window, and saw King David leaping and dancing before the LORD; and she despised him in her heart [*va-tibaz be-libah*].... David returned to bless his household. But Michal, the daughter of Saul, came out to meet David, and said, 'How honored [*nikhbad*] is the king of Israel today, uncovering himself today before the eyes of his servants' slave girls, as any vulgar fellow might shamelessly uncover himself!' David said to Michal, 'It was before Yhwh, who chose me in place of your father and all his household, to appoint me as prince [*nagid*] over Israel, the people of Yhwh, that I have danced before Yhwh. I will make myself yet lighter [*u-neqaloti*] than this, and I will be abased in my own eyes; but by the slave girls of whom you have spoken, by them I shall be held in honor [*'ikavedah*]' (2 Sam. 6.14-16, 20-22, author's trans.).

Here, Michal is significantly identified by the epithet 'Saul's daughter' (v. 16)—her lot as princess chosen by the narrator, her position framed by the window. In the earlier scene by the window, she is identified as David's wife [*ishto*] (1 Sam. 19.11). Yet, as Klein points out, 'the window which provided David with freedom and saved his life becomes a window which confines Michal, evidenced by the bitter tone of her words. The window "frames" each of these scenes, much as it "frames" David's earlier speechless passivity, and his later surge of uninhibited activity. The window also "frames" the sexual content of each of the scenes....'[35]

In the earlier scene, Michal is the passionate one, David silent and passive (represented by the mute *teraphim* that remain coldly wooden in their shared abandoned marital bed); their roles, here, are reversed. As he leaps

---

35. Klein, 'Michal, the Barren Wife', p. 42.

6. *Michal*

and cavorts (vv. 14, 16), uninhibited in his linen tunic before the presence of the ark, David is in full form—the farm boy, shepherd, poet, musician—all heart. She now stands, statuesque, the bronze figure of a princess turned green, watching from the window. At that moment, we know that her love has turned to disdain [*bzh*] (v. 16), though no reason is given. Perhaps she is appalled by his undignified display, or she is envious of this moment of glory, or resentful of his indifference to her all those years (as he acquired other wives) when she was wrested from a man who clearly loved her. As Alter points out, 'by suppressing any causal explanation in his initial statement of Michal's scorn, [the biblical author] beautifully suggests the 'overdetermined' nature of her contemptuous ire, how it bears the weight of everything that has not been said but obliquely intimated about the relation between Michal and David'.[36]

In their bitter exchange, Michal opens with a sarcastic barb: 'How honored [*nikhbad*] is the king of Israel today . . .' (v. 20)—so 'honored, heavy, weighty [*kbd*]',[37] while, in truth, lightly/dishonorably exposing himself to slave girls. David answers her with an equally sarcastic repartee, only adding gall to her wound as he refers to God, before whom he dances, as the deity who chose him over her father (v. 21). He responds to her insistence on honor/weight [*kbd*] with a desire to be even 'lighter/more dishonored or debased [*u-neqaloti*]'[38] in the eyes of God, while heavier/more honorable in the eyes of the slave girls of whom she spoke. In this witty play on the terms *kbd* and *qll,* David inadvertently echoes his own obsequious words to Saul, when Michal was first promised in marriage to him: 'Does it seem a light thing [*ha-neqalah*] to be the king's son-in-law, seeing that I am a poor man, and lightly esteemed [*va-niqleh*]?' (1 Sam. 18.23). Clearly the tables have turned. Where once he had been deferential (perhaps feigning), now David is openly disdainful of his marriage to the princess; he revels, rather, in his honor in slave girls' eyes.

The narrator is given the last word in this bitter sequence. 'And Michal, daughter of Saul, had no child till her dying day' (2 Sam. 6.23). Barren?[39] Or abandoned as a 'grass widow' in her tower? Frozen as she stands by the window frame? We are left to ponder why she is served this tragic fate. One might justifiably conclude that David simply stopped having conjugal relations with her. Or that Michal's fate is merely collateral in covert curse

---

36. Alter, *Biblical Narrative*, p. 123.

37. Based on the root *kbd,* which in the qal (a stative verb) suggests 'being heavy or weighty', though in the niphal (passive form) it implies 'being honored' (See BDB entry 4318, p. 458).

38. From the root *qll*, which in the niphal means 'to appear trifling' or 'lightly esteemed' (see BDB entry 8589, p. 886).

39. The MT on 2 Sam. 21.8 records that 'Michal had fives sons' whom she bore to Adriel, but this is clearly an error in textual transmission (see n. 11 of this chapter).

on Saul's monarchy; this is the end of the Saulide line. Perhaps the biblical author implies the workings of retributive justice, divine disapproval in response to Michal's disdain for the king. Yet the parataxis of the Hebrew 'and' suggests an ambiguity about consequences. As Alter suggests, 'we may presume too much altogether in seeing here any definite relation of cause and effect: we cannot be entirely certain that Michal's childlessness is not a bitter coincidence, the last painful twist of a wronged woman's fate'.[40] Our sympathies remain with her, as she is bound to and torn between father and husband. In the androcentric world of king making, she ultimately has little say.

Conclusion: Michal, Princess of Broken Promises

As the daughter of King Saul, Michal serves as a wager in the rivalry between the incumbent monarch and his archrival, David, and is tragically deprived of autonomy over the course of the narrative. She is the only woman in the Hebrew Bible who is said to love a man, yet that very love becomes her undoing. Her father positions her as the pretext for David's fall, when she displaces her older sister (as Leah had displaced her younger sister, Rachel, in the House of Laban), sending him out to the front to win the gruesome bride price of a hundred Philistine foreskins. Like Rachel, the matriarch, she is 'sentenced to' a 'literary death' when she sides with her husband against her father, by helping David escape 'through the window'. She reports a supposed threat, 'Why should I kill you?' (1 Sam. 19.17), which metaphorically rings true to her end. For though David later reclaims her as his wife, they never seem to resume marital relations. She speaks no oath nor is she the subject of one, though her father and brother, Saul and Jonathan, both make oaths invoking the divine presence, and lose or win according to their alliance with 'the man after God's heart'. Michal, on the other hand, is only the princess of promise, of broken promises, the woman who meets an embittered fate. Bereft of father, brother, husband-of-her-bed, no children born to her. She thus stands in dramatic contrast to David's other wives—Abigail and Bathsheba—who wield oaths as autonomous agents in their own right.

---

40. Alter, *Biblical Narrative*, p. 125.

7

ABIGAIL: WOMAN OF VALOR OR WOMAN OF WILE?

Weigh oath with oath, and you will nothing weigh:
Your vows to her and me, put in two scales,
Will even weigh, and both as light as tales.
                Shakespeare, *Midsummer Night's Dream* III.ii

Introducing Abigail

Astute character studies of Abigail's story are surprisingly rare in the corpus of biblical scholarship. Bar-Efrat, for example, entitles his commentary on this chapter 'Woman of Valor [*'eshet hayil*]', as if her finesse in shifting allegiance from husband to future king is wholly virtuous and not the least self-serving. Similarly, Fokkelman calls this chapter 'A Woman's Intervention Stops David from a Bloodbath', as if *that* were the sole purpose of the chapter; she lacks motive. Berlin describes her as merely a 'type', not a full-fledged character, who has a limited and stereotyped range of personality traits, characterizing her as 'the perfect wife'.[1] In this epithet, however, lies the crux of *her* personal drama. The perfect wife of whom? David or Nabal? True, she saves her husband and household from David's vengeful wrath. But the husband mysteriously dies soon after the near conflagration, and the future king of Israel, whom she 'saves' from committing the moral outrage of a bloodbath, summons her to become his third wife. Caution, perhaps, about imputing a psychological motive or full agency to Abigail has led scholars to systematically *under-read* her story. Yet it is Abigail's complex motivation and verbal eloquence that make the story so compelling. She plots her way out of a socially constricted union to a boor of a husband into a marriage to David, artfully deploying oath language. It certainly takes wit to wend one's way out of a terrible marriage without suffering social

---

1. Bar-Efrat, *I Shmuel*, p. 309, Fokkelman, *Crossing Fates*, p. 474, and Berlin, *Poetics*, p. 30.

disapprobation. In my reading, Abigail is a cross between Chaucer's Wife of Bath and Shakespeare's Portia of *The Merchant of Venice*.² Both these literary figures, like Abigail, are at first bound, but then released from their bonds, through the power of oath.

Abigail is the sole woman in the Hebrew Bible who is introduced as both wise and beautiful, which, in itself, must give us pause. The biblical narrative sets her up in clear contrast to her husband:

> A man [was] in Maon, and his business [was] in Carmel. And the man [was] very rich; he had three thousand sheep and a thousand goats. And at the time, he was shearing his sheep in Carmel. And the man's name was Nabal, and his wife's name was Abigail. And the woman was of good-mind and beautiful of form [*tovat-sekhel vi-yfat to'ar*], but the man was hard and evil in his doings; He was a Calebite/dog-like [*khalibi*, acc. to *qere*], as his heart [*kha-libo*, acc. to *kethib*] (1 Sam. 25.2-3, author's trans.).

In this opening, the conventional introduction, 'And there was a man of [*va-yehi 'ish*], from the country of . . .', is conspicuously absent; Nabal's naming is notably delayed.³ What is highlighted, instead, is his wealth, the expanse of his estate (his home in Maon, his affairs in Carmel), and the season of the story—sheep-shearing, a time renowned for feasting, perhaps also drunken debauchery.⁴ The sequence of names—the man, Nabal; his wife, Abigail—is followed, inversely, by their characterization. The doubled term for her intelligence [*tovat-sekhel*] and beauty [*yfat-to'ar*] inadvertently sets up a contrast with other biblical beauties: Rachel (*yfat to'ar vi-yfat mar'eh*, Gen. 29.17) and Esther (*yfat-to'ar ve-tovat mar'eh*, Est. 2.7). Unlike these beauties, Abigail is a graduate of Eve's finishing school; Eve, the 'first intellectual', was drawn to eat of the Tree, seeing it as 'desirable to the mind [*ve-nehmad ha-'etz le-haskil*]' (Gen. 3.6). It is Abigail's forethought [*sekhel*] that leads her to avert disaster and plot her way out of marriage.

Nabal, by contrast, is hard, evil, befitting his name, which means 'fool', 'churl' or 'cur', as Abigail will later aver (v. 25).⁵ Resonant with the term

---

2. For a brilliant feminist analysis of this episode in Chaucer's *Canterbury Tales*, see Mary Carruthers, 'The Wife of Bath and the Painting of Lions', *PMLA* 94 (1979), pp. 209-22. On the role of oath in Shakespeare's *Merchant of Venice*, see William Kerrigan, *Shakespeare's Promises* (Baltimore, MD: Johns Hopkins University Press, 1999), pp. 92-150.

3. Consider Elkanah (1 Sam. 1.1.), Job (1.1), Kish and Saul (1 Sam. 9.1-2).

4. Later we are told that he returns from the festivities exceedingly drunk (v. 36). Consider also Gen. 38.13 and 2 Sam. 13.23-38 (see Chapter 3 n. 18).

5. '. . . for just like his name he is, his name means base and baseness is with him' (1 Sam. 25.25) (see BDB entry 5860, p. 615). He is also called a scoundrel or worthless man [*ben-bliya'al/'ish-habliya'al*] (vv. 17, 25). The term *nabal* is translated variously

for wineskin, *nevel,* his name also anticipates the drunken stupor following the sheep-shearing festival (v. 36). Bibulous, he becomes the empty wineskin from which he guzzles. He is also identified, by the *qere,* as a Calebite [*khalibi*]—perhaps a potential rival from that clan of Judah in claiming a right to the Judean monarchy.[6] This epithet also suggests another counterpoint to Abigail's beauty—he is dog-like [*khalibi*],[7] and according to the *kethib,* just like his heart [*kha-libo*]. Later, the narrative informs us that 'his heart [*libo*] died within him and he became stone [*le-'aven*]' (v. 37). Obtuse to ethical claims as a cur [*naval*], he is answered, measure for measure, by the petrification of his stony heart.

The following lines carefully juxtapose the dialogue between David's messengers and Nabal (vv. 5-13) and the exchange between one of Nabal's lads and Abigail (vv. 14-19). While the repartee between the men is inflammatory, Abigail and the servant plot to quench the flames. A gendered lens is clearly operative here—the men up in arms, the woman placating. When David hears of the sheep-shearing festivities, he sends word to Nabal asking for sustenance as pay for the protection he and his four hundred men provided to the shepherds in Carmel (vv. 7-8). Despite Nabal's dismissal—'Who is David and who is the son of Jesse? These days, many are the slaves breaking away from their masters' (v. 10)—these warriors are no mere 'ragtag band of dispossessed men and malcontents'.[8] In essence, they are running a mafioso protection racket.[9] We are adjured by the narrative to take their services seriously, deserving compensation, according to David and his men's report (vv. 7-8, 21), which is then corroborated by the servant (vv. 15-16). Yet when the rich landowner refuses to comply with the

---

as 'base' (Alter, *David Story,* p. 156), 'cur' (Fokkelman, *Crossing Fates,* p. 482), and 'churl' (Jon D. Levenson, '1 Samuel 25 as Literature and as History', *CBQ* 40 [1978], p. 13). In wisdom literature it connotes 'fool' (as in Prov. 17.21), a 'glutton' (Prov. 30.22), a hoarder (Jer. 17.11). Most significantly, the term alludes to a man who refuses to feed the hungry and give drink to the thirsty (Isa. 32.6). Resonant with *nevalah,* meaning 'corpse', his name also anticipates his coma and subsequent death (1 Sam. 25.37-38).

6. Both Alter (*David Story,* p. 153), and Bar-Efrat (*I Shmuel,* p. 314) identify him with the Kenizzites who joined the tribe of Judah (cf. Num. 32.12; Josh. 14.6, 14; and Gen. 15.19). More likely, he is linked to Judah directly, as a descendant of Caleb, and therefore constitutes a potential rival to the throne. See the discussion in Jon D. Levenson and Baruch Halpern, 'The Political Import of David's Marriages', *JBL* 99 (1980), pp. 507-518; also Levenson, '1 Samuel 15 as Literature', pp. 11-28.

7. See LXX on 1 Sam. 25.3: *khalibi* is translated in the Greek as *anthropos kunikos* ('dog-like man').

8. Alter, *David Story,* p. 154. He alludes to the description of David's band of four hundred warriors in 1 Sam. 22.2.

9. As Meir Shalev suggests in his provocative essay 'Protection in Carmel', from *The Bible Now* [*Tanakh 'Akhshav*] (Tel Aviv: Schocken, 1985), p. 20 (Heb.).

demand, David's response seems beyond the ethical pale. He and his men gird themselves for slaughter.

Simultaneously, Abigail gathers together a feast—two hundred loaves of bread, two jugs of wine, five dressed sheep, five seahs of parched grain, a hundred raisin cakes, and two hundred fig cakes—and loads them onto donkeys. As she rounds the corner, under the cover of the mountain, riding her donkey side-saddle (presumably), she bears an invisible placard: 'Make food not war'. (Or is it love?)

> And she told her young men, 'Go on ahead of me, and I'll follow you'; but she did not tell her husband, Nabal. She was riding on the ass and descending along a crag in the hill [*be-seter ha-har*], when, behold, David and his men were descending toward her; and she met them (1 Sam. 25.19-20).

She knows well enough not to tell Nabal her plans—but what are her plans? The scene is carefully staged—she, with her servant ahead of her, rounding one side of the mountain, while David and his men round the other—setting up the contrast between masculine and feminine modes of response. The 'crag in the hill [*be-seter ha-har*]' is suggestive of secrecy,[10] of erotic response,[11] the womb itself.[12] The staging of her offering is a particularly feminine form of appeasement—'her goal is more than the safety for Nabal's household: she offers victuals to David's men (v. 27); for David she offers herself (v. 31)'.[13]

Meanwhile, we are privy to a view of David in all his machismo, bolstering his intent with an oath, a kind of war cry of crude phallic proportions:

> For David had said: 'All in vain did I guard everything that belonged to this [man] in the wilderness and nothing was missing from all that was his, and he paid me back evil for good! This may God do to David and even more [*koh ya'aseh 'Elohim ve-koh yosif*],[14] if I leave from all that is

---

10. From the root *str*, meaning 'to hide, conceal' (BDB entry 6700, p. 712); the nominal form *seter* refers to 'a hiding place, covering, secrecy' (BDB entry 6701, p. 712), as in David's place of hiding from Saul (1 Sam. 19.2).

11. As Cant. 2.14: 'O my dove, in the clefts of the rock, in the covert of the cliff [*be-seter ha-madregah*], let me see your face, let me hear your voice; for your voice is sweet, and your face is lovely'.

12. As in Ps. 139.15: 'My frame was not hidden from you, when I was being made in secret [*va-seter*], intricately woven in the depths of the earth'.

13. Levenson, '1 Sam. 25 as Literature', p. 19.

14. The text here literally says, 'So may God do to the *enemies* of David . . .', but this is clearly an amendment on the part of the Masoretes (*leshon sagi nahor*, lit., 'language of great light', an ironic euphemism referring to one who cannot see. The term refers to occasions in the Bible and the Talmud where the opposite expression is used in order to avoid speaking/writing coarsely). The oath implies a punishment that will befall the speaker if he fails to fulfill the conditions of the oath (as in 1 Sam. 14.44, discussed

his by morning [*'ad ha-boqer*], a single pisser against the wall [*be-qir*]!' (vv. 22-23).

The threat is emphatically expressed by the 'rough vivid epithet' particular to curse language;[15] all the males in Nabal's household would be slaughtered, made even harsher by the fricatives: *koh... ve-khoh... ha-boqer... be-qir.* As Levenson points out, 'the episode of Nabal is the very first revelation of evil in David's character. He is a killer. This time he stops short. But the cloud that chapter 25 raises continues to darken our perception of David's character'.[16] The question, for the literary reader, is why we hear of this vicious oath only *after* seeing Abigail round the corner (v. 20). Focalization is upon her, initially, as the antidote to David's aggression. Before we are struck by its full force, we anticipate its undoing.

Upon seeing David, she 'hurried and got down from the donkey and flung herself on her face before David, and bowed to the ground, and fell upon his feet [*'al raglav*]' (vv. 23-24a). The sheer hyperbole in this expression, 'falling upon his feet', suggests not only theatricality but also quivers of *Eros,* of intimacy.[17] This series of downward motions, five carefully choreographed gestures of supplication, continue her descent in rounding the crag in the hill. They also set the tone for her eloquent speech, which I present in two parts, following Fokkelman's lead: (1) the supplication (vv. 24-27) with regard to the present; the last three of these verses are punctuated by the urgent expression 'and now therefore' [*ve-'atah*]; (2) and the appeal to the future (vv. 28-31), alluding to the long-term consequences of bloodshed (for Nabal and his clan, as well as Saul, the anointed one), at the hands of David, the 'prince [*nagid*] over Israel' (v. 30). She is the first to publicly

---

earlier). Having never followed through on the threat, a danger hovers over the House of David as a consequence of this religious speech act, which the tradition takes very seriously. Notably, the LXX (version-L) omits the term 'enemies' in the self-imprecation.

15. David reiterates the formula of the curse, once averted, in 1 Sam. 25.34. The epithet for the decimation of all males as they 'that pisseth against the wall' (KJV), is found in 1 Kgs 14.10 (House of Jeroboam I), 1 Kgs 16.11 (House of Baasha), 1 Kgs 21.21 and 2 Kgs 9.8 (House of Ahab). It is reserved for the Israelite regnal line that is wiped out and is invoked by the prophet's doom toll. This resonance reinforces Levenson and Halpern's theory that the House of Nabal represented a rival Judean line to the Davidic claim to the throne (Levenson and Halpern, 'Political Import', pp. 507-18).

16. Levenson, '1 Sam. 25 as Literature', p. 22.

17. The term *regel* may be a euphemism for male genitalia, as in Isa. 6.2 (or *margelotav*, in Ruth 3.4, 7, 8 and 14). While the scene between Boaz and Ruth is fraught with erotic overtones (see the discussion in Chapter 4), the suggestion here is more subtle. The rabbis make explicit the erotic overtones in this scene, suggesting that Abigail 'bared her thigh and [David] leapt three pharasangs by the light of it' (*b. Meg.* 15a).

address him with this title, and perhaps this is why the rabbis include her in the list of 'seven prophetesses'.[18]

An Oath for an Oath

> 'Me, mine, my lord is the blame [*bi 'ani 'adoni ha-'avon*]; please let your servant [*'amatekha*] speak in your ears, and hear the words of your servant [*'amatekha*]. My lord [*'adoni*], do not pay attention to his heart, to this scoundrel of a man, Nabal; for as his name is, so is he; Nabal is his name, and baseness is with him; but I, your servant [*'amatekha*], did not see the young men of my lord, whom you sent. Now then, my lord, as Yhwh lives, and as you yourself live, since Yhwh has restrained you from bloodguilt and from taking vengeance with your own hand, now let your enemies and those who seek to do evil to my lord be like Nabal' (1 Sam. 15.24-26).

She opens her address by taking on the transgression of her husband, but then carefully dissociates herself from blame, in letting David know her ignorance of the request and in disparaging her husband (v. 25). As Alter points out, 'it is hard to think of another instance in literature in which a wife so quickly and so devastatingly interposes distance between herself and her husband'.[19] She does so by making herself into the pivotal point, with her emphatic opening: 'Me, mine, my lord is the blame [*bi 'ani 'adoni ha-'avon*]' (v. 24).[20] She refers to herself, obsequiously, as 'your maidservant' [*'amatekha*], though she is obviously a wealthy aristocrat.[21] While she

---

18. *b. Meg.* 14a-b. Surprisingly, the prooftext for her prophetic status is found in the expression *seter ha-har* (v. 20, the crags of the hill), *not* in her calling David the future leader of Israel (v. 30). According to the Talmud, the term *seter* is a code word for 'covert things'. She showed him two bloods (*damim*)—her own menstrual blood and the potential bloodshed of Nabal, as well as Saul, and male progeny of their households. With wit, she prevents him from transgressing both sexual and military matters (temptation he does not resist in the story of Bathsheba). As prophet, she doesn't predict the future but serves as a voice of conscience to the king.

19. Alter, *David Story*, p. 156.

20. The supplication *bi 'adoni/'adonai* is common enough (see Judah's speech, for example, to the supposed Egyptian viceroy, Gen. 44.18; cf. 43.20; Exod. 4.10, 13), but the added *'ani* is unique to this instance.

21. Abigail refers to herself six times as *'amatekha* (vv. 24 [2x]; 25, 28, 31, and 41) and twice as *shifhah* (vv. 27 and 41). On the term 'your maidservant' as a rhetorical device in women's speech, see Hannah (with respect to God in 1 Sam. 1.11 (2x); in addressing the priest, Eli, in v. 16). Hannah also refers to herself as *shifhah* in 1 Sam. 1.18, as does the witch of Endor (1 Sam. 28.21, 22), the wise woman of Abel of Bethmaacah (in addressing the general, Joab, 2 Sam. 20.17), and the wise woman of Tekoa (addressing herself as *shifhah* to King David (2 Sam. 14.6, 7, 12, 15, 17 and 19).

addresses David as 'my lord' [*'adoni*] no less than fifteen times,[22] initially he is but the leader of a band of guerillas. By the end of her speech, David has been elevated to God's anointed one (v. 30). Later, when he takes her in matrimony after the death of her husband, she offers herself as his slave woman [*shifḥah*], ready to wash his feet (v. 41). Yet as she hurries after him, riding a donkey, she has five maidservants accompany her on foot.[23]

With a keen sense of her own agency and the power of speech, she treads a fine line between loyalty to her household, whom she wishes to save from a bloodbath, and disdain for her husband, whom she identifies as 'a scoundrel of a man [*'ish ha-bliya'al*]'.[24] She rattles off her dismay with a wordplay on his name, in the form of rhyming couplet: 'for as his name is, so is he; Nabal is his name, and baseness is with him [*ki khishmo ken h'u naval shmo u-nevalah 'imo*]'. Once she exonerates herself, the path is paved not only for the counteroath that will save her people but also for the request to 'remember your maidservant' (v. 31)—that will save her.

> And now [therefore], my lord, as Yhwh lives and as you live—Yhwh who prevented you from coming into blood guilt, delivering you from your own hand—And now, like Nabal may your enemies be who seek evil against my lord (v. 26).

Unlike David's oath of self-imprecation, the language here foregrounds the living God, along with the very alive David, as life-giving forces. Fokkelman notes that 'David is now put next to Yaweh and such good company helps to restrain him from murder'.[25] Oddly, though, God's power is seen through a pluperfect lens;[26] having prevented David from bloodguilt, the reward is retribution for his enemies. Her powers of persuasion seem to be on a prophetic order. In leaving the identity of the enemy, 'like Nabal', open, she alludes to David's restraint with Saul in the cave at Ein Gedi

---

22. See vv. 24, 25 [2x], 26 [2x], 27 [2x], 28 [2x], 29, 30, 31 [3x] and, in the follow-up, v. 41; she is operating in the rhetorical mode of her predecessor, Hannah, who also addresses Eli as 'my lord' (1 Sam. 1.15).

23. See Moshe Garsiel, 'Wit, Words, and a Woman: 1 Samuel 25', in *On Humour and the Comic in the Hebrew Bible* (ed. Yehuda Radday and Athalya Brenner; Sheffield: Almond, 1990), p. 168.

24. In characterizing Nabal as *ben-bliya'al* in v. 17 and *'ish ha-bliya'al* in v. 25, he is lumped with the gang rapists of Gibeah (Judg. 19.22; 20.13), the corrupt priests of Shiloh (1 Sam. 2.12), and those who disdain Saul as the chosen king of Israel (1 Sam. 10.27).

25. Fokkelman, *Crossing Fates*, p. 501.

26. The perfect form of the verbs—God who *prevented* you [*mena'akha*] . . . and saved [*ve-hoshe'a*] your hand . . .'—seems to allude to events that have already occurred.

(ch. 24) and in the Wilderness of Ziph (ch. 26).[27] The phrase 'and now [*ve-'atah*]' serves as a bridge between appeasement in the here and now and intimations of the future. In the very next verse, also punctuated by 'and now [*ve-'atah*]', she offers him gifts—literally blessing (*brakhah*)[28]—of food for his lads who walk about in the footsteps 'of my lord' (v. 27). This resolves the immediate demand David had made but leaves the impending threat trembling in the air.

After her initial burst of confidence, she promises even more . . .

> 'Please forgive the trespass of your **maidservant**; for **Yhwh** will certainly make **my lord** a sure house [*bayit ne'eman*], because **my lord** is fighting the battles of **Yhwh**; and evil shall not be found in you so long as you live. If anyone should rise up to pursue you and to seek your life, the life of **my lord** shall be bound in the bundle of the living with **Yhwh** your God; but the lives of your enemies he shall sling out as from the hollow of a sling. When **Yhwh** has done to **my lord** according to all the good that he has spoken concerning you, and has appointed you prince over Israel [*nagid 'al yisrael*], this will not be a trembling or stumbling block of the heart to **my lord**, to have shed blood for no cause, or for **my lord** having saved himself. And when **Yhwh** has dealt well with **my lord, then remember your maidservant**' (1 Sam. 25.28-31, author's trans.).

The reference to herself as 'your maidservant' frames the speech—a call to forgive and a call to remember. Again she obsequiously takes on her husband's sin but holds out reward for David's forgiveness. The central protagonists in the larger scheme are Yhwh ('the LORD') and David ('my lord'), mentioned contiguously (in the Hebrew) as if in one breath. In these four verses, 'my lord [*'adoni*]' appears seven times, and 'Yhwh' five. They form a chiastic structure: *Yhwh 'adoni . . . 'adoni Yhwh*, in v. 28, juxtaposing the reward—*bayit ne'eman*—and the reason: because David fights God's battles. In v. 30, the alignment of Yhwh and then *'adoni* also speaks of reward, while heralding a warning (v. 31). The careful placement of words reflects the ultimate promise, that 'my lord be bound in the bundle of the living with Yhwh . . .' The central image revolves around stones in a sling

---

27. This double entendre is also suggested by the vague 'those who pursue you and seek your life' (v. 29)—hardly befitting Nabal. The 'near miss' of Saul in the caves of Ein Gedi (ch. 24) and the wilderness of Ziph (ch. 26) clearly 'frame' this chapter, where David twice restrains himself from slaying the king. As Polzin points out, Nabal becomes 'an obvious replacement or stand-in for Saul so that David's mercy toward him in chapter 25 is as toward Saul is chapters 24 and 26' (Robert Polzin, *Samuel and the Deuteronomist* [Bloomington, IN: Indiana University Press, 1993], pp. 206).

28. Similarly, Jacob offers Esau gifts (*minḥah*, in Gen. 32.14, 19, 21, 22), hoping that he will 'accept his appearance' (*'ulai yis'a penai*, in v. 21) just as Abigail offers gifts (food as *brakhah* in v. 27), and David responds, 'I have heard your voice and accepted your appearance [*sham'ati ve-kolekh va-'es'a panayikh*]' (v. 35).

or pouch—bundled or flung—which is David's trademark. It alludes to past heroism, in slaying Goliath (1 Sam. 17.49), but it also anticipates human restraint taken up by divine retribution. Nabal's heart will be turned to stone at the hand of God (1 Sam. 25.37).[29]

Again, Abigail's speech proves oracular on three accounts—two promising and one foreboding. She is the first to state, publicly, that David will be chosen as 'prince [*nagid*] over Israel' (v. 30). But this is hardly surprising! Rumors may have run rampant since the private anointing in Bethlehem (1 Sam. 16). David will refer to himself as ruler over Israel in his counter to Michal, 'God chose me over your father and all his household to appoint me as prince [*nagid*] over Israel, the people of Yhwh' (2 Sam. 6.2), and the prophet Nathan confirms this title (2 Sam. 7.8). Her speech also anticipates the establishment of a dynasty, *bayit ne'eman* (v. 28), also confirmed by Nathan after David moves his capital to Jerusalem (2 Sam. 7.16). Most ominous, though, is her veiled warning that 'this [*z'ot*]' not be a cause for 'trembling or stumbling block of the heart to my lord [*le-puqah u-lemikhshol lev la-'adoni*], to shed blood for no cause' (v. 31). On the proximate level, 'this [*z'ot*]' refers to the potential slaughter of Nabal and all the males of their household. On another level, the words foreshadow a time when David would not refrain from shedding blood gratuitously (the murder of Uriah) and save himself (from adultery with Bathsheba). For then it would *not* go well for him by Yhwh.

Just as she, 'the maidservant (*'amah*, lit., extended arm)', frames the opening and closing of her own speech, so she delineates both the boundary to David's action and the extension of God's hand. Ziegler points out that, in blessing her, David repeats the specific words used in Abigail's oath (v. 26): 'Blessed be *your* good sense and blessed be *you yourself*, who restrained me this very day from bloodguilt and from taking vengeance with my own hand' (v. 33).[30] That is, David attributes to Abigail what she had attributed to the LORD. David then responds with a third oath, 'by the *life* of Yhwh, the God of Israel, who has kept me from harming you—had you not come quickly to meet me, not one by morning [*'ad ha-boqer*] would have remained, not a single pisser against the wall [*be-qir*]!' (v. 34). This overturns his first oath; he has clearly internalized her message that saves him from bloodguilt by his own hands.[31] The question is: who really 'saved' him?

In the same vein, Abigail's injunction, 'and remember your maidservant' (v. 31), is fraught with ambiguity, as it follows, 'when Yhwh deals well with my lord'. In the proximate time frame, the 'good deal' is the death of

---

29. See Polzin, *Deuteronomist*, pp. 211-12.
30. Ziegler, *Promises to Keep*, p. 114.
31. See the discussion in Bar-Efrat, *I Shmuel*, p. 323.

Nabal at the hands of God and marriage to her—but here, too, agency is blurred as to how this comes about. In the dénouement, the narrator informs us that Abigail returned that very night and found Nabal in a drunken stupor. She waited until he was sober in the morning and told him all that had transpired, 'and his heart died within him and he became as stone' (v. 37). Yet the obituary can only be published 'some ten days later', when 'Yhwh struck Nabal and he died' (v. 38).

How did he die? Why the delay? If she is imputed with agency (in God's stead) by David in preventing the bloodbath, could she also play a role in the bloodless death of Nabal? When Abigail accedes to the summons, she is mysteriously silent about the cause of her husband's death, while David identifies it as retributive justice (v. 39). Rashi, almost comically, suggests that he was struck by a heart attack or stroke in response to the news of all that food and drink given away for free. Perhaps Abigail was aware that he had a heart condition, as Alter suggests. 'If this assumption is correct she would be using her knowledge of his physical frailty to carry out the tacit contract on his life—bloodlessly, with God Himself left to do the deed'.[32] Ibn Caspi, drawing on the ambiguity 'he/it became as stone', suggests that Nabal himself turned to stone. Just as his heart had been hard (like Pharaoh's hard heart),[33] so his whole body became petrified, comatose. Yet why the delay? Radak disambiguates. For ten days he was deathly ill, and at the end of that period he died, as if by divine decree, as a natural consequence of his sin. Measure for measure, this stone-man is slung out as from the hollow of a sling, alone into the grave.

Most compelling is Meir Shalev's version of the story. The Israeli novelist audaciously suggests that by killing off her ornery husband, Abigail would, of course, be free to marry David. In her speech, she dissuades David from killing Nabal and assures him (repeatedly) that the 'final reckoning' lay with the LORD, hinting that she will serve as God's agent. She is proposing, effectively, a kind of contract killing (*Dial M for Murder*), where the reward is matrimony to the future king of Israel. As Shalev so provocatively suggests, 'she is many times more dangerous than her two "lords" put together'.[34] Lady Macbeth-like, she poisons her husband with hemlock upon returning home. The weed grows rampant in Judea and was well known in ancient Greece for inducing a fatal coma.

32. Alter, *David Story*, p. 160
33. The narrative (MT) informs us that he was *kha-libo*, in the *kethib*, v. 3, as Abigail adjures David, 'do not pay attention to his heart [*libo*]' v. 25. In the Hebrew Bible, the heart is the site of the psyche/mind/intentionality (as in Gen. 6.5; Exod. 31.6; Deut. 20.8). It hearkens to the Old French meaning of *coeur*, of courage, and the corollary to that, in English, 'to dishearten, to lose heart, to lose one's will'. Nabal's fate, his heart smitten to stone, contrasts with the *lev tov* of his drunken stupor (v. 36).
34. Shalev, *The Bible Today*, p. 21.

Yet Shalev's midrash, so audacious in its secular reading, ostensibly undermines the theological tenor of the text and the central principle of divine retributive justice. To remove God from the story is to impose modern literary criteria (namely, realism), fundamentally at odds with 'the Book,' to the reading of Bible as literature. It also chafes at an essential tenet of the female ruse: how God works in circuitous ways through female agency. The text is deliberately ambiguous as to the cause of Nabal's death precisely because the line between God's will and the woman's is blurred.

Ironically, the epithet 'Nabal's wife' still clings to Abigail, even after she bears David a son. Perhaps because the question of paternity lingers. Not one month had passed after her husband's death when she was summoned, as another queen was summoned with 'most wicked haste, to post with such dexterity to incestuous sheets' (*Hamlet* I.ii).

8

BATHSHEBA: WOMAN OF OATH

A shudder in the loins engenders there
The broken wall, the burning roof and tower
And Agamemnon dead.
Being so caught up,
So mastered by the brute blood of the air,
Did she put on his knowledge with his power
Before the indifferent beak could let her drop?

William Butler Yeats, 'Leda and the Swan'

Preamble

In his epic poem 'Leda and the Swan', William Butler Yeats depicts the fall of Troy in terms of a trauma engendered at conception. According to the Greek myth, Zeus, in the form of a swan, rapes Leda, wife of the Spartan king Tyndareus. She then bears Helen and Polydeuces, the children of Zeus, as well as Castor and Clytemnestra, conceived by her husband on that same night. Her daughters, Helen and Clytemnestra—one spawned by the immortal, the other by the Spartan king—are separated, divided between nations at war. Helen, 'the face that launched a thousand ships', becomes the pretext for the Trojan War, and Clytemnestra kills her husband, King Agamemnon, when he returns with Cassandra, the Trojan princess, as a war prize after the sack of Troy. Yeats traces the origin of Troy's bloody fate and the tragic aftermath of war to that initial violation of Leda as a trauma 'engendered there'. 'Did she put on his knowledge with his power before the indifferent beak could let her drop?' The question probes the moment of the rape, not only with regard to the progeny conceived in the womb, 'this field of double sowing', but also in terms of the mother's psyche, shuddered to her core there. By putting 'on his knowledge with his power', Yeats asks whether Leda transforms the act of sexual possession into a feminine force, a field of vengeance, bloodshed sewn into the daughters' souls upon conception.

8. *Bathsheba*

I wonder, too, whether Bathsheba put on King David's 'knowledge with his power' when she was *taken* by him, sexually possessed as a married woman. Seeing her from the rooftop, naked at her bath, David summons her, intent on satisfying his desire in just one tryst. She is then sent home, but pregnancy betrays them. Unlike Leda, there is no ambiguity about conception, her womb no 'field of double sowing'. When Uriah, her husband, is summoned from the battlefield to cover for the conception, he refuses to comply (knowingly?), and so is sent to his death at the front. David then marries Bathsheba. Though he is exposed for his heinous sins, soundly rebuked by the prophet with a doom toll, the king never loses his hold over the Judean dynasty. That first child conceived in adultery dies, but their second son, Solomon, becomes the next king on the throne. Bathsheba, though passive in the initial scene, plays a pivotal role in colluding with the prophet to set her son up to succeed David as king. Is this the same woman? And if so, why does God (or the prophet as his proxy) ally with Bathsheba? What wrong was seeded there that the woman transforms by taking on 'his knowledge with his power'? The sequel suggests an alternative narrative of mastery.

In this chapter, I focus on the question of Bathsheba's shifting agency, and the critique that she implicitly poses of power politics in the founding narratives of the Judean monarchy. 'Would you murder and then dispossess?' asks the prophet.[1] Indeed the king does both, maneuvering the pieces across the chess board at will for his own sexual pleasure and collateral in war. The pawn becomes queen while the knight is sacrificed. Radically at odds with the idealization of David until this point in the history, the story is nevertheless foundational, hinging on the confluence of gender, violence and power. As Meir Sternberg notes, 'within the composition of the book, therefore, [it] is a central chapter in that it pinpoints the where and why of David's change of fortune'.[2] The consequences of the adultery and murder form the turning point in David's life. What follows is a series of tragic episodes within David's family—the death of the son conceived in adultery (ch. 12.), the rape of Tamar, David's daughter (ch. 13), fratricide (ch. 14), Absalom's insurrection and civil war between father and son (chs. 15-18), ending with an aged, impotent monarch, divided loyalties among his henchmen, and contentions for the throne (1 Kgs 1–2).

Robert Polzin further argues that this episode is not only the turning point in David's life but the pivot of the entire Deuteronomistic Histo-

---

1. 1 Kgs 21.19. The context is Elijah's rebuke of Ahab, king of the northern tribes, following the confiscation of Naboth's vineyard and his trumped-up execution. The narratives are parallel, insofar as the prophets—Elijah and Nathan—both rebuke the kings—Ahab and David—for an abuse of power, one for confiscating another man's field, the other for taking another man's wife.

2. Sternberg, *Poetics of Biblical Narrative*, p. 529.

ry.³ For David abrogates the law, three of the Ten Commandments: 'Thou shalt not murder; Thou shalt not commit adultery; Thou shalt not covet thy neighbor's wife'.⁴ As Acton's dictum avers, 'Power corrupts; absolute power corrupts absolutely'. And so the history tells us about the corruption that is endemic to the kings of Israel and Judah. In this instance, the woman 'tries' the limits of the king's power; she is the cause of 'trembling and the stumbling block' for David's heart (1 Sam. 25.31).⁵ She 'tests' him, not as

3. Robert Pozin, *David and the Deuterononomist* (Bloomington, IN: Indiana University Press, 1993), p. 119. See also Frymer-Kensky, who suggests that the purpose of this chapter is 'to teach David about the limitation of the rights of kings and the accountability of the king to God's law and God's prophet' (*Reading the Women of the Bible*, p. 156). On the relationship between the Deuteronomic law code and the historical books (Joshua–2 Kings), see Martin Noth, *The Deuteronomistic History* (trans. J. Doull; Sheffield: JSOT Press, 1981), originally published as *Überlieferungsgeschichtliche Studien* (Tübingen: Max Niemeyer, 1943). I follow Joel Rosenberg's call that 'the text's meaning as literature' is 'dependent on the weight and moment of its deliberations as history' (*King and Kin: Political Allegory in the Hebrew Bible* [Bloomington, IN: Indiana University Press, 1986], p. 106). Literary readings such as Fokkelman's and Sternberg's do not adequately consider the context of this narrative within the larger rubric of the sacred history. Even David Gunn, who claims to analyze the relationship between 'the man' and the 'monarchy', is 'overly aestheticized and contemplative towards his subject' (Rosenberg, *King and Kin*, p. 107). He is primarily concerned with the literary features of the text, 'its quality as a work of art and entertainment' (David Gunn, *The Story of King David* (JSOTSup, 6; Sheffield: JSOT Press, 1978], p. 38). Gerhard von Rad suggests that this narrative explains the exclusion of the older brothers (Amnon, Absalom and Adonijah, who sin 'in the image of their father'), and Solomon's accession to the throne ('The Beginnings of Historical Writing in Ancient Israel', in *The Problem of the Hexateuch and Other Essays* [Edinburgh: Oliver & Boyd, 1965], pp. 166-205). Yet the question remains as to why this must be done through recounting the king's heinous crimes. Surely an original act of adultery would delegitimize the union of Solomon's parents rather than justify the displacement of his older brothers! The book of Chronicles, also concerned with the legitimacy of David and Solomon (redacted much later, in the fourth century BCE), omits the story of David's adultery with Bathsheba and Uriah's murder altogether. Consequently, Van Seters argues that these events contradict the historiographic and ideological perspective of the overall Deuteronomistic History. He reads it as a 'bitter attack upon the whole royal ideology of a "sure house" for David' (*In Search of History* [New Haven, CT: Yale University Press, 1983], p. 290). See James W. Flanagan's summary of the issues in 'Court History or Succession Document? A Study of 2 Samuel 9–20 and 1 Kings 1–2', *JBL* 91 (1972), pp. 172-81. Flanagan claims that it is a composite of two sources—one (2 Sam. 12–20) accounting for the rejection of the elder brothers, in which David maintains the powers of office as the legitimate king of Judah and Israel, while the other recounts the Bathsheba episode and the succession of Solomon to the throne (2 Sam. 11–12; 1 Kgs 1–2), which is later integrated into the Court History. I assume the integrity of the narrative unit and will argue along those lines.

4. Deut. 5.17-18; cf. Exod. 20.13-14.

5. Uriel Simon notes, 'Once David had become embroiled in the affair with Bathsheba he forgot the ruling which Abigail had so eloquently commended to him: "that this

a seductress, but as the object of his unchecked desire, a seemingly passive rather than an active player in his fall. Yet why does *this* woman, Bathsheba, of all David's wives, become the mother of Solomon, the successor of the Judean kingship and founder of the messianic dynasty? What turns the source of the king's condemnation into one of continuity? The mystery lies in the continuity of character between the woman, illicitly taken by the king, and the woman who becomes queen mother.

In this chapter, I engage in a close literary and psychological reading of the biblical narrative in alignment with the 'Succession History'.[6] Here, the religious presentation of history and the feminist critique of androcentric structures of power align. It is precisely from the weaker party that the sharpest critique resounds. My discussion revolves around the nexus of gender and power, with a focus on four pivotal points in the narrative, where the pitch of irony rises incrementally along the temporal axis. The further from David's sins of adultery and murder, the sharper the goad to the king's conscience. The first is found in the betrayal of the body—in Bathsheba's pregnancy. The second occurs when Uriah fails to comply with the coverup. The third is found in the general Joab's report of Uriah's death, alluding to the story of a man 'felled by a woman' (vv. 20-21; Judg. 9.52-54). The effect of irony, for the reader, hinges on the knowledge gap between the king and the other players. As a literary device, it prods the thickness of David's skin until finally, in the fourth pivotal point, the 'play within the play' of Nathan's parable of the little ewe lamb, the king sentences the rich man to death, and therein stands condemned. Breaking down in response to the prophet's accusation and rebuke (vv. 7-12), the king confesses to his sin (2 Sam. 12.13). This poignant moment allows a redemptive trajectory to rise, despite the series of tragic episodes that follow. In my analysis, I show how questions of gender and the theological tenets underlying the history coincide. Both 'speak truth to power'. The purpose for God, as the purported author of the history, is 'to catch the conscience of the king' so that he may stand before the law condemned as guilty yet, ultimately, redeemed.

---

be no stumbling block of the heart to thee . . . that thou hast shed blood without cause"' (1 Sam. 25.31) (Uriel Simon, 'The Poor Man's Ewe-Lamb: An Example of a Juridical Parable', *Biblica* 48 [1967], p. 236). The same allusion is found in the Babylonian Talmud: '"Let this not be a trembling or stumbling block of the heart to my lord" (1 Sam. 25.31). The word "this" alludes to another story, and what was that? The incident of Bathsheba; and so it was eventually' (*b. Meg.* 14b).

6. I date the first stage of the Court History (2 Sam. 9–1 Kgs 2) to the latter half of the ninth century BCE, before the destruction of the Northern Kingdom at the hands of the Assyrians. On controversies of dating, see the discussion in P. Kyle McCarter, *II Samuel* (AB, 9; Garden City, NY: Doubleday, 1984), pp. 6-8. See also John Van Seters, *The Biblical Saga of King David* (Winona Lake, IN: Eisenbrauns, 2009), pp. 3-52.

Of Messengers and Kings

David's sin takes up all of one verse in the narrative—in the bat of an eyelid, the loss of a lifetime. The problem begins in a moment of leisure, when the king remains home while his troops are deployed at the front. The city of Rabbah is under siege, while Jerusalem is secure; the danger, for David, lies within.[7] While the Ammonite city is surrounded by soldiers for months of waiting, with occasional skirmishes over the wall, David penetrates the boundary of one forbidden to him, inviting her *into* his palace. She is his own personal Trojan Horse; brought in, she penetrates his 'wall', and with the breakdown of his boundaries, the man and king come tumbling down.

> And it happened at the turn of the year, at the time the kings (or messengers) [*ha-mal'akhim*] sally forth, that David sent out Joab and his servants with him and all Israel, and they ravaged the Ammonites and besieged Rabbah. And David remained in Jerusalem (v. 1).
>
> And it happened at the evening time, when David rose from his couch [*mishkavo*] and was walking [*va-yithalekh*] about on the roof of the king's house that he saw from the roof a woman bathing [*roḥetzet*]; the woman was very beautiful (v. 2).
>
> David sent to inquire [*va-yishlaḥ lidrosh*] about the woman. And he [the one sent] said, 'Is this not Bathsheba daughter of Eliam, the wife of Uriah the Hittite?' (v. 3).
>
> So David sent messengers, and took her [*va-yiqaḥeha*], and she came to him [*va-tav'o 'elav*], and he lay with her [*va-yishkav 'imah*]. (She was purifying herself of her impurity—*mitqadeshet mi-tum'atah*.) And she returned [*va-tashov*] to her house (v. 4).
>
> The woman conceived; and she sent [*va-tishlaḥ*] to David, and she said, 'I am pregnant' (v. 5, author's trans.).

The passage opens with a peculiar 'misspelling' in the MT—*mal'akhim* (messengers) instead of the understood *malakhim* (kings)—which points to a central motif in the chapter. The power of the king is conveyed through messengers, as they traverse the boundary between private and public domains.[8]

---

7. Joel Rosenberg sees this chapter, the 'going indoors', as 'a shift from body politic to body paradigmatic', where 'the fate of kingship in Israel must be seen as the vehicle of a reflection on Israelite society as a whole' (Rosenberg, *King and Kin,* pp. 124-25). When David returns 'outdoors', to the public domain, that is to the military front (2 Sam. 12.26-31), the corrective is made.

8. See the remarks of Jan Fokkelman, *Narrative Art and Poetry in the Books of Samuel: A Full Interpretation Based on Stylistic and Structural Analyses: King David* (Studia Semitica Neerlandica, 20; Assen: Van Gorcum, 1981), pp. 50-51; Polzin, *David and the Deuteronomist,* pp. 109-12; Alter, *David Story,* p. 249; Frymer-Kensky, *Reading the Women of the Bible,* pp. 143-44.

The same juxtaposition between palace and front, between private and public domain, is conveyed by the temporal phrase 'And it happened . . . at the time . . .' (v. 1), echoed in v. 2. In the plain sense, the season refers to spring, when kings sally forth in battle.[9] The repeated phrase suggests a contrast between David's withdrawal from fighting the 'battles of Yhwh' and his 'conquest' of a woman. In fulfilling his lust with Bathsheba, David fails to play the role of king, the one he was chosen for: to fight the LORD's battles.[10] As Fokkelman quips, 'the devil finds work for idle hands'.[11]

When the king stays home, he *sends* the general and troops out to the front and sends forth messengers; he summons people to and from the palace, to and from the front, envoys dispatching letters, letters dispatching envoys. Messengers inquire after the identity of the beautiful woman; they send for Bathsheba. She in turn sends word to the king, who then sends for Uriah, who is then sent out to the front again; and Joab sends a damning message back to the king.[12] In the gap between kings and messengers lies the first hint of irony in our narrative—the powerful David is peculiarly sedentary as he remains behind in Jerusalem. All his actions are done with a sleight of hand. He is, paradoxically, both sexually charged and figuratively impotent. Bal remarks, 'Power makes its objects passive, since the powerful use other agents as instruments. In all his absolute power, David is basically passive. The superman of verse 4 comes to resemble a non-man in the rest of the fabula.'[13]

The lying or laying [*shkb*], as both an intransitive and transitive verb, also serves as a *Leitwort* throughout the narrative. At his leisure, David rises from a late afternoon siesta, from his couch [*mishkavo*], the word proleptic for his 'lying with' Bathsheba (v. 4)[14] and Uriah's refusal to 'lie with' his

---

9. Bar-Efrat, *II Shmuel*, p. 110 (he cites R. Yosef Karo). The LXX records 'when the kings went out . . .'; similarly, 1 Chron. 20.1 records 'kings' (not 'messengers'). The spelling of 2 Sam. 11.1 in the MT may be matter of *matres lectionis* (where a consonant is used for vocalization), as in the variant spelling for 'poor man [*rash/ra'sh*]' (cf. 2 Sam. 12.1, 4).

10. The whole purpose of establishing a monarchy was so that the king would unite the tribes, leading them in war (1 Sam. 8.20), fighting the battles of Yhwh, as Abigail had reminded David (1 Sam. 25.28). This is what he was lauded for by the people (2 Sam. 3.17-18).

11. Fokkelman, *King David,* p. 51.

12. As Polzin points out, the key verb in all these transaction is *shlḥ*, which is found twelve times in this chapter, more often than in any other chapter in the History (cf. 2 Sam. 11.1, 3, 4, 5, 6 (3x), 12, 14, 18, 22). See Polzin, *David and the Deuteronomist*, pp. 115 and 223 n. 11; and Simon, 'The Poor Man's Ewe-Lamb', p. 209.

13. Bal, *Lethal Love*, p. 29.

14. As Fokkelman points out, it 'shows the development of idleness into fornication' (*King David,* p. 51). In following the ambiguous use of these key words [*Leitwörten*], I

wife (vv. 9, 11), 'lying abed', instead, with the troops (v. 13). This key word [*shkb*] also anticipates Nathan's oracle of doom, when his rival will, *quid pro quo,* take his wives and 'lie with them' for all to see (12.11). The king strolls along the roof [*va-yithalekh*];[15] just as God did in the Garden of Eden at the breezy time of day (Gen. 3.8), and he sees a woman bathing. This 'meandering' could serve his conscience or feed the desire of his eyes. But 'to see her is, for a man in his position, to possess her'.[16] Though the text never mentions she is naked, her exposure to his gaze while she is bathing implies as much; initially he is the voyeur. Exum comments, 'Nakedness makes her more vulnerable, and being observed in such a private, intimate activity as bathing, attending to the body, accentuates the body's vulnerability to David's and our shared gaze. A woman is touching herself and a man is watching.'[17] He sees her from a height, as a 'despot who is able to survey and choose as he pleases'.[18] The roof, as literal higher ground, is metonymic for power; on that roof Absalom will subvert his father's authority by taking David's ten concubines, presumably by force as the oracle of doom presaged (2 Sam. 16.21-22).[19]

When David sends to inquire after her identity, he is told, 'Is this *not* Bathsheba daughter of Eliam, the wife of Uriah the Hittite?' (v. 3). The stage directions might read: 'the messenger raises his eyebrows'. Both these names, Eliam and Uriah, are presumably recognizable to the king as two of his closest henchmen.[20] In committing adultery with the woman, as the daughter and wife of other men, he not only violates the law, but betrays the soldiers who fight the LORD's battles. In taking Bathsheba, he acts treacher-

---

draw insight from Gale A. Yee, '"Fraught with Background": Literary Ambiguity in II Samuel 11', *Interpretation* 42 (1988), pp. 240-53.

15. The verb is then echoed by the term for traveler [*helekh*, a near *hapax legomenon* based on the root *hlkh*] in Nathan's parable (2 Sam. 12.4). Uriel Simon notes the parallel as well, 'The Poor Man's Ewe-Lamb', pp. 226-27 n. 3.

16. Bal, *Lethal Love,* p. 29.

17. Exum, *Fragmented Women,* p. 174.

18. Fokkelman, *King David,* p. 51.

19. As Exum points out, 'Absalom does in the sight of the sun and all Israel what David had done in secret, he openly rapes ten of David's wives in a tent pitched for him on the roof—the roof, of course, serving as a reminder that this is where David's crime began' (Exum, *Fragmented Women,* p. 176). But the parallel is not between the 'rape' of Bathsheba and the concubines but in the sexual nature of the transgression insofar as the women belonged to another man. See the discussion to follow.

20. Both Eliam and Uriah are identified as members of the thirty elite warriors in David's army (2 Sam. 23.34 and 39); the former, Bathsheba's father, is also identified as 'son of Ahithophel'—Ahithophel, who later serves as Absalom's advisor in the insurrection and civil war against his father. If Ahithophel is, indeed, Bathsheba's grandfather then his alliance with Absalom may be understood as vengeance for David's possession of her.

ously against them, her father and her husband, betraying the kingship and the divine election that lies therein.

Does the narrative suggest that Bathsheba, too, is complicit in the adultery? Bible scholars in recent decades have profusely debated the role Bathsheba plays.[21] Does she place herself on the roof within view of the palace in the mode of an intended seduction—as Tamar set herself up as the crossroads to waylay Judah? Or is Bathsheba ostensibly raped? While the debate has been generative, it has led to a distorted binary reading of Bathsheba's role as either a conniving seductress or a hapless victim. The truth is that we are not privy to anything she feels, what her response to the summons might have been, whether she was complicit or resistant, or whether she took pleasure in her tryst with the king. As the object of his gaze and the subject of his summons, she is bereft of agency. The discrepancy in their positions of power implies that she could not have refused his missive. Furthermore, if she were conniving, either lustful for the king (like Potiphar's wife for Joseph) or hankering to become the progenitrix of an heir for the monarchy, she too would have been judged guilty by the narrative. Yet she is never held culpable for the transgression. Only David is condemned, in the end, by the prophet, and only he suffers the punishment meted out for *his* sins.[22] While Bathsheba suffers consequences, first the loss of her hus-

---

21. For example, Nicol considers 'Bathsheba's action of bathing in such close proximity to the royal palace . . . deliberately provocative' (George C. Nicol, 'The Alleged Rape of Bathsheba: Some Observations on Ambiguity in Biblical Narrative', *JSOT* 73 [1997], pp. 43-54, p. 44). Other scholars suggest that she was trying to wheedle herself into the kingly lineage in light of her role in 1 Kings 1 (see H.W. Hertzberg, *1 and 2 Samuel* [Old Testament Library; London: SCM Press, 1964], p. 310; and R.C. Bailey, *David in Love and War* [JSOTSup, 75; Sheffield: JSOT Press, 1990], p. 88). Exum, on the other hand, argues that Bathsheba is deprived of voice and portrayed in an ambiguous light, and thus she is metaphorically 'raped' by the androcentric biblical narrator ('Raped by the Pen', in *Fragmented Women*, pp. 170-201; and J. Cheryl Exum, 'Bathsheba Plotted, Shot, and Painted', *Semeia* 74 [1996], pp. 47-73, esp. p. 53). Frymer-Kensky challenges Exum's reading. The tendency to understand her actions as 'seductive' comes from the porous nature of the biblical narrative, 'from the readers own projections and fears rather than from any hints in the text . . . the scheming, manipulative Bathsheba comes from a set of gender stereotypes essentially alien to the biblical author' (*Reading the Women of the Bible*, p. 395 and note on p. 144). Abisili argues, and I concur, that the text does not present relations between David and Bathsheba as rape, which entails forced sexual relations and humiliation, often associated with the verb *'nh* [piel] (Alexander Izuchukwu Abasili, 'Was it Rape? The David and Bathsheba Pericope Re-examined', *VT* 61 [2011], pp. 1-15). For a discussion of the ambiguity, see Sara M. Koenig, *Isn't This Bathsheba?: A Study in Characterization* (Eugene, OR: Wipf & Stock Publishers, 2011), pp. 69-72.

22. According to the norms of the ancient Near East and the Pentateuch, the punishment for adultery (stoning to death) devolves upon both parties. Tikvah Frymer-Kensky goes to great length to show the danger Bathsheba is in, once she discovers she is pregnant (*Reading the Women of the Bible*, pp. 148-50). Abisili points out that, given the con-

band[23] and then the death of the child conceived of the adulterous union, she is condemned neither by society, when she later reenters the palace as David's wife, nor by the principles of divine justice. As Fokkelman points out, 'the text shows her merely as an object of desire (vv. 2-4) and David's choice (v. 27)'.[24]

Yet the sequence of actions suggests that Bathsheba is not *totally* without agency. The series of paratactic verbs (in the *va-yiqtol* form) alternate between man and woman, masculine and feminine subject, in the one verse accounting for their sexual union (v. 4): *he* sent [*va-yishlaḥ*], *he* took *her* [*va-yiqaḥeha*], *she* came [*va-tav'o*], *he* lay with her [*va-yishkav 'imah*], and *she* returned [*va-tashov*]. Against the grain of gender norms in the Bible, the woman is the one who *comes* to the man.[25] A grey area lies between the binary of 'active' and 'passive' subject, which disrupts the categorical reading of their intercourse as either seduction or rape. In coming into the king's private domain, she is the means of a divine trial, which, like the

sequences, she would not have gone willingly: 'Bathsheba cannot deliberately will her own destruction. She knows the disastrous implications of marital infidelity (it includes the death penalty [Lev. 20.10; Deut. 22.22], trial by ordeal [Num 5.11-31], stripping of the adulteress naked, and stoning [Hos. 2.5; Ezek. 16.37])' (Abisili, 'Was It Rape?', p. 7).

23. Bathsheba is not, in any way, party to the murder of Uriah. The text records that she 'lamented over her husband' (2 Sam. 11.26), and only after the period of mourning was over was she brought into the palace to become David's wife (v. 27). One might read this as a mere formality or dissimulation on her part. However, in contrast to Abigail and her role in the death of Nabal (the text records no lament or mourning period), Bathsheba is not suspect.

24. Fokkelman, *King David*, p. 53. Similarly Adele Berlin emphasizes Bathsheba's passivity; she is merely an agent (in the Aristotelian sense), merely a function of the plot: 'the plot . . . calls for adultery, and adultery requires a married woman. Bathsheba fills that function. Nothing about her which does not pertain to that function is allowed to intrude into the story' (Berlin, *Poetics*, p. 27, based on her article 'Characterization in Biblical Narrative: David's Wives', *JSOT* 23 [1982], pp. 69-85). Koenig, however, understands Bathsheba as a complex character (*Isn't This Bathsheba?*, pp. 11-17). Her discussion (like my own) hinges on the ambiguity implied by Bathsheba as the subject of the verb *bw'*.

25. In particular, the combination 'he took' [*lqḥ*] and 'came into' [*bw'*] is strictly attributed to male subjects (cf. Gen. 29.23 and 38.2). There are only two examples where the female is the subject of the verb 'to come [*bw'*]' (with possible sexual connotations): the story of Lot's daughters (Gen. 19.34) and the story of Bathsheba (2 Sam. 11.4). In most instances, it is the man who 'comes into/in [*bw' 'el/'al*]' the tent, the home, or the woman herself (see Gen. 6.4; 16.2; 30.3; 38.8; 39.14; Deut. 22.13; 2 Sam. 12.24; 16.21; 20.3; BDB entry 1054, p. 99). See Alter, *David Story*, p. 251. The Septuagint, interestingly, 'corrects' this (or testifies to a textual variant) on 2 Sam. 11.4: 'And David sent messengers, and took her, and *he* went in to her . . .' See the discussion in Tarja S. Philip, *Menstruation and Childbirth in the Bible: Fertility and Impurity* (Studies in Biblical Literature, 88; New York: Lang, 2006), p. 26.

Trojan Horse, bodes terrible consequences for David, as a 'gift' that is both bidden yet forbidden.[26]

The asymmetry in movement—he blithely sedentary while she probes inadvertently—is further reinforced by a parenthetical remark inserted into the action-packed verse: 'She was purifying herself of her impurity [*mitqadeshet mi-tum'atah*]'. The verb (in the participial form) contrasts with the series of paratactic verbs, and raises questions about the timing of her purification. Most commentators suggest that it refers back to her bathing on the roof; she had been cleansing herself from menstrual impurity. Radak (almost comically) lauds David for his good timing; at least he didn't transgress the laws of family purity![27] At the level of simple physiology, it guarantees that the conception is a natural consequence of their adultery.[28] In addition, it exonerates Bathsheba of seductive intentions; presumably she had been bathing on the roof in order to resume sexual relations with her husband. That is, her purity contrasts with the blind passion of David.[29]

Frymer-Kensky, however, argues that Bathsheba's bathing on the roof (v. 2) was simply that, a bath, and her purification (v. 4) *follows* their sexual relations. She notes that the bathing of a menstruant woman (*Niddah*) is not described in Leviticus in terms of a rite of purification. 'The phrase, "He [or she] shall wash his [or her] clothes and bathe in water", used regularly in Leviticus for the end of periods of impurity, is conspicuously absent in the

---

26. Based on *b. Sanh.* 107a. I am grateful to Leigh Ann Hildebrand, at the Harvard Divinity School, for this brilliant insight in her paper 'The Ruse Embodied: Bathsheba as a Divine Dangerous Gift' (unpublished, 2012). Her paper centers on the rabbinic reading of Bathsheba and David's relationship, drawing upon the work of Deborah Lyons, 'Dangerous Gifts: Ideologies of Marriage and Exchange in Ancient Greece', *Classical Antiquity* 22 (2003), pp. 93-131.

27. Both the verb 'bathing [*rohetzet*]' (v. 2) and 'purifying [*mitqadeshet*]' (v. 4) are participles, introducing a circumstantial clause (as in Judg. 13.9; 2 Sam. 4.7; see GKC §141e; see also the discussion in Simon, 'The Poor Man's Ewe-Lamb', p. 213). Radak and Rashi (on 2 Sam. 11.4, 11) both exculpate David of transgressing Niddah, and also cite the rabbinic tradition that exonerates David of adultery. Soldiers would give their wives a conditional divorce [*get kritut*] when they went out to war, and so Bathsheba was 'retroactively divorced' upon Uriah's death (cf. *b. Shab.* 56a). Sternberg as well claims that the text wishes to justify David for not transgressing the laws of menstrual purity (*Poetics of Biblical Narrative*, p. 198). This claim is supported by the textual variant on 2 Sam. 11.4 in 4QSam² (albeit fragmentary): 'she had purified herself from her impurity and came to him [*ve-h'i mitqadeshet mi-tum'ata va-tav*[']'; that is, it does not read 'she returned', but 'she came . . .', presumably *after* her purification. See the analysis of this passage in Philip, *Menstruation and Childbirth,* pp. 25-28. I am grateful to my colleague Michael Rosenberg for pointing out this source to me.

28. Berlin, *Poetics,* p. 144 n. 8; Fokkelman, *King David,* p. 52; Alter, *David Story,* p. 251; Bar-Efrat *II Shmuel,* p. 111.

29. Fokkelman, *King David,* pp. 52-53.

passage on menstruation'.³⁰ Furthermore, in contrast to rabbinic law, which requires that a woman immerse herself in a ritual pool [*mikvah*] seven days after the *cessation* of her menstrual bleeding, biblical impurity entails only seven days of waiting after the *onset* of menstruation before the resumption of sexual relations. This time period is unlikely to result in conception. So, rather than purification *before* relations, Frymer-Kensky claims that purification must have occurred *after* Bathsheba and David lay with one another. 'When Bathsheba purifies herself, she is washing off the impurity that comes with all sexual relations, even licit ones'.³¹ According to Leviticus, *both* the man and the woman are deemed impure/unclean [*tam'eh*] after intercourse; both must wash, and are then deemed pure again with nightfall (Lev. 15.17-18). If Bathsheba alone purifies herself after sexual relations, as Frymer-Kensky suggests, the effect of the narrative aside is to highlight the contrast between king and female subject even further. While he presumes to rise from the bed with no lasting residue on his body or conscience, she tries to wash away the emissions, the consequences that both physically and psychically cling to her.

The scene might have concluded here, as David intended—a mere fling—except for the indemnifying pregnancy.³² Now it is her turn to send for the king.³³ She speaks but two words in this whole chapter: 'I am preg-

---

30. Frymer-Kensky *Reading the Women of the Bible*, p. 147. She points out that women, in the Bible, do not ritually wash after menstruation as an act of purification so that they may resume martial relations. Rather, they merely wait the requisite seven-day time period; 'time itself, rather than water, brings an end to the period of impurity' (see Lev. 15.19, 28). This is true of a woman who has just given birth as well; she simply waits, as in her Niddah period, for one week after the birth of a male and two weeks after the birth of a female before resuming sexual relations, but 33 or 66 days respectively before purification (see Lev. 12.2-6). For further scholarship on these passages in Leviticus, see Tikva Frymer-Kensky, 'Pollution, Purification, and Purgation in Biblical Israel', in *The Word of the Lord Shall Go Forth: Essays in Honor of David Noel Freedman in Celebration of his Sixtieth Birthday* (ed. Carol L. Meyers and M. O'Connor; ASOR Special Volume Series, 1; Winona Lake, IN: Eisenbrauns, 1983), pp. 399-414. Jacob Milgrom, however, argues that the omission of an immersion requirement is incidental; the biblical text does not consistently state that cleansing in a ritual bath is necessary in every verse where it might be relevant; sometimes the immersion requirement is simply assumed, as in Lev. 11.40. See the discussion in Jacob Milgrom, *Leviticus: A New Translation with Introduction and Commentary.* Vol. 1 (AB, 3; New Haven, CT: Yale University Press, 1991), p. 667. I am grateful to my colleague Michael Rosenberg for pointing out these sources to me.

31. Frymer-Kensky, *Reading the Women of the Bible*, p. 147.

32. Exum points out that 'the scene is the biblical equivalent to "wham bam, thank you, ma'am": he sent, he took, she came, he lay, she returned' (*Fragmented Women*, p. 175).

33. Frymer-Kensky points to other women in the Bible who 'send [*va-tishlah*]'— Rahab and Deborah and Delilah and Jezebel (see Josh. 2.21; Judg. 4.6; 16.18; 1 Kgs

nant [*harah 'anokhi*]' (v. 5). In sending and then speaking,[34] she echoes the discretion of Tamar, who first sends the tokens of Judah's identity before confronting him directly:

> As she was being brought out, she sent to her father-in-law, saying, 'I am pregnant [*'anokhi harah*] by the man to whom these belong'. And then she said, 'Please discern/recognize these, whose signet and cord and staff are these?' (Gen. 38.25).

The words—Tamar's *'anokhi harah* and Bathsheba's *harah 'anokhi*—are inversely related. Tamar's pregnancy, a consummation devoutly wished for, is marked by a paternity that needs proving, while Bathsheba's needs a cover. The stakes for both women are very high indeed. One woman is accused of 'harlotry [*znunim*]' and sentenced to the stake (Gen. 38.24).[35] The other would have been sentenced to death by stoning if her pregnancy had become public in the husband's absence. As Frymer-Kensky points out, 'pregnancy may "prove" the woman's adultery, but it does not indict the father, and public rumor would not be sufficient to convict a man . . . it is the woman who is in danger'.[36] The woman alone would bear the shame, just as the heroine in Nathaniel Hawthorne's novel alone wore the scarlet letter sewn to her cloak in the absence of an admission of paternity from the father.

The turning point hinges on the demand women make of men to take responsibility. In dire straits, both Tamar and Bathsheba challenge father-in-law and king. While Tamar prompts an 'ethical epiphany' in Judah, whereby he acknowledges his responsibility toward her and his 'seed',[37] Bathsheba's announcement only embroils David further in sin as he looks to her husband for a false alibi. To his credit, the king does not deny her implied appeal. He does not allow Bathsheba to be marked by the letter 'A', as the heroine

---

19.2; and 21.8) (*Reading the Women of the Bible*, p. 149). She also notes the parallel between Bathsheba and Tamar: 'The pregnancy of both women precipitates male action: they each use the emphatic "I", *'anoki*, to emphasize their situation' (p. 280).

34. Presumably, she speaks directly to him and not through a messenger, as the sequence of verbs suggests: 'and she sent to David and she said . . . [*va-tishlaḥ leDavid va-to'mer*]' (v. 5). See Bar-Efrat, *II Shmuel*, p. 111.

35. The term 'harlotry [*znunim*]' does not refer to a woman who provides sex for hire, but a woman who is faithless, either to her husband or to the man to whom she is promised in matrimony; or it may refer to a young woman who has sex out of wedlock (based on the verb *znh*, as in Gen. 34.31; Deut. 22.21; Lev. 21.9; Hos. 1.2; 4.13-14, BDB entry 2675, p. 276). See the discussion in Frymer-Kensky, *Reading the Women of the Bible*, pp. 270-71.

36. Frymer-Kensky, *Reading the Women of the Bible*, p. 149.

37. On Judah's moral transformation in terms of Aristotle's narrative theory of *anagnorisis* (recognition), see the discussion in Chapter 3, and Adelman, 'Ethical Epiphany', pp. 51-76.

in Hawthorne's novel. David, at least, admits to his paternity privately, and then acts to spare them both ignominy. Plan B ensues—where Plan A (if one can call it a plan) was simply to have a one-night stand. David had been hoping to get away with it, a mere 'misdemeanor'.[38] As king, he can cover for her pregnancy and his paternity by calling Uriah back from the front. People might then ascribe the pregnancy to the husband. That is, if Uriah concedes to sleep with his wife.

'Would You Murder and Also Dispossess?'[39] *The Fate of Uriah*

Yet Uriah does 'not go down' to sleep with his wife! Three times, in v. 6, the verb 'to send [*shlh*]' is deployed, comparable to the three times it is associated with the adultery (vv. 3, 4, 5), which reinforces the symmetry between 'sending' for Bathsheba and 'sending' Uriah to his doom. To justify the summons, the king asks Uriah after the welfare [*shalom* 3x] of Joab, the troops and the war.[40] The chit-chat is essentially a pretext, wherein the king casts Uriah into the role of a messenger from the front. Yet David's query resounds jarringly in retrospect—for how can there be *shalom* (welfare, wholeness) when David breaks faith with the man? Because Uriah does not fulfill the *real* reason for his return to the capital—that is, to cover for the adulterous conception—he must be sent back to the front as a messenger of his own demise; the king's question about *shalom* turns sinister. Uriah is sent back to the front, carrying the letter to Joab that decrees his own death and, like Rosencrantz and Guildenstern, is hoisted with his own petard.

David demands that Uriah cross the boundary from public front to the private domain, from soldier to husband, in conformity to military and domestic norms, just as the king had done inversely and illicitly in violating those norms when he lay with Bathsheba. The order is veiled with innuendo: 'Go down to your *house* and bathe your feet' (2 Sam. 11.8). The king does not speak of going to his *wife* but of his *house* [*beitekha*], not of lying

---

38. I allude to the name of Woody Allen's movie, *Crimes and Misdemeanors* (1989), which is a take-off on Dostoyevsky's *Crime and Punishment*, in that it pivots around the theme of conscience (or, rather, lack thereof).

39. 1 Kgs 21.19. See n. 1.

40. Similarly, David invokes the term *shalom* three times: in the greeting he sends to Nabal via ten of his men: 'To life! May you fare well [lit. be at peace, *shalom*], your household fare well [*shalom*], and all that you have fare well [*shalom*] . . .' (1 Sam. 25.6). Ironically, these tidings of 'life' and 'peace' [*shalom*] anticipate the violent threat to Uriah. See Alter, *David Story*, p. 153. Rosenberg comments on the 'threefold use of the term' *shalom* in both passages, reading the former 'as a serious oath, sincere of intention, and signifying David's good faith towards the household of Nabal' (*King and Kin*, p. 150). I am more equivocal about the overtone in both instances; if read ironically, it bodes the inverse of *shalom*: treachery, fracture and violent death.

[*shkb*] with his wife but of washing [*rḥtz*] his feet. The latter expression may be a euphemism for sexual relations,[41] and resonates with the bathing beauty [*'ishah roḥetzet*] that the king had spied from his rooftop (v. 2).[42] When Uriah leaves the palace, the king's provisions follow, the eating of which may lead to further comestibles.[43] Dissimulation compels the king to prevaricate; he cannot be direct, lest he arouse suspicion. Only by hints and innuendo may suspicion be stymied, the winds of gossip waylaid. The return of Uriah to his house is all that matters.

But...

> Uriah slept at the entrance of the royal palace [*beit ha-melekh*], along with the other officers of his lord, and did not go down to his house [*beito*]. When David was told that Uriah had not gone down to his house [*beito*], he said to Uriah, 'You just came from a journey; why didn't you go down to your house [*beitekha*]?' Uriah answered David, 'The Ark and Israel and Judah are dwelling in Sukkot (or huts),[44] and my lord Joab and my lord's men are camped in the open; how can I go home and eat and drink and lie with my wife? As you live, by your very life [*hayekha, ḥay nafshekha*], I will not do such a thing!' (2 Sam. 11.9-11).

In his explanation for why he did not go down to his home to lie with *her*, Uriah swears on oath that he would not sleep with his wife but with the troops. The question is: Does Uriah know about the adultery and is he provoking the king by refusing to comply? Is he daring fate? Or, in his naïve fealty to the men, does he inadvertently become a foil to the king?[45]

---

41. Yee suggests that the feet here are euphemistic for male genitalia, as in Exod. 4.25; Isa. 6.2; 7.20; Ruth 3.4, 7, 8, 14 (Yee, 'Fraught with Background', p. 245).

42. As Mieke Bal points out, 'David sends Uriah home but he does not name the real destination: the woman. Similarly, v. 15, the content of the letter does not specify the reason for Uriah's death: the woman. In both cases, the addressed other man has to complete the message himself. David does not specify the location of his interest. In v. 11, Uriah names the woman and in v. 21, Joab names her . . . David as a subject is so weak that he needs others to speak his mind' (Bal, *Lethal Love*, p. 35). I think she rather misses the point of the prevarication. It is not that David is 'weak'; rather, he must not mention Bathsheba, the locus of his concern, lest he reveal his intentions. She is displaced from his speech because she weighs on his conscience.

43. The term *mas'et ha-melekh* derives from the verb *ns'* ('to carry or bear'), and is used as a nominal form to refer to a meal, as in Gen. 43.34.

44. The term *sukkot* here may refer to the temporary dwellings (a hut or booth), which contrasts with a permanent dwelling—*bayit*, house (either David's or Uriah's). The *sukkot* subject the private man to public domain. So Uriah, in alluding to these *sukkot*, is also refusing to cross that line. Alternatively, Succoth may refer to a town (as in Gen. 33.17; Exod. 12.37; 13.20; 1 Kgs 7.33) that served as a strategic base for the army's encampment (see Yigal Yadin, 'Some Aspects of the Strategy of Ahab and David', *Biblica* 36 (1955), pp. 332-51.

45. See the discussion in Sternberg, *Poetics of Biblical Narrative*, pp. 201-209; Alter, *David Story*, pp. 252-53; Bal, *Lethal Love*, pp. 26-38. Moshe Garsiel argues that

Given the opaque nature of the biblical text, we cannot be certain what Uriah knows and what he intends. In not sleeping with his wife, he may be observing a tradition, lost to the contemporary reader, of maintaining ritual purity during 'holy war'.[46] As Rosenberg notes, Uriah plays the role of 'orthodox Israelite, quietly observing the wartime soldier's ban against conjugal relations (cf. 1 Sam. 21.4-7). The significance is double; it compounds the enormity of David's crime (a violation of a marriage is bad enough; a violation of a marriage under sacred conjugal suspension is a particularly cruel and nasty offence)'.[47] Further, Uriah's statement may mean more than he intends as the second agent of dramatic irony in the narrative. When he identifies Joab as 'my lord', Uriah suggests that authority lies *not* with the king but elsewhere.[48] Whether he intends the barb or not, the narrative sides with the soldier, for 'lordship', as ascribed to David, is undermined the moment the king does not sally forth in battle with his troops. Lordship is further lost when David commits adultery with the wife of one of his most loyal soldiers and then has him slain in battle. The trait associated with the king as 'lord' is contingent upon military mastery of the battle at the front, as well as ethical mastery of the boundary between the public and private man in the palace and home. Through Bathsheba and Uriah, David violates both domains.

---

when Uriah first arrives from the front he does not know why he has been summoned, but after the first night sleeping at the entrance to the palace with the servants, he finds out about the adultery and, in the second conversation with the king, subtly accuses him (*2 Samuel*: *'Olam ha-Tanakh* [The World of the Bible] [Tel Aviv: Revivim, 1993], p. 106).

46. See the discussion in Simon, 'The Poor Man's Ewe-Lamb', p. 214 n. 1. He cites G. von Rad, *Der heilige Krieg im alten Israel* (Göttingen: Vandenhoeck & Ruprecht, 1958), p. 7; J. Pedersen, *Israel: Its Life and Culture* (London: Oxford University Press, 1940), vols. 3-4, pp. 8-11.

47. Rosenberg, *King and Kin,* p. 132. Frymer-Kensky, on the other hand, argues that this verse only refers to the ban on eating consecrated food after sexual relations. According to the passage in Deut. 23.10-14, ritual impurities must be removed from the war camp, but there is no taboo on sexual relations outside the camp. So it would be permissible for a soldier to have relations with his wife when on furlough. Uriah's refusal to go down to his house even to say hello to his wife is then rather striking (Frymer-Kensky, *Reading the Women of the Bible,* p. 397 n. 150).

48. The ascription 'my lord' is used to refer both to the general, Joab, in v. 11, and to the king, in the next verse: 'the servants of my lord [*'avdei 'adoni*]'—clearly a reference to David's men. That is, Uriah is equivocal about David's 'lordship'. The Talmud picks up on the irony (only to undermine it) by suggesting that Uriah committed treason in defying the king, and therefore deserved the death sentence (*b. Shab.* 56a). In this passage, according to Rashi, Uriah commits treason when he calls Joab 'my lord', while Rashbam (Rabbenu Meir quoted by the Tosafot) argues it was because he did not obey the king's command to go home (commenting on *b. Shab.* 56a)).

Failing to convince him verbally, the king tries another instrument of seduction on the next night: inebriation. Even after plying him with drink, Uriah does not comply, but 'went out to sleep in the same place [*lishkav mishkavo*] with his lord's servants [*'avdei 'adonav*]; to his home [*'el beito*] he did not go down' (2 Sam. 11.13). Whether he intends to goad David or not, the text presents Uriah as a loyal soldier of consummate integrity, who remains in control of himself within the male/military/public sphere. The husband does not cross the boundary between public and private space; he does not 'go down' (literally and figuratively) as David had done, to his home to sleep with his wife. As a consequence, he makes a fatal mistake.[49] He hazards on oath, ironically, and loses: 'As you live, by your very life [*ḥayekha, ḥay nafshekha*], I would not do such a thing!' (v. 11). Strangely, Uriah swears on the king's life (who is mortal!) rather than in the name of the (immortal) God—the more common biblical trope. Imbedded within the oath lies an implied curse: 'Just as you [David] live (and will continue to live), I would never dare do such a thing. . . . And if I *were* to do so, it would be at peril of my life'. Or does he put David's life at risk by invoking the king, *ḥayekha, ḥay nafshekha*, as the irrevocable, authoritative witness to the oath? Either his own life or David's is on the line in the implied imprecation. The veiled threat ironically rebounds against him as he remains loyal to his word. Like Saul, Uriah tragically hazards on oath and loses. He forfeits his life while David lives on, for we, the readers of this history, know that God is bound in an irrevocable covenant with David (2 Sam. 7.12-16). Indeed, 'the arrows of the Almighty' imbedded in Uriah's words 'are arrayed against him'; his 'spirit absorbs their poison'.[50]

'*How have the mighty fallen?*'[51]

The king now resorts to Plan C, to have Uriah slain in the battle as the army lays siege to the Ammonite city of Rabbah. Two agents must bear out his will—Uriah, knowingly or unknowingly, by carrying his own death warrant in the form of a letter to Joab, and the general, in strategically setting the soldier up to be killed. David's order, however, is rather vague: 'Put Uriah

---

49. If he knows, as one reading suggests, then he acts defiantly against David and speaks sarcastically in addressing him as 'lord', and perhaps deliberately martyrs himself when the king sends him to be killed in battle. If he does not know, then David is sending an innocent man of integrity and a loyal soldier to his death (Sternberg, *Poetics of Biblical Narrative*, pp. 207-12).

50. Based on Job 6.4.

51. The expression 'How are the mighty fallen!', essentially a rhetorical question, is deployed by David in his eulogy praising the heroic deaths of Saul and Jonathan in battle (2 Sam. 1.19, 25, 27), but I mean to read it ironically as a real question. How is the hero fallen? Ignominiously, by the hand of a woman.

in the face of the fiercest fighting and draw back, so that he will be struck down and die' (2 Sam. 11.15). But there is no real battle 'front' in siege warfare, only skirmishes across the wall. In addition to a defense against external forces, the wall becomes metonymic for the boundary between the public and the private sphere of the monarchy—the boundary the king breached in taking Bathsheba and transgresses again in the murder of her husband.

A contrast between the narrative (vv. 16-17), the message (vv. 18-21) and the king's response (v. 25) sets the sin in stark relief where the general is agent of yet a third moment of dramatic irony. To isolate Uriah by the wall would be to expose the king's nefarious plot. So the general modifies the order. The narrative records, 'He deployed Uriah in the place where he knew there were valiant men', and when the enemy came out to battle, 'some of the troops, some of David's servants [*'avdei David*], fell and Uriah the Hittite also died' (vv. 16-17). As Alter notes, 'Joab . . . coldly recognizes that in order to give David's plan some credibility, it will be necessary to send a whole contingent into a dangerous place and for many others beside Uriah to die. In this fashion, the circle of lethal consequences of David's initial act spreads wider and wider.'[52] Several soldiers die, as collateral damage, along with Uriah. These 'valiant men', redundantly and ironically called '*David*'s servants [*'avdei David*]', acted in solidarity with Uriah, just as Uriah had done in lying with 'his lord's servants [*'avdei 'adonav*]' and *not* sleeping with his wife (v. 13). As a consequence, like Uriah, they forfeit their lives. David, on the other hand, acts in '*desolidarity*' by felling his soldiers to cover for the adultery and by forcing his general into complicity with him.[53]

Joab, laden with ambivalence about the loss of his troops, anticipates a reproach from the king in the form of a question of strategy, while ironically levelling a rebuke at him (v. 25):[54]

> And Joab charged the messenger saying, 'When you finish reporting all the details of the battle to the king, if it should happen that the king's wrath is roused and he says to you, "Why did you approach the city to fight? Did you not know they would shoot from the wall? Who struck down Abimelech son of Jerubbesheth? Did not a woman fling down upon him an upper millstone from the wall, and he died in Thebez? Why did you approach the wall?" Then you shall you say, "Your servant Uriah the Hittite also died"' (vv. 18-21).

---

52. Alter, *David Story*, p. 254.
53. This term, 'desolidarity', is Mieke Bal's in *Lethal Love*, p. 30.
54. See the discussion in Sternberg, *Poetics of Biblical Narrative*, pp. 212-22; Fokkelman, *King David*, pp. 64-69; Alter, *David Story*, pp. 254-55; Simon, 'The Poor Man's Ewe Lamb', pp. 218-20; and Bal, *Lethal Love*, pp. 30-35. The version in the LXX records this report as integral to the narrative, not the dialogue, thereby closing the ironic gap by suggesting that this was indeed the way Uriah had been killed.

The double entendre in the allusion to Abimelech's death, 'felled by a woman', refers not only to *how* the troops (presumably) died, 'in going too close to the wall', but harks back to David's breach across that figurative wall in taking a married woman. The general sees in Bathsheba the woman who, with more than manly strength, dropped an upper millstone from the wall that crushed the king's skull (cf. Judg. 9.50-54). In response to the fatal injury, Abimelech pleads with his arms bearer to draw a dagger and kill him: 'Let it not be said of me, "A woman killed him!"' (Judg. 9.54). As a *femme fatale,* the woman becomes an agent not only of death but of ignominy. Similarly, Deborah, the judge, answers Barak's request to go into battle with him: 'There will be no glory for you in the course you are taking for Yhwh will deliver Sisera into the hands of a woman' (Judg. 4.9).[55] Likewise Rahab, the 'harlot', is the source of Jericho's downfall, in betraying the Canaanite city to the spies who escape across a similar town wall (Josh. 2). It is from the boundary defined by a wall, a tower, or, in David's case, a rooftop within the city walls that great leaders are shamefully laid low. So Yeats penned, what began as a 'shudder in the loins', with the rape of Leda, engenders 'the broken wall, the burning roof and tower' in the fall of Troy. How are the mighty fallen? By the lethal woman, when the man goes 'too close to the wall', here, by illicitly crossing the boundary it defines between the public and private spheres.

In contrast to Joab's pangs of conscience, expressed in anticipation of the king's wrath, David's response is glib. It seems that the messenger never relayed these words to David (vv. 23-24), so the general's subtle rebuke of the king (whether intended or not) is lost. The general is presented as the foil to the king, strangely, through a speech never relayed. As Fokkelman points out, 'The paradox is that Joab allows that very David, the man who consistently acts in Ch. 11 as though he has no conscience, to be the voice of his [that is, the general's] own bad/good conscience'.[56] Joab had adjured the messenger to placate David, who, contrary to expectation, is rather sanguine: 'Thus shall you say to Joab, "Let this thing not seem evil in your eyes, for the sword devours this way and that . . ."' (v. 25). Perhaps David intends to exonerate Joab, to convey that he accepts the necessary price paid—the collateral damage in the execution of Uriah. But the effect is chilling. Following the mourning period,[57] David sends for her, 'gathers her [*va-ya'asfah*] to his house', and she becomes 'wife to him' (v. 27).

---

55. Deborah's statement is doubly ironic because, in consenting to go with the general, Barak, into battle, she invokes this misogynist view as a *female* prophet and strategist. But her own words then double back upon her, for it is not Deborah but Jael who wins the glory in slaying the general of the Canaanite army.

56. Fokkelman, *King David*, p. 68.

57. Most probably seven days (see Gen. 50.10; Job 2.13; 1 Sam. 31.13; as in David's 'mourning/penitence' for his dying infant, 2 Sam. 12.18-23).

Bathsheba remains unnamed, designated merely as 'Uriah's wife' (v. 26) in this seeming resolution. The epithet emphasizes the *attempt* to make the illicit licit. Further, the term *va-ya'asfah* (root: *'sf*), which connotes care, responsibility or protection toward the widow,[58] is used rather than the more common biblical euphemism for marriage, 'to take [*lqḥ*]', perhaps because David has already sexually 'taken' her. Initially he had no intention of marrying Bathsheba before her pregnancy and Uriah's refusal to play the cuckold. When the king summons her now, it is with a protective feelings toward her. Is it love? We do not know; the Bible is characteristically terse. Bathsheba then bears David the bastard son of their adulterous union as though legitimate. All I's dotted, T's crossed. Crimes become mere misdemeanors when the king presumes to stand above the law. That is, until God intervenes. The narrator introduces the omniscient deity, who echoes David's own words to his general, 'let this thing not seem *evil* in your eyes' (v. 25): 'But the thing that David had done was evil in the *eyes of Yhwh*' (v. 27).[59]

'She was like a daughter to him':
Nathan's Parable and the Oracle of Doom

The prophet Nathan is sent by God to rebuke David through the famous 'parable of the poor man's ewe lamb'. This is the fourth stage of dramatic irony, 'the play within the play', designed to 'catch the conscience of the king'. It is important to note that the king does not hear the story as a tall tale but as a real case presented to him for judgment.[60] Psychologically, it is a ploy used to galvanize David's conscience by enabling him to recognize evil in another's actions before he, himself, stands accused.

> And Yhwh sent Nathan to David. He came to him and said to him: 'There were two men in the same city, one rich and one poor. The rich man had sheep and cattle, very many, but the poor man had only one little ewe lamb that he had bought. He nurtured it and it grew up together with him and his children: it would eat of his bread, drink from his cup, and in his lap it would lie [*tishkav*]; it was like a daughter to him [*va-tehi lo ke-vat*]. One

---

58. See Deut. 22.2; Ps. 27.10; Isa. 40.11; BDB entry 695, p. 63.

59. Or 2 Sam. 12.1a (as in the LXX, which the NJPS and NRSV translations adhere to). This is one of the few theologically explicit statements in the Court History (the others being 12.24 and 17.14). See the discussion in McCarter, *II Samuel*, p. 298.

60. What Uriel Simon calls a 'juridical parable', similar to the parable of the Tekoite woman (2 Sam. 14.4-17), the parable of the captive who escaped from his keeper (1 Kgs 20.35-43), the parable of the vineyard (Isa. 5.1-7) and that of the divorced woman who returned to her first after leaving her second husband (Jer. 3.1-5) (Uriel Simon, 'The Poor Man's Ewe-Lamb', pp. 207-42). David M. Gunn, on the other hand, argues that the parable draws from a classic folklore motif rather than a legal formulation ('Traditional Composition in the Succession Narrative', *VT* 26 [1976], pp. 218-20).

day, a traveler [*helekh*] came to the rich man, but he found it a pity to take [*va-yaḥmol laqaḥat*] any of his own flock or herd to prepare a meal for the guest who had come to him; so he took the poor man's lamb and prepared it for the man who had come to him' (2 Sam. 12.1-4).

Many scholars have commented on the gap between the parable and the reality to which it alludes. They argue that the inability to map the allegorical figures onto the historical narrative is an artefact of the story's genre.[61] But, in characterizing the story as a kind of fable, they fail to see the significance of the parable's complexity in its psychological impact on the listener (David) as a fictionalized case, and the reader (us) as dramatic irony. The rich man, who had very many sheep and oxen, is obviously the king, who has many wives; the poor man (Uriah) has but 'one little ewe lamb' (v. 3). But who is the ewe lamb?[62] Is it Bathsheba, 'taken' from the tender lap of her master for the king's pleasure, or Uriah, slaughtered like the lamb on the battlefield? At first blush, the lamb corresponds to the woman, given the feminine gender of *kivsah*, and the resonance with her name, *Bat-sheva*; the lamb 'was like a *daughter* to him [*va-tehi lo ke-vat*]'.[63] Yet the verbs—eat, drink and lie [*'kl, shth, shkb*]—are all associated with Uriah's refusal to go home to sleep with his wife (11.11; cf. v. 13), which prompts his death orders. It is he who is slaughtered (presumably like the lamb), while Bathsheba is elevated to the status of queen. Furthermore, the identity of the traveler [*helekh*],[64] whose visit prompts the rich man to take the poor man's lamb, does not correspond to any figure in the historical narrative.

---

61. For example, Simon, 'The Poor Man's Ewe-Lamb', pp. 226-32; Gunn, 'Traditional Composition', pp. 218-220; and Bar-Efrat, *II Shmuel*, p. 118.

62. Bar-Efrat, *II Shmuel*, p. 118; Regina Schwartz, 'Adultery in the House of David: The Metanarrative of Biblical Scholarship and the Narratives of the Bible', *Semeia* 54 (1991), pp. 35-56. Frymer-Kensky (*Reading the Women of the Bible*, pp. 154-54) argues that Bathsheba is the 'poor man' and Uriah 'the lamb' (see p. 399 n. on 155).

63. *Bath-sheva*, literally 'daughter of seven', suggests yet another double entendre—with 'oath [*shevu'ah*]' and 'seven [*shev'ah*]'. The LXX testifies to an alternative version of David's decree; instead of paying 'fourfold [for the stolen sheep]' (12.6), the Greek records sevenfold [*shivatayim*]. Many scholars hold that the LXX is the original version here, which the MT 'corrects'. The term 'oath' and 'seven' are linguistically related also in Abraham's oath and the exchange of seven ewes in the etiological narrative on the naming of Beersheba (Gen. 21.28-33). See the discussion in Moshe Garsiel, *Biblical Names*, pp. 129-30.

64. The term *helekh* is a near *hapax legomenon* (based on the root *hlkh*, 'to go/walk'), parallel to the term *'oreaḥ*, 'visitor', later in the verse. The only other occurrence is found in 1 Sam. 14.26, *helekh devash* ('flow of honey'), which, perhaps, should be amended to *halaḥ devash* ('dripping with honey'); see BDB entry 2402, p. 237. Read psychoanalytically, the *helekh* may be an external projection of evil inclination, what Freud might call the Id (in rabbinic parlance, the *yetzer*), which arouses his desire for another's wife (the ewe-lamb) and compels him to spare his own sheep and oxen (v. 4).

The nominal form (based on the verb *hlk*, meaning 'to go or walk') is rare and harks back to the image of David wandering [*mithalekh*] in lust and lassitude on the roof (11.1); the visitor is Desire personified. The king is then split, symbolically, between the 'rich man' and the wayfarer [*helekh*], whom he feels compelled to feed. In the parable, the rich man's actions come from a positive impulse, of generosity [*hakhnasat 'orhim*], but ethics go awry when the rules of hospitality trump the boundaries of another's property. In splitting David into two figures, the one manifest as Desire (the traveler), who is not culpable for the sin though he prompts it, and the 'rich man', who slaughters the sheep to feed him, the truth is effectively obscured. The conscience of the king, as the one who judges and (ironically) stands judged, can thus be aroused. I suggest that the blurring of identities in the parable lies at the crux of the gendered critique of power in the narrative. The wayfarer is both David *and* his pangs of conscience, split between his private desires and his public self. The lamb, likewise, is both Uriah and Bathsheba. These double identifications of the figures in the parable—the female lamb denoting both the husband and wife, as victims, and the male figures denoting both the king and his conscience—present a critique of the masculine illusion of omnipotence. In the patriarchal world, the wife belongs to the protective domain of her husband. In breaching the line between palace and home, both become vulnerable. When that boundary is violated by the rich man's whims, both female and male are prey; both wife and husband are at risk under the aegis of the king's illusion of absolute power.

Consider, for example, the stories of the patriarchs, Abraham and Isaac, who present their wives as sisters to protect themselves as they sojourn in foreign lands.[65] In the ancient Near East, it seems that murder was less grievous than adultery. It was preferable to take a 'widow' (after killing the husband) than to take a man's wife. Upon remarking on Sarai's great beauty, for example, Abram adjures her, 'When the Egyptians see you, they will say, "This is his wife"; then they will kill me, but they will let you live' (Gen. 12.12; cf. 20.13). So the founding fathers pass their wives off as sisters in Egypt and in Gerar.[66] Only by dint of divine intervention are Sarah and Rebekah spared and returned to their husbands without being violated. By contrast, Greek and ancient Near Eastern legends recount the stories of wife abduction without any protective higher hand toward the woman. Helen, 'the face that launched a thousand ships', was married to Menelaus and then abducted by Paris, spurring the Trojan War. As Sarna

---

65. See Gen. 12.10-20; 20.1-18; and 26.6-11, known as the wife-sister tales. For a cogent feminist analysis of these passages, see Susan Niditch, *Underdogs and Tricksters* (San Francisco: Harper & Row, 1987), pp. 23-69.

66. Indeed, in the second episode, he tells Abimelech, king of Gerar, that she is his half-sister (20.12).

recounts, 'From Ugarit comes the story of King Keret who lost his lovely spouse Hurrai (or Hurriya), through whom he was supposed to be destined to carry on his line, and had to mount a military campaign to recover her'.[67] While the stories in Genesis may draw on these or similar sagas, according to Sarna, the biblical author engages in a polemic against them, where 'the sensuality and immorality of the pagan nations contrasts with the values of the patriarchs'. And, 'of major concern, is the emphasis placed on God's protective intervention on behalf of the women—just at the moment when all human resources have failed and it appears that the divine promises are to be aborted. The matriarch is recovered by the action of God, not as a result of warfare waged by the outraged husband.'[68] In a similar vein, Uriel Simon argues that David is *not* like these Oriental monarchs (Pharaoh of Egypt and Abimelech of Gerar), 'who resorted to stealing wives from their husbands or who sought to do away with husbands in order to gain their wives'.[69] At least initially, the Israelite king does not intend to take the wife away from the husband or murder him, but only attempts to erase the consequences of the affair by summoning Uriah from the front in order to have relations with Bathsheba. But does this make David somehow better? In retrospect, the difference between Paris of Troy and David, king of Israel, is narrow. Divine intervention *before* the transgression is painfully absent in the David–Bathsheba–Uriah episode; both the wife and husband are subject to the whims of the king of Israel. One is taken; the other killed. Only after committing the two transgressions is the king's power checked through the prophet's rebuke. One might say: too little too late! What do we gain in hindsight as we read the prophet's rebuke? The history, as a theocentric narrative of events, testifies to a divine voice, as articulated by the prophet, that checks the political power of the king in the absence of miraculous intervention.

The parable and rebuke have a humanizing impact on the monarch that is unparalleled in Greek and ancient Near Eastern legends. David responds, in fury, with two judgments against the 'rich man' (himself), demonstrating that his conscience, his 'good side' that has been repressed by heinous crimes and coverups, is indeed alive and well:

> David flew into a rage against the man, and said to Nathan, 'As Yhwh lives, the man who did this should die [*ben mavet h'u*]! He shall pay for the lamb fourfold because he did this thing and because he showed no pity [*l'o ḥamal*]' (2 Sam. 12.5-6).

---

67. Sarna, *JPS Commentary: Genesis,* p. 94.
68. Sarna, *JPS Commentary: Genesis,* p. 94.
69. Simon, 'The Poor Man's Ewe-Lamb', p. 212.

The first sentence, issued in the form of an oath, is clearly not proportional to the crime,[70] whereas the second aligns with Mosaic law: the demand that the man pay fourfold for the stolen sheep.[71] The first death sentence is mitigated by God's compassion in response to David's penitence (vv. 13-14); the latter, more measured judgment is reinforced by Nathan's rebuke (vv. 10-12) and irrevocably played out in the events that ensue. The fourfold recompense is meted out in the series of tragedies that unfold within his own family: the rape of Tamar by her half-brother, Amnon (ch. 13); she, condemned as a 'ruin' to live in Absalom's house (13.20); Absalom's vengeance upon his sister's rape through fratricide (13.28-33); and Absalom's insurrection and the civil war that ensues between father and son (chs. 14–18).[72]

David gives two rather vague reasons for the double sentence: 'because he did this thing' and because he had no compassion [*l'o ḥamal*]. The inclination of the rich man 'to have pity [*va-yaḥmol*]' in wishing to spare his own flock (v. 4) rebounds, ironically, in the reason for condemning 'the man' who showed '*no* pity [*l'o ḥamal*]' in taking another man's sheep (v. 6).[73] Only when David responds with indignation and a call for justice, can Nathan, the prophet, confront him. He tears the veil away with two words: 'You (are) the man [*'atah ha-'ish*]!' (v. 7). The psychological continuity between David (as judge) and David (as judged), according to Uriel Simon, 'indicates how the juridical parable served the prophet as a medium of both reproof and repentance, at the same time. For David not only sentenced himself by these words of indignation, his spontaneous reaction also bore evidence of the sincerity of his own admission of guilt. The words:

---

70. A similar phrase can be found in David's reproof of Abner: 'As the LORD (Yhwh) lives, you deserve to die, because you have not kept watch over your lord [King Saul], Yhwh's anointed' (1 Sam. 26.16). Abner indeed dies at the hands of Joab, avenging the death of his brother (Asahel), though David dissociates himself from the murder (2 Sam. 3.27-37). See also Gen. 31.32, where Jacob inadvertently sentences Rachel to death for stealing Laban's household idols, fulfilled in her premature death while giving birth (35.18).

71. According to Exod. 21.37, 'When someone steals an ox or a sheep, and slaughters it or sells it, the thief must pay five oxen for an ox, and four for a sheep'. The LXX on 2 Sam. 12.6 has him decree 'seven times', as in Prov. 6.32 (MT): 'Yet if [the thieves] are caught, they will pay sevenfold'. The Septuagint's version further reinforces the play on Bathsheba's name.

72. The Talmud enumerates the four as the child (of David and Bathsheba's adulterous union), Amnon, Tamar and Absalom (*b. Yom.* 22b).

73. As Fokkelman observes, 'This sensitivity towards his own property has insensitivity and cruelty as the other side of the coin. David sees this by consummating the '*ḥamal* ("he spared") (v. 4) into a paradox; pusillanimous self-pity is transformed into a grave lack of sympathy and even into an obdurate egoism and crime. . . .' He is indeed 'a Nabal *redivivus*' (*King David*, p. 75).

"Thou art the man!" tore the veil of probity from the righteous judge, but the accused who thus stood unmasked was not presented as worthless.'[74]

What hangs in the balance is the impact of the oath, a speech act that calls for the living God to affirm whether the judgment (however fictional the case may be) against 'the man' will be fulfilled in the unraveling of historical events as divine retribution for David's sin. To the prophet's accusation, 'You are the man [*'atah ha-'ish*]' (v. 7), and the oracle of doom (vv. 9-12) David's answers two words: 'I have sinned to the LORD [*hat'ati le-Yhwh*]' (v. 13). His expression of remorse and repentance enables God to mitigate the initial harsh judgment that the king had (inadvertently) decreed upon himself on oath, 'the man who did this should die' (v. 5)—with compassion—'you shall not die' (vv. 13-14). Instead, the death sentence will be displaced onto the innocent child, conceived of the adulterous union. The infant's death will then haunt David, as he rises prematurely from mourning: 'While the child was still alive, I fasted and wept because I thought: "Who knows? Yhwh may be gracious to me and let the child live." But now that he is dead, why should I fast? Can I bring him back again? I *go* to him [*'ani holekh 'elav*], but he will not return to me' (2 Sam. 12.22-23). Bereft, David now moves irrevocably toward death as though condemned. He will not go 'gently into that good night', but will rage, rage against the dying of light', limping in the Valley of Death's shadow, doom looming over him.

As in the king's double verdict, Nathan's oracle of doom suggests two indictments (vv. 10-11).[75] In the first, as a consequence of Uriah's murder, punishment is meted out by the proverbial sword [*herev*, 3x] that will never depart from David's house.[76] It is the fiery ever-turning sword that guards the way of no return to Eden (Gen. 3.24). In the second, as a response to the sexual transgression, punishment will be visited upon David with a 'calamity' from 'within his house' [*ra'ah mi-beitekha*] when another man 'will lie [*ve-shakhav*]' with his wives 'in the eyes of this sun' (v. 11). What

---

74. Simon, 'The Poor Man's Ewe-Lamb', p. 232. See also Fokkelman: 'The one parable with its duality of good and evil speaks to the one David and brings about a curative change in the duality, the discord, and the positions, hardened by suppression and self-condemnation of his good and evil side. So the whole parable begins to restore wholeness to a chaotic soul' (*King David*, p. 80).

75. Fokkelman observes that the division into verses by the Masoretes has misled exegesis, where the parallels between Uriah's murder and the sword and the sin of adultery with the taking of David's wives has been obscured. He suggests that vv. 9a-10a address the murder, and the latter half of the verse, 'because...' (v. 10b), pertains to the second part of the oracle (vv. 11-12) (Fokkelman, *King David*, pp. 83-85).

76. The oracle opens with echoes of David's blithe remark: 'for the sword devours this way and that...' (11.25).

began as a transgression committed 'in secret [*va-seter*]'[77] will be exposed and amplified through an act of rape, incest and treason in public, 'in the sight of all Israel and in broad daylight' (v. 12), when Absalom sexually possesses David's ten concubines on the very roof where the sin began (2 Sam. 16.21-22).[78] Ineluctable justice assures that what is observed by God in private, deemed 'evil' in the divine eye,[79] will now be exposed to the public eye, measure for measure. So the slogan goes, 'the personal is political'. As a result of the king's transgression of boundaries through power politics, crossing the line of another man's 'home' (his wife), David's own personal boundaries will be violated in the confluence of 'house' as dynasty and kingship, manifest in progeny and palace.

The Birth of Solomon—Return to Broken Wholeness

Though divine comeuppance is meted out from *within* David's own family, the house (that is, the Davidic dynasty) remains standing. His immediate wish for God's compassion (v. 22) is not answered with the infant son, conceived in adultery, who dies tragically as a consequence of his father's displaced death sentence. However, the second child born of David and Bathsheba's union will thrive. The son is named for peace or wholeness by both parents, and for the return to God's grace:

> Then David consoled [*va-yinahem*] his wife Bathsheba, and went [*va-yav'o*] to her, and lay with her [*va-yishkav 'imah*]; and she bore a son, and he/she named [*va-yiqr'a/va-tiqr'a*] him Solomon [*Shlomoh*]. Yhwh loved him ['*ahevo*], and sent a message by the prophet Nathan; so he named him Jedidiah [*Yedidyah*] because of Yhwh (2 Sam. 12.24-25).

This is the first time we have seen real tenderness between David and Bathsheba, who is now called, for the first time, 'his wife'.[80] He consoles her, just as Isaac is consoled after the death of his mother in his love for Rebekah (Gen. 24.67).[81] It is love that turns the heart away from grief and gives hope

---

77. The term *seter* is full of erotic resonance, as in Abigail's first encounter with David, when she rounds the 'crag in the hill [*seter ha-har*]' (1 Sam. 25.20; cf. Cant. 2.14). See the discussion in the previous chapter, nn. 10-12.

78. These ten women are taken by force, and then tragically condemned to the status of grass widows (2 Sam. 20.3). In comparing the sin of Bathsheba and David to Absalom's taking his father's ten wives/concubines, the transgression is intensified: private versus public, one to ten, adultery to incest/adultery/treason, coercion as opposed to force.

79. As in 2 Sam. 11.27 and 12.9.

80. In contrast to vv. 11.5, 26 and 12.10, 15, where is she called 'the woman' or 'the wife of Uriah'.

81. Both David and Isaac, however, are unlike Jacob (bereft of both his beloved wife, Rachel, and their son, Joseph), who *refuses* to be comforted (*va-yema'en lehitnahem*, in

to the bereaved soul. David *comes* [*va-yav'o*] to her and lies with her [*va-yishkav 'imah*], an inversion of the original act of forbidden relations where she had come [*va-tav'o*] to him (11.4).[82] Where he had once summoned her as an object of his own lust, now he goes to her as a subject to answer her needs, to comfort her, lie with her, and enable her to bear a son that will replace their infant who died. Compassion, comfort in the wake of mourning, is what Solomon comes to mean to her.

Once the child of this tenderness is born, both parents engage in naming him, that is, if we acknowledge the tradition preserved in the MT.[83] Agency in the act of naming is not necessarily either/or; there is no tension between mother and father in the meaning they wish to bestow on the child born in the aftermath of their adultery.[84] David and Bathsheba name him *Shlomoh* in concert with each other. The meaning of his name might be construed as 'his peace', 'his wholeness' or 'his well-being' (from *shlm*)—but is it God's or David's? In the aftermath of sin and rebuke, David is a broken man. The narrator interjects to tell us that 'Yhwh loved him ['*ahevo*]', and it is corroborated by Nathan's naming of the child, 'Jedidiah [*Yedidyah*]', literally, 'beloved of God'.[85] Perhaps the name foreshadows the future status of the

---

37.35), and the mythic matriarch, Rachel, who *refuses* to be comforted for her children who have gone into exile (*me'anah lehinnahem*, Jer. 31.15).

82. Bar-Efrat points out that this collocation is unique in the Hebrew Bible (*II Shmuel*, p. 123).

83. We acknowledge the double act of naming as preserved in the MT: 'and she named [*va-tiqr'a*]' in the pronounced form (*qere*), as in the Syriac and Aramaic *Targum Jonathan*, and 'he named [*va-yiqr'a*]' in the written form (*kethib*). Most often it is mothers who name their children, as in Gen. 29.32, 33, 35; 30.11, 13, 18, 20-21, as well as 1 Sam. 1.20. Karla G. Bohmbach points out, 'In the Hebrew Bible women outnumber men as name-givers. Of the approximately forty-seven instances in which a name-giver is specified, twenty-nine involve women' ('Names and Naming in the Biblical World', in *Women in Scripture* [ed. C. Meyers, T. Craven and R.S. Kraemer; Boston: Houghton Mifflin, 2000] p. 37). There are a few significant outliers, however. Abraham names Ishmael and Isaac (Gen. 16.15; 21.3); both parents name Esau (25.25), though only Isaac names Jacob (25.25); and Jacob names Levi (29.34). For an excellent analysis of this trend of paponymy in the priestly source (P), see Isaac Sasson's article 'Baby Naming: Biblical Rites and Mother's Rights' (http://thetorah.com/baby-naming-biblical-rites-and-mothers-rights, 2014).

84. As reflected in the naming of Benjamin, who is named both by Rachel, as 'son of my sorrow [*ben 'oni*]', and by Jacob, as 'son of my right hand [*binyamin*]' (Gen. 35.18).

85. Alter understands 'Jedidiah' to mean 'God's friend', and reads it in accordance with the phrase that follows 'by the grace of the LORD [*ba'avur Yhwh*]' (based on McCarter's reading [*II Samuel*, pp. 294, 304]). Though the term *ba'avur* may suggest a reason or cause (as in 2 Sam. 13.2: 'Amnon was so distressed that he made himself ill because of [*ba'avur*] his sister Tamar'; cf. Ps. 106.32), Alter understands it as purpose— 'for the sake of', and reads a political motive behind the name: 'Perhaps, the second name, indicating special access to divine favor, reflects a political calculation on the part

prince and the role that the prophet Nathan (as agent of God) will play in determining the successor to the throne. But the name of the son serves as a counterpoint to his father's, resonant with the lover of Song of Songs (*dwd*). David is beloved by many but never loves until, perhaps, this moment. God, as the 'author' of this theocentric history, hints at a resolution in this second act of naming, reflecting from on high the return to wholeness below in the reconciliation of love between husband and wife.

The chapter ends as it began, with reference to the battle against the Ammonites in the siege upon Rabbah. Joab again sends messengers [*mal'akhim*] to the king and offers him the victory if he gathers the soldiers and takes upon himself, once again, the role of king at the army's helm. And so David rises from despair to win the battle and to collect the myriad of wealth from the spoils (including the crown of Milcom now placed on his own head). He also expels the residents of Rabbah, as well as other Ammonite cities, and subjects them to harsh work, presumably as corvée labor: 'Then David and all the people returned to Jerusalem' (v. 31c). This return to Jerusalem suggests that the king has not only proved himself victorious, once again, but has restored his reputation both in the political and personal sphere. The name of the city resonates with the naming of the prince, Solomon [*Shlomo*]. As Fokkelman remarks, 'These correspondences permit our saying that, after long and painful turmoil, Jerusalem has become "the city of peace", looking from the inside outward, now that the *shalom* of the war (11.7b!) has been attained, and looking inward from the outside through the birth of the "prince of peace", Solomon'.[86]

The final word of the chapter, *Yerushalam*, is spelled and even pronounced conspicuously without a yod, suggestive of a return to wholeness or completion.[87] Yet can wholeness ever be wholly recovered? The name, as a portmanteau, contains at its very core a paradox; *yeru-shalem* means 'he *contends* [*yrh*] for *peace* [*shalom*]'. David, as the one who conquered and established Jerusalem as the capital of the united Israelite kingdom, embodies that very paradox. How can a man so shattered be put together again? How does one *contend* for *peace*? Return to broken wholeness? The scars of his treachery, like seams along a precious porcelain bowl that has

---

of Nathan: he is already aligning himself with Solomon (and with Bathsheba), figuring that in the long run it will be best to have a successor to David under some obligation to him. In the event, Nathan's intervention will prove crucial in securing the throne for Solomon' (Alter, *David Story*, p. 263). This reading, however, ignores the narrative voice and its theological directive, which explicitly state that 'God loved him' and that God sent the prophet to name him Jedidiah.

86. Fokkelman, *King David*, p. 96.

87. In the MT, the name of the city appears 664 times; 660 do not include a yod, and the name is vocalized, for the most part, as *Yerushalem*. Here, because it ends a verse, the vocalization concludes with a *patah*.

been broken and then carefully sealed again, will show. In the man. In his children. In his dynasty. And in his beloved city, Zion. Yehuda Amichai, the modern Israeli poet, questions why the holy city, *Yerushalayim*, has a suffix that connotes doubling:

> Why is Jerusalem always two, Jerusalem on High and Jerusalem Below?
> I want to be in the Jerusalem of the middle,
> Without craning my neck upward, without injuring my feet below.
> Why is Jerusalem in the language of pairs—*Yerushala-yim*?
> Like two hands—*yadayim*—and two feet—*raglayim*.
> I just want to be in one *Yerushal*.
> For I am just one me, '*'ani*' and not '*'anayim*'.[88]

We now turn to that very city, in the aftermath of civil war between King David and his son, Absalom (whose very name, ironically, means 'father's peace'). The kingdom is divided; the yod has wedged its way back into the integrity of Jerusalem.

Woman of Oath: The Role of Bathsheba in the Succession Narrative

In the unraveling of David's household, Bathsheba has been conspicuously absent from the narrative for some two decades since her fatal affair with the king. Her role in determining the successor to the monarchy now stands in marked contrast to her passive position in chs. 11 and 12 of 2 Samuel.[89] Where once she had been acted upon, summoned for the fulfillment of the king's desire, silent except for the testimony to her pregnancy, she will 'show herself', as Robert Alter avers, 'a mistress of language—shrewd, energetic, politically astute'.[90] Her agency hinges upon the dramatic fulfillment of her name, *Bat-shevu'ah*, as 'woman of oath', which will take place over the course of two scenes. The first entails Nathan's initiative to send her to the ailing and aged king in order to remind him of the promise he had supposedly made to her that their son, Solomon, would succeed him on the throne. She not only urges David to fulfill the oath but prompts him to *swear* again to do so. In the second scene, Adonijah, who had set himself up as king and his brother's usurper, turns to the queen mother to request that Solomon, now king, grant him the beautiful Abishag, David's latest consort, as a wife. When she presents the request, again Bathsheba prompts

---

88. Yehuda Amichai, *Open Closed Open* [*Patuach Sagur Patuach*] (Tel Aviv: Schocken, 1998), p. 144 (Heb., author's trans.).

89. As Adele Berlin points out, 'she is a "real" person', here 'a mother concerned with securing the throne for her son. She emerges in these episodes as one of the central characters, important in affairs of state as well as in family matters (the two are inseparable)' (Berlin, *Poetics*, p. 27).

90. Alter, *David Story*, p. 366.

an oath in response, but this time with fatal consequences, for Solomon condemns his brother and rival to death. Does she understand the implications—that the request for the father's wife or concubine suggests a latent desire to repossess the throne? Does she know how Solomon will respond? Though the queen plays the role of mere messenger in both episodes, her adaptation of the script suggests political acumen and feminine wile on par with her biblical predecessors. Sarah and Rebekah, likewise, forward their sons as heir to the covenant and blessing, and God concurs (Gen. 21.10-12 and 27.6-7). The question of succession lies at the crux of the drama, where 'natural right' is pitted against divinely sanctioned choice, as advanced by the prophet and mother.

The chapter opens with a portrait of the king—frail, aged and shivering under his bed covers. Impotent, not even the young, beautiful Abigshag, the Shunammite, can keep him warm. He is also dangerously oblivious to the political intrigues surrounding his court. David does *not know*, both in body and mind. As Fokkelman notes, 'the reiteration of the word *yd'*', 'to know' in both the carnal and the cognitive sense (1 Kgs 1.4, 11, 18 and 27), 'pairs his sexual impotence with general powerlessness—the loss of his grip on political reality'.[91] The scene sets up a contrast between David's relations with Abishag, the virgin summoned to minister to him, and his illicit relations with the wife of Uriah, Bathsheba, at the height of his passion and power.

David's fourth son, Adonijah, now steps into the power vacuum. He is, apparently, next in line for the throne following the death of Amnon and Absalom,[92] and assumes that *he* is the rightful heir. Pretender, he takes the initiative, announcing, '*I* shall be king' (v. 5). Taking advantage of his father's frailty, he 'exalts himself [*mitnas'e*]', with fifty men running before his chariot and horsemen. Like Absalom, he is handsome and similarly unrestrained by his father (v. 6).[93] He then holds a sacrificial feast to confirm his own coronation at Ein-rogel by the Zoheleth stone (lit. 'eye-of-the-spy' and 'creeping stone'). Those allied with Adonijah are listed: Joab and Abiathar the priest (v. 7);[94] all his brothers, the king's sons (with the exception of Solomon), and the tribe of Judah attend the feast (v. 9). Those in the

---

91. Fokkelman, *King David*, p. 350.

92. See the genealogy in 2 Sam. 3.2-6. Chileab, the third son born to Abigail, is never a contender for the throne, and I suggest why that may be the case in the previous chapter. Adonijah proclaims that his right is based on primogeniture (1 Kgs 2.15), but we, the readers, know that God consistently plots to overturn that natural right.

93. The parallel between Absalom and Adonijah are quite explicit (1 Kgs 1.5 echoes 2 Sam. 15.1).

94. Joab, the former general of David's army, in allying with Adonijah, presents an overt critique of David and the pro-Solomon faction. Ever since he was forced into complicity with the king in the Bathsheba affair, he has been critical of David's weakness. He is rebuked for the slaying of Absalom, though with no dire consequences (2 Sam.

pro-Solomon faction are Zadok, the priest, Benaiah son of Jehoiada, Shimei and Rei, David's warriors, and, Nathan, the prophet (v. 8). Bathsheba, as a political player, is only mentioned when the prophet requires her diplomatic services. The most effective means of checking Adonijah's grab for power rests in making David *aware* of the political intrigues in the kingdom.

So Nathan appeals to Bathsheba to address the king:

> Have you not heard that Adonijah son of Haggith has become king and our lord David *does not know it*? Now therefore come, let me give you advice, so that you may save your own life and the life of your son Solomon. Go in at once to King David, and say to him, **'Did *you not, my lord the king,* swear to your servant, saying, Your son Solomon shall succeed me as king, and he shall sit on my throne? Why then is Adonijah king?'** Then while you are still there speaking with the king, I will come in after you and confirm your words (1 Kgs 1.11-14).

Nathan invokes a promise that David had supposedly made to Bathsheba that their second son, born in the wake of repentance and comfort after the infant conceived in sin died, would succeed him on the throne. The problem is that the text never records such an oath, even at the scene of Solomon's propitious birth when one would most expect it. Is Nathan urging Bathsheba to remind the king, whose memory is fading, of a promise that simply was never recorded?[95] Or is it a political fiction concocted to protect Bathsheba, Nathan and the pro-Solomon faction?[96] Or are human machinations pointing to a higher hand?

The oath, as it modulates from Nathan to Bathsheba (v. 13), Bathsheba to David (v. 17), and then is affirmed by David in yet another iteration of the promise to Bathsheba (vv. 29-30), exploits an ambiguity that is central to the plot. The gaps, ironic fissures between narrative and dialogue, invite 'God', the ultimate Knower and Adjudicator to witness the oath, to attest to the truth of the original utterance or affirm the ruse on the part of prophet and queen mother. Bathsheba, when she prostrates herself before the king, alters the script ever so subtly, drawing on God as her alibi: 'My lord, you

---

19.5-13). Now he will pay for his alliance against Solomon with his life, in fulfillment of the father's vendetta (1 Kgs 2.5-6, 31).

95. See Radak on 1 Kgs 1.13. See the discussion and review of the literature in Ziegler, *Promises to Keep,* pp. 250-51, especially n. 209. She cites 'Provan, *Kings,* p. 26', who 'downplays the formality of the oath, suggesting that it is nothing more than "pillow-talk" between the king and Bathsheba'.

96. For a list of scholars who suggest that the oath is a ruse on the part of the prophet and queen, see Ziegler, *Promises to Keep,* p. 250 n. 208. Alter suggests that the ambiguity 'opens up a large, though by no means certain, possibility that Nathan the man of God has invented the vow [*sic*] and enlists Bathsheba's help in persuading the doddering David that he actually made this commitment' (Alter, *David Story,* p. 366). Fokkelman concludes that there is no evidence to support either theory (*King David,* pp. 353-54).

yourself swore *by Yhwh your God* to your handmaid, saying, "Indeed, your Solomon shall reign as king after me, and he shall sit on my throne"' (v. 17). As Alter observes, Bathsheba adapts the script to her own ends: 'The vow [*sic*] is said to have been made solemnly "by the LORD your God." If in fact the vow [*sic*] is a fabrication, perhaps Nathan the prophet was leery of invoking God's name in connection with it.'[97] This is a notable *under-reading* of her agency. Bathsheba invokes the name of God in the oath because she wants to align her words and the king's promise that follows with the divine plot. Similarly, Rebekah invokes blessing in the presence of God when she urges Jacob, as an imposter, to go before his father in Esau's stead. Where the father had commanded his older son to hunt, prepare the venison and feed him, 'so that I may bless you before I die' (Gen. 27.4), Rebekah reports Isaac's words to Jacob as 'that I may bless you *in the presence of Yhwh* before I die' (v. 7). God's presence, in the blessing, was not necessary or anticipated by the blind, aging father. It is Rebekah who infers it. So too Bathsheba deliberately invokes God, whether David ever made such a promise or not, even if it was just sweet 'pillow talk'. Whether David had uttered an oath in the name of the LORD or not, Bathsheba brings God into the picture. Knowing her husband's idiom, she hazards the presence of the deity and wins.

After Bathsheba describes the lay of the political land, the divided factions and the danger both she and Solomon are in, Nathan enters the chamber, bowing low in obeisance, and affirms her report. He ends his words with a plea: 'Has this thing been brought about by my lord the king and you have not let your servants know [*l'o hoda'ta*] who should sit on the throne of my lord the king after him?' (v. 27). His follow-up speech differs from Bathsheba's report in four significant ways: (1) he lists the events and persons who have allied with Solomon; (2) he does not invoke the oath (respecting its original, though perhaps fantasized, intimate iteration); (3) he implies that David *might have* designated Adonijah as king but did not *make known* that initiative to him; (4) he does not imply that David does not know what is going on, as Bathsheba did (v. 18). That is, the prophet 'nettles' the king, provokes him to correct his negligence. He is much less direct than the wife, who unsettles him altogether. It is only in the presence of Bathsheba that the record can be set straight. David summons her into the chamber again! He runs with it, reiterating and reinforcing the oath with lucidity:

> The king *swore* [*va-yishv'a*] saying, 'As Yhwh lives, who has saved my life from every adversity, for just as I *swore* [*ki ka'asher nishb'ati*] to you by Yhwh, the God of Israel, that [*ki*] "Your son Solomon shall succeed me

---

97. Alter, *David Story*, p. 367. Alter uses the term 'vow' (hence my corrective *sic*), when what he refers to is the 'oath'. See the distinction between 'oath [*shevu'ah*]' and 'vow [*neder*]' in Chapter 5.

as king, and he shall sit on my throne in my place", so [*ki*] will I do this day' (vv. 29-30).

He swears on oath that he had sworn to her, this time by the LORD (Yhwh), God of Israel, and then swears again to fulfill it! As Fokkelman notes, 'In the O.T. [*sic*] the oath, along with its counterpart, the curse, is religiously and psychologically the most weighty and severe manner of speech. The oath of 1.29-30 is, due to its threefold use of *ki* and its opening clause, fully deployed, unlike the abbreviated quotations in vv. 13/17. Its central importance is indicated structurally by the narrator. The entire *scene structure in 1.5-53 points towards the oath and revolves around it.*'[98] Whether the oath had ever been uttered, the king now affirms its truth and expands upon the identity of the divinity to reinforce its verisimilitude—in the name of Yhwh, who is God *of* the Israelite people. So, too, the people twice aver, 'Yhwh *is* the [one] God! Yhwh is the [one] God!' (1 Kgs 18.39), in response to Elijah's contest with the prophets of Ba'al at Mt Carmel. This dual affirmation is reenacted, liturgically, at the conclusion of the Yom Kippur service. The oath here both invokes and affirms the presence, urged on by the woman's word, of God in history.

Adonijah's Appeal to Bathsheba

In the sequel to the short-lived insurrection, Adonijah (son of Haggith)—the 'rightful' heir to the throne—appeals to Bathsheba, mother of Solomon, for compensation for his displacement. But his request is either terribly naïve or he does not know with whom he contends: his brother, the king and the queen mother. A juxtaposition between Adonijah, on the one hand, and Bathsheba, on the other, is imbedded in the verses, and forms the basis for alliances throughout the succession narrative:

> Then Nathan said to Bathsheba the mother of Solomon,
> 'Have you not heard that Adonijah the son of Haggith
> has become king and David our lord does not know it?' (1 Kgs 1.11).

The same apposition introduces this scene:

> Then *Adonijah the son of Haggith* came to *Bathsheba the mother of Solomon* . . . (1 Kgs 2.13)

It is the son of one of his father's other wives that appeals to the mother of his rival. Why does Adonijah approach Bathsheba, of all people, with his request to have Abishag as his wife? Perhaps he is appealing to her maternal side. Perhaps he has no inkling of the role Bathsheba played in assuring Solomon's succession to the throne. Yet claiming a former king's concubine

---

98. Fokkelman, *King David*, p. 364.

is tantamount to claiming the throne.⁹⁹ Is this Adonijah's intention? Does Bathsheba know and anticipate Solomon's reaction? Not all scholars see Adonijah's request as a bid for the kingship.¹⁰⁰ Fokkelman and Berlin both consider Abishag's status as ambiguous, since King David never 'knew' her (in the biblical sense). Adonijah may then think he has a right to her, desires her as 'a consolation prize; having lost one thing (the kingship), he childishly comes forward to be pacified with something else'.¹⁰¹

I present the 'screenplay adaptation' of their dialogue:

> B: Do you come peaceably [*ha-shalom bo'ekha*]?
> A: Peaceably [*shalom*].
> A: May I have a word with you?
> B: Say on.
> A: You know that the kingdom was mine, and that all Israel expected me to reign; however, the kingdom has turned about and become my brother's, for it was his from Yhwh. And now I have one request to make of you; do not refuse me.
> B: Say on.
> A: Please ask King Solomon, for he will not refuse you, to give me Abishag the Shunammite for a wife.
> B: Very well [*tov!*]; I will speak to the king on your behalf. (1 Kgs 2.13-18).

The dialogue opens with a tenuous query, a bid for *shalom* in the wake of civil war and insurrection, ominously prescient of a breach of that peace with fratricide. What 'fatal naïveté'! To offer *shalom*, to risk *shalom*, in expecting his request for Abishag to be provided by *Shlomo*! His mistake lies precisely in asking for that which is associated with kingship—the wife or concubine. Though, as Fokkelman points out, 'Abishag has had no intercourse with the old king—and so Adonijah is under the illusion that he may ask for her. [She] has known great intimacy with the old David, has shared his bed (literally, and not in the usual figurative, i.e. sexual sense) and this suits Solomon perfectly.'¹⁰² It becomes a pretext for the eradication of his rival. Adonijah, in his plea, invokes the rights of primogeniture, 'the kingdom was mine (by right)', only to concede that God's choice trumped that

---

99. See Solomon's reaction (1 Kgs 2.22). Following Ahithophel's advice, Absalom blatantly sleeps with his father's concubines (2 Sam. 16.21-22), confirming his insurrection against his father/king. Reuben sleeps with Jacob's wife Bilhah (Gen. 35.22) and is soundly rebuked (49.4)—his loss of the status of firstborn is attributed to this blunder. Ish Bosheth, similarly, accuses Abner of coveting the kingship in taking Rizpah, Saul's concubine (2 Sam. 3.7).

100. Gunn, *King David*, p. 137 n. 4: 'both Adonijah and Bathsheba are to be viewed as imbeciles' in naively presuming that Solomon would interpret this request as innocuous.

101. Fokkelman, *King David*, p. 394; and Berlin, *Poetics*, p. 28.

102. Fokkelman, *King David*, pp. 392 and 394.

natural right (v. 14). In this way, he voices and affirms the antinomian trend that underlies the Davidic dynasty.

So why not take it further? Why not use the queen, whom King David bedded illicitly, to be his emissary before the son, King Solomon, conceived in the wake of their adulterous union? Yet Bathsheba, as 'woman of oath', will not balk at using the request to her own ends. Twice she urges him on (vv. 14, 16), suggesting that she is carefully considering the implications. 'Why', as Berlin asks, 'would Bathsheba have agreed to carry Adonijah's request to Solomon? Was it only to placate Adonijah so that he would cause no further trouble, or was it perhaps that Bathsehba was a bit jealous of Abishag and did not want Solomon to have her? Or did she, even more cunningly, anticipate Solomon's reaction and see this as a way to get rid of her son's opposition permanently?'[103] I rather favor the last interpretation. She knows her son, and just as she provoked an oath that catalyzes action in her husband, the aging king, so she anticipates the young king's outrage will lead to the eradication of his rival. She then approaches Solomon on behalf of Adonijah, and in full deference, the king bows to her and sets up a royal throne for her to his right (v. 19), establishing Bathsheba as queen mother and his right-hand woman. She importunes him, minimizing the request while demanding his compliance:

> B: I have one small request to make of you; do not refuse me.
> S: Make your request, my mother; for I will not refuse you.
> B: Let Abishag the Shunammite be given to your brother Adonijah as his wife.
> S: And why do you ask Abishag the Shunammite for Adonijah? Ask for him the kingdom as well! For he is my elder brother; ask not only for him but also for the priest Abiathar and for Joab son of Zeruiah!

She turns Adinojah's request (v. 16) into 'one small request' (v. 20), and points to the familial ties with 'your brother' (v. 21).[104] Yet, in commanding (and eliciting) the king's acquiescence, methinks the lady doth protest too much! For Solomon responds, almost on cue, as his father did, with yet another oath, breaking his former promise to her, 'I will not refuse you'[105]:

---

103. Berlin, *Poetics*, p. 29. The suggestion that Bathsheba might have been jealous seems rather inconsequential here. There is not a tinge of that sentiment, even when she first approaches David, the king, with the young beautiful Abigshag attending him. Rather it is pity (and the contrast of their respective experiences) that informs the relations between the two women.

104. Based on this placating tone, Fokkelman conjectures, 'She really does her best and nothing in the text justifies speculations concerning her having secret intentions or even counting on a bad outcome' (*King David*, p. 395).

105. Both Bathsheba and Solomon, in demanding and promising, echo Adonijah's naïveté: 'do not refuse me' and 'he will not refuse you' (vv. 16-17).

Then King Solomon swore by Yhwh, 'So may God do to me, and more also, for Adonijah has devised this scheme at the risk of his life! Now therefore as Yhwh lives, who has established me and placed me on the throne of my father David, and who has made me a house [*bayit*] as he promised, today Adonijah shall be put to death' (1 Kgs 2.23-24).

Solomon's words echo his father's oath, 'As Yhwh lives', and hark back to the supposed original promise made to Bathsheba 'by Yhwh, the God of Israel' (1 Kgs 1.29). Furthermore, he invokes his divine right to the throne, in God's original promise to establish a dynasty [*bayit*, lit., house] for his father and a kingdom that would endure forever (2 Sam. 7.11-16). Adonijah, he suggests, threatens that very divine right. While his brother had conceded that divine privilege in his dialogue with Bathsheba (v. 15), she did not repeat his conciliatory tone in her report to her son. Solomon's oath as a speech act is hyperbolic, intensified by the implied imprecation if the vow to execute Adonijah is not fulfilled. As Fokkelman observes, 'this heavily laid-on talk in the form of oath formulas is once more a type of over-reaction, indicating that for Solomon much more is involved than the request alone. The request touches on a negative charge already present in Solomon, causing it to be suddenly released.'[106] This is why he dismisses her plea, sarcastically along with any others that may come in its wake: 'ask not only for him but also for the priest Abiathar and for Joab son of Zeruiah!' (v. 22).[107] The oath, in response to the 'woman of oath', then prompts a command—'Off with his head'—and the fulfillment of David's vendetta, bequeathed to him on his father's deathbed. The first round of executions ensues: Adonijah (vv. 13-25), the priest Abiathar (vv. 26-27) and finally Joab, the general (vv. 28-35). In one fell swoop, the king eradicates all those who allied with the rival faction.

Conclusion: The Handmaid of History

The story of David and Bathsheba is at the crux of Israelite biblical history, from the conquest of the land to the Babylonian exile through the vicissitudes of the Judean monarchy. It both reinforces the notion of retributive divine justice, in the harsh judgment upon the king and the tragic events that ensue, and the irrevocable nature of God's covenant with David. The author (or redactor, rather) of the history would be remiss to conclude the story with David's confession and punishment for his sins. It is incomplete

---

106. Fokkelman, *King David*, p. 396.
107. The Hebrew is ambiguous here. The simplest and most literal reading renders it: 'Ask for him the kingdom also, for he is my older brother, and *on his side* [*ve-lo*] are Abiathar the priest and Joab the son of Zeruiah' (v. 22 ESV; cf. NJPS as well). This is corroborated by the LXX's version. Whether we 'interpolate in the elliptical phrase 'why not also ask for . . .' or not, the sarcasm is indeed very sharp in both readings.

as the 'biography' of an individual alone. The king made the city, Jerusalem, into the center of cultic worship, and laid the foundations for the House of Yhwh (the Temple). The prophet, in turn, had assured the king of Judah that he would establish a dynasty, 'the House of David', in terms of an everlasting covenant (2 Sam. 7.12-16). As Jon Levenson points out, these principles are at the center of the Deuteronomist's 'Zion theology'.[108] So the fruition of David's repentance, the boy conceived in the wake of sin and named, 'Solomon [*Shlomoh*]' (by his parents) and *Yedidiyah* (beloved of God) by the prophet (2 Sam. 12.24), represents both the critique of power and its restoration, on a humbled footing. Bathsheba is a pivotal player at both stages. As an embodied critique of power, she is David's nemesis, the powerless one who speaks a somatic truth. Her pregnancy, her very body, exposes David in his 'double self', split between body and mind, between desire and moral conscience endemic to man. But Bathsheba also reminds him of his higher calling. In the succession narrative, she moves from a passive, embodied testimony against him to a full-fledged player when she and the prophet Nathan collude in guaranteeing Solomon's place upon the throne. Nathan urges her to remind David of the oath he had supposedly made to her that Solomon would be the dynastic heir. But Bathsheba deviates from script by bringing God's name into the vow (1 Kgs 1.29-30). Herein lies the crux of the female ruse, where the duplicity of woman aligns with the divine will. For as we have shown, the impact of an oath invoking 'the Name' is either vindicated or subverted by God's presence in their midst. Bathsheba and the prophet hazard on oath and, unlike Saul, triumph. The woman moves from an embodied truth to a verbal, divinely endorsed one, from carnal knowing to full consciousness in the redemptive arc of history.

---

108. Levenson demonstrates how Jerusalem was inextricably associated with King David from the tenth century through the destruction of the Temple and the Babylonian Exile (587 BCE): 'the fortunes of Jerusalem and of the house of David were to rise and to fall together' (Jon D. Levenson, *Sinai and Zion* [Minneapolis, MN: Winston Press, 1985], p. 97). The return to Jerusalem and the reestablishment of the Davidic line was guaranteed by the covenant in 2 Samuel 7, and reiterated throughout 1–2 Kings (see 1 Kgs 8.20, 25; 9.5; 11.5, 13, 32, 36; 15.4; 2 Kgs 2.4; 8.19; 19.34; 20.6).

9

'Passing Strange': Gender Crossing in the Story of Joseph and Esther*

My story being done,
She gave me for my pains a world of sighs;
She swore, in faith 'twas strange, 'twas passing strange;
'Twas pitiful, 'twas wondrous pitiful,
She wish'd she had not heard it, yet she wish'd
That heaven had made her such a man . . .
                              Shakespeare, *Othello* I.iii.158-63

This chapter engages in a close study of the analogies between the Joseph and Esther narratives in the Hebrew Bible, drawing on the methods of feminist hermeneutics and rabbinic exegesis. Until this point, I have argued that deceit is a particularly feminine art of subterfuge, the way the weaker 'sex' seizes the reins of power from her male counterpart in the social hierarchy. But as Simone de Beauvoir once famously asserted, 'One is not born a woman, but, rather, becomes one'.[1] The traits associated with 'woman' and 'feminine' are social and cultural constructs integral to patriarchy; 'woman' is passive, corporeal, irrational, emotional, the quintessential objectified 'other'. But these traits may equally map onto a man, culturally or socially defined as *'femme'*. And so the art of discretion or deceit as a feminine mode of subterfuge is not bound to the second sex; it is engendered, but not biologically determined. Joseph and Esther are both feminine figures.

---

* This chapter was originally presented on the panel 'Comparative Feminist Studies of Scripture' at the SBL Annual Meeting in Baltimore, MD, November 24, 2013. A version of this chapter was published as '"Passing Strange"—Reading Transgender across Genre: Rabbinic Midrash and Feminist Hermeneutics on Esther', in *JFSR* 30 (2014), pp. 81-97.

1. Simone de Beauvoir, *The Second Sex* (New York: Vintage Books, 1973), p. 301. For a critique of de Beauvoir's characterization of 'feminine' and 'woman', see the discussion in Judith Butler, *Gender Trouble* (New York: Routledge, Chapman & Hall, 1990), esp. pp. 8-34.

They engage with political power hierarchies as beautiful 'strangers', as the quintessential 'other' (Hebrew or Jew), rising to prominence in the foreign court. While many biblical scholars have noted the parallels between these stories of prominent Jewish figures in the Diaspora, none have addressed the gendered aspect of their character development.[2] As beautiful orphans who 'find favor in the eyes' of others, Esther and Joseph aim to please. They use the art of discretion, concealing their identity, for the salvation of their people. But, over the course of the drama, Joseph's and Esther's so-called femininity molts into a more complex personhood as the mask is sloughed off.

Esther is ostensibly planted in the imperial court as a kind of mole, married off to the Persian king, only later revealing her identity as a Jew to save her people from Haman's decree of genocide. Joseph, too, conceals his identity from his brothers behind the mask of viceroy in Pharaoh's court in order to draw his family down to Egypt and save them from famine. In comparing the 'Persian' queen to her male counterpart, the 'Egyptian' viceroy, I highlight how the role of Jew in the imperial court is transformed through the lens of gender. Because the position of Jew as 'other' in the Diaspora is concealed, while gender (at least in the biblical text) is not, the comparison compels us to deconstruct deceit or discretion as an essentially 'feminine' mode of subterfuge. In the act of disclosure, when the face behind the mask is revealed, there is a deeper truth that emerges, which ultimately probes the power dynamics for both women, as subject to patriarchy, and Hebrew/Jew, as the denigrated 'other' in the Diaspora.

In this reading, I draw on the insights of rabbinic midrash—a method of filling in gaps in the biblical text that is over two millennia old; characters can be hyperbolically valorized or demonized and ironies made explicit, as they are pitched at sharper angles. The rabbis, however, had their own agenda with respect to the MT of the Esther scroll—preoccupation with assimilation, the absence of divine providence, the dearth of prayer and Jewish practice—and thus felt compelled to fill in the lacunae in the biblical text for their own purposes.[3] Likewise, with respect to the Joseph saga, the aggadic corpus fills in the gaps: as patriarch and prophet, Jacob must have

---

2. Sandra B. Berg, *The Book of Esther: Motifs, Themes and Structure* (Missoula, MT: Scholars Press, 1979), pp. 123-42; Adele Berlin, *The JPS Bible Commentary: Esther* (Philadelphia, PA: Jewish Publication Society, 2001), p. xxxvii; Moshe Gan, 'The Book of Esther in the Light of Joseph's Fate in Egypt', *Tarbiz* 31 (1961–62), pp. 144-49 (Heb.); Michael V. Fox, *Character and Ideology in the Book of Esther* (Grand Rapids, MI: Eerdmans, 2001), pp. 147 n. 17, 239 and 250. For a chart summarizing the parallels, see the addendum to this chapter.

3. For an overview of the midrashic sources, see Leila Leah Bronner, 'Esther Revisited: An Aggadic Approach', in *A Feminist Companion to Esther, Judith and Susanna* (ed. Athalya Brenner; Sheffield: Sheffield Academic Press, 1995), pp. 176-98.

had some inkling of his favorite son's sale into slavery; how was Joseph able to resist the solicitations of his master's wife? What kind of 'man' is that? I am intrigued by the rabbis' answers, and adopt their exegetical method and insights as a means to a feminist hermeneutical end. I assume a 'conscious partiality', as advocated by Elisabeth Schüssler Fiorenza, where the 'view from below' is privileged, posing a critique of the one from above—the one that claims hegemony and objectivity under the assumption of the male gaze.[4] My goal is to show how midrash highlights the gender-encoded motifs, which are only covert in the biblical text. In comparing Esther's and Joseph's stories, I present a critique of the essentially deterministic categories of man/woman and Hebrew/Jew. In this way, the feminist midrashic reader emulates the palimpsest, writing a new script between the fading letters of an old manuscript as an alternative story emerges in the *inter*-text.

Esther and Vashti: Speculum of the Other Woman

The first chapter of Esther in the Hebrew Bible features no Jews, and so one might query: wherefore was it written? We are told, auspiciously, that Ahasuerus, king of Persia, reigned over one hundred and twenty-seven provinces, from India to Ethiopia, over an empire of many peoples and tongues—the people of Judea but one. It is *this* people who supposedly 'do not obey the king's laws' and are therefore sentenced to destruction by Haman (Est. 3.8-9). The autocratic rule, the extent of the empire's hegemony, and the very arbitrariness, indeed absurdity, of the king's rules are laid out in the first chapter as critical background to Haman's decree.

Furthermore, the decree of genocide is foreshadowed by the displacement of Vashti, the queen, and the oppression of women that follows. Esther is introduced only in the wake of the first queen's removal. As vilified as her successor is lauded, Vashti plays the foil to Esther's passive and pleasing demeanor. But her brief role in the opening chapter must be read ironically against the backdrop of the narrative as a whole. As a kind of proto-feminist, her role makes a parody of the king's 'honor [*yaqar*]' and the assertion of male authority.[5] At the end of the seven-day feast in Shushan, King

---

4. Elisabeth Schüssler Fiorenza, 'On Feminist Methodology', *JFSR* 1.2 (1985), p. 75. Much of what she articulates here is further developed in her books: *Bread Not Stone: The Challenge of Feminist Biblical Interpretation* (Boston: Beacon Press, 1984); and *But She Said: Feminist Practices of Biblical Interpretation* (Boston: Beacon Press, 1992).

5. For a brilliant analysis of the significance of this first chapter, see Timothy K. Beal, 'Tracing Esther's Beginnings', in *A Feminist Companion to Esther, Judith and Susanna* (ed. A. Brenner; Sheffield: Sheffield Academic Press, 1995), pp. 87-110. In contemporary Jewish feminist circles, she has become somewhat of a heroine. See Jeffrey M. Cohen, 'Vashti—An Unsung Heroine', *JBQ* 24.2 (1996), pp. 103-106; Norma

Ahasuerus orders his queen to be brought before him in her royal diadem to show her beauty off to the people and officials (1.11). His request parallels the desire to show off the vast riches of his kingdom during the hundred-and-eighty-day feast (v. 4). Vashti, however, refuses. No explicit reason is given in the biblical text. Michael Fox suggests that she is 'a woman of dignity, too proud to allow herself to be put on display alongside other pieces of royal property before a bunch of bibulous males'.[6] The midrash amplifies her sense of pride, suggesting that the king demanded she appear in nothing *but* her royal diadem—naked, that is.[7] Her refusal provokes alarm among the courtiers; the queen's behavior will set a precedent for all the ladies in the kingdom, 'and there will be no end of scorn and provocation' (v. 18). Simply her absence, her refusal to be the object of the 'male ogle', prompts anxiety about control over women. As Timothy Beal notes, 'Like a pebble dropped in a puddle, the queen's offense is first against the king, but moves out "against all the chiefs", and ultimately threatens to upset the entire social order. Male fixation on/of her is central.'[8]

Her refusal then prompts the first series of pernicious royal edicts that are absurdly irreversible.[9] Vashti is sent away, by decree, never to 'come into the king's presence' again, and the advisors counsel the king to 'choose

---

Rosen, 'Midrash, Bible, and Women's Voices', *Judaism* 45 (1996), pp. 422-45; also Norma Rosen, *Biblical Women Unbound: Counter-Tales* (Philadelphia, PA: Jewish Publication Society, 1996), p. 170. Mary Gendler, 'The Restoration of Vashti', in *The Jewish Woman: New Perspectives* (ed. Elizabeth Koltun; New York: Schocken, 1976), pp. 241-47. See also Gail Twersky Reimer, 'Eschewing Esther/Embracing Esther: The Changing Representation of Biblical Heroines', in *Talking Back: Images of Jewish Women in American Popular Culture* (ed. Joyce Antler; Hanover, NH: Brandeis University Press, 1997), pp. 207-19; Wendy Amsellem, 'The Mirror Has Two Faces: An Exploration of Esther and Vashti', *JOFA Journal* 4 (2003), p. 7.

6. Fox, *Character and Ideology*, p. 164.

7. See *b. Meg.* 12b; *Est. R.* 3.13. According to the Talmud, however, the king's demand is poetic justice for her treatment of her Jewish slave girls. 'Just as she caused the daughter of Israel to be stripped naked and work on the Sabbath so was the command to appear naked her downfall' (*b. Meg.* 12b, Bronner's paraphrase, 'Esther Revisited', p. 189). Another opinion suggests that it was not modesty but shame that prompted her refusal—she was stricken with leprosy or she had grown a tail (*b. Meg.* 12b).

8. Beal, 'Tracing Esther's Beginnings', p. 97.

9. The first edict actually concerns the people in the capital of Shushan, during the seven-day feast: 'And the drinking was by law, without compulsion [*'ein 'ones*]' (1.8). This paradoxical order (for how can you have a decree without enforcement/compulsion?) seems to emphasize Ahasuerus's benevolence. In fact, it only highlights his character as a buffoon and foreshadows the ominous and lethal nature of the edict to annihilate the Jews (3.9-11), which is also significantly called a 'law [*dat*]' (4.8). However, it is not qualified as being 'without compulsion [*'ein 'ones*]'. It is, nevertheless, absurdly irreversible. Therefore another 'law [*dat*]' is issued to allow the Jews to defend themselves on the day their enemies rise up to destroy them (8.13).

another more pleasing than her' (v. 19). She becomes, in Beal's words, 'quite literally *abject,* neither subject nor object within the social and symbolic order, and therefore must be pushed outside its boundaries'.[10] As a consequence of this decree, the advisors adjure 'all women to give honor/respect [*yaqar*] to their husbands' (v. 20), and 'every man will rule his house, speaking the language of his own people' (v. 22).[11] Every woman is to become a 'Stepford wife'.[12] In honoring her husband, her mother tongue becomes forbidden in her own home; she is effectively silenced. How this latter part of the decree was to be enforced is left open, but the effective gist of it, in addition to the deposition of the queen and the search for her 'better', entails an attempt to reassert male hegemony; rule is imposed *through* language. Essentially the assertion of one woman's will leads to her displacement and the subversion of *all* women in the kingdom.

Once the queen is displaced, the Jew, as victim, is next when Haman, the king's viceroy, issues the decree of genocide against Mordecai's people (ch. 3). First the women, then the Jews.[13] There are three aspects of this authoritarian regime that are highlighted and parodied by the juxtaposition of woman and Jew. First, the characters must 'dress up' to become an object of desire in others' eyes (contra Vashti, who is asked to present herself 'undressed'). Second, there is a consequent exile of self and ethnic identity (in Kristeva's terms, becoming abject). Third, the language of the oppressed

10. Beal, 'Tracing Esther's Beginnings', p. 99. The category 'abject' is drawn from Julia Kristeva, *Powers of Horror: An Essay on Abjection* (trans. L. Roudiez; New York: Columbia University Press, 1982).

11. The phrase 'and speak in the language of his own people' is omitted in the Greek. Adele Berlin relates it back to the language of the decree (as in 8.9), which must be dispatched to every province in its own script and to every nation in its own language (Berlin, *Esther*, pp. 20-21). Yet the phrase seems redundant and hardly follows from the edict that the husband will be 'ruler [*sorer*]' in his own home (v. 22). Furthermore, how would the decree relate to Vashti's unruly behavior as undermining the king's honor with its potential repercussions (vv. 18 and 20)? My reading follows Rashi, who claims that the husbands may compel their wives to learn their native language and speak it in the home. This reading is corroborated in Neh. 13.24, which is concerned with the same anxiety over which language was to be spoken in the home. Here, too, we find the similar phrase, 'in the language of various people [*kilashon 'am va-'am*]'. See the discussion in Jon D. Levenson, *Esther: A Commentary* (London: SCM Press, 1997), p. 52.

12. The term 'Stepford wife' refers to an artificially docile and submissive wife, based on the satirical novel *Stepford Wives* (1972), by Ira Levin, made into a movie in 1975.

13. Edward Greenstein points out that the generalization of the decree from the particular and petty is characteristic of the story: 'Here, one wife disobeys one order from the king, so the king commands all wives to obey all husbands. Later, one Jew, Mordecai, will similarly trespass one law—to bow to Haman—and Haman will seek to execute all Jews' (Edward L. Greenstein, 'A Jewish Reading of Esther', in *Judaic Perspectives on Ancient Israel* (ed. Jacob Neusner; Philadelphia, PA: Fortress Press, 1987), p. 228.

subject is subverted. In the unfolding of the drama, Esther (as both woman and Jew) gradually sheds each of these layers as she moves from a passive to an active role, eventually revealing her ethnic and religious identity to obvert the genocidal decree, and finally assuming full agency as a commanding subject. The *Megillah* concludes with Esther, the eponymous heroine of our story, *writing* the scroll (Est. 9.29).

Joseph too negotiates the terrain of personal transformation though a process of being an object in the eyes of others, then abject (beyond the purview of sight), and finally the subject of sight, 'the seer'.[14] At first he assumes a position of high visibility, the object of others' desires and enmity (the 'apple of his father's eye', magnet for his brothers' envy, and victim of the wife of Potiphar's lust). He is then cast below the surface of visibility (into the dungeon) as abject and moves back to a position of prominent visibility again, where (as the subject) *he* controls how he is to be seen, by whom and when. He mediates this control as the self-proclaimed siphon of the divine will, initially as dream interpreter for the cup-bearer and baker, and then for Pharaoh: 'For do not interpretations belong to God [*'Elohim*]? Please tell me your dreams!' (Gen. 40.8; cf. 41.16; 50.19). Invoking 'interpretation' as the provenance of God, he dons the cloak of invisibility. When his brothers descend to Egypt, he occludes himself and speaks to them *through* a translator, such that they do not recognize him. The permutations of his agency seem highly personal, but they are in the service of a political, historical and spiritual line—the formative move from family to nation in the Egyptian exile, the pretext being the salvation of Jacob and sons from famine. Both Esther and Joseph undergo a radical character transformation, moving from object to subject, from a position of passivity to powerful agency, from disguise/occlusion to the revelation of identity that effects the release of their people from the decree of death. How do the parallel biblical narratives depict this character transformation? And how does the nexus of identity for the Hebrew/Jew (*qua* Egyptian/Persian) map itself out along gendered lines?

Esther's and Joseph's Beauty

Esther is notably passive in ch. 2 when we are first introduced to her, and this passivity is strangely amplified in rabbinic sources. She, like Joseph, is described as 'shapely and beautiful' (Est. 2.7; cf. Gen. 39.6).[15] But unlike

---

14. I owe this insight about the trajectory of Joseph's life to my deeply perceptive rabbinical student Gray Myrseth, at Hebrew College.

15. They are both, literally, 'beautiful of form and of pleasing sight [*yfat-to'ar ve-tovat mar'eh*]' (Est. 2.7), in the masculine formation: *yfeh-to'ar vi-yfeh mar'eh* (Gen. 39.6). See also the description of Rachel's beauty (Gen. 29.17). According to *Gen. R.* 86.6, p. 1059, Joseph inherits his beauty from his mother—perhaps this is one of the reasons Jacob favored him over his brothers (cf. Josephus, *Ant.* 2.2.1).

her ancestor (bereft only of his mother), she is an orphan who has neither mother nor father. Joseph and Esther are then vulnerable to abduction at the hands of brothers, slave traders or king's henchmen.[16] She is taken (*lqḥ*) three times—first by Mordecai 'as a daughter' (2.7), then, perhaps forcibly, to the king's palace by the officers along with all the virgins in Shushan (v. 8), and finally by the king (v. 16). The verb 'take [*lqḥ*]' also connotes marriage (as in Deut. 24.1), an active, seemingly unilateral male assertion of possession of the woman. In rabbinic tradition, Esther's passivity is amplified as the 'object of the taking'. Mordecai is presumed to have taken Esther not as a daughter [*bat*] but as a wife [*bayit*].[17] This complicates their relationship and her position in the royal palace, in the rabbinic mind, for not only does she marry a heathen king but she becomes an adulteress by doing so. To salvage Esther's (and Mordecai's) integrity, it is presumed that she was taken by force to the royal palace, and she assumed a wholly passive position, like 'the ground of the earth' [*qarqa' 'olam*], when she engaged in sexual relations with the king.[18] Because intercourse with the Persian monarch was nonconsensual (ostensibly rape), in the rabbinic understanding, she may remain wife to Mordecai, her Jewish husband.

Furthermore, she does only what Mordecai bids her to do and does not tell of her people or her kindred (vv. 10, 20), though no reason is given for such secrecy. Haman's decree of genocide is issued only after Esther is well ensconced in the palace precincts. In contrast to Esther, Mordecai is overtly known as 'the Jew',[19] and he refuses 'to kneel and bow low to Haman' (3.2, 5)—yet another inexplicable detail of the plot. Only a hint of a historical vendetta is implied in the text.[20] As a result, Haman 'disdained to lay his

---

16. Joseph is passive, insofar as he is sold into slavery and 'taken down' to Egypt (37.28, 36; and 39.1; in this last verse, the passive form of *yrd* [descend] rather than *lqḥ* [take] is used).

17. *b. Meg.* 13a. The Septuagint also reads 'as a wife' instead of 'as a daughter'. See the commentary of Berlin, *Esther*, p. 26. On the use of the metaphor 'home [*bayit*]' as wife in rabbinic sources, see the discussion in Gail Labovitz, *Marriage and Metaphor: Constructions of Gender in Rabbinic Literature* (Plymouth: Lexington Books, 2009), p. 119.

18. *b. Sanh.* 74a-b. See Bronner, 'Esther Revisited', pp. 183-84. Labovitz points out that the image of *qarq'a 'olam* ('natural earth') always refers to *un*-cultivated fields in rabbinic discourse. That is, the expression refers to land that is not put to productive agricultural use. 'Esther, by being common earth, resists being "field", resists being owned, bounded, domesticated, and/or cultivated by Ahasuerus' (Labovitz, *Marriage and Metaphor*, pp. 114-15).

19. See Est. 2.5; 5.13; 8.7; 9.29, 31; 10.3.

20. Mordecai is linked to the House of Saul (of Benjamin) (Est. 2.5-6), and Haman is identified as an Agagite—that is from Amalek (3.1). According to biblical law, Jews are eternally obligated to 'blot out the remembrance of Amalek' because they attacked the weak, as they lagged behind, in the journey out of Egypt (Exod. 17.14-16; Deut. 25.17-

hand on Mordecai alone... and plotted [instead] to destroy all the Jews...' (3.6). Why Esther remains hidden, with respect to her Jewish identity, while Mordecai sits in the palace gates as a prominent and outspoken 'male Jew' [*'ish Yehudi*], is one of the great mysteries of the plot. But it plays into the gender alignment: she (female) is covert/hidden/passive; he (male) is open/overt/active, until this dichotomy is realigned. Esther's hiddenness and the openness of Mordecai 'the Jew' highlight the theme of how Jewish identity is negotiated in the Diaspora. It emphasizes that there are multiple and double-edged roles. Initially, however, the older father-figure/husband and the younger woman collude in the royal court—she by covert, he by overt channels.

Esther is well poised for the plot to unfold with her ethnic identity concealed. She is endowed with two names, a Jewish one—Hadassah (lit. myrtle, and so, 'pleasing of scent')—and a Persian one—Esther, the Persian name for Ishtar or Astarte, the goddess of love, who, like Venus, is associated with the morning star.[21] Joseph as well is given an Egyptian name before his brothers descend to Egypt—Zaphenath-paneah (Gen. 41.45). Both names hint at a double hiding. Joseph, who decodes divine secrets as an interpreter of dreams,[22] is himself in hiding from his family; his name is a Hebrew homonym for 'you hid your face [*tzafanta panekha*]'. Similarly, Esther not only plays the role of secret Jewess but also becomes the agent of the hidden face of God. The Talmud, playing with the vocalization of Esther as *'astir*, suggests that she is the fulfillment of the curse in Deuteronomy when the Jews—suffering hardship, prey to their enemies, subject to exile—will experience the absence of divine providence:

> My anger will be kindled against them in that day. I will forsake them and hide [*ve-histarti*] my face from them; they will become easy prey, and many terrible troubles will come upon them. In that day they will say, 'Have not these troubles come upon us because our God is not in our

---

19). The rabbinic tradition draws on this vendetta as 'unfinished business' between Saul and Agag, which becomes liturgically inscribed by the *Maftir* (Deut. 25.17-19) and *Haftorah* (1 Sam. 15), both read on *Shabbat Zakhor* before Purim.

21. See *Midr. Teh.* 22—where Esther is presumed to be the author of Psalm 22, attributed to 'the hind of the dawn [*ayelet ha-shahar*]' or the dawn star. See the discussion in Bronner, 'Esther Revisited', p. 180.

22. Nahum Sarna suggests that the name, Zaphenath-paneah, is a transcription of an Egyptian expression meaning 'God speaks, he lives'; the Septuagint transcribed it *psonthomphenech*, perhaps related to the Late Egyptian word *psontenpa'anh*, 'the creator/sustainer of life' (Sarna, *JPS Torah Commentary: Genesis*, pp. 287-88). The Aramaic translation, however, interprets Joseph's Egyptian name in terms of the Hebrew—to decode [*phe'aneah*] secrets [*tsfn*, lit. 'to hide']: '*guvr'a demitamran galyan leih*—the man to whom hidden (or mysterious) things are revealed' (*Targ. Onq.* Gen. 41.45; cf. Josephus, *Ant.* 2.6.1 (Loeb Classical Library, p. 297), Peshitta and Saadiah Gaon (*loc. cit.*) and *Gen. R.* 90.4, pp. 1103-1104.

midst?' On that day I will surely hide my face [*haster 'astir*] on account of all the evil they have done by turning to other gods' (Deut. 31.17-18 NRSV).

The Talmud comments, 'Where is Esther indicated in the Torah? R. Matan replied, "Then I will indeed hide My face [*haster 'astir*] on that day . . ."' (*b. Hul.* 139b). Avivah Zornberg suggests that 'the word-play [*haster 'astir*/Esther] defines Esther and her world as embodying the terror foreshadowed in the biblical verse: in her time, God hides his face. God is absent, occluded from her world, as his name is, in fact, absent from her text'.[23] Yet the Talmud is ambiguous as to *how* the absence of God is to be experienced in exile. Is the divine presence refracted through the lens of the *Megillah* in which the name of God never appears, or will divine providence be manifest through Esther herself? As the plot unravels, Esther moves into full view as a main player, from the occluded, passive position into a fully actualized self. God's hidden face is made palpable through her. Does Esther reveal herself *in spite of* or, paradoxically, as a result of ontological absence?

But first, Esther and her male counterpart, Joseph, must themselves undergo complete occlusion. Endowed with disarming charm, a trait developed perhaps in response to their vulnerability as orphans, they are both groomed (or groom themselves) to please. In the House of Potiphar and in prison, Joseph 'finds favor' [*hen*] in his master's eyes, 'grace and favor' [*hen va-hesed*] in the eyes of the prison guard (Gen. 39.4, 21). When taken to the 'house of women' (the harem) under the supervision of Hegai, Esther is propitiously found 'pleasing in the [eunuch's] eyes', and 'won his favor [*hesed*]' (Est. 2.9). Later, we are told that she 'won the admiration [*hen*] of all that saw her' (v. 15). For the king she bears both 'grace and favor' [*hen va-hesed*] (v. 17). Not only does she obey Mordecai, but she follows the suggestions of the king's eunuch in charge of the women. The reader is told that the woman could ask for anything for her night with the king (v. 13), in the so-called beauty competition for the position of queen; but 'Esther did not ask for anything but what Hegai, the king's eunuch, guardian of the women, advised' (v. 15). In his role of exalted pimp in charge of the harem, would not the eunuch know best how to please the king!

As feminine figures whose sense of self revolves around how they are perceived by others Joseph's and Esther's greatest strength serves also as their most poignant source of vulnerability. Beautiful like his mother, beloved by his father, yet marked as a moving target by his 'coat of many colors', Joseph becomes the victim of fratricidal ire. When his brothers see him coming from afar, it must be the cloak that catches their eye, and

---

23. Avivah Zornberg, 'Esther—Mere Anarchy Is Loosed upon the World', in *Murmuring Deep*, pp. 108-109.

they turn to one another saying, 'Here comes *that there* [*ha-lazeh*] master of dreams' (Gen. 37.19). The demonstrative preposition, 'that there [*ha-lazeh*]', positions him as the distant target of their fury, a bulls-eye. They fear his mastery of the future as a 'seer/prophet' through the dominion that his dreams portend.[24] And so they plot to slay him and throw him into a pit, sarcastically remarking, 'and we will see what will become of his dreams' (v. 20). Their statement is fraught with dramatic irony, for it is precisely their plot to do away with Joseph that enables his ascent to power and facilitates the fulfillment of those dreams. The plot to kill him is amended; the lad is stripped of his 'coat of many colors', thrown into a pit [*bor*] and sold into slavery. The coat is dipped in goat's blood and presented, torn, to their distraught father. As he is cast into the pit, Joseph descends below the surface, beyond the purview of any passer-by. And when he is sold into slavery and taken down to Egypt, he is lost to family,to all those who would recognize him. Though Jacob, upon seeing the bloodied cloak, presumes Joseph has been torn apart by a wild animal, he has inklings of this pit, figured as the underworld into which his favored son has been cast. His father identifies Joseph as having 'gone down to Sheol'—the world of the dead, the land of no return—where he too will go down mourning him (37.35). Though Joseph is alive and well, only presumed dead, there is a sense in which he has really 'gone underground'—into the pit, Sheol, the land of the dead, metonymic for Egypt itself.

Joseph in Potiphar's House

Stripped of the external mark of distinction and sold as a slave, Joseph is still vulnerable as the object of others' ire *and* desire. In the next episode, he enters the House of Potiphar, 'an officer of Pharaoh, captain of the guard [*seris Pharaoh, sar ha-tabahim*]' (Gen. 39.1),[25] where, like Esther, he is seen as beautiful and charming in the eyes of others (39.4, 6, 21). In certain midrashic traditions, Potiphar lusts after Joseph, but God intervenes to castrate the master.[26] Joseph is thus hyperfeminized; 'well built and hand-

---

24. In the end, Joseph owes his prophetic 'sight/insight' and his meteoric rise to power *not* primarily to his role as dreamer but, rather, to his role as dream interpreter in the prison and in Pharaoh's palace, and to his role as provider in rationing the food out during the years of famine (Gen. 40–41). Joseph also alludes to his supposed powers as a diviner with regard to the goblet that he plants in Benjamin's sack (Gen. 44.15).

25. Cf. Gen. 37.36 (based on ESV, KJV, NRSV translations); the Aramaic targum renders: 'minister of Pharaoh, chief executioner' (*Targ. Onq.* Gen. 37.36).

26. See *b. Sot.* 13b; *Gen. R.* 86.3, p. 1054; *Tanh.* (ed. Buber) *VaYeshev* 14; and *Targ. Ps.-J.* on Gen. 39.1. This explains both the term *saris* (understood as 'eunuch'), and Potiphar's wife's sexual frustration in lusting after Joseph. The term *saris*, in Biblical

some' (v. 6), his beauty becomes a source of fatal attraction for the lord *and* the lady. Potiphar grants him full reign of the house, though his wife is presumably off limits.[27] According to rabbinic tradition, Joseph, as a result of his meteoric rise to power, becomes smug and vainglorious; he begins to eat and drink and curl his hair, acting the dandy.[28] The narrative mentions Joseph's beauty here (v. 6), not when he is first introduced to the reader (in 37.2), as if to alert us to what is to come. We are auspiciously told, 'His master's wife cast her eyes upon him' (v. 7). The midrash suggests that his vanity leads to her undesirable solicitations:

> 'And his master's wife cast her eyes upon Joseph' (39.7). What is written just before this? 'Now Joseph was well built and handsome' (v. 6). (This is) like a man/hero [*gever/gibor*], who would stand in the market, making up (or fluttering) his eyes, fixing his hair, and lifting up his heel, saying: 'See how good-looking, how pleasing I am! Such a handsome man/hero [*gever/gibor*]!' They said to him: 'If you're such a "man" [*gever/gibor*], and (also) so pleasing, here is the bear (i.e. Potiphar's wife) standing before you, (ready to) pounce!'[29]

Hebrew, can mean simply 'officer, chief, or high military captain' (as in Gen. 37.36; 39.1; and 40.2, 7, attributed to the 'E' source; 2 Kgs 18.17; Jer. 39.3, 13). Rabbinic tradition, however, understands *saris* to mean 'eunuch', according to Late Biblical Hebrew (cf. 2 Kgs 20.18; Isa. 39.7; Isa. 56.3, 4; Est. 2.3, 14, 15; Dan. 1.3 [BDB entry 5591, p. 710]). The motif that Joseph may have been sold into sexual service shows up later as well. When the brothers go down for food during the famine, they go in search of their brother in the red light district (lit. market of prostitutes [*shuq shel zonot*]) (*Gen. R.* 91.6, pp. 1122-23). That Potiphar has been castrated is suggested by his identification with Potiphera (Gen. 41.45, both called Pentephres in the Septuagint; Josephus *Ant.* 2.4.1 and 6.1; cf. *Gen. R.* 86.3). Aseneth is then an adopted daughter, perhaps the progeny of Dinah and Shechem (*Targ. Ps.-J.* 41.45 and *PRE* 38). See V. Aptowitzer, 'Asenath, the Wife of Joseph: A Haggadic Literary-Historical Study', *HUCA* 1 (1924), pp. 239-305, and the discussion in Kugel, *In Potiphar's House,* pp. 75-76, and p. 90 n. 15.

27. Joseph is given jurisdiction over everything '*but the bread* which he [Potiphar] ate' (v. 6). Rashi understands this to be a euphemism [*lashon naqi*] for the wife (cf. *Gen. R.* 86.6, p. 1059); presumably she was forbidden to him. As Joseph protests, in response to the importuning of Potiphar's wife: '". . . nor has he kept back anything from me *but you* because you are his wife"' (Gen. 39.9).

28. *Tanḥ. VaYeshev* 8, paraphrased by Rashi on Gen. 39.6. See also the comment on Gen. 37.2, 'Joseph being seventeen years old . . . being a lad [*na'ar*] with the sons of Bilhah and Zilpah': 'He behaved like a young lad, fluttering his eyelashes (or using eyeliner [*memashmesh be-'eynav*]), curling his hair [*metaqen be-sa'aro*], and lifting his heel [*matleh be-'aqivo*] . . .' (*Gen. R.* 84.7, p. 1008).

29. *Gen. R.* 87.3, p. 1068. See the discussion of this source in Lori Hope Lefkovitz, *In Scripture: The First Stories of Jewish Sexual Identities* (Plymouth: Rowman & Littlefield, 2010), pp. 88-91, and Kugel, *In Potiphar's House,* pp. 77-78.

Does the midrash implicate Joseph for the unsolicited attention of Potiphar's wife? This is a familiar misogynist trope: the victim of nonconsensual sexual advances or rape must have been 'asking for it', an allegation often directed at women, rarely at men.[30] As a man (*gibor/gever*), presumably Joseph can physically resist.

Rather than seeing this narrative expansion in contemporary terms as 'blaming the victim', a more nuanced reading points to the gender ambiguity of Joseph's identity. The midrash highlights the dissonance between Joseph's feminine posturing and his boast—'What a man!' He is tested precisely on that demarcation between man/woman, masculine/feminine, *through* his sexuality. As the feminine object of unwanted sexual attention *and* the masculine 'Jewish' hero [*gibor*], Joseph must prove himself by resisting the attentions of his master's wife, that is, by fighting off 'the bear'. It is Joseph's beauty, amplified by his own vanity in the rabbinic tradition, that makes him visible, feminine, vulnerable and therefore a magnet for Mrs Potiphar's attentions, which must be counteracted by extreme (mas-

---

30. For example, there is a rabbinic tradition in which Dinah is blamed for the rape by Shechem, based on the verse, 'And Dinah, daughter of Leah whom she had borne to Jacob, *went out* [*va-tetz'ei*] to see the daughters of the land' (Gen. 34.1). Going out [*ytz'*] to the market place (that is, in public) is the male prerogative, and when a woman does so, she 'invites' calamity upon herself (*Gen. R.* 8.12; 79.8; 80.1). In this misogynist reading, Dinah is likened to her mother, Leah, who went out 'as a harlot [*zonah*]' to meet Jacob (Gen. 30.16). See the discussion in Lefkovitz, *In Scripture,* p. 96. In yet another midrashic tradition, Dinah underwent a 'sex change' in utero. When Leah was pregnant, she realized that if she bore a son (her seventh), the prophecy that twelve sons would be born to Jacob would make Rachel 'less than the maidservants' (who each bore two sons). 'So she prayed and it [i.e. the fetus] was transformed into a female' (*Gen. R.* 72.6, pp. 844-45]; *b. Ber.* 60a, based on the ambiguous *'aḥar,* 'afterwards/other', in Gen. 30.21; see also Rashi, Radak and Ibn Ezra on Gen. 30.16). Erik Bittner gave a fascinating talk, in which he suggested that one could substitute 'transgender' for 'embryo transformation in utero'. Dinah should have been a male but was born female, and chafed at that gender designation. He likens her to Joy Ladin, author of *Through the Door of Life: A Jewish Journey between Genders* (Madison, WI: University of Wisconsin Press, 2012). Similarly, Bittner argues that Joseph departed from gender norms and suggests that Rachel's son, as well, may have undergone a 'gender transformation in utero', given that the two matriarchs were pregnant at the same time (Erik Bittner, 'Speaking for Dinah', Congregation Shaarei Tefillah, Newton, Massachusetts, December 6, 2014). Ladin, born a biological male, identifies as female and, later in life, undergoes a sex change just as, inversely, Dinah should have been born 'male' but is turned female in utero. As 'transgender', she crosses that socially encoded boundary again when she *goes out* 'to see the women of the land' (Gen. 34.1). Joseph, as well, crosses gender boundaries as an effeminate man. But I could not find corroboration, among the rabbinic sources, for the idea that he may have undergone a sex change before his birth. The idea, nevertheless, is evocative and certainly plays into a central motif in his character development.

culine) self-restraint, when he proves himself a 'true' hero.[31] In the biblical text, he does so by invoking loyalty to his master and God [*'Elohim*]: 'He [Potiphar] is not greater in this house than I am, nor has he kept back anything from me but yourself, because you are his wife. How then could I do this great wickedness, and sin against God?' (Gen. 39.9).

Yet Mrs Potiphar persists, tempting him to lie with her day after day (v. 10), and, finally, when she sequesters him alone in the house and he refuses, she frames him with attempted rape:

> And it came to pass on this day, when he went into the house to do his work [*mal'akhto*] and none of the men of the house was there in the house, she caught him by his garment [*bigdo*], saying, 'Lie with me'. But he left his garment [*bigdo*] in her hand and fled and got out of the house. And as soon as she saw that he had left his garment [*bigdo*] in her hand and had fled out of the house, she called to the men of her household and said to them, 'See, he has brought among us a Hebrew [*'ivri*] to mock us [*letzaheq banu*]. He came in to me to lie with me, and I cried out with a loud voice. And as soon as he heard that I lifted up my voice and cried out, he left his garment [*bigdo*] beside me and fled and got out of the house' (Gen. 39.11-15).

Several questions arise: How did Joseph and the mistress find themselves alone in the house? Where were all the other residents and servants? How did she manage to grab hold of his cloak? Auspiciously, the garment is here called a *beged*; with this as her alibi, she can *betray* [*bgd*] him.[32] For Joseph, the test resides in fealty to his master, whose identity is bounded by jurisdiction over his wife, and loyalty to mores of his God. Thereupon, later rabbinic tradition identifies him as 'the faithful one [*ne'eman*]'.[33] She, on the

---

31. In the *Chapters of the Fathers* (a collection of wisdom sayings attributed to the Tannaitic rabbis), the 'hero' [*gibor*] is described in particularly rabbinic terms: 'Ben Zoma would say . . . What is a hero [*gibor*]? A man that controls his desires!' (*m. 'Av.* 4.1). See Michael Satlow, '"Try to be a Man": The Rabbinic Construction of Masculinity', *HTR* 89 (1996), pp. 19-40; Daniel Boyarin, *Unheroic Conduct: The Rise of Heterosexuality and the Invention of the Jewish Man* (Berkeley, CA: University of California Press, 1997); Peter Brown, *The Body and Society: Men, Women, and Sexual Renunciation in Early Christianity* (New York: Columbia University Press, 1988), pp. 9-12. See also the discussion in Joshua Levinson 'An-other Woman: Joseph and Potiphar's Wife. Staging the Body Politic', in *JQR* 3/4 (1997), pp. 269-301.

32. Kugel comments on Gen. 39.12, 'by using the term *beged* (rather than, say, *simlah*, used in connection with Joseph in Gen. 41.14), Scripture wished further to imply something about Joseph's own attitude at this crucial moment with Mrs. Potiphar. She seized him not by his "garment" but "in his faithlessness" . . .' (Kugel, *In Potiphar's House*, p. 98).

33. See the midrashic tradition on Serah bat Asher, who connects the 'faithful to the faithful [*ne'eman la-ne'eman*]', that is, Joseph to Moses (*Gen. R.* 94.9, pp. 1182-83, and *Pes. K., Beshallah* 11.13, ed. Mandelbaum, p. 189; *Tanh. Va-Yeshev* 5. The

other hand, betrays both her husband and her would-be lover, identifying Joseph as a Hebrew, *'ivri* (lit. 'one who crosses over')—the quintessential 'other' in the Egyptian court.³⁴ Deploying a rhetoric of alliance with the servants, they are all presumably 'mocked [*tzhq*]' by his presence.³⁵ Interestingly, she drops the 'us' when she tells her husband about the attempted rape (vv. 17-18). Though Potiphar, as recounted by the narrator, is furious, he does not sentence Joseph to death; perhaps he doubts her report. Instead, the master casts his Hebrew slave in prison, 'the place where the king's prisoners were bound' (v. 20). It is an elite cell, but, nevertheless, below the surface of the earth where he may be abandoned again (cf. 40.23). Despite his performance as 'hero [*gibor*]', in order to emerge out of the feminized 'object' status, he must be reduced to being totally *abject*, forgotten, as if dead, in yet another pit/dungeon.

epithet *ne'eman* ['faithful'] is based on an attribute associated with Moses: 'He [the prophet] is trusted throughout my household' (Num. 12.7). Joseph may also be identified as *ne'eman* because he was 'keeper of the keys' in Potiphar's house and in the prison (Gen. 39.4, 21-22). Early Jewish texts, similarly, downplay his femininity and emphasize, rather, his sagacity, forbearance, and self-restraint. In these sources, his piety is augmented (Philo, *On Joseph* 9.40–10.53; Josephus, *Ant.* 2.4.1-5; and, in *The Testament of the Twelve Patriarchs*: *T. Reub.* 4.8-9; *T. Sim.* 4.4-5; 5.1-3; *T. Jos.* 2.1–9.5; and *T. Benj.* 4.9). As James Kugel has observed, in these sources 'his behavior in the face of temptation is exemplary—so much so that one might even say he was *not* tempted!' (*In Potiphar's House*, p. 23). For a review of the Second Temple literature, see Maren Niehoff, *The Figure of Joseph in Post-Biblical Jewish Literature* (Leiden: Brill, 1992).

34. The term 'Hebrew [*'ivri*]' is used to identify the Israelite (or proto-Israelite) as alien with respect to the people indigenous to a land, for they originally 'lived beyond the [Euphrates] River [*be-'ever ha-nahar*]' (Josh. 24.2). For example, Abram is an *'ivri* with respect to the Canaanites in Gen. 14.13; the Israelites are identified as 'Hebrews' from the perspective of the Egyptians in Exod. 1.15, 16, 19; 2.7 and 11; Jonah identifies himself as *'ivri* to the sailors in Jon. 1.9; Joseph is identified as an *'ivri* by Potiphar's wife (Gen. 39.14, 17) and by the cup-bearer (41.12). From the perspective of the 'natives', the term *'ivri* seems to have a strong negative valence. In ancient Near Eastern sources, the term has been associated with the Hapiru/Habiru, who are either a social caste of unruly people or a seminomadic ethnic group (perhaps, in terms of the biblical Table of Nations, descendants of Eber [Gen. 10.21, 24-25; 11.14-17]). See the now classic article by Moshe Greenberg, *The Hab/piru* (New Haven, CT: American Oriental Society, 1955), and John Bright, *A History of Israel* (Philadelphia, PA: Westminster Press, 3rd edn, 1981), pp. 92-95.

35. The verb *tzhq*, 'to mock, dally, play, or laugh', has strong sexual overtones (as in Gen. 26.8), and thus becomes the basis for the midrashic motif 'The Assembly of Ladies', where many women are besotted by Joseph's beauty. See the discussion in Kugel, *In Potiphar's House*, pp. 28-65. This motif is highly developed in the Qur'an, Sura 12. For the Islamic reception of the story, see Shalom Goldman, *The Wiles of Women/The Wiles of Men: Joseph and Potiphar's Wife in Ancient Near Eastern, Jewish, and Islamic Folklore* (Albany, NY: SUNY Press, 1995).

In the Image of the Father

The rabbinic tradition in the Talmud expands upon the ethnic divide between the Egyptian woman and the Hebrew man, transforming the trial in the sexual arena into a contest of cultural values encoded in gender terms. The narrative expansion in the Talmud conforms, as Levinson points out, to the classic Hellenistic seduction/adultery plot 'of the romance and the mime, where women are associated with lack of control (especially sexual) and men with self-mastery'.[36]

> 'And it came to pass on this day, when he [Joseph] went into the house to do his work [*mal'akhto*]' (Gen. 39.11). R. Yochanan said, this teaches that they both intended to sin. 'When he [Joseph] went into the house to do his work [*mal'akhto*]' (v. 11). Rav and Shmuel—One said: it means literally to do his work [*mal'akhto*], the other said that he went to satisfy his desires.[37] 'And not one of the members of the household were present in the house' (v. 11). Is it possible that there was no man in the large house of this wicked man (Potiphar)? It was taught in the School of R. Ishmael: that particular day was their festival, and they had all gone to their idolatrous rites, and she (Potiphar's wife) told everyone that she was ill, saying [to herself] she has no day to fornicate [*nizaqeq*] with Joseph like this day. 'And she seized him by his garment saying, "lie with me"' (v. 12). This teaches that they both went to bed naked.[38] At that moment the image of his father appeared to him in the window, and said, 'Joseph, in the future your brothers will have their names written on the priestly breastplate [*'efod*],[39] and yours amongst them. Do you want it effaced, and yourself called a shepherd of prostitutes?' as it says, '[A

---

36. Levinson, 'An-other Woman', p. 293; cf. pp. 290-91. Levinson focuses on the narrative expansion of the story in rabbinic literature as embedded within Greco-Roman historical/cultural context. Because his interest lies in reading the sexual scene in terms of a trial of cultural continence, the comparison between the Hellenistic genre and rabbinic aggadah is germane to his argument. But the antecedents to the 'seduction plot', in midrash, lie in the biblical text. In fact, it is a near-universal motif of folklore. Stith-Thompson has described the motif as 'A woman makes vain overtures to a man and then accuses him of attempting to force her' (Stith Thompson, *Motif Index of Folk Literature* [Bloomington, IN: University of Indiana Press, 1955–58], motif K 2111).

37. That is, *his* work, not his master's work.

38. This comment is missing in certain manuscripts of the Talmud (MSS Vatican 110 and Munich 95). Levinson points out that 'this daring innovation seems to be based in the fact that Potiphar's wife holds Joseph's garment, or alternatively, on a word play whereby "his garment" (*bigdo*) can be read as "his betrayal" (*bagdo*)' ('An-other Woman', p. 278 n. 31).

39. 'Most interpreters (Cassuto, Noth, Childs)', as Levinson notes, 'see [the *'ephod*] as a garment similar to a loincloth with a double shoulder strap held in place by two stones, one on each shoulder, upon which were engraved the names of the twelve tribes (Exod. 28.6-12)' (Levinson, 'An-other Woman', p. 279 n. 37).

man who loves wisdom will please his father] but a shepherd of prostitutes loses his wealth' (Prov. 29.3). At once 'his bow remained taut [*va-teshev be-'eitan qashto*]' (Gen. 49.24). R. Yochanan in the name of R. Meir said, this teaches that his bow returned to its natural state [*shavah qashto la-'eitano*]. 'And his arms were made firm' (v. 24). He thrust ten fingers into the ground and his seed was excreted from between his fingernails. 'By the hands of the Mighty One of Jacob' (v. 24). Who caused his name to be inscribed upon the stones of the breastplate? None other than 'the Mighty One of Jacob, from there, the Shepherd, the Rock of Israel' (v. 24), from there was he worthy to be called a 'shepherd of Israel', as it says, 'Give ear, O Shepherd of Israel who leads Joseph like a flock' (Ps. 80.2) (*b. Sot.* 36b).[40]

In this aggadic rendition, all the servants have left for the idolatrous festivities; in the parallel midrash it was the Festival of the Nile or, in another opinion, 'a day of theater and everyone went to watch' (*Gen. R.* 87.7). This accounts for how Joseph and Potiphar's wife found themselves alone in the house. But it also alerts us to a central theme; Egypt is steeped in lewdness and idolatry, from which the Hebrew servant must refrain. The trial is set against the background of 'cultural continence', in which the battle for ethnic and religious identity is intertwined with the struggle over gender and sex.

The lascivious wife with whom Joseph, according to this aggadah, *does* lie, is juxtaposed with his father, Jacob, as his savior. *Deus ex machina*, the image of the patriarch appears to rescue his son from completing the sexual act. Like the ghost of Hamlet's father whose 'visitation is but to whet [his] almost blunted purpose', Jacob's face hovers in the window, perhaps as a reflection of Joseph's own idealized self.[41] The patriarch threatens him with the loss of 'wealth' if he were to succumb to become a 'shepherd of prostitutes' (Prov. 29.3), and offers him a reward: to be etched on the stones of the priestly breastplate, along with his brothers. This is the 'rock of

---

40. Based on Levinson's translation, 'An-other Woman', pp. 278-79, according to MSS Oxford 2675.2, Vatican 110, Munich 95, *Aggadot ha-Talmud*. It is a reworking of the Palestinian tradition in *Gen. R.* 87.7, pp. 1071-74, and *y. Hor.* 2.4, 46d.

41. Joseph's face is the spitting image of his father's, according to midrash (*Gen. R.* 84.8, p. 1010), playfully rereading the phrase 'son of his old age [*ben zqunim*]' in Gen. 37.3 as *ziv 'iqonin* (lit. splendor of countenance). The term *'iqonin* is a Greek loan word (like the English 'icon') from *eikonion*, meaning 'countenance' (Jastrow p. 60). According to R. Samuel bar Nahman, in *Gen. R.* 87.7, he sees the image of his father [*'iqonin*], and 'did not find himself to be a man' (playing on the expression 'there was no man' in Gen. 39.11). That is, he experiences temporary impotence; his bow *returned* to its natural state (Gen. 49.24). See Kugel's analysis of this motif of 'the image [*'iqon*]' or 'countenance of the father' (*In Potiphar's House*, pp. 69-71 and 106-12; and my discussion in Chapter 1 nn. 8 and 9).

Israel', the promised 'wealth' of being inscribed on the priestly breastplate, alluded to in Jacob's blessing to Joseph at the end of his life: 'Yet his bow remained taut [*va-teshev be-'eitan qashto*]; his arms were made firm by the hands of the Mighty One of Jacob (from there is the Shepherd, the *Stone* of Israel)' (Gen. 49.24). What paradoxically effects *coitus interruptus* is the 'stone' image of the father's features and the reward of having his named engraved on one of the twelve stones of the *'ephod*. This cools Joseph's ardor, softens the phallus so that it 'returns' to its former 'natural state' [lit. his vigor, *'eitano*].[42] It is not firmness in body but a resoluteness of mind that preserves his integrity. 'It would almost seem', as Levinson points out, 'that Jacob is offering himself as a surrogate object of desire'.[43] It is a homoerotic alliance, or rather fealty to a 'socially sanctioned homosocial community' (allied with father and brothers, all male), that displaces the power of the seductive foreign female. Perhaps Boyarin's term 'homotopia' is more appropriate here.[44] 'Given the projection of the other as woman, Potiphar's wife's uncontrolled passion and its attendant loss of cultural identity is counterbalanced by Jacob's offer of a spiritual fraternity'.[45] In the midrash, Joseph does not succumb to sexual transgression but remains resolutely loyal to the image of his father.

In the biblical text, while he refrains from sexual relations with Potiphar's wife, Joseph does *not* return to his 'natural state', in alliance with his father and brothers. Rather, the converse happens. Joseph attempts to assimilate in Egypt. Marrying Asenath, the daughter of Potiphar, priest of On (Gen. 41.45), he names his firstborn Manasseh [*Menashe*], 'For God has made me forget [*nashani*] all my hardship and all my father's house' (41.51). Over the course of the more than twenty years that Joseph resides in Egypt, while his father grieves, the son never sends word home—not even when lifted out of prison and elevated to viceroy. The image of the father, in reality, is held aloof and fading. Only after he rises from the second pit (prison) and sees his brothers face to face, while ensconced behind his Egyptian mask, can he begin to make the slow journey homeward.

---

42. As Levinson points out, this is based on Exod. 14.27, where the sea returns to its previous condition, 'And the Sea returned to its natural state/flow [*va-yashov . . . la-'eitano*]'.

43. Levinson, 'An-other Woman', p. 280.

44. Daniel Boyarin, 'Homotopia: The Feminized Jewish Male and the Lives of Women in Late Antiquity', *Differences* 7.2 (1995), pp. 41-81.

45. Levinson, 'An-other Woman', p. 297.

Joseph in the Pit/Prison

Potiphar, in response to his wife's allegations, condemns him to the dungeon (lit. 'pit [*bor*]' in 40.15). This second 'pit' recalls the one into which he was thrown by his brothers (37.24), below the surface of the earth. As Avivah Zornberg points out,

> The full terror of the *bor* is precisely that of disappearing, without explanation, down a hole, to be forgotten by the world. . . . Joseph, therefore, becomes invisible when he is thrown into the *bor*, into both *borot*-pit and prison. In the fullest sense, he is forgotten by the world.[46]

His visibility had put him at risk, wherein he became not only an object of envy but of dangerous attraction. So he descends back down to the underworld to learn a different kind of seeing, to be transformed from object to subject, through an *abject* state of invisibility.

In the next scene, Joseph moves beyond being the object of admiration, 'beautiful in the eyes of beholder', where the internal is occluded by an external image of self. He learns to read *other* people's faces. In the prison, he positions himself for the ascent out of prison, where he inhabits a locus of invisibility. There he learns to see/read others (40.6), instead of being the one who is seen/read. He turns to Pharaoh's courtiers who were with him in prison, 'Why do you appear downcast today?' (v. 7),[47] prompting them to tell him their dreams. Now, instead of the dreamer, he becomes a dream interpreter—master of the inchoate narrative that must unfold. He urges them, 'Do not interpretations belong to God? Please tell me [your dreams]' (Gen. 40.8). His interpretations of both the cup-bearer's and baker's dreams become the hook that will lift him up out of the prison, out of the pit, into visibility again. Though he is forgotten for, presumably, another two years, after the cup-bearer is reinstated in his role (40.23), he is eventually recalled for his remarkable ability to interpret dreams (41.9-13). Again, he urges Pharaoh to tell him the dreams as a conduit of the divine will: 'It is not I [*bil'adai*]; God will give Pharaoh a favorable answer' (41.16; cf. v. 25). At that point, he moves from being the object of others' plots—sold as a slave, favored by Potiphar, framed for rape by the thwarted wife—to an active role in Pharaoh's court as dream interpreter and eventually viceroy and provider over the years of famine. He moves from object to subject, through the phase of being abject (neither subject nor object), below the purview of the visible, beyond sight of the public eye.

---

46. Zornberg, *Beginning of Desire*, p. 291.
47. In Hebrew, literally, 'Why are your *faces* bad today [*madu'a paneikhem ra'im ha-yom*]?' (Gen. 40.7).

Esther in the Eyes of the Beholder

Esther, too, moves from object, the one who is acted upon, to subject as prime mover over the course of the drama. In describing her charm, the rabbis seem to relativize her beauty, as 'beautiful in the eyes of the beholder'. The Talmud remarks on the verse 'that she bore grace [*ḥen*] in the eyes of all who saw her' (Est. 2.15) that everyone imagined her in the likeness of their own people.[48] Given the expanse of empire, 'from India to Ethiopia, over one hundred and twenty-seven provinces' (1.1), she may have looked Malaysian or North African, Persian or Greek—as the song from *Cabaret* goes, 'If you could see her through *my* eyes, she wouldn't look Jewish at all'.[49] The Talmudic passage, however, does not present a burlesque commentary on anti-Semitism (forgive the anachronism), but, rather, provides us with psychological insight into Esther's character. It is not *looking Jewish* that is problematic, but looking authentically true to oneself, to one's ethnicity *qua* Jew, that is inherently problematic for her. Esther is the inverse of Vashti, who refused to be displayed as an extension of the king's honor and the object of others' admiration. Instead, Esther (Vashti's foil) is the mirror of others' desires, and as mirror, she loses her singularity, the ability to be identified externally as a Jew. She cannot be 'fixed' but is, rather, malleable, permeable to the projections of others. The more feminine she is, that is, the more 'beautiful' as the object of the male ogle, the more she becomes a fantasy of the viewer, and the less 'Jewish', the less distinctively *other* in terms of her ethnicity.

The beauty of Joseph and Esther is, both literally and figuratively, 'in the eyes of the beholder'—as objects, mirrors, displaced selves. This feminine identity is inversely related to their visible Jewish one as we cross genders. When Esther dons royal apparel (5.1), she assumes an active, 'masculine' stance in presenting herself unbidden before the king, and eventually moves from covert to overt Jew. Joseph, on the other hand, as he is 'masculinized', rising to power as Pharaoh's viceroy, becomes less 'Hebrew' and more deeply ensconced behind the Egyptian mask, until it finally cracks open in a display of intense emotion.

48. *b. Meg.* 13a.

49. The ambiguity about Esther's Jewish identity is still quite prevalent in contemporary circles. Alice Bach, in a workshop at a Jewish feminist conference on the book of Esther, pointed out that the participants all imagined Esther as petite and doll-like, or tall, stately, and elegant, blue-eyed or green-eyed, and blonde (unanimously)—something like Grace Kelly. In these women's imagination, while Esther was quintessentially feminine, she did not look Semitic at all. The exercise exposes a degree of internalized anti-Semitism, which Bach, strangely, does not comment on. See Alice Bach, 'Mirror, Mirror in the Text: Reflections on Reading and Rereading', in *Ruth and Esther: A Feminist Companion to the Bible* (ed. A. Brenner; Sheffield: Sheffield Academic Press, 1999), pp. 81-86.

Passing Strange: The Motif of Clothing

For Joseph, the dynamic between being Jewish and being feminine is quite the reverse of Esther's. Vulnerable in the House of Potiphar to the lascivious gaze of his master's wife, he is repeatedly referred to as a 'Hebrew' [*'ivri*], the quintessential other (39.14, 17). To be a Hebrew, a slave, and feminized as the object of another's lust is to be the ultimate victim, the quintessential puppet in another's plot. Twice he is betrayed by clothing, *beged* as *biggud*.[50] Twice Joseph is stripped bare—once at the hands of his brothers, when they strip him of his tunic and throw him into the pit (Gen. 37.23), and another time, at the hands of Potiphar's wife (39.12). Where clothing had made him visible, vulnerable, subject to being stripped, Joseph later deploys clothing to reconstruct himself behind a mask. With his rise to power, he covers up his identity; he will 'dress for success', as the adage goes, rather than be stripped, exposed, bared.

When taken out of prison, he is shaved and dressed as an Egyptian lord, heavily made-up, almost mummified. He gains a new face—*il fait face*. Pharaoh gives him the signet ring, dresses him in fine robes of linens, and parades him around on a chariot as his second-in-command, for all to proclaim ruler over the land (Gen. 41.42-46). Similarly, Mordecai is dressed in royal apparel and paraded around on the king's horse, led by the humiliated Haman, who is forced to proclaim, 'Such is done for the man whom the king desires to honor!' (Est. 6.11). Later, when Haman is deposed and hanged, Mordecai (like Joseph) is given the royal signet and again dressed in royal garments (8.2, 15).[51] But while Mordecai maintains his image, consistently 'the Jew', Joseph's particularity is occluded.

As Egyptian viceroy, he is so well masked that his brothers fail to recognize him when they come down to Egypt.

> When Joseph saw his brothers, he recognized them [*va-yakirem*], but he made himself strange [*va-yitnaker*] and spoke harshly to them. . . . And Joseph recognized [*va-yaker*] his brothers, but they did not recognize him [*l'o hikiruhu*] (Gen. 42.7-8).

The double-edged verb *nkr*, meaning 'to recognize' (in the causative, hiphil) and to 'make strange/alien' (in the reflexive, hitpael), is deployed four times over the course of this short passage. Avivah Zornberg comments on the paradoxical use of the term:

---

50. See the discussion of this theme in Chapter 3, particularly on Gen. 39.16-18, and n. 38 in this chapter.
51. The linguistic resonances between these passages in the Esther and Joseph stories are quite striking (see n. 2 for the list of secondary sources tracing these parallels and the addendum to this chapter). The midrash picks up on these intertextual allusions (*Gen. R.* 87.6, pp. 1069-70).

> Beyond the asymmetrical drama of recognition and non-recognition, there is the enigma of 'He made himself strange to them'. This reflexive verb suggests a more-than-tactical move of self-disguise on Joseph's part. Within himself, he becomes alien to himself. . . . The result is that he cannot know himself, cannot relate to his past in compassion for himself. Only through a radical act of self-cauterization can he proceed to a limited experience of memory.[52]

Later, the brothers refer to him, in recounting the story of their sojourn to their father, as simply 'the man who is lord of the land' (vv. 30, 33). He speaks Egyptian to them, through the use of a translator (v. 23), though to the Egyptians, Joseph remains a Hebrew and retains his outsider status (cf. 43.32). But the mask is not only to test them, as Uriel Simon suggests.[53] With Joseph's rise to prominence, he conscientiously strives to shed his ethnic identity and to forget familial ties. He names his firstborn son *Menashe*, for the anodyne of forgetting (41.51), and his second, Ephraim, for 'God has made me fertile in the land of my affliction' (v. 52). Numb to his early trauma, he embraces his 'otherness', the occluded self in a fecund but foreign land. In assuming the role of Egyptian viceroy, Joseph becomes more *masculine*, master of his own narrative, less a projection of others' desire and concomitantly *less* Hebrew, until the point of crisis.

Joseph Resurfacing

The revelation of Joseph's identity, as it maps across gender, is both more complex and more personal than Esther's process of revelation. It entails a perplexing delay; Joseph does not reveal himself to his brothers until their second descent to Egypt. As I pointed out, the more firmly Joseph is ensconced behind his 'Egyptian' mask, the less vulnerable and the less feminine he becomes, whereas for Esther, the more feminine (that is pleasing and passive) she is, the less visibly Jewish. The nexus between Hebrew/ Jew and masculine/feminine are inversely related in the two narratives. And in the final revelation, for both Esther and Joseph, there is a complete breakdown of essentialist gender categories. Esther writes. Joseph weeps.[54] The cracking of the viceroy's mask, however, is complicated, drawn out over

---

52. Zornberg, *Murmuring Deep*, p. 303.
53. Uriel Simon, *Joseph and his Brothers: A Story of Change* (trans. David Louvish; Ramat Gan: Lookstein Center, 2001); also in Uriel Simon, *Seek Peace and Pursue It: The Bible in the Light of Topical Issues* (Tel Aviv: Yediyot Ahronot, 2004) (Heb.), pp. 58-85.
54. He actually weeps on a few occasions before the final revelation (Gen. 42.24 and 43.30) but never in public, where he must 'restrain himself [*yit'apeq*]', that is, keep the horizons ['*opheq*], the boundaries of his mask, firmly delineated. The reflexive of the verb 'to restrain/control oneself' ('*pq*) is quite unusual—used twice in the Joseph narrative (Gen. 43.31 and 45.1) and once with reference to Haman—who 'restrained himself [*va-yit'apeq*]' upon his return from the first feast when he saw the recalcitrant

the course of four chapters in the book of Genesis (chs. 41–44). When the brothers first go down to Egypt during the years of famine, Joseph recognizes them, but they fail to recognize him and he concocts a plot, a trap, a 'male ruse' (if you will) by which to test their conscience and perhaps his own place within the family.[55]

In the first act of masking, Joseph sets up a pretext for bringing Benjamin down to Egypt upon the second round. When the brothers first came down to procure food, he recognized them, but they did not recognize him; and he made himself strange to them (vv. 7-8). Speaking harshly . . .

> He said to them, 'You are spies; you have come to see the nakedness of the land [*lir'ot 'ervat ha-'aretz*]!' They said to him, 'No, my lord; your servants have come to buy food. We are all sons of one man; we are honest men; your servants have never been spies.' But he said to them, 'No, you have come to see the nakedness of the land [*ki 'ervat ha-'aretz ba'tem lir'ot*]!' And they replied, 'We, your servants, were twelve brothers, sons of a certain man in the land of Canaan; the youngest, however, is now with our father, and one is no more ['*einenu*]' (Gen. 42.9-13).

This is an odd accusation, construed in a strange turn of phrase: that they are spies come 'to see the *nakedness* of the land' [*lir'ot 'ervat ha-'aretz*]. The verb to 'see' or 'uncover' nakedness [*glh 'ervah*] is usually associated with the incest laws of Leviticus (chs. 18 and 20); the collocation *'ervat ha-'aretz* is found nowhere else in the Hebrew Bible. What is the 'nakedness of land' that he suspects they might discover? The accusation reverberates with irony; it is *himself* that they are in danger of discovering. He is the 'nakedness of the land' they have come to expose. Twice he has been stripped—once at the hands of his brothers (37.23) and then again at the hands of the lascivious Potiphar's wife (39.12); twice he has been submerged below the surface of the earth, into a pit. Now he fears exposure again, and thickens the layers between them.

Mordecai 'the Jew' yet again refusing to bow down (Est. 5.10). See also 1 Sam. 13.12; Isa 42.24; and 64.11.

55. Several commentators address the question as to why Joseph postponed the revelation of his identity until the second descent to Egypt. Some argue that he was testing to see whether his brothers repented of what they had done (Simon, *Joseph and his Brothers*, p. 20; and Nechama Leibowitz, *Studies in Bereshit* [Jerusalem: World Zionist Organization, 1972], pp. 457-61). Others wager that he wanted to guarantee the fulfillment of his dreams (Ramban on Gen. 42.9). Yoel bin Nun argues that Joseph assumed he was the 'rejected' son, like Esau and Ishmael, both excluded from the patriarchal covenant (Yoel bin Nun, 'Division and Unity: Duplication of a Bitter Mistake and the Shock of Discovery—Why Did Joseph Not Send (an Emissary) to his Father?', *Megadim* 1 [1986], pp. 20-31 [Heb.]). I follow Avivah Zornberg's reading that Joseph was bound by a pact of silence; he himself went into exile and must, paradoxically, become aware of his own absence and overcome the blanked memory caused by trauma in order to surface again (Zornberg, 'The Pit and the Rope', in *Murmuring Deep*, pp. 297-312).

The accusation of spying, furthermore, is not unfamiliar to Joseph. In addition to the gift of the ornamented tunic, it is his role as tattletale that first infuriates his brothers, as it says, 'and Joseph brought a bad report about his brothers to their father' (Gen. 37.2). Jacob seems to even encourage this role. He sends Joseph to Shechem, to 'see if it [is] well with [his] brothers and with the flock', and bring back word to him (v. 14). Perhaps the principle of poetic justice is operative here. Playing the family spy results in Joseph being stripped bare, uncovered, placed in a pit below the surface of the ground, where he is covered over, so to speak, by a false tale.[56] So he, in turn, accuses them of spying out 'the nakedness of the land', throws them all in jail for three days, and releases them (with the exception of Simeon), on condition that they promise to bring down the youngest son, Benjamin, when they return. This is the pretext that will crack open the cover story, the frozen land of winter, the wasteland of exile and family estrangement from which Joseph must be recovered.

The midrash brings this reading to the fore, succinctly paraphrased by Rashi:

> 'You have come to see the nakedness of the land' (Gen. 42.9)—For you have entered by way of the ten gates of the city. Why did you not enter [together] through one gate? And they said, 'We, your servants, . . . for the "one who is no more" [*'einenu*] (vv. 12-13), we scattered in the city *to seek him*'.

The question is why Joseph, as viceroy, noticed the entrance of ten brothers into Egyptian territory in the first place. What pretext does he have to single them out, ask them about their land of origin, and then accuse them of spying? Was he not governor, second only to Pharaoh, in charge of distributing the grain to multitudes? Surely he was a busy man! According to the midrash from which Rashi draws,[57] Joseph anticipated that his brothers would eventually come down to buy grain in Egypt; the famine, caused by drought, inevitably strikes Canaan.[58] And he had them arrested as they entered the city through ten different gates, ostensibly to find *him*, accusing them of being spies.

Does the midrash take the *irony* out of the dramatic irony in the biblical narrative? I think not. This is the story not told, the consummation devoutly to be wished. (Midrashim, just as dreams, can express wish fulfillment.) It

---

56. I owe the trajectory of this argument to a telephone conversation with Jeremy Milgrom, who first posed the question to me: 'Why does Joseph accuse his brothers of spying?'

57. *Tanḥ. Buber, Miqetz* 17.

58. As in Abraham's lifetime (Gen. 12.10-20) and in Isaac's (26.1). While the first patriarch does descend to Egypt, Isaac is told by God *not* to go down, but to stay in Gerar, as an alien among the Philistines (26.2-5).

is a fantasy on Joseph's part: 'If only my brothers would be so stricken with pangs of conscience for having sold me into slavery that they would come to Egypt in search of me'. But Joseph's fantasy is fraught with ambivalence. He remembers the trauma of the pit and wishes fervently to forget (as his naming of Manasseh reflects), while he also yearns to be found and reclaimed by the family, to return to an integrated self. The accusation of spying out the land is a pretext for discovering the truth, a truth born of conscience on the part of his brothers and a truth about himself. What was their mission, according to the midrash? To find the 'one who is no more [*'einenu*]'—that is, to redeem Joseph from slavery. Yet, according to the biblical narrative, Joseph has to wait another few years before he would discover their willingness to release the *other* brother (that is, Rachel's youngest son, Benjamin, who becomes his stand-in) from the threat of slavery. At that moment, he sees the real 'nakedness of the land' and uncovers the truth, healing the earth cracked open and scarred by near fratricide, drought and famine.

When Judah finally steps forward in his address to the Egyptian viceroy, Joseph experiences *his own* absence [*'einenu*] for the first time through another's eyes. Throughout the saga, Joseph is perpetually referred to as 'absent [*'einenu*]', the missing one—first by Reuben when he returns to the pit (37.30), then by his brothers in reporting that they had once been a band of twelve (42.13, 32), and then (like Simeon in jail) by his own father (42.36). Now, if Benjamin is taken, he too will become *'einenu*, absent to his father (44.30, 34). Joseph sees himself on the edge of disappearing (once again) in the patriarch's eyes through Benjamin (his stand-in), as Jacob said, fatalistically, when he relented in allowing his youngest son to go down to Egypt: 'And if/when I am to be bereaved, I shall be bereaved [*ka'asher shakholti shakhalti*]' (Gen. 43.14). Like Esther, the turning point for Joseph hinges on *imagining* a disappearance of self. The 'Persian' queen risks her life in presenting herself, unsummoned, to the king, invoking, 'And if/when I perish, I perish [*ka'asher 'avadeti 'avadeti*] . . .' (Est. 4.16). At this 'if/when' pivotal point,[59] the subject wavers on the verge of death or near erasure of identity. 'A strange lostness/Was palpably present' (Paul Celan).[60] Both Joseph and Esther undergo a complete occlusion to the point of 'strange lostness' before they can surface again as fully human, man/woman and Hebrew/Jew. Joseph is only 'redeemed', that is figuratively freed from the slavery into which he was sold, when he sees himself mirrored in Benjamin. As Judah avers, 'For how can I go back to my father if the boy is not with me? Let me

---

59. The term *ka'asher* means, in Hebrew, not 'if' but 'when'. Only in these two instances, Gen. 43.14 and Est. 4.16, does it acquire a conditional sense.

60. From Paul Celan's poem, 'Dumb Autumn Smells', *Poems of Paul Celan* (trans. Michael Hamburger; New York: Persea, 2002), p. 139.

not be witness to the evil that would befall my father' (v. 34). At that point Joseph can no longer restrain himself (45.1). He orders all the Egyptians out, and weeping, cries out, 'I am Joseph. Is my father still alive?' For the earth, winter always seems longer than it can endure.

Esther Concealed/Esther Revealed

Esther, in contrast to Joseph's guise, must reclaim her Jewish self by abandoning the hall of mirrors, the world of images and appearances. In the woman's house, she seems oblivious to the genocidal decree. The people of Shushan are dumbfounded (3.15), Mordecai tears his clothing, puts on sackcloth and ash, crying a loud and bitter cry, and sits prominently in his rags of mourning before the palace gate (4.1-2). Yet Esther seems to ignore the cause of his cry, trembling in fear on account of his inappropriate dress. She sends him a new suit, which he refuses to take (v. 4). Willfully oblivious or caught up in the web of veils in the harem, she is true to the role for which was groomed—to be passive and please, smile and pose. Mordecai sends her a copy of Haman's decree, urging her to plea for her people. But, she protests, none may approach the king without an invitation.[61] There is but one law for that person, man or woman—'that he be put to death' unless the king extends his golden scepter to him, and 'I have not been summoned to the king for thirty days now' (4.11).

So Mordecai is compelled to deliver a wrenching wake-up call, with a view of the precipice her people hover over:

> 'Do not imagine that you, of all the Jews, will escape with your life by being in the king's palace. On the contrary, if you keep silent in this crisis, relief and deliverance will come to the Jews from another place, while you and your father's house will perish [*to 'vedu*]. And who knows [*mi yode'a*], perhaps you have attained to royal position for just such a crisis' (4.13-14).

Mordecai's words resound more like a threat than a challenge. While he is sure that, if she remains silent, 'relief and deliverance will come to the Jews' from another place, he guarantees her no such salvation. All that Mordecai can offer her is a perhaps. 'What', then, in Avivah Zornberg's words, 'is to impel her to risk her life? No providential knowledge, no prophecy, not even an intuition—merely a *who knows*. . . . Moreover, while Mordecai

---

61. The rule that one may enter the Persian king's presence unsummoned at peril of one's life is found only in Herodotus (*Histories* 1.99; 3.72, 77, 84, 118, 140), with the important caveat that individuals could request an audience with the king. Historical fact aside, the emphasis in the Megillah is that Esther invokes a 'rule' that she must abrogate and thereby risk her life. See the discussion in Levenson, *Esther*, p. 80; Berlin, *Esther*, p. 48; and Fox, *Character and Ideology*, p. 62.

does have faith that the people will be saved in one way or another, he cannot cover Esther with that mantle of confidence.'[62]

At that moment, she must do a radical about-face, transform herself from a pretty, pliant, charming Persian queen into an active, political player among courtiers and kings. It is not incidental that she risks *everything* in going unbidden before the king—not only death but even her relations with Mordecai. If the king extends his scepter, she will be spared execution, yet something else is doomed. And so she concedes to go before the king and enigmatically avers, 'If/when I perish, I perish [*ka'asher 'avadeti 'avadeti*]!' (v. 16).[63] The emphatic doubling of the verb and the fatalism implied by *ka'asher* ['when', not 'if'] suggests that, indeed, something inevitably will be lost. Drawing on the language of Mordecai's threat,[64] the rabbis of the Talmud imply that she stands to lose him as her husband. As soon as she abandons her sexually passive position as *qarqa' 'olam*, the earth's ground, she is culpable for adultery, and her Jewish husband becomes forbidden to her.[65] She may never return to his embrace. This is by way of metaphor. She is indeed lost... lost to her former self. Gone is the pliant pose, the shuttling between men—between husband/father-figure, Mordecai 'the Jew', and the Persian king. No longer can she play the passive female role, mere chattel, wares in a high-stakes game of power politics. As Zornberg poignantly comments, 'When [Mordecai] replies, *Who knows*?, he cuts the traces of her dependency and springs her free'.[66]

She now commands him to declare a three-day fast for the people, while she and her maidservants too would fast before presenting herself unbidden to the king. 'And he went about and did just as Esther had commanded' (4.17)—a sharp reversal of their former roles (2.10, 20). From this point onward, the plot hinges on her plan. At this moment, Esther assumes power by adopting Vashti's defiance—not in *refusing* to appear, but, rather, in dar-

---

62. Zornberg, *Murmuring Deep,* 123.
63. Echoing Jacob's words in Gen. 43.14. See the discussion in Levenson, *Esther,* p. 82.
64. 'Relief and deliverance will come to the Jews from another place, while you and your father's house will perish [*to'vedu*]' (v. 14). The verb 'will perish [*to'vedu*]' is based on the same root, *'bd*, as in Esther's expression: 'If/when I perish, I perish [*ka'asher 'avadeti 'avadeti*]' (v. 16). It is echoed again at Esther's challenge of the death decree: 'And how can I bear to see the annihilation [*'avadon*] of my kindred!' (8.6). In Mordecai's threat, the plain sense of 'her father's house' may indeed be an allusion to himself. After all, she is an orphan. As her cousin and adoptive parent, Mordecai *has become* her 'father's house'. See the discussion in Fox, *Character and Ideology,* pp. 62-63. The Talmud, however, assumes that they are married, and it is the marriage that is at stake. See nn. 17-18.
65. *b. Meg.* 15a.
66. Zornberg, *Murmuring Deep,* p. 124.

ing to appear before the king unbidden.[67] As Fox points out, 'this is the turning point in Esther's development. She moves from being a dependant of others (all of them men) to an independent operator who, whatever the objective restrictions on her freedom, will work out her own plans and execute them in order to manipulate one man and break another.'[68]

On the third day, she literally 'dons royalty [*va-tilbash Esther malkhut*]' (5.1) and steps through that looking glass into the reality of selfhood as she presents herself unbidden before the king. Ahasuerus responds by extending his golden scepter to her (v. 2). The midrash elaborates, 'R. Yochanan said: three ministering angels came to her aid at that moment: one extended her neck, another stretched the scepter, and the third wrapped her with a thread of charm'.[69] The commentary imbues the scene with divine providence, embellished by miracles, but an expanding royal rod is a stand-in for another image. (Sometimes a snake is *more* than just a snake, a scepter more than a symbol of imperial rule.) Esther learns to master that male organ of power, the scepter metonymic for monarchy and patriarchal power.

The Reversal of Fate in Esther

But as she is galvanized into an active stance, wearing the masculine garb of 'royalty', she does not altogether abandon feminine wile. The plot twists around one perplexing detail. Why does Esther not reveal the consequences of Haman's decree and her Jewish identity right away, as Mordecai adjured her to do? After all, the king promises her 'half his kingdom' (5.3). At this point, standing in the inner court before the royal throne, she simply invites the king and Haman to a private wine feast, a strange *ménage à trois* (v. 5). Then, in the first feast, she prevaricates when the king again offers her 'half his kingdom', and merely invites him to the next feast (v. 6). The delay is perplexing. It is not because she is fearful or indecisive—'frailty thy name is' not 'woman'!—but because she deploys the female ruse in line with her biblical predecessors. As Michael Fox points out, Esther plots not only to undermine the decree but to bring Haman and his house down as well.[70] She does so, over the course of several scenes, by transforming herself into a subtle seductress. Critical to the plot is the build-up of Haman's ambition

---

67. See Amsellem, 'The Mirror Has Two Faces', p. 7.
68. Fox, *Character and Ideology*, p. 66.
69. *b. Meg.* 15b. See also *Midr. Teh.* 22.27.
70. See the discussion in Fox, *Character and Ideology*, pp. 71-73. The rabbis also ponder why Esther delays the revelation until the second feast, and offer several reasons. The best explanations, in the Talmudic discussion, are that Esther was setting a trap for Haman (R. Eleazar), that she wished to make the king and others jealous of Haman (R. Eliezer of Modi'in), and that she wanted Haman to be at hand for an accusation (R. Jose) (*b. Meg.* 15b).

and the jealous ire of the king. This second exclusive invitation may even explain why Ahasuerus was beset by insomnia that night (6.1).

Following the first feast, Haman returns home drunk, perhaps literally but most certainly metaphorically, on the tryst with the king and queen (5.9, 11-12). Yet, in dismay upon seeing Mordecai stubbornly refusing to bow down to him again, he orders gallows to be made for the Jew, following his wife's advice. That night, unable to sleep, the king reads in the annals that Mordecai had never been rewarded for uncovering the earlier plot of treason (2.21-23), and so Ahasuerus summons his viceroy in from the courtyard to advise him, 'What should be done for a man whom the king desires to honor?' (6.6). At the apex of dramatic irony, thinking it is himself the king intends to honor, Haman exposes his covetous desire for the crown. He suggests the man be dressed in royal garb, with a diadem placed on his head, while being paraded about on the king's horse, a courtier proclaiming, 'This is what is done for the man whom the king desires to honor!' (vv. 8-9). In a whiplash turn-about, Haman becomes the courtier designated to parade his Jewish enemy about on the king's horse—and, once fulfilled, it is *his* face that is, literally, 'covered in mourning [*'avel ve-ḥafui ro'sh*]' (v. 12).[71] The reversal of fate is now assured, as his wife intones upon Haman's return: 'If Mordecai, before whom you have begun to fall [*linpol*], is of Jewish stock, you will not overcome him; you will surely fall before him [*naphol tipol*] to your ruin' (6.13).

Haman then stumbles to the second feast, where Esther finally exposes the evil decree to massacre her people and the villain behind it. The king responds by storming out of the room in anger, and Haman falls prostrate on her couch to plead for mercy. Upon the king's return, he finds the obsequious Haman 'lying prostrate [*nophel*, lit., falling] upon the bed upon which Esther was lying' (7.8).[72] The stage directions echo his wife's ominous words that he would surely fall at the hands of the Jew (6.13). Just as Mordecai secured the reversal of fate in the public sphere, Esther now seals Haman's fate in the private *tête-à-tête*. In a jealous fury, mistaking his prostrations for sexual advances (as Esther must have planned), the king sentences Haman to be impaled on the very same stake built for Mordecai. Indeed the villain is 'hoisted with his own petard'.

One must note, however, that Esther never identifies herself as 'Jewish' in this scene, as if the detail would be completely lost upon the king. (Does Ahasuerus even know *which* nation was condemned by the decree?) Only in

---

71. This is poetic justice, *quid pro quo*, for the response of mourning Haman induced in Mordecai, who dons the symbols of mourning—tearing his clothes, dressing in sackcloth and ashes, and wailing bitterly as he goes about the city (4.1). Again, Haman's face is covered, *u-phanei Haman ḥafu*, when he stands condemned before the king (7.8).

72. The verb form *nophel* (participle of *npl*), implies that Haman is here pleading for mercy, but it is understood (by the king) as an attempt to ravish the queen.

the dénouement, when she presents herself again without being summoned (8.3), does she request that the edict to annihilate the Jews be repealed (vv. 5-6). But since the king's rule cannot be rescinded, Ahasuerus simply abdicates responsibility and hands the signet ring to Esther and Mordecai to write their 'letters' authorizing the Jews to defend themselves. Because Esther had advocated for Mordecai's promotion to the position of viceroy (vv. 1-2), he can now wield this signet ring as the arbiter of law (decrees/ edicts/letters/dispatches) for the Persian Empire (vv. 9-14). Yet it is Esther who asks for a second day of self-defense for the Jews of Shushan and for the sons of Haman to be impaled on the stake (9.13, 25), and Esther writes the letter confirming all the customs associated with the holiday of Purim, incumbent on all 127 provinces and on all future generations of Jews (9.29). The complete reversal of fate in the plot is particular to the genre of the *Megillah* as burlesque.[73] Yet the effectiveness of the reversal hinges on character development. Esther is transformed from puppet to puppeteer in the careful timing of her revelation, delayed until the second feast when the inversion of Haman and Mordecai is secured in the portent of a woman's word.

What the midrash uncovers is a subtext of sex beyond the purview of the reader, using hyperbole in the service of subversive reading. Like other warrior women in the Hebrew Bible such as Deborah, Jael and Rachab, the Jewish/Persian queen uses feminine wile, the 'unconventional weaponry of women', to undermine the pernicious sources of power—Haman and his evil decree. Over the course of the story, Esther undergoes a radical character transformation from object to subject, from a position of passivity to powerful agency, from disguise/occlusion to the revelation of identity that effects the release of her people from the decree of death. She gradually sheds layers of alienation—no longer merely the object of desire in the eyes of others, in exile from herself and her people, where language, for the oppressed subject, is dubbed. The *Megillah* concludes with Esther, the eponymous heroine of our story, *writing* the scroll (9.29; cf. v. 32).[74] Uniquely, she becomes the one female author in the biblical canon, engaging in writing as a mode of reflexivity, the means by which the self is reclaimed

---

73. On the genre of the book of Esther as farce, or 'festive comedy' related to the carnival-like holiday of Purim, see Berlin, *Esther,* xvi-xxii. She, however, argues that the characters must be understood as two-dimensional 'type-characters', given the nature of the genre. I beg to differ, at least with regard to Esther.

74. The Hebrew actually attributes the writing of this second letter, confirming the practice of Purim, to both Esther and Mordecai, but the verb is in the feminine singular, *va-tikhtov* . . . (Est. 9.29). Mordecai, according to the biblical text, writes the first letter (9.20), and Esther affirms it; but some exegetes attribute the latter act of writing primarily to Esther (see the commentary on Gen. 24.5 and 1 Kgs 17.15 by Radak, who cites the verse in Esther, where the grammar suggests that the woman is really the 'main player [*ha-'iqar*]').

as subject, free from the view of male ogle, released from the husband's rule in palace or home.⁷⁵ She moves from silence to *author*-ity, not only as author of the *Megillah*, but also as a maker of laws and customs incumbent upon her people ever after.

Conclusion: 'Esther and Joseph—c'est moi'

Through a careful reading of the resonances between the Joseph saga and the Esther scroll, I set the ironies in high relief. New aspects of these Diaspora heroes emerge. Esther is transformed from a flat, two-dimensional, Barbie-doll character into three or even four dimensions, crossing the boundaries of gender and time into the contemporary interpretive context. Joseph, a dandy and a snitch, is also transformed from a feminine figure, beautiful and charming in the eyes of others, to a master of his own narrative, provider for many peoples, and ultimately the source of salvation for his family. Yet, in both stories, God is conspicuously absent. There are no miracles. No prayers. No direct messages from heaven. God is only seen to be 'with' Joseph and invoked by him, principally through dreams and the attribution of their interpretation and fulfillment to the divine will.⁷⁶ Yet it is the characters operating in the seeming absence of divine providence that characterize these stories as tales of Jewish courtiers in the imperial palace. They are narratives of exile—both for Israel, as a people, and for *'Elohim*/Yhwh, as their God.⁷⁷

Gustav Flaubert once wrote, in reflecting on his great novel: '*Madame Bovary, c'est moi*'. Of course, the assertion is absurd. What does the reclusive French author have in common with the main character of his story—the bourgeois wife of a country doctor, bored, self-indulgent, preoccupied with her love affair, who ultimately takes her life? This statement conveys something about the nature of literary realism, where the author's voice is occluded, made perfectly invisible: 'since no one can ever give the exact measure of his needs, nor of his conceptions, nor of his sorrows, and since human speech is like a cracked tin kettle, on which we hammer out tunes to

---

75. See Mieke Bal on writing as reflexivity in the book of Esther: 'Lots of Writing', in *Ruth and Esther: The Feminist Companion to Bible* (ed. A. Brenner; second series; Sheffield: Sheffield Academic Press, 1999), pp. 212-38.

76. See Gen. 39.2-3 and 23 (Yhwh, 4x); and God as *elohim* in 39.9; 40.8; 41.16, 25, 32 (2x), 38-39, 51-52 and so forth. The only direct divine revelation occurs in 46.2, to Jacob in Canaan, before his descent to Egypt.

77. On the disappearance of God in the book of Esther, see the discussion in Richard Elliott Friedman, *The Hidden Face of God* (New York: HarperSanFrancisco, 1997), pp. 27-28.

make bears dance when we long to placate the stars'.[78] God, like Flaubert, as 'author' of the Esther and Joseph narrative is perfectly invisible. His main characters, like Madame Bovary, become the lens through which the divine light is refracted, through serendipity, chance encounters, covert plotting and radical reversals. In exile, his courtiers—the 'Egyptian' viceroy and 'Persian' queen—journey to near oblivion and back again when they finally reveal themselves as Jew/Hebrew and as fully human. Upon unmasking, the hidden face of God is revealed. Not in a whirlwind that splits mountains, a fire, or an earthquake. Not in blinding light. But in 'tunes hammered' on a 'cracked tin kettle'. It is in the sound of murmuring silence, near lost, heard behind the viceroy's mask, beneath the queen's royal diadem—in the arousal of conscience and terrible vulnerability.

ADDENDUM: ANALOGIES BETWEEN THE JOSEPH AND ESTHER NARRATIVES[79]

Motif	Book of Esther	Genesis (The Joseph Saga)
Passivity	Esther 'taken' (Est. 2.8, 15, 16).	Joseph 'brought down' 37.28, 36; and 39.1.
Beauty	'The maiden was shapely and beautiful' (Est. 2.7).	Joseph was well built and handsome (Gen. 39.6).
Grace and favor—*hen* and *hesed*	'The girl pleased [Hegai] and won his *favor* . . .' (Est. 2.9). 'Yet Esther won *favor* in eyes of all who saw her' (Est. 2.15). 'And the king loved Esther more than all the women, and she won *grace and favor* more than all the virgins' (Est. 2.17).	'And Joseph found *favor* in [Potiphar's] eyes . . .' (Gen. 39.4). 'The Lord was with Joseph: He extended *kindness* to him, and he found *favor* in the eyes of the minister of the jail' (Gen. 39.21).
Double naming	Esther /Hadassah (Est. 2.7): Esther as signifying the hidden face of God (Deut. 31.18).	'Pharaoh then gave Joseph the name *Zaphenath-paneah*' (Gen. 41.45) (homonym: your face is hidden).

---

78. Gustave Flaubert, *Madame Bovary* (trans. Eleanor Marx-Aveling; Zurich: Limited Editions Club, 1938), pp. 196-97.

79. See n. 2 for the list of secondary sources, which have addressed many of these parallels.

The attempted 'seduction' and resistance	'When they spoke to him *day after day* and he would not listen to them, they told Haman, in order to see whether Mordecai's resolve would prevail; for he had explained to them that he was a Jew' (Est. 3.4).	'And much as she coaxed Joseph *day after day*, he did not yield to her request to lie beside her, to be with her' (Gen. 39.10).
Dressed in royal apparel; given the signet ring; made *second* to the king.	'On the third day Esther put on her *royal robes* . . .' (Est. 5.1). 'So Haman took the *robes* and the horse and robed Mordecai and *led him riding* through the open square of the city, proclaiming, "Thus shall it be done for the man whom the king wishes to honor"' (Est. 6.11). 'Then the king took off his *signet ring,* which he had taken from Haman, and gave it to Mordecai' (Est. 8.2). 'Then Mordecai *went out from the presence* of the king, wearing *royal robes* of blue and white, with a great golden crown and a mantle of *fine linen* and purple, while the city of Susa shouted and rejoiced' (Est. 8.15). 'For Mordecai the Jew was made second [*mishneh*] to King Ahasuerus' (Est. 10.3).	'Removing his *signet ring* from his hand, Pharaoh put it on Joseph's hand; he arrayed him in *garments of fine linen,* and put a gold chain around his neck. He had him *ride in the chariot* of his *second-in-command* [*mishneh*]; and they cried out in front of him, "Bow the knee!" Thus he set him over all the land of Egypt . . .' (Gen. 41.42-43). 'And Joseph went out from the presence of Pharaoh, and *went out through* all the land of Egypt' (v. 46).
The appointments—*peqidim*	'And let the king appoint commissioners [*peqidim*] . . .' (Est. 2.3).	'Let Pharaoh proceed to appoint overseers [*peqidim*] over the land' (Gen. 41.34).

The risk that Esther, Jacob and Judah take	"'Go, assemble all the Jews who live in Shushan, and fast in my behalf; do not eat or drink for three days, night or day. I and my maidens will observe the same fast. Then I shall go to the king, though it is contrary to the law; *and if/when I am to perish, I shall perish!*'" (Est. 4.16). "'For we have been sold, my people and I, to be destroyed, massacred, and exterminated. Had *we only been sold as bondmen and bondwomen [slaves]*, I would have kept silent; for the adversary is not worthy of the king's trouble'" (Est. 7.4). "'For *how can I* bear to see the disaster which will befall my people! And how can I bear to see the destruction of my kindred!'" (Est. 8.6).	"'And may El Shaddai dispose the man to mercy toward you, that he may release to *you your other brother*, as well as Benjamin. As for me, *if/when I am to be bereaved, I shall be bereaved*'" (Gen. 43.14). "'Therefore, please let your servant remain *as a slave* to my lord instead of the boy, and let the boy go back with his brothers. For *how can* I go back to my father unless the boy is with me? Let me not be witness to the woe that would overtake my father!'" (Gen. 44.33-34).
What prompts the revelation of identity?	Est. 4.13-14: the threat of oblivion ['*bd*]; echoed in 8.6.	Gen. 45.3-5: "'I am Joseph! Is my father still alive?'" The image of the father's face

Other parallels include the following:

- Main action set in a foreign court
- 'On the third day'—Esther's fast (Est. 5.1) and the fulfillment of the baker's and cup-bearer's dreams (Gen. 40.20; 42.18)
- 'After these things [*'aḥar ha-devarim*]' (Gen. 40.1 and Est. 2.1)
- Dreams as effecting reversal of fate (Pharaoh in Gen.41.1-8 and Ahasuerus, Est. 6.1)
- Punishment by impalement [*tlh 'al 'etz*]
- Feast as the locus for concealed/revealed identity (Gen. 43.16-34 and Est. 7)
- The terms 'eunuch/officer [*saris*]'
- The reflexive form of the verb 'to restrain himself [*'pq*]' (Gen. 43.31; 45.1; Est. 5.10)
- The two characters in the subplot—cup-bearer and baker; kings guards, Bigthan and Teresh—are functionaries in the reversal of fate

BIBLIOGRAPHY

Abasili, Alexander Izuchukwu, 'Was it Rape? The David and Bathsheba Pericope Re-examined', *VT* 61 (2011), pp. 1-15.

Ackerman, Susan,'Child Sacrifice: Returning God's Gift', *BR* 9.3 (1993), pp. 20-28, 56.

Adelman, Rachel, 'Ethical Epiphany in the Story of Judah and Tamar', in *Recognition and Modes of Knowledge: Anagnorisis from Antiquity to Contemporary Theory* (ed. Teresa Russo; Edmonton: University of Alberta Press, 2013), pp. 51-76.

—'On Laughter and Re-membering', *Nashim* 8 (2004), pp. 230-44.

—'"Passing Strange"—Reading Transgender across Genre: Rabbinic Midrash and Feminist Hermeneutics on Esther', *JFSR* 30.2 (2014), pp. 81-97.

—'Seduction and Recognition in the Story of Judah and Tamar and the Book of Ruth', *Nashim* 23 (2012), pp. 87-109.

Adler, Rachel, *Engendering Judaism: An Inclusive Theology and Ethics* (Philadelphia: Jewish Publication Society, 1998).

Allen, Christine Garside, 'Who Was Rebekah? "On Me Be the Curse, my Son"', in *Beyond Androcentrism: New Essays on Women and Religion* (ed. Rita M. Gross; Missoula, MT: Scholars Press, 1977), pp. 183-216.

Alter, Robert, *The Art of Biblical Narrative* (New York: Basic Books, 1981).

—*The David Story* (New York: Norton, 1999).

—*Genesis* (New York: Norton, 1996).

—'How Convention Helps Us Read', *Prooftexts* 3 (1983), pp. 115-30.

—'Sodom as Nexus: The Web of Design in Biblical Narrative', in *The Book and the Text: The Bible and Literary Theory* (ed. Regina M. Schwartz; Oxford: Blackwell, 1990), pp. 146-60.

Amichai, Yehuda, *Open Closed Open* [*Patuach Sagur Patuach*] (Tel Aviv: Schocken, 1998) (Hebrew).

Amsellem, Wendy, 'The Mirror Has Two Faces: An Exploration of Esther and Vashti', *JOFA Journal* 4 (2003), pp. 7-10.

Aptowitzer, V., 'Asenath, the Wife of Joseph: A Haggadic Literary-Historical Study', *HUCA* 1 (1924), pp. 239-305.

Aschkenasy, Nehama, *Woman at the Window* (Detroit, MI: Wayne State University Press, 1998).

Ashley, Kathleen, 'Interrogating Biblical Deception and Trickster Theories: Narratives of Patriarchy or Possibility', *Semeia* 42 (1988), pp. 103-16.

Auden, W.H., 'Brothers and Others', in *The Dyer's Hand and Other Essays* (London: Faber & Faber, 1963), pp. 218-37.

Auerbach, Erich, *Mimesis: The Representation of Reality in Western Literature* (trans. Willard Trask; Garden City, NY: Doubleday, 1957).

Austin, J.L., *How to Do Things with Words* (Cambridge, MA: Harvard University Press, 1975).

Bach, Alice, 'Mirror, Mirror in the Text: Reflections on Reading and Rereading', in *Ruth and Esther: A Feminist Companion to the Bible* (ed. A. Brenner; Sheffield: Sheffield Academic Press, 1999), pp. 81-86.

—'Reading Allowed: Feminist Biblical Criticism Approaching the Millennium', *Currents in Research: Biblical Studies* 1 (1993), pp. 191-215.

—'Rereading the Body Politic', in *Women in the Hebrew Bible* (ed. Alice Bach; New York: Routledge, 1999), pp. 389-401.

Bailey, Randall C., *David in Love and War: The Pursuit of Power in 2 Samuel 10–12* (JSOTSup, 75; Sheffield: Sheffield Academic Press, 1990).

Bal, Mieke, *Lethal Love: Feminist Literary Readings of Biblical Love Stories* (Bloomington, IN: Indiana University Press, 1987).

—'Lots of Writing', in *Ruth and Esther: The Feminist Companion to the Bible* (ed. Athalya Brenner; second series; Sheffield: Sheffield Academic Press, 1999), pp. 212-38.

—*Narratology* (Toronto: University of Toronto Press, 2nd edn, 1999).

—'Tricky Thematics', *Semeia* 42 (1988), pp. 133-55.

—(ed.), *Anti-Covenant: Counter-reading Women's Lives in the Hebrew Bible* (Sheffield: Almond Press, 1989).

Bar-Efrat, Shimon, *I Shmuel: With an Introduction and Commentary* (Tel Aviv: Am Oved, 1996) (Hebrew).

—*II Shmuel: With an Introduction and Commentary* (Tel Aviv: Am Oved, 1996) (Hebrew).

Beal, Timothy K., 'Tracing Esther's Beginnings', in *Ruth and Esther: A Feminist Companion to the Bible* (ed. A. Brenner; Sheffield: Sheffield Academic Press, 1999), pp. 87-110.

Beauvoir, Simone de, *The Second Sex* (trans. H.M. Parshley; New York: Vintage Books, 1973).

Benjamin, Walter, *Understanding Brecht* (trans. Anna Bostock; London: Verso, 1983).

Berg, Sandra Beth, *The Book of Esther: Motifs, Themes and Structure* (Missoula, MT: Scholars Press, 1979).

Berlin, Adele, 'Characterization in Biblical Narrative: David's Wives', *JSOT* 23 (1982), pp. 69-85.

—*The JPS Bible Commentary: Esther* (Philadelphia: Jewish Publication Society, 2001).

—'Legal Fiction: Levirate "cum" Land Redemption in Ruth', *Journal of Ancient Judaism* 1 (2010), pp. 3-18.

—*Poetics and Interpretation of Biblical Narrative* (Winona Lake, IN: Eisenbrauns, 1999).

Bigger, S.F., 'The Family Laws of Leviticus 18 and their Setting', *JBL* 98 (1979), pp. 87-93.

Bin Nun, Yoel, 'Division and Unity: Duplication of a Bitter Mistake and the Shock of Discovery—Why Did Joseph Not Send (an Emissary) to his Father?' *Megadim* 1 (1986), pp. 20-31 (Hebrew).

Bird, Phyllis, 'To Play the Harlot', in *Gender and Difference in Ancient Israel* (ed. Peggy L. Day; Minneapolis, MN: Augsburg Press, 1989), pp. 75-94.

Blenkinsopp, Joseph, *The Pentateuch* (New York: Doubleday, 1992).

Bohmbach, Karla G., 'Names and Naming in the Biblical World', in *Women in Scripture* (ed. C. Meyers, T. Craven and R.S. Kraemer; Boston: Houghton Mifflin, 2000), pp. 33-39.

Bos, Johanna, 'Out of the Shadows: Genesis 38; Judges 4:17-22; Ruth 3', in *Reasoning with the Foxes: Female Wit in a World of Male Power* (ed. Cheryl Exum and Johanna Bos; Semeia, 42; Atlanta, GA: Scholars Press, 1988), pp. 37-67.

Boyarin, Daniel, 'Homotopia: The Feminized Jewish Male and the Lives of Women in Late Antiquity', *Differences* 7.2 (1995), pp. 41-81.
—*Unheroic Conduct: The Rise of Heterosexuality and the Invention of the Jewish Man* (Berkeley, CA: University of California Press, 1997).
Brenner, Athalya, *The Israelite Woman: Social Role and Literary Type in Biblical Narrative* (Sheffield: Sheffield Academic Press, 1985).
—*The Social Role and Literary Type in Biblical Narrative* (Sheffield: JSOT Press, 1985).
Bright, John, *A History of Israel* (Philadelphia: Westminster Press, 3rd edn, 1981).
Bronner, Leila Leah, 'From Veil to Wig: Jewish Women's Hair Coverings'. *Judaism* 42 (1993), pp. 465-77.
—'Esther Revisited: An Aggadic Approach', in *A Feminist Companion to Esther, Judith and Susanna* (ed. A. Brenner; Sheffield: Sheffield Academic Press, 1995), pp. 176-98.
Brown, Peter, *The Body and Society: Men, Women, and Sexual Renunciation in Early Christianity* (New York: Columbia University Press, 1988).
Brueggemann, Walter, *Genesis* (Interpretation: A Bible Commentary for Teaching and Preaching; Atlanta, GA: John Knox Press, 1982).
Buber, Martin, *Hasidism and Modern Man* (trans and ed. Maurice Friedman; New York: Horizon Press, reprint, 1966).
Buber, Martin, and Franz Rosenzweig, *Scripture and Translation* (trans. Lawrence Rosenwald with Everett Fox; Bloomington, IN: Indiana University Press, 1994).
Butler, Judith, *Gender Trouble* (New York: Routledge, Chapman & Hall, 1990).
Bush, F.W., *Ruth/Esther* (WBC 9; Dallas, TX: Word Books, 1996).
Campbell, Edward, *Ruth* (AB, 7; New York: Doubleday, 1975).
Carruthers, Mary, 'The Wife of Bath and the Painting of Lions', *PMLA* 94 (1979), pp. 209-22.
Clines, David J.A., 'The Story of Michal, Wife of David, in its Sequential Unfolding', in *Telling Queen Michal's Story: An Experiment in Comparative Interpretation* (ed. David J.A. Clines and Tamara C. Eskenazi; Sheffield: Sheffield Academic Press, 1991), pp. 129-40.
Cohen, Gerson, 'Esau as Symbol in Early Medieval Thought', in *Jewish Medieval and Renaissance Studies* (ed. Alexander Altmann; Cambridge, MA: Harvard University Press, 1967), pp. 19-48.
Cohen, Jeffrey M., 'Vashti—An Unsung Heroine', *Jewish Bible Quarterly* 24.2 (1996), pp. 103-106.
Cover, Robert, 'The Supreme Court, 1982 Term—Foreword: Nomos and Narrative', *Harvard Law Review* 97.4 (1983), pp. 4-68.
Cott, Nancy, *Public Vows: A History of Marriage and the Nation* (Cambridge, MA: Harvard University Press, 2001).
Craven, Toni, *Artistry and Faith in the Book of Judith* (Chico, CA: Scholars Press, 1983).
—'Women Who Lied for the Faith', in *Justice and the Holy: Essays in Honor of Walter Harrelson* (ed. D.A Knight and P.J. Paris; Atlanta, GA: Scholars Press, 1989), pp. 35-59.
Daly, Mary. *Beyond God the Father: Toward a Philosophy of Women's Liberation* (Boston: Beacon Press, 1973).
Davies, Eryl W., 'Inheritance Rights and the Hebrew Levirate Marriage', *VT* 31 (1981), pp. 138-44, 257-69.
Deen, Edith, 'King Saul's Daughter—David's First Wife', in *Telling Queen Michal's Story: An Experiment in Comparative Interpretation* (ed. David J.A. Clines and Tamara C. Eskenazi; Sheffield: Sheffield Academic Press, 1991), pp. 141-44.

Doniger, Wendy, *The Bedtrick: Tales of Sex and Masquerade* (Chicago: University of Chicago Press, 2000).
Driver, Samuel Rolles, *The Book of Genesis: With Introduction and Notes* (London: Methuen, 2nd edn, 1904).
Eliade, Mircea, *The Sacred and the Profane: The Nature of Religion* (trans. Willard R. Trask; New York: Harcourt Brace, 1959).
Emerton, J.A., 'An Examination of a Recent Structuralist Interpretation of Genesis xxxviii', *VT* 26 (1976), pp. 79-98.
Engar, Ann W., 'Old Testament Women as Tricksters', in *Mappings of the Biblical Terrain: The Bible as Text* (ed. Vincent L. Tollers and John Maier; Lewisburg, PA: Bucknell University Press, 1990), pp. 143-57.
Eskenazi, Tamara Cohn, and Andrea L. Weiss (eds.), *The Torah: A Women's Commentary* (New York: Women of Reform Judaism, Federation of Temple Sisterhood, 2008).
Exum, J. Cheryl, 'Bathsheba Plotted, Shot, and Painted', *Semeia* 74 (1996), pp. 47-73.
—*Fragmented Women: Feminist (Sub)versions of Biblical Narratives* (Sheffield: Sheffield Academic Press, 1993).
—*Tragedy and Biblical Narrative: Arrows of the Almighty* (Cambridge: Cambridge University Press, 1992).
Fewell, Danna Nolan, and David M. Gunn, *Gender, Power, and Promise: The Subject of the Bible's First Story* (Nashville, TN: Abingdon Press, 1993).
Fisch, Harold, 'Ruth and the Structure of Covenant History', *VT* 32 (1982), pp. 425-37.
Fishbane, Michael, *Text and Texture: A Literary Reading of Selected Texts* (New York: Schocken Books, 1979).
Fishbane, Mona DeKoven, 'Ruth: Dilemmas of Loyalty and Connection', in *Reading Ruth: Contemporary Women Reclaim a Sacred Story* (ed. Judith Kates and Gail Reimer; New York: Ballantine, 1994), pp. 298-309.
Flanagan, James W., 'Court History or Succession Document? A Study of 2 Samuel 9–20 and 1 Kings 1–2', *JBL* 91 (1972), pp. 172-81.
Flaubert, Gustave, *Madame Bovary* (trans. Eleanor Marx-Aveling; Zurich: Limited Editions Club, 1938).
Fokkelman, Jan, 'Genesis', in *The Literary Guide to the Bible* (ed. Robert Alter and Frank Kermode; Cambridge, MA: Belknap Press, 1987), pp. 36-55.
—*Narrative Art in Genesis: Specimens of Stylistic and Structural Analysis* (Sheffield: JSOT Press, 2nd edn, 1991).
—*Narrative Art and Poetry in the Books of Samuel: A Full Interpretation Based on Stylistic and Structural Analyses: The Crossing Fates* (Studia semitica neerlandica, 23; Assen/Maastricht: Van Gorcum, 1986).
—*Narrative Art and Poetry in the Books of Samuel: A Full Interpretation Based on Stylistic and Structural Analyses: King David* (Studia semitica neerlandica, 20; Assen/Maastricht: Van Gorcum, 1981).
—*Narrative Art and Poetry in the Books of Samuel: A Full Interpretation Based on Stylistic and Structural Analyses: Throne and City* (Studia semitica neerlandica, 27; Assen/Maastricht: Van Gorcum, 1990).
—*Narrative Art and Poetry in the Books of Samuel: A Full Interpretation Based on Stylistic and Structural Analyses: Vow and Desire* (Studia semitica neerlandica, 31; Assen/Maastricht: Van Gorcum, 1993).
Fonrobert, Charlotte Elisheva, 'The Handmaid, the Trickster, and the Birth of the Messiah: A Critical Appraisal of the Feminist Valorization of Midrash Aggadah', in *Current Trends in the Study of Midrash* (ed. Carol Bakhos; Leiden: Brill, 2006), pp. 245-75.

Fox, Everett, *The Five Books of Moses: A New English Translation with Commentary and Notes* (New York: Schocken Books, 1995).
Fox, Michael V., *Character and Ideology in the Book of Esther* (Grand Rapids, MI: W.B. Eerdmans, 2001).
Friedman, Richard Elliott, *The Hidden Face of God* (New York: HarperSanFrancisco, 1997).
Frymer-Kensky, Tikva, 'Pollution, Purification, and Purgation in Biblical Israel', in *The Word of the Lord Shall Go Forth: Essays in Honor of David Noel Freedman in Celebration of his Sixtieth Birthday* (ed. Carol L. Meyers and M. O'Connor; ASOR Special Volume Series, 1; Winona Lake, IN: Eisenbrauns, 1983), pp. 399-414.
—*Reading the Women of the Bible* (New York: Schocken Books, 2002).
Frymer-Kensky, Tikva, and Tamara Cohn Eskenazi, *The JPS Bible Commentary: Ruth* (Philadelphia: Jewish Publication Society, 2011).
Fuchs, Esther, '"For I Have the Way of Women": Deception, Gender, and Ideology in Biblical Narrative', *Semeia* 42 (1988), pp. 68-83.
—'Marginalization, Ambiguity, Silencing: The Story of Jephthah's Daughter', in *A Feminist Companion to Judges* (ed. Athalya Brenner; Sheffield: JSOT, 1993), pp. 116-30.
—'Reclaiming the Hebrew Bible for Women: The Neoliberal Turn in Contemporary Feminist Scholarship', *JFSR* 24.2 (2008), pp. 45-65.
—*Sexual Politics in the Biblical Narrative: Reading the Bible as a Woman* (Sheffield: Sheffield Academic Press, 2000).
—'Structure and Patriarchal Functions in the Biblical Betrothal Type-scene: Some Preliminary Notes', *JFSR* 3.1 (1987), pp. 7-13.
—'Who Is Hiding the Truth? Deceptive Women and Biblical Androcentrism', in *Feminist Perspectives on Biblical Scholarship* (ed. Adela Yarbro Collins; Chico, CA: Scholars Press, 1985), pp. 137-44.
Gan, Moshe, 'The Book of Esther in the Light of Joseph's Fate in Egypt', *Tarbiz* 31 (1961-62), pp. 144-49 (Hebrew).
Garsiel, Moshe, *2 Samuel: 'Olam ha-Tanakh* [The World of the Bible] (Tel Aviv: Revivim, 1993) (Hebrew).
—*Biblical Names: A Literary Study of Midrashic Derivations and Puns* (trans. Phyllis Hackett; Ramat Gan: Bar-Ilan University Press, 1991).
—'Wit, Words, and a Woman: 1 Samuel 25', in *On Humour and the Comic in the Hebrew Bible* (ed. Yehuda Radday and Athalya Brenner; Sheffield: Almond Press, 1990), pp. 161-68.
Gendler, Mary, 'The Restoration of Vashti', in *The Jewish Woman: New Perspectives* (ed. Elizabeth Koltun; New York: Schocken, 1976), pp. 241-47.
Ginsberg, Harold Louis, 'Hosea's Ephraim, More Fool Than Knave: A New Interpretation of Hosea 12:1-14', *JBL* 80 (1961), pp. 339-47.
Goldman, Shalom, *The Wiles of Women/The Wiles of Men: Joseph and Potiphar's Wife in Ancient Near Eastern, Jewish, and Islamic Folklore* (Albany, NY: SUNY Press, 1995).
Greenberg, Moshe, *The Hab/piru* (New Haven, CT: American Oriental Society, 1955).
—'Another Look at Rachel's Theft of the Teraphim', JBL 81 (1962), pp. 239-48.
Greenstein, Edward L., 'A Jewish Reading of Esther', in *Judaic Perspectives on Ancient Israel* (ed. Jacob Neusner; Philadelphia: Fortress Press, 1987), pp. 225-43.
—'Reading Strategies in the Book of Ruth', in *Women in the Hebrew Bible* (ed. Alice Bach; New York: Routledge, 1999), pp. 211-31.

Grottanelli, Cristiano, 'Tricksters, Scapegoats, Champions, Saviors', *History of Religions* 23 (1983), pp. 117-39.
Grubin, Eve, *Morning Prayer* (Riverdale-on-Hudson, NY: Sheep Meadow Press, 2005).
Gunkel, Hermann, *Genesis* (Macon, GA: Mercer University Press, 3rd edn, 1997).
Gunn, David, *The Fate of King Saul: An Interpretation of a Biblical Story* (Sheffield: Sheffield Press, 1980).
—*The Story of King David* (JSOTSup, 6; Sheffield: Sheffield Press, 1978).
—'Traditional Composition in the Succession Narrative', *VT* 26 (1976), pp. 218-20.
Hadas-Lebel, Mireille, 'Jacob et Esaü ou Israël et Rome dans le Talmud et le Midrash', *Revue de l'histoire des religions* 4 (1984), pp. 369-92.
Handelman, Susan, 'Facing the Other: Rosenzweig, Levinas, Perelman', in *Divine Aporia: Postmodern Conversations about the Other* (ed. John C. Hawley; Lewisburg, PA: Bucknell University Press, 2000), pp. 263-85.
—*Fragments of Redemption* (Bloomington, IN: Indiana University Press, 1991).
Hartman, David, *A Living Covenant: The Innovative Spirit in Traditional Judaism* (New York: Free Press, 1985).
Hasan-Rokem, Galit, *The Web of Life: Folklore and Midrash in Rabbinic Literature* (Stanford, CA: Stanford University Press, 2000).
Haughwout, Mark S., 'Ruth 3:3' (2010), http://markhaughwout.com/Bible/Ruth_3_3.htm.
Hendel, Ronald, Chana Kronfeld and Ilana Pardes, 'Gender and Sexuality', in *Reading Genesis* (ed. Ronald Hendel; Berkeley, CA: University of California Press, 2010), pp. 71-91.
Hertzberg, H.W., *1 & 2 Samuel* (Old Testament Library; London: SCM Press, 1964).
Hobbes, Thomas, *Leviathan* (Indianapolis, IN: Bobbs-Merrill, 1958).
Huddleston, John R., 'Unveiling the Versions: The Tactics of Tamar in Genesis 38:15', *Journal of Hebrew Studies* 3: article 7 (2001), http://www.arts.ualberta.ca/JHS/Articles/article_19.htm.
Hume, David, *A Treatise of Human Nature* (Harmondsworth: Penguin, 1969).
Irwin, Brian, 'Removing Ruth: tiqqune sopherim in Ruth 3.3-4?', *JSOT* 32 (2008), pp. 331-38.
Jacobs, Louis, 'Vows and Oaths', http://www.myjewishlearning.com/practices/Ethics/Talk_and_Gossip/Types_of_Speech/Vows_and_Oaths.shtml.
Jagendorf, Zvi, '"In the morning, behold it was Leah"; Genesis and the Reversal of Sexual Knowledge', *Prooftexts* 4 (1984), pp. 187-92.
Josipovici, Gabriel, *The Book of God: A Response to the Bible* (New Haven, CT: Yale University Press, 1988).
Kallai, Zecharia, 'Rachel's Tomb: A Historiographical Review', *Studies in Biblical Historiography and Geography* (Frankfurt am Main: Peter Lang, 2011), pp. 142-49.
Kaplan, Aryeh, *Made in Heaven: A Jewish Wedding Guide* (New York: Moznaim, 1983).
Kara-Ivanov, Ruth Kaniel, '*Gedolah Averah Lishmah*—Mothers of the Davidic Dynasty, Feminine Seduction and the Development of Messianic Thought from Rabbinic Literature to Luzzatto', *Nashim* 24 (2013), pp. 27-52.
—*Motherhood and Seduction in the Myth of David's Messianic Dynasty: The Hebrew Bible, Rabbinic Literature and the Zoharic Corpus* (PhD diss., Hebrew University of Jerusalem, 2010) (Hebrew).
—'Seed from Another Place: Transformation of the Account of Lot's Daughters', in *Jerusalem Studies in Jewish Thought* 22 (2011), pp. 91-119 (Hebrew).

Kates, Judith A., 'Women at the Center: Ruth and Shavuot', in *Reading Ruth* (ed. Judith A. Kates and Gail Twersky Reimer; New York: Ballantine Books, 1994), pp. 187-98.
Kerrigan, William, *Shakespeare's Promises* (Baltimore, MD: Johns Hopkins University Press, 1999).
Kiel, Yehuda, *Sefer Bereshit* (3 vols.; Jerusalem: Mosad ha-Rav Ḳuḳ, 1997–2003) (Hebrew).
Klein, Lillian R., 'Michal, the Barren Wife', in *A Feminist Companion to Samuel and Kings* (ed. Athalya Brenner; second series; Sheffield: Sheffield Academic Press, 2000), pp. 37-46.
Klitsner, Judy, *Subversive Sequels in the Bible* (Philadelphia: Jewish Publication Society, 2009).
Koenig, Sara M., *Isn't This Bathsheba?: A Study in Characterization* (Eugene, OR: Wipf & Stock Publishers, 2011).
Kristeva, Julia, *Powers of Horror: An Essay on Abjection* (trans. L. Roudiez; New York: Columbia University Press, 1982).
Kugel, James, —'Appendix 1: Apologetics and Bible Criticism Lite', http://jameskugel.com/read.php.
—*The Bible as It Was* (Cambridge, MA: Harvard University Press, 1997).
—*How to Read the Bible: A Guide to Scripture, Then and Now* (New York: Free Press, 2007).
—*The Ladder of Jacob* (Princeton, NJ: Princeton University Press, 2006).
—*In Potiphar's House* (Cambridge, MA: Harvard University Press, 1994).
Labovitz, Gail, *Marriage and Metaphor: Constructions of Gender in Rabbinic Literature* (Plymouth: Lexington Books, 2009).
LaCocque, André, *Ruth: A Continental Commentary* (trans. K.C. Hanson; Minneapolis, MN: Fortress Press, 2004).
Ladin, Joy, *Through the Door of Life: A Jewish Journey between Genders* (Madison, WI: University of Wisconsin Press, 2012).
Lamm, Maurice, *The Jewish Way in Love and Marriage* (San Francisco: Harper & Row, 1980).
Lauterbach, Jacob Zallel, 'The Ceremony of Breaking a Glass at Weddings', *HUCA* 2 (1925), pp. 351-80.
Leach, Edmund, *Genesis as Myth and Other Essays* (London: Jonathan Cape, 1969).
Lefkovitz, Lori, 'Eavesdropping on Angels and Laughing at God: Theorizing a Subversive Matriarchy', in *Gender and Judaism: The Transformation of Tradition* (ed. T.M. Rudavsky; New York: New York University Press, 1995), pp. 157-68.
—*In Scripture: The First Stories of Jewish Sexual Identities* (Lanham, MD: Rowman & Littlefield, 2010).
Leibowitz, Nechama, *Studies in Bereshit* (Jerusalem: World Zionist Organization, 1972).
Leibtag, Menachem, 'Parshat Toldot: Yitzschak's Blessing of Yaakov and Esav', http://www.tanach.org/breishit/toldot/toldots1.htm.
Levenson, Jon D., '1 Samuel 25 as Literature and as History', *CBQ* 40 (1978), pp. 11-28.
—*The Death and Resurrection of the Beloved Son: The Transformation of Child Sacrifice in Judaism and Christianity* (New Haven, CT: Yale University Press, 1993).
—*Esther: A Commentary* (London: SCM Press, 1997).
—*Sinai and Zion* (Minneapolis, MN: Winston Press, 1985).
Levenson, Jon D., and Baruch Halpern, 'The Political Import of David's Marriages', *JBL* 99 (1980), pp. 507-18.

Levinas, Emmanuel, *Difficult Freedom* (trans. Seán Hand; Baltimore, MD: Johns Hopkins University Press, 1990).
—*The Levinas Reader* (ed. and trans. Seán Hand; Oxford: Blackwell, 1989).
Levine, Baruch, *JPS Torah Commentary: Leviticus* (Philadelphia: Jewish Publication Society, 1989).
Levinson, Bernard, *Legal Revision and Religious Renewal in Ancient Israel* (New York: Cambridge University Press, 2008).
Levinson, Joshua, 'An-Other Woman: Joseph and Potiphar's Wife. Staging the Body Politic', *JQR* 3/4 (1997), pp. 269-301.
—'Dialogical Reading in the Rabbinic Exegetical Narrative', *Poetics Today* 25 (2004), pp. 497-528.
Licht, Jacob, *Storytelling in the Bible* (Jerusalem: Magnes Press, 1978) (Hebrew).
Lockyer, Herbert H., 'Michal', in *Telling Queen Michal's Story: An Experiment in Comparative Interpretation* (ed. David J.A. Clines and Tamara C. Eskenazi; Sheffield: Sheffield Academic Press, 1991), pp. 227-28.
Lyons, Deborah, 'Dangerous Gifts: Ideologies of Marriage and Exchange in Ancient Greece', *Classical Antiquity* 22 (2003), pp. 93-131.
Mandel, Pinchas, 'On Pataḥ and the Petiḥah: A New Study', in *Higayon l'Yona: New Aspects in the Study of Midrash, Aggaah and Piyut, in Honor of Professor Yona Fraenkel* (ed. Y. Elbaum, G. Hasan-Roken, and J. Levinson; Jerusalem: Magnes Press, 2007), pp. 49-82.
Mann, Thomas, *Joseph and his Brothers* (trans. H.T. Lowe-Porter; 4 vols.; London: Sphere Books, 1968); orig., *Joseph und seine Brüder* (Berlin, 1933).
May, Simon, *Love: A History* (New Haven, CT: Yale University Press, 2011).
McCarter, P. Kyle, *II Samuel* (AB, 9; Garden City, NY: Doubleday, 1984).
McNamara, Martin (ed. and trans.), *The Aramaic Bible Targum* (2 vols.; Collegeville, MN: Liturgical Press, 1994).
Meacham, Tirzah, 'The Missing Daughter: Leviticus 18-20', *ZAW* 109 (1997), pp. 254-59.
Menn, Esther Marie, *Judah and Tamar (Genesis 38) in Ancient Jewish Exegesis: Studies in Literary Form and Hermeneutics* (Leiden: Brill, 1997).
Milgrom, Jacob, *Leviticus: A New Translation with Introduction and Commentary* (AB, 3; 3 vols.; New Haven, CT: Yale University Press, 1991).
Millet, Kate, *Sexual Politics* (Garden City, NY: Doubleday, 1970).
Murphy, Roland E., *Wisdom Literature: Job, Proverbs, Ruth, Canticles, and Esther* (FOTL, 13; Grand Rapids, MI: Eerdmans, 1981).
Myers, Carol, *Discovering Eve* (New York: Oxford University Press, 1988).
Newsom, Carol A., and Sharon H. Ringe (eds.), *The Women's Bible Commentary* (Louisville, KY: Westminster/John Knox Press, 1992).
Nicol, George C., 'The Alleged Rape of Bathsheba: Some Observations on Ambiguity in Biblical Narrative', *JSOT* 73 (1997), pp. 43-54.
Niditch, Susan, *Underdogs and Tricksters: A Prelude to Biblical Folklore* (San Francisco: Harper & Row, 1987).
—'The Wronged Woman Righted: An Analysis of Genesis 38', *HTR* 72 (1979), pp. 143-49.
Niehoff, Maren, *The Figure of Joseph in Post-Biblical Jewish Literature* (Leiden: Brill, 1992).
Noth, Martin, *The Deuteronomistic History* (trans. J. Doull; Sheffield: JSOT Press, 1981); orig., *Überlieferungsgeschichtliche Studien* (Tübingen: Max Niemeyer, 1943).
Nygren, Anders, *Agape and Eros* (New York: Harper & Row, 1969).

Otwell, John H., *And Sarah Laughed: The Status of Woman in the Old Testament* (Philadelphia: Westminster Press, 1977).

Pardes, Ilana, *Countertraditions in the Bible: A Feminist Approach* (Cambridge, MA: Harvard University Press, 1992).

Philip, Tarja S., *Menstruation and Childbirth in the Bible: Fertility and Impurity* (Studies in Biblical Literature, 88; New York: Lang, 2006).

Polzin, Robert, *David and the Deuteronomist* (Bloomington, IN: Indiana University Press, 1994).

—*Samuel and the Deuteronomist* (Bloomington, IN: Indiana University Press, 1989).

Prouser, Ora Horn, *The Phenomenology of the Lie in Biblical Narrative* (PhD diss., Jewish Theological Seminary of America, 1991).

—'The Truth about Women and Lying', *JSOT* 61 (1994), pp. 14-28.

Provan, I.A., *1 and 2 Kings* (New International Biblical Commentary, 7; Peabody, MA: Hendrickson Publishers, 1995).

Rad, Gerhard von, *The Problem of the Hexateuch and Other Essays* (Edinburgh: Oliver & Boyd, 1965).

Rapoport, Sandra E., *Biblical Seductions* (Jersey City, NJ: Ktav Publishing House, 2011).

Reimer, Gail Twersky, 'Eschewing Esther/Embracing Esther: The Changing Representation of Biblical Heroines', in *Talking Back: Images of Jewish Women in American Popular Culture (*ed. Joyce Antler; Hanover, NH: Brandeis University Press, 1997), pp. 207-19.

Ricoeur, Paul, *The Symbolism of Evil* (New York: Harper & Row, 1967).

Rosen, Norma, *Biblical Women Unbound: Counter-Tales* (Philadelphia: Jewish Publication Society, 1996).

— 'Midrash, Bible, and Women's Voices', *Judaism* 45 (1996), pp. 422-45.

Rosenberg, Joel, *King and Kin: Political Allegory in the Hebrew Bible* (Bloomington, IN: Indiana University Press, 1986).

Roubach, Sharon, '"Two who donned the veil": The Image of Twins in the Bible', *Beit Mikra* 50 (2004), pp. 366-90 (Hebrew).

Sarna, Nahum M., *JPS Torah Commentary: Genesis* (Philadelphia: Jewish Publication Society, 1989).

—*Understanding Genesis* (New York: Schocken Books, 1966).

Sasson, Issac, 'Baby Naming: Biblical Rites and Mother's Rights', http://thetorah.com/baby-naming-biblical-rites-and-mothers-rights, 2014.

Sasson, Jack M., 'Farewell to "Mr. So and So" (Ruth 4.1)?' in *Making a Difference: Essays on the Bible and Judaism in Honor of Tamara Cohn Eskenazi* (ed. David J.A. Clines, Kent Harold Richards, and Jacob L. Wright; Sheffield: Sheffield Phoenix Press, 2012), pp. 251-56.

—*Ruth: A New Translation with a Philological Commentary and a Formalist–Folklorist Interpretation* (Sheffield: Sheffield Academic Press, 2nd edn, 1989).

—'The Servant's Tale: How Rebekah Found a Spouse', *JNES* 65 (2006), pp. 241-65.

Satlow, Michael, '"Try to be a Man": The Rabbinic Construction of Masculinity', *HTR* 89 (1996), pp. 19-40.

—*The Jewish Marriage in Antiquity* (Princeton, NJ: Princeton University Press, 2001).

Schaberg, Jane, Alice Bach, and Esther Fuchs (eds.), *On the Cutting Edge: The Study of Women in Biblical Worlds: Essays in Honor of Elisabeth Schüssler Fiorenza* (New York: Continuum, 2004).

Scholem, Gershom Gerhard, *On the Kabbalah and its Symbolism* (trans. Ralph Manheim; New York: Schocken Books, reprint, 1965).

—*Major Trends in Jewish Mysticism* (New York: Schocken Books, reprint, 1954).
Schüssler Fiorenza, Elisabeth, *Bread Not Stone: The Challenge of Feminist Biblical Interpretation* (Boston: Beacon Press, 1984).
—*But She Said: Feminist Practices of Biblical Interpretation* (Boston: Beacon Press, 1992).
—'On Feminist Methodology', *JFSR* 1.2 (1985), pp. 73-88.
—*Sharing her Word* (Boston: Beacon Press, 1995).
Schwartz, Regina, 'Adultery in the House of David: The Metanarrative of Biblical Scholarship and the Narratives of the Bible', *Semeia* 54 (1991), pp. 35-56.
Scott, James C., *Domination and the Arts of Resistance: Hidden Transcripts* (New Haven, CT: Yale University Press, 1992).
Searle, John, *Speech Acts: An Essay in the Philosophy of Language* (Cambridge: Cambridge University Press, 1969).
Seeman, Don, 'The Watcher at the Window: Cultural Poetics of a Biblical Motif', *Prooftexts* 24 (2004), pp. 1-50.
Segal, Alan F., *Rebecca's Children: Judaism and Christianity in the Roman World* (Cambridge, MA: Harvard University Press, 1986).
Shalev, Meir, *The Bible Now* [*Tanakh 'Akhshav*] (Tel Aviv: Schocken, 1985) (Hebrew).
Sharvit, S., *Tractate Avoth through the Ages* (Jerusalem: Bialik Institute, 2004) (Hebrew).
Shinan, Avigdor, and Yair Zakovitch, *Ma'aseh Yehudah ve-Tamar* [The Story of Yehuda and Tamar] (Jerusalem: Magnes Press, 1992) (Hebrew).
Simon, Uriel, *Joseph and his Brothers: A Story of Change* (trans. David Louvish; Ramat Gan: Lookstein Center, 2001).
—'The Poor Man's Ewe-Lamb: An Example of a Juridical Parable', *Biblica* 48 (1967), pp. 207-42.
—*Seek Peace and Pursue It: The Bible in the Light of Topical Issues* (Tel Aviv: Yediyot Ahronot, 2004) (Hebrew).
Speiser, E.A., *Genesis: Introduction, Translation, and Notes* (AB, 1; Garden City, NY: Doubleday, 1964).
Spiegel, Shalom, *The Last Trial* (New York: Schocken Books, 1969).
Stanton, Elizabeth Cady, *The Women's Bible* (New York: Arno Press, reprint, 1972).
Steinberg, Naomi, 'The Genealogical Framework of the Family Stories in Genesis', *Semeia* 46 (1989), pp. 41-50.
—'Israelite Tricksters, their Analogues and Cross-Cultural Study'. *Semeia* 42 (1988), pp. 1-13.
—*Kinship and Marriage in Genesis: A Household Economics Perspective* (Minneapolis, MN: Fortress Press, 1993).
Steinmetz, Devora, *From Father to Son: Kinship, Conflict, and Continuity in Genesis* (Louisville, KY: Westminster/John Knox Press, 1991).
Stern, David, *Midrash and Theory: Ancient Jewish Exegesis and Contemporary Literary Studies* (Evanston, IL: Northwestern University Press, 1996).
Sternberg, Meir, *The Poetics of Biblical Narrative* (Bloomington, IN: Indiana University Press, 1985).
Swidler, Leonard, *Biblical Affirmations of Women* (Philadelphia: Westminster Press, 1979).
Syrén, Roger, *The Forsaken First-Born: A Study of a Recurrent Motif in the Patriarchal Narratives* (Sheffield: JSOT Press, 1993).
Teugels, Lieve, *Bible and Midrash: The Story of 'The Wooing of Rebekah' (Gen. 24)* (Dudley, MA: Peeters, 2004).

—'"A Strong Woman Who Can Find?" A Study of Characterization in Genesis 24 with Some Perspectives on General Presentation of Isaac and Rebekah in the Genesis Narrative', *JSOT* 63 (1994), pp. 89-104.

Theodor, J., and H. Albeck, *Midrash Bereshit Rabba: Critical Edition with Notes and Commentary* (Jerusalem: Wahrmann, reprint, 1965).

Todorov, Tzevetan, *The Poetics of Prose* (Ithaca, NY: Cornell University Press, 1977).

Thompson, Stith, *Motif Index of Folk Literature* (Bloomington, IN: Indiana University Press, 1955–58).

Toorn, Karel van der, 'The Significance of the Veil in the Ancient Near East', in *Pomegranates and Golden Bells: Studies in Biblical, Jewish, and Near Eastern Ritual, Law, and Literature in Honor of Jacob Milgrom* (ed. David P. Wright, David Noel Freedman and Avi Hurvitz; Winona Lake, IN: Eisenbrauns, 1995), pp. 327-39.

Trible, Phyllis, *God and the Rhetoric of Sexuality* (Philadelphia: Fortress Press, 1978).

—*Texts of Terror* (Philadelphia, PA: Fortress Press, 1984).

Tsevat, Matitiahu, 'The Husband Veils a Wife', *Jewish Chautauqua Society* 17 (1975), pp. 235-40.

Turner, Victor Witter, *The Ritual Process: Structure and Anti-Structure* (Chicago: Aldine, 1969).

Van Seters, John, *The Biblical Saga of King David* (Winona Lake, IN: Eisenbrauns, 2009).

—*In Search of History* (New Haven, CT: Yale University Press, 1983).

Vawter, Bruce, *On Genesis: A New Reading* (Garden City, NY: Doubleday, 1977).

Viezel, Eran, 'The Influence of Realia on Biblical Depictions of Childbirth', *VT* 61 (2011), pp. 685-89.

Weisberg, Dvora, Levirate Marriage and the Family in Ancient Judaism (Hanover, NH: University Press of New England, 2009).

Wenham, Gordon J., *Genesis 16–50* (Dallas, TX: Word Books, 1994).

Westbrook, Raymond, *Property and Family in Biblical Law* (Sheffield: JSOT Press, 1991).

Westermann, Claus, *Genesis: A Commentary* (Minneapolis, MN: Augsburg Press, 1985).

Wilde, Oscar, 'The Critic as Artist', in *The Artist as Critic* (ed. Richard Ellman; Chicago: University of Chicago Press, 1968), pp. 341-407.

Wolde, Ellen van, 'Texts in Dialogue with Texts: Intertextuality in the Ruth and Tamar Dialogues', *BI* 5 (1997), pp. 1-28.

Yee, Gale A.,'"Fraught with Background": Literary Ambiguity in II Samuel 11', *Interpretation* 42 (1988), pp. 240-53.

Yuval, Israel Jacob, *Two Nations in your Womb: Perception of Jews and Christians in Late Antiquity and the Middle Ages* (trans. from Hebrew by Barbara Harshav and Jonathan Chipman; Berkeley, CA: University of California Press, 2006).

Zakovitch, Yair, ''aqevat Ya'aqob [Jacob's Heel]', in *Baruch Ben-Yehudah Festschrift* (ed. B.Z. Lurie; Tel Aviv: Ha-ḥevrah le-ḥeqer ha-miqra, 1981), pp. 125-27 (Hebrew).

—*An Introduction to Inner-Biblical Interpretation* (Even Yehudah: Rekhes, 1992).

—*Ruth: Introduction and Commentary* (Tel Aviv: Am Oved, 1990) (Hebrew).

Zakovitch, Yair, and Avigdor Shinan, *Ma'aseh Yehuda ve-Tamar: Breshit 39 ba-Mikra, ba-targumim ha'atikim uva-sifrut ha-Yehudit* (Jerusalem: Mifalei ha-meḥqar shel ha-makhon le-mada'ei ha-yahadut, 1992) (Hebrew).

Zevit, Z., 'Dating Ruth: Legal, Linguistic and Historical Observations', *ZAW* 117 (2005), pp. 574-600.

Ziegler, Yael, *Promises to Keep* (Leiden: Brill, 2008).
—*Ruth: From Alienation to Monarchy* (Jerusalem: Koren/Maggid, 2015).
Ziskind, Jonathan, 'The Missing Daughter in Leviticus xviii', *VT* 46 (1996), pp. 125-30.
Zornberg, Avivah Gottlieb, *The Beginning of Desire: Reflections on Genesis* (New York: Doubleday, 1996).
—*The Murmuring Deep: Reflections on the Rabbinic Unconscious* (New York: Schocken Books, 2009).
—*The Particulars of Rapture: Reflections on Exodus* (New York: Doubleday, 2001).
Zucker, David J., 'What Sarah Saw: Envisioning Genesis 21:9-10', *JQR* 36 (2008), pp. 54-62.

Index of Biblical References and Other Ancient Texts

OLD TESTAMENT
Genesis
1.1–2.4a   13
1.5, 8ff.   45
2.4b–26   13
2.4   12, 13, 91
2.7   13
3.6   9, 28, 152
3.8   168
3.15   23
3.22   28
3.24   185
4.1   94, 95
4.3-5   22
4.17   95
4.24   95
5.1   12, 91
6.4   170
6.5   160
6.9   12, 13, 91
10   13
10.1   12, 91
10.21   211
10.24-25   211
11.10-11   13
11.10   12, 91
11.14-17   211
11.27–25.11   13
11.27   12. 13, 91
11.29   33, 34
11.30   14
12.1   33, 98
12.7   18
12.10-20   182, 220
12.12   182
13.15   18
14.13   211
14.20   65
15.2   72
15.9   153
15.13-16   132
15.18   18
16.2   170
16.13-14a   30
16.15   187
17.8   18
17.18-21   28
18   17, 124
18.13   19
18.15   18
18.18   108
18.20   131
19   90, 121
19.5   95
19.8   95
19.30-38   105, 106
19.31-32   106
19.33, 35   124
19.34   170
20.1-18   15, 182
20.12   33, 28, 182
20.13   182
21.1   15
21.2, 7   15
21.3   187
21.9-10   25
21.10-12   190
21.12   18, 26, 62
21.28-33   181
22.14   30
22.17-19   18
22.19   31, 32
22.20-24   11, 34
22.23   16
23.1-2   11
24.3-4   72
24.5   33, 226
24.8-9   133
24.10-28   41, 42
24.12, 26   98
24.16   95
24.41   133
24.50-60   60
24.60   34
24.62-63a   30
24.63b-67   31, 37
24.64   46
24.65   36, 69
24.67   12, 17, 186
25.2   16
25.3   25
25.11   31
25.12   12, 91
25.18   32
25.19–35.19   13
25.19-20   154
25.19   12, 13, 14, 15, 91
25.20   16
25.21   17
25.22   21, 28
25.23   12, 17, 18, 19, 20, 25, 28, 42, 52, 62
25.25-27   43
25.25-26   22, 23, 85
25.25   85, 123, 187
25.26   16
25.27-34   55
25.27-28   47
25.27   24, 47, 55
25.28   27
25.29-34   17

The Female Ruse

Genesis (continued)

26.1	220	29.22-23, 25-26	44	35.22	47, 194
26.2-5	220	29.23-26	116, 127	35.27-28	25, 26
26.3-4	18, 34	29.23	170	36.1, 9	12, 91
26.8	211	29.25	49, 65, 146	37	70, 110
26.34-35	18, 72	29.30-35	50-51, 187	37.2–50.26	14
26.35	26	29.31	48, 50, 52	37.2	12, 13, 14, 91, 208, 220
27.1-2, 3, 6-7, 8, 13, 43	25	29.35	84	37.3	15, 16, 47, 48, 213
27.1	45	30.1	56		
27.11	43	30.3-13	58		
27.12	55	30.3	170	37.18-19	32
27.15, 42	44	30.8	56	37.23	217
27.16	76	30.11, 13, 18, 20-21	187	37.25	66
27.18-29	45			37.26-27	81, 84, 112
27.19	24, 45	30.14-15, 16, 18, 28	57	37.28, 36	204, 228
27.22	60, 65			37.31-33	76
27.28-29	18, 28	30.16, 21	209	37.32-33	111
27.29, 37, 40	42	30.18-19	59	37.32	71
		30.22	52, 66	37.33	72
27.33	18, 28	30.24	61	37.35	66, 187
27.36	55, 57	30.25-43	59	37.36	204, 207, 208
27.40	20, 21	31.1, 15	59		
27.41-42	18	31.11-13	58-59	38	70, 90, 109
27.43-45	41	31.13	131	38.1	71, 72
27.46	18, 41, 72	31.14	59	38.2	70, 110, 170
28.1-3	41	31.19-20, 26	59	38.7, 8	72-73
28.1-2	72			38.8	100, 101, 170
28.3-4	18, 28	31.19, 32	61, 145, 184	38.9	102
28.8-9	72	31.31-37	59-60	38.11	73
28.13-14	18	31.38	42	38.12	124
28.20-22	61	32.5	20	38.13	152
28.20	131	32.14, 19, 21, 22	158	38.14-19, 24, 25-26	111
29–30	17	32.15	42	38.14-19	74-75
29.1	46	32.25	54	38.14, 19	36, 69, 170, 207
29.3, 8	38	32.29	39, 57		
29.6, 10-11, 17	41	33.13	20	38.15	75
29.11	42	33.17	175	38.16, 18	44
29.12	54	34.1	209	38.18	88
29.15, 18, 20, 27	42	34.31	173	38.21	75, 77
		35.1-14	61	38.24-26	77-78
29.15	57	35.11-12	18	38.24, 25	71, 88
29.16-18	43	35.16-19, 20	52, 63, 64, 145	38.24	
29.17	43, 47, 152, 203			38.25	79, 112, 173
29.18, 23, 25	45	35.17	61	38.26	81, 84, 95, 112, 123
		35.18	72, 187	38.27-30	22, 70

38.29-30	83, 85, 86, 89, 92	44.15	207	18.6, 7, 17	103
38.29	112	44.18	156	18.10, 15	74, 103
39	70	43.31	218	18.15-16	110
39.1	71, 204, 207, 208, 228	43.33-34	175, 230	18.18	40, 65
		44.30	138	19.11	59
39.2-3, 23	227	44.32-34	71, 81, 83, 112	19.18	139
39.4, 6, 21	207	45.1	218, 230	20.10	74, 170
39.4, 21-22	211, 228	45.3-5	230	20.17	102
		48.4	18	20.21	110
39.6	203, 208, 228	48.5	18	21.9	173
39.9	210	48.12	22	25.23-28	101, 102, 120
39.10	210, 229	49.3	18, 22	26.40	84
39.11-15	210	49.8-10	83, 84, 86		
39.11	212, 213	49. 10	110	*Numbers*	
39.12	210, 217, 219	49.11-12	74, 88	3.1	13, 91
39.14, 17	211, 217	49.24	213, 214	5.7	84
39.14	170	50.19	203	5.11-31	170
39.16-18	76, 211, 217			10.9	65
39.20	211	*Exodus*		12.7	211
40–41	207	1.15, 16, 19	211	15.38-39	87
40.1-8	230			22.33	28
40.1	230	2.7, 11	211	24.8	65
40.2, 7	208, 215	2.15-21	41	25.1-9	92, 107
40.8	203, 215	4.9	28	30.3	131
40.20	230	4.10, 13	156	31.16, 18, 35	95
40.23	211, 215	4.25	175	32.12	153
41.9-13	215	12.37	175		
41.12	211	13.20	175	*Deuteronomy*	
41.14	210	14.27	214	2.9, 17	103, 107
41.16, 25	203, 215	17.3	19	4.20	83
41.34	229	17.4-16	204	5.6	24
41.42-43	215, 229	17.7	136	5.17-18	164
41.45	205, 208, 214, 228	19.4	118	7.8	132
		20.2	24	7.9, 12	97, 98
41.46	229	20.13-14	164	8.1, 18	132
41.51	214	21.37	184	20.8	160
42.7-8	95, 96, 217	28.6-12	212	21.15-17	17, 22, 48, 99
42.8-10	71, 81, 83	31.6	160	22.2	180
42.9-13	219, 220	34.6	97	22.13, 22	170
42.18	230	34.33-35	36	22.21	173
42.21-22	71			22.22	74, 170
42.24	218	*Leviticus*		23.1	118
43.9	81, 112	5.5	84	23.4-5	92, 94, 102, 103, 107
43.14	221, 223, 230	11.40	172		
		12.2-6	172	23.10-14	176
43.16-34	230	15.17-18, 19, 28	172	23.18	77
43.31	230			24.1	204
43.34	175	16.21	84		

Deuteronomy (*continued*)		1.15	157	18.7	143
25.5-10	73, 94, 100, 101	1.18	156	18.10-11, 16	140, 144
		1.19	95		
25.5	110	1.20	187	18.13	140
25.9-10	101	2.3	29	18.17-22	140
25.17-19	205	2.12	157	18.17, 19-22, 25	127, 141
26.14	72	3.17	135		
31.17-18	206, 228	6.8	86		
32.11	118	8.20	167	18.17, 21, 25	141
32.15	39	9.1-2	54, 152		
32.27	65	10.2	63	18.17, 21, 26	138
33.5, 26	39	10.16	53, 54	18.18, 23	141
33.7	65	10.27	157	18.20, 28	127, 141, 143
		13	138	18.21	141-42
Joshua		13.12-44	133	18.22	142 144
2	179	13.12	219	18.23	149
2.15	89, 147	14	133, 138	18.25, 26, 27	142
2.21	147, 172	14.24-30, 49	133		
6.25	89	14.24, 39	131	18.30	141
6.26	131	14.26	181	19.1	143-44
7.1	133	14.32-35, 37	134	19.2-7	138
7.15-18	134			19.6	144
7.21-22	134	14.39, 44	144	19.9-10	144
7.24-25	131, 133	14.39	134	19.10-18	145
14.6, 14	153	14.41, 42, 43	134	19.10-17	128
24.2	211			19.11	148
		14.44	135, 154	19.12	146
Judges		14.49	138	19.15	147
4.6	172	15	135, 205	19.17	44, 146, 150
4.9	179	15.22-24a	155	20	139
5.28, 30	147	15.22-23	133	20.13-16	136
9.50-54	179	16	139, 159	20.13	135
9.52-54	165	16.7	22, 70, 99, 123	20.14-17, 41-42	139
11.30-31	131				
11.35	132, 133	16.12	43, 122, 123	20.17	126, 138
11.39	95	16.21	126	20.33	144
13.9	171	17.17	141	20.41	138
13.20	30	17.25	127, 140	21.3	101
16.18	172	17.26, 30	140	21.4-7	176
17.2	133	17.26, 36	142	22.2	153
19.22, 25	95, 157	17.49	159	23.16-18	136
20.13	157	18	145	24	144, 158
21.11	95	18.1-16	140	25	128, 147, 155
21.15	86	18.1, 3, 16, 20, 28	126, 138, 140	25.2-3	152, 153
				25.2, 36	74
1 Samuel		18.1, 3	139	25.5-13, 14-19	153
1.1	152	18.3	136, 138, 139		
1.6	65	18.4	138	25.6	174
1.11	131, 156				

25.7-8, 21	153	6.2	159	12.9-12	185
25.10	153	6.8	86, 92	12.9	186
25.15-16	153	6.14-16,		12.10-12	184-86
25.17, 25	152, 157	20-22	148	12.10, 15	186
25.19-20	154	6.14, 16	149	12.13-14	184-85
25.20	186	6.16	139, 146	12.22-23	185
25.22-23	154-55	6.20, 31	149	12.24-25	188-87
25.22	135	6.23	139, 146	12.24	197
25.24-31,		7.8	159	12.31	188
41	157	7.11-16	196	13	163, 184
25.24-27	155	7.12-16	132, 197	13.2	187
25.24-26	156	7.15	97	13.20	184
25.24, 25,		7.16	159	13.23-28	74, 152
28, 31,		7.18	140	13.28-33	184
41	156	7.29	159	14–18	184
25.26, 31,		8.12-14	20	14	163
33, 34	159	9–1 Kgs 2	165	14.6, 7,	
25.27, 31	153	9.7	97	12, 15,	
25.27, 35	158	11–12	164	17, 19	156
25.27, 41	156	11.1-5	166-67	15–18	163
25.28-31	155, 158	11.2-4	170	15.1	190
25.28	167	11.2, 4	171	15.30	35
25.30	155, 157, 159	11.2, 8	175	16.21-22	168, 186, 194
25.31	159, 164, 165	11.3, 4,		17.10	28
25.36	153, 160	5, 6	174	19.4	135
25.37,		11.4	6, 187	19.5-13	191
38, 39	160	11.5	172-73	19.14	135
25.37	153, 159	11.5, 26	186	20.3	186
25.41	157	11.7	188	20.17	156
25.44	128, 141, 147	11.8	174	21.8	141, 149
26	144, 158	11.9-11	175	22.26	56
26.16	184	11.9, 11,		22.27	54, 55
28.12	44	13	168	23.34, 39	168
28.21, 22	156	11.11,			
31	138	15, 21	175	*1 Kings*	
31.4	142	11.11	176	1–2	163, 164
31.13	179	11.20-21	165	1.5-53	193
		11.25	185	1.5-9	190
2 Samuel		11.26, 27	170	1.11	193
1.20	142	11.27	170, 186	1.13, 17	128, 132
1.26	139	12–20	164	1.4	95
3.2-6	190	12	163	1.4, 11,	
3.7	194	12.1-4	180-81	18, 27	190
3.9	135	12.4	168	1.11-14	191
3.14-16	147-48	12.4-7	184	1.29-30	192-93,
3.14	142	12.5	185		197
3.17-18	167	12.6	184	1.29	196
3.27-37	184	12.7-12,		2.5-6, 31	191
5.20-22	85, 92	13	165	2.7	97

1 Kings (continued)

2.13-25	196
2.13-18	194
2.13	19
2.15	190, 196
2.22	194, 196
2.23-24	196
2.23	135
2.26-27	196
2.28-35	196
3.5	98
4.5-6	96
7.33	175
8.20, 25	197
8.23	97
8.31	133
8.51	83
9.5	197
11.5, 13, 32, 36	197
11.27	85
14.10	155
14.21	108
16.11	155
17.1	133
18.17	133
18.27	30
18.39	193
19.2	135, 172-73
20.10	135
20.35-43	180
21.8	173
21.19	163, 174
21.21	155

2 Kings

2.4	197
6.8	101
6.31	135
8.19	197
9.8	155
9.30, 33	147
19.34	197
20.6	197

Isaiah

1.9-10	104
3.9	104
3.19	36
5.1-7	180
6.2	155, 175
13.19	104
22.12	64
32.6	153
39.7	208
40.11	180
44.2	39
47.2-3	36, 37, 56
54.13	x
56.3	208

Jeremiah

2.33	28, 116
3.1-5	180
3.4	116
4.19	116
9.3	23
11.4	83
14.3	35
17.11	153
23.14	104
31.15-17	52, 63, 65-67, 187
31.21	116
32.6-8	120
39 3, 13	208
49.18	104
50.40	104

Ezekiel

5.3	118
13.5	86
16.8	57, 118
16.37	170
16.49-50	104-105
23.17	118

Hosea

1.2	173
2.5	170
4.2	92, 133
4.13-14	173
4.14	77
10.4	133
12.4 [3]	17, 23, 86

Amos

3.11	65
4.3	85
4.11	104

Jonah

1.9	211

Micah

2.13	86
9.32	97

Zephaniah

2.9	104

Zechariah

5.9	118
10.2	60

Psalms

22	205
22.2	19
27.10	180
44.25	19
45.14	92
45.18	84
49.19	84
51.7	123
62.13	98
80.2	213
102.1	30
106.32	187
116.16	123
132.11	132
132.12	28
139.15	154
144.14	85

Proverbs

6.32	184
7.4	114
7.18	57
14.13	28
14.34	103
17.21	153
23.29	30
25.10	103
29.22	213
30.22	153

Job

1.1	152
2.13	179
3.10	19
6.4	177
10.18-19	19
13.24	19
14.19	20
16.14	86
23.2	30
30.14	85
36.7	53, 54
40.14	84

Song of Solomon (Canticles)

2.2	39
2.14	154, 186
3.1	56
4.1, 3	36
4.1, 9	43
6.7	36
7.13-14	57

Ruth

1.1	93
1.4	92
1.8	97, 98
1.15	100
1.16-17	98
1.17	135
1.19	113
1.20	113
1.21	119
1.22	92, 113
2.1	113
2.2, 6, 21	92
2.5	113
2.8-12	98
2.8-9	114, 116
2.10	114, 125
2.10, 19	95
2.11-12	115
2.12	118
2.13	117
2.20	97
3–4	40
3	58
3.1-4	98
3.2	113
3.3-4	116
3.3	115, 116
3.4	115, 116
3.4, 7, 8, 14	155, 175
3.7	115
3.8-9	117
3.8	113, 115
3.9	118, 119, 125
3.10	97
3.12-13	101
3.14	95, 115
3.15	89, 119
3.16	113, 119
3.17	119
3.18	116
4.1-10	98
4.1	95, 101
4.3-4	120
4.5, 10	92
4.5ff.	120
4.5	101
4.6	102, 110
4.7	101
4.10	121
4.11-12	91, 98, 117
4.14-16	121
4.15	113
4.16	116
4.18-22	83, 86, 91
4.18	13, 91, 108

Lamentations

4.6	104

Ecclesiastes (Kohelet)

4.12	87
10.5	61

Esther

1	200
1.1	216
1.4	201
1.8	201
1.11	201
1.18	201, 202
1.19	202
1.20	202
1.22	202
2.3	229
2.3, 14, 15	208
2.5-7	54
2.5	204
2.7	152. 203, 204, 228
2.8	204
2.8, 15, 16	228
2.9	206
2.9, 15, 17	228
2.10, 20	204, 223
2.13	206
2.15	206, 216
2.16	204
2.17	206
2.20	53
2.21-23	225, 230
3	202
3.2, 5	204
3.4	229
3.6	205
3.8-9	200
3.9-11	201
3.15	222
4.1-2	222
4.1	225
4.4	222
4.8	201
4.11	222
4.13-14	222, 230
4.14	223
4.16	221, 223, 230
4.17	223
5.1	224, 229, 230
5.2	224
5.3	224
5.4	224
5.6	224
5.9	225
5.11-12	225
5.13	204
5.10	219, 230
6.1	225, 230
6.6	225

Esther (continued)		2 Chronicles		1 Samuel	
6.8-9	225	6.14	97	18.17-19	142
6.11	217, 229			18.27	142
6.12	35, 225	Apocrypha		25.3	153
6.13	225	Tobit		25.23	155
7	230	3.7-17	73	2 Samuel	
7.4	230	6.9-8.21	73	11.1	167
7.8	35, 225			11.4	170
8.1-2	226	Judith		11.18-21	178
8.2	229	10.2	75	12.1	180
8.2, 15	217	16.9	75	12.6	181, 184
8.3	226			13.21	126
8.5-6	226	New Testament		21.8	141
8.6	230	Matthew		1 Kings	
8.7	204	1.2-16	109	2.22	196
8.9	202			Isaiah	
8.13	201	Romans		47.2	24
8.15	229	9.10-11	22	Esther	
9.13, 25	226	11.23-24	100, 108-109	2.7	204
9.20	226				
9.29, 31	204	Pseudepigrapha		Targums	
9.29, 32	226	Testaments of the		Targum Jonathan	
9.29	203, 226	Twelve Patriarchs		ben Uziel	
10.3	204, 229	T. Reuben		1 Samuel	
		4.8-9	211	18.21	142
Daniel				2 Samuel	
1.3	208	T. Simon		12.24	187
1.6	79	4.4-5	211		
3.14-27	79	5.1-3	211	Targum Pseudo-Jonathan	
8.13	101			Genesis	
9.20	84	T. Judah		38.8	72
		12.5-6	78	38.15	75
Nehemiah		12.6	81	39.1	207
1.5	97			41.45	208
6.1	85	T. Joseph			
9.32	97	2.1-9.5	211	Targum Neofiti	
11.17	84			Genesis	
12.24	84	T. Benjamin		38	79
13.1	92	4.9	211	38.15	75
13.24	202			38.21, 24	75
		Septuagint (LXX)		38.25	79
1 Chronicles		Genesis		38.26	81
2.3-15	83, 86	21.9	25		
5.1	18, 22, 47	25.25-26	24	Targum Onqelos	
13.11	86	29.17	43	Genesis	
14.11	85	41.45	205, 208	29.17	43
16.4	84	Ruth		37.36	207
20.1	167		93	38.26	81
23.30	84			41.45	205

Biblical References and Other Ancient Texts

PESHITTA
Genesis
41.45   205
38.21, 24   75
2 Samuel
12.24   187

MISHNAH
'Avot
3.11   78
4.1   210
5.10   105
Ketubot
2.1   31
Yebamot
8.3   92

TALMUD
(Babylonian [b.] and Palestinian [y.])
b. 'Avodah Zarah
7b   30
b. Berakhot
24a   66
26b   30
43b   79, 81
60a   209
y. Berakhot
4.1   30
b. Baba Bathra
12b   105
59a   105
60b   36
123a   47, 53
168a   105
b. Baba Metzi'a
3b   84
30b   122
58b   79
87a   15
b. 'Eruvin
49a   105
y. Horayot
2.4, 46d   213
b. Ketubot
17b   35
67b   78
103a   105

b. Megillah
10b   75
12b   201
13a   204, 216
13b   45, 54
14a-b   18, 26, 156
14b   165
15a   155, 223
15b   224
16b-17a   25
b. Pesaḥim
53b   79
119b   40
b. Sanhedrin
74a-b   204
93a   79
93b   119
107a   171
107b   15
b. Soṭah
10b   78, 79, 81, 112
13b   207
36b   213
y. Soṭah
1.4   84
b. Shabbat
56a   171, 176
b. Yebamot
63a   100, 108
77a   92
b. Yoma
13b   34
22b   184

TOSEFTA (t.)
t. Berakhot
4.17   84, 112

MIDRASHIM
Genesis Rabbah
(= *Bereshith Rabbah*)
8.12   209
53.6   15
53.6, 9   15
57.3   11
57.10   106
60.14   30, 32
60.15   69

63.4   39
63.6   18
63.7   18, 20
63.10   24
67.9   18, 26, 30
68.3   46
68.9   30
68.18   24
70.12   42
70.16   44, 47
70.19   50
71.2   52
72.6   209
74.4   61, 145
74.5   60
79.8   209
80.1   209
82.10   64
84.6, 8   15, 16
84.7   208
84.8   213
85.1   71, 81, 86
85.2   72
85.7   69
85.8   75
85.10   74
85.11   81
85.12   82
85.13   86
86.3   207, 208
86.6   203, 208
87.3   208
87.6   217
87.7   213
90.4   205
91.6   208
94.9   210

Numbers Rabbah
(= *Bemidbar Rabbah*)
1.3   56

Canticles Rabbah
(= *Shir ha-Shirim Rabbah*)
3.2   56

Ruth Rabbah
4.6   92
2.14   96

Lamentations Rabbah
(= *Eikhah Rabbah*)
24   64, 65

Ecclesiastes Rabbah
(= *Kohelet Rabbah*)
60.4   26

Esther Rabbah
3.13   201

Aggadat Bereshit
(*Midrash Aggadat Bereshit*, ed. Buber)
49   48
73   18

'Avot deRabbi Natan Bet
38   78

Seder Eliyahu Rabbbah
(also *Tanna de'bei Eliyahu*)
6   40
28   64

Mekilta de-Rabbi Ishmael BeShallaḥ
5 [106]   84

Midrash ha-Gadol
Genesis
22.19   32
38.25   79

Midrash Tehillim
(also *Shoḥer Tov*)
22   205
22.27   224
42   26
54.4   48
90.18   32

Midrash Yashar
Toledot
43a-b   40

Pirqe deRabbi Eliezer [PRE]
31   32

38   208
37   20

Pesiqta de-Rav Kahana BeShallaḥ
11.3   210

Pesiqta Rabbati
3   64
42   92

Seder 'Olam Rabbah
1   16

Sifre Deut.
405   84

Tanḥuma Yelammdenu
Toledot
1   15
8   24
Vayetzei
4   48, 50
12   60
Vayeshev
5   210
8   208

Tanḥuma Buber (ed. Buber)
Vayetzei
11   48
Vayeshev
14   207
Miqetz
17   220

Yalkut Shimoni
Genesis
93   40
109   32
116   26
117   40
125   48
136   64
145   79

PHILO
On Joseph
9.40–10.53   211

JOSEPHUS
Antiquities of the Jews
2.2.1   203
2.4.1-5   211
2.4.1   208
2.6.1   205

MEDIEVAL AND LATER EXEGETES ON THE TORAH, TANAKH AND TALMUD

Ibn Ezra
Genesis
25.23   19
30.16   209

Or haḥayyim
Genesis
48.7   61

Maharal
Hilkhot Nissu'in
    34

Maharal [*Gur Ariyeh*] on Rashi
Genesis
48.7   65

Maharsha on *b. B. Bat.*
123a   54

Netziv (*Ha'ameq Devar*, commentary of R. Naftali Zvi Yehuda Berlin)
Genesis
24.66   30, 32-33
25.23   20

Radak (R. David Kimḥi)
Genesis
19.31-32   106
24.5   226
30.16   209
1 Samuel
25.38   160
2 Samuel
11.4, 11   171

1 Kings		24.63	30	*Ruth*	
1.13	191	25.2	16	3.9	118
17.15	226	25.19	15	*Esther*	
		25.23	18, 19	1.22	202
Ramban (Naḥmanides)		25.25-26	23	*b. Ketubot*	
Genesis		25.25	85	17b	35
25.23	19	25.28	24	*b. Shabbat*	
27.33	29	27.1	28, 31	56a	176
27.4	28-29	27.19	24		
38.8	101	28.9	25	Tosafot (Commentary	
42.9	219	29.11	42	on the Talmud)	
48.7	61, 63	29.25	45	*b. Yoma*	
		30.16	209	13b	34
Rashbam		35.8	27	*b. Shabbat*	
Genesis		35.29	26	56a	176
30.18	57	39.6	208		
b. Shabbat		42.29	220	Saadiah Gaon	
56a	176	48.7	63, 64, 65	*Genesis*	
		1 Samuel		41.45	205
Rashi		25.37-38	160		
Genesis		*2 Samuel*			
22.23	11	11.4, 11	171		

Index of Authors

Abisili, A. I.   169
Adelman, R.   10, 17, 75, 90, 173, 198
Alter, R.   17, 22, 24, 26, 30, 41, 43, 45,
    48, 50, 58, 70, 93, 104, 137, 138,
    139, 140, 141, 142, 143, 144, 145,
    146, 149, 150, 153, 156, 160, 163,
    166, 170, 171, 174, 175, 178, 187,
    188, 191, 192
Amichai, Y.   189
Amsellem, W.   201, 224
Aptowitzer, V.   208
Ashley, K.   3
Auden, W. H.   130
Auerbach, E.   7
Austin, J. L.   5, 129

Bach, A.   104, 216
Bailey, R. C.   169
Bal, M.   3, 5, 60, 61 73, 94, 102, 117,
    167, 168, 175, 178, 227
Bar-Efrat, S.   140, 151, 153, 159, 167,
    171, 173, 181, 187
Beal, T. K.   200, 201, 202
Beauvoir, S. de   198
Benjamin, W.   114
Berg, S. B.   199
Berlin, A.   101, 116, 138, 139, 151, 170,
    171, 189, 194, 195, 199, 202, 204,
    222, 226
Bigger, S. F.   103
Bin Nun, Y.   219
Bird, P.   77
Blenkinsopp, J.   14
Bohmbach, K. G.   187
Bos, J.   94
Boyarin, D.   210, 214
Bright, J.   211
Bronner, L. L.   32, 199, 201, 204, 205
Brown, P.   210

Brueggemann, W.   70, 107, 108
Buber, M.   8, 53
Budick, S.   3, 46
Bush, F. W.   93
Butler, J.   198

Campbell, E.   93, 114, 115
Carruthers, M.   152
Clines, D. J. A.   127
Cohen, G.   21
Cohen, J. M.   200
Cohen, L.   37
Cott, N.   118
Cover, R.   98, 99, 100, 121, 122
Craven, T.   2

Davies, E. W.   73
Deen, E.   127
Doniger, W.   1, 2, 49 116, 117
Driver, S. R.   20, 135

Eliade, M.   30
Emerton, J. A.   109
Eskenazi, T.   98, 101
Exum, C. J.   136, 138, 146, 168, 169,
    172

Fisch, H.   94, 119, 120, 121, 124
Fishbane, M.   18, 56, 57, 61
Fishbane, M. D.   116
Flanagan, J. W.   164
Flaubert, G.   227, 228
Fokkelman, J.   13, 14, 42, 44, 51, 57,
    60, 61, 138, 139, 142, 143, 151,
    153, 155, 157, 164, 166, 167, 168,
    170, 171, 178, 179, 185, 185, 188,
    190, 91, 193, 194, 195, 196
Fox, E.   8, 14, 16, 23, 24, 30, 43, 57,
    85, 94

Fox, M. V.   199, 201, 222, 223, 224
Friedman, R. E.   227
Frymer-Kensky, T.   2, 33, 34, 62, 63, 72, 75, 77, 81, 92, 93, 94, 98, 101, 102, 103, 104, 106, 164, 166, 169, 171 172, 173, 176, 181
Fuchs, E.   2, 27, 59, 60, 61

Gan, M.   199
Garsiel, M.   128, 157, 175, 181
Gendler, M.   201
Ginsberg, H. L.   17
Goldman, S.   211
Greenberg, M.   60, 211
Greenstein, E.   93, 95, 102, 114, 202
Grubin, E.   34
Gunkel, H.   20
Gunn, D.   136, 164, 180, 181, 194

Hadas-Lebel, M.   21
Halpern, B.   153, 155
Handelman, S.   84, 98
Hartman, D.   118
Hasan-Rokem, G.   63, 64, 65, 66
Haughwout, M. S.   116
Hendel, R.   105, 106, 107
Hertzberg, H. W.   169
Hobbes, T.   132
Huddleston, J. R.   75
Hume, D.   132

Irwin, B.   116

Jacobs, L.   131
Jagendorf, Z.   45, 46, 75, 82, 94, 95, 106

Kallai, Z.   63
Kaplan, A.   34, 35
Kara-Ivanov, R. K.   96, 107
Kates, J.   118
Kerrigan, W.   130, 152
Kiel, Y.   20
Klein, L. R.   127, 148
Klitsner, J.   23, 24, 25, 26
Koenig, S. M.   169, 170
Kristeva, J.   202
Kronfeld, C.   105, 106, 107
Kugel, J.   15, 70, 71, 74, 78, 79, 81, 82, 105, 208, 210, 211, 213

Labovitz, G.   204
LaCocque, A.   97
Ladin, J.   209
Lamm, M.   34, 35
Lauterbach, J. Z.   35, 36
Leach, E.   14, 33, 109
Lefkovitz, L.   58, 208, 209
Leibowitz, N.   219
Leibtag, M.   18
Levenson, J. D.   22, 25, 70, 153, 154, 155, 197, 202, 222, 223
Levinas, E.   80, 84, 98
Levine, B.   40
Levinson, B.   95, 101, 102
Levinson, J.   2, 44, 45, 53, 55, 56, 58, 210, 212, 213, 214
Licht, J.   95
Lockyer, H. H.   127
Lyons, D.   171

Mandel, P.   63, 64
Mann, T.   68, 69
May, S.   97
McCarter, P. K.   165, 180, 187
McNamara, M.   75, 79
Meacham, T.   103
Menn, E. M.   79, 82
Milgrom, J.   172, 220
Murphy, R. E.   93

Nicol, G. C.   169
Niditch, S.   2, 34, 94, 182
Niehoff, M.   211
Noth, M.   164, 212
Nygren, A.   97

Pardes, I.   44, 51, 52, 59, 60, 61, 105, 106, 107
Philip, T. S.   170, 171
Polzin, R.   158, 159, 163, 166, 167
Prouser, O. H.   2
Provan, I. A.   191

Rad, G. von   176, 164
Reimer, G.   201
Ricoeur, P.   136
Rosen, N.   201
Rosenberg, J.   164, 166, 174, 176
Rosenberg, M.   171, 172

Rosenzweig, F. 8, 9
Roubach, S. 69

Sarna, N. M. 17, 18, 22, 36, 39, 42, 43, 57, 73, 74, 110, 182, 183, 205
Sasson, I. 187
Sasson, J. M. 35, 37, 93, 101, 114, 115, 117, 118
Satlow, M. 35, 210
Scholem, G. G. 52, 53
Schüssler Fiorenza, E. 200
Schwartz, R. 104, 181
Searle, J. 129
Seeman, D. 146
Segal, A. F. 21
Shakespeare, W. 1, 21, 71, 126, 130, 137, 139, 151, 152, 198
Shalev, M. 153, 160, 161
Sharvit, S. 78
Shinan, A. 85, 86
Simon, U. 164, 165, 167, 168, 171, 176, 178, 180, 181, 183, 184, 185, 185, 218, 219
Speiser, E. A. 60, 70
Spiegel, S. 32
Steinberg, N. 14
Stern, D. 66
Sternberg, M. 3, 22, 25, 44, 73, 163, 164, 171, 175, 177, 178
Syrén, R. 22

Thompson, S. 212

Todorov, T. 14
Toorn, K. van der 36, 37
Trible, P. 94, 104, 112, 118
Tsevat, M. 35, 36
Turner, V. W. 2, 137

Van Seters, J. 164, 165
Vawter, B. 70
Viezel, E. 85

Weisberg, D. 73
Wenham, G. J. 20
Westbrook, R. 73
Westerman, C. 20, 70
Wilde, O. 1
Wolde, E. van 94

Yeats, W. B. 11, 13, 162, 172
Yee, G. A. 168, 175
Yuval, I. J. 21

Zakovitch, Y. 23, 85, 86, 93, 102, 115, 118
Zevit, Z. 93
Ziegler, Y. 93, 129, 132, 133, 134, 135, 136, 159, 191
Ziskind, J. 103
Zornberg, A. 8, 17, 19, 21, 24, 25, 27, 29, 31, 40, 46, 47, 50, 53, 63, 65, 99, 206, 215, 217, 218, 219, 222, 223
Zucker, D. 26